"An essential contribution to the development of studies on the global law of public contracts."

Jean-Bernard Auby,
Emeritus Professor, Sciences Po Paris

Global Contract Law in the Middle East and North Africa

Public Law Constraints

This book comprehensively covers the interplay between cultural and legal globalization and the impact this has on contract law, with a particular focus on state contracts within the MENA region.

The book discusses the roles assumed by Supreme Courts in Egypt and MENA countries in creating unified principles of international contract law in states' contracts which are consistent with international commercial contracts' principles. It makes a powerful argument for further harmonization of contract law in the area, and how this can be achieved. The book forms a case study of how international harmonization can be achieved through a number of routes, such as codification, digitalization of processes and contracts, private-public arbitration, and further use of international instruments. It also considers the implications of comparative European law, convention law, and other legal domains, particularly international standards, on contract law in the MENA region. The book suggests how international legal standards can be integrated within contract law, and how a harmonious contract law framework can thus be achieved. Through analyzing ICSID case law, the book argues that unification of contract law principles in the MENA region is a considerable step towards achieving legitimate expectations of foreign investors. It argues, further, that global contract law is underway.

The book will be is of interest to students and scholars in the field of international contract law, public law, and international law in Egypt and MENA countries.

Mohamed A.M. Ismail, *PhD (Cairo); FCIArb (London)* is the vice president of the Conseil d'État and judge at the Supreme Administrative Court, Egypt. He is an arbitrator in international commercial disputes. Dr. Ismail is affiliated with several global legal bodies/organizations. He is a Member of the Comité Française De L'Arbitrage (Paris) and a member of the 'Public Contracts in Legal Globalization' as a global research network at Sciences Po University, Paris. He has been appointed as an expert member to the Working Group of the ICC and UNIDROIT on International Investment Contracts. Dr. Ismail was a visiting research fellow at Max Planck Institute for Comparative and International Private Law, Hamburg.

Global Contract Law in the Middle East and North Africa

Public Law Constraints

Mohamed A.M. Ismail

With a foreword by Louise Gullifer, QC, University of Cambridge

Routledge
Taylor & Francis Group
LONDON AND NEW YORK

First published 2024
by Routledge
4 Park Square, Milton Park, Abingdon, Oxon OX14 4RN

and by Routledge

605 Third Avenue, New York, NY 10158

Routledge is an imprint of the Taylor & Francis Group, an informa business

British Library Cataloguing-in-Publication Data
A catalogue record for this book is available from the British Library

ISBN: 978-1-032-71601-5 (hbk)
ISBN: 978-1-032-73863-5 (pbk)
ISBN: 978-1-003-46635-2 (ebk)

DOI: 10.4324/9781003466352

Typeset in Times New Roman
by Deanta Global Publishing Services, Chennai, India

To Rania Koura;
To Youssef Ismail;
To Ahmed Ismail.

Contents

Foreword by Louise Gullifer, QC, University of Cambridge

I am very pleased to have been asked to write a foreword for this important and interesting book. The book covers a number of themes, only some of which I am familiar with, and focuses on the law of Egypt and MENA, with which I have very little knowledge. I have therefore learned a great deal from reading the book, and I am sure that it will prove a valuable source of information for many. However, its importance also lies elsewhere, in the pulling together of a number of themes in pursuit of a particular goal: the development of a harmonized business contract law in the region, both generally but particularly for contracts between private actors and state authorities. The practical driver for this goal is the increase of foreign direct investment.

The first theme, therefore, is that of harmonization based on international standards. The standard chosen by Dr. Ismail is that of international commercial contract principles, exemplified by the instruments of international organizations such as UNIDROIT and UNCITRAL. The focus on this standard, though, necessitates discussion of the second theme, which is the tension between administrative law, and the extent to which it governs 'administrative contracts,' and the international commercial law standards. While Dr. Ismail argues strongly for the removal of what he calls 'public law barriers' to the achievement of harmonized contract law, he also recognizes the purpose of some public law restrictions in relation to 'administrative contracts' and carefully charts both where the existing balance lies, and where he thinks it should lie. Another theme, perhaps covered with a lighter touch, is that of variance of legal culture, particularly between the common law and civil law traditions, which Dr. Ismail argues, persuasively, has been mitigated in the area of international commercial contract law by harmonization instruments.

The substance of the book contains a detailed examination of the factors which Dr. Ismail has identified as either already contributing to the level of harmonization that exists (such as some court decisions, the legal treatment of specialized contracts such as PPP contracts, and the use of international arbitration to resolve disputes arising in relation to 'administrative contracts') or which he argues can play a significant role in the drive towards harmonization (such as codification, including some reform, digitization of processes and contracts, and further use of international instruments). There is a wealth of detailed analysis of cases and legislation in Egypt and a number of MENA countries, including some very useful case studies to illustrate the points made.

The book therefore functions on a number of levels, all of which are very valuable. It provides some very interesting information about the current state of the law and practice in relation to PPP and other administrative contracts in the Egypt and the MENA region. It makes a clear and powerful argument for further harmonization of contract law in the area, and how this can be achieved. And, at a more theoretical level, it forms a case study itself of how international harmonization can be achieved through a number of routes, and why it is important. I recommend it to anyone interested in any or all of these.

Louise Gullifer FBA, QC (hon)
Rouse Ball Professor of English Law, University of Cambridge
Rome, January 2024

Preface

Contract law developments are an important factor behind economic growth in any country. A developed legal system of contract law is a fundamental tool to increase the inward flow of Foreign Direct Investments (FDI) in developing countries. Further, it is an important tool to achieve progress in the socio-economic life of the ordinary citizens in Egypt and the Middle East and North African (MENA) region. This vision is valid for both private law contracts which are civil and commercial contracts, and state contracts whether administrative contracts or private law contracts. Enhancements to the socio-economic lifestyle of citizens are not only in healthcare, education, housing, or social lifestyle in general, but also in reducing the unemployment rate in developing countries, in particular in Egypt and the MENA countries. Unemployment is one of the main factors behind the increase of the crime rate, in particular terrorism crime.

The influence of cultural, policy, and legal globalization upon Egyptian and MENA countries' legal systems, in particular Egypt and the Gulf region, is clear in recognizing new contractual patterns such as Build/Operate/Transfer (BOT), Build/Own/Operate/Transfer (BOOT) and Public Private Partnerships (PPPs), and in the developments in legislation and case law.[1] Many crucial questions arise: How far is contract law, whether public or private, in Egypt and the MENA countries consistent with international contract law substantive principles? How far is contract law in Egypt and the MENA countries consistent with the global diversity of contract law principles, in particular international commercial contracts' substantive principles? How can coherent contract law principles, which are consistent with global principles of contract law, be achieved in international states' contracts in Egypt and the MENA countries? What are the tools to achieve such unification? What are the public law barriers and constraints? What is the ideology behind creating a special legal framework of administrative contracts in Egypt and the MENA countries? To what extent is the traditional theory of administrative contracts, in the respective jurisdictions, an obstacle to achieving global contract law and unified principles in contract law, for both private and public contracts? The

1 Mohamed A.M. Ismail, *Globalization and New International Public Works Agreements in Developing Countries, An Analytical Perspective* (Routledge 2011 and 2016, pp, 1–8, with a foreword by HH Humphrey Lloyd QC).

question why? is also of fundamental importance. Why is unification of contract law principles needed in the respective jurisdictions?

The courts' intervention explores the various judicial approaches by Egyptian courts, as the leading jurisdiction in the MENA region, and portrays the need for global contract law. The expected global contract law, in Egypt and the MENA countries, unifies the substantive principles of administrative contracts to be consistent with the international commercial contracts' substantive principles. PPPs and energy contracts play an important role to achieve unification and global contract law. Digitalization of public contracts and codification of administrative contracts' principles are considerable steps towards achieving global contract law, both in public and private contracts.

Private-public arbitration also plays a significant role towards the unification of contract law principles, to achieve coherent and global substantive principles of contract law. It is worth noting that:

- The permissibility of private-public arbitration as a dispute resolution system has been transmitted to the Egyptian legal order by influencing factors such as international normative convergence and regulatory standardization. The apparent constitutional stance in relation to private-public arbitration has been the source of inconsistency in the legal treatment of alternative dispute resolutions which threaten the jurisdictional exclusivity of the administrative court system.
- The prohibition of private-public arbitration was justified on the nature and character of administrative contracts as the backdrop of the relevant disputes between private actors and the state. The causal link between jurisdictional exclusivity of the administrative court system and administrative contracts has been the condition of public interest which is present only in administrative contracts. On the other hand, the explicit permissibility of private-public arbitration has been conditioned on ministerial consent which serves as a system for compatibility approval of private-public arbitration with public interest, with a view to settling disputes that otherwise are reserved for the exclusive jurisdiction of administrative court system.
- A *lex lacuna* emerged by the extraction of PPP contracts from administrative jurisdiction. Such treatment of PPP contracts as commercial contracts does not run contrary to international practice, since the civil justice courts could have jurisdiction in settling disputes arising therein. The principle of party autonomy also offers the optionality of recourse to private-public arbitration, however without any control system for public interest assurance.
- Private-public arbitration has created, through decades, a new transnational set of substantive contractual principles, as international arbitrators have different backgrounds, whether civil law or common law, or non-legal arbitrators. Global contract law exists in practice, to some extent, and the private-public arbitration jurisprudence is a step towards the unification of substantive principles of contract law to achieve a coherent set of substantive principles of global contract law.

International organs such as the United Nations Commission on International Trade Law (UNCITRAL) and the International Institute for the Unification of Private Law (UNIDROIT) play an important role in the international sphere to achieve the unification of contract law principles. The UNIDROIT principles of International Commercial Contracts 2016 are clear example to achieve unification of contract law and to create a set of substantive principles of global contract law.

Global contract law, in Egypt and the MENA countries, is expected to contain a coherent set of substantive principles of contract law, both private and public contracts, which is consistent with international commercial contracts' law and practice. Further, global contract law will not violate the legitimate expectations of foreign investors, in the respective jurisdictions, as legal approaches and substantive principles adopted in the global contact law will lead to judicial and arbitral approaches which are acceptable to foreign investors. Such judicial and arbitral approaches will not violate the economic expectations of foreign investors in the respective jurisdictions and they are considered an important factor to increase the inflow of FDI to the MENA region. Global and unified contract law is a tool to avoid inconsistent findings by national courts and arbitral tribunals.

It is expected that codification of administrative contracts' principles in Egypt and the MENA countries will adopt liberal approaches which supersede the party autonomy principle. Adam Smith and the Chicago school in economics have reduced the role of states to the minimum.[2] The contracting state has to be only an observer or a regulator. This view is consistent with the substantive principles in international commercial contracts. It is assumed that codification of administrative contracts' principles will adopt international commercial contracts' principles, which are accepted in developed legal systems. Therefore, in light of the trajectory of states' legislation in Egypt and the MENA region, state contracting law and public procurement law should not promulgate legislative provisions containing liquidated damages calculations and caps and should leave such clauses to party autonomy.

It is worth noting that private law is a multilevel legal system where the traditional boundaries between public law and private law and also the boundaries between the law and other structuring instruments are not only shifting, but are sometimes also blurred. This monograph aims at analyzing interaction between legal systems, and exploring the connection and interaction between the different areas of the law and the various 'layers' of the international legal order. In addition, legal culture is an intangible value. The flow of legal culture in contract law from Anglo-American jurisdictions to Egypt and MENA civil law countries created new PPP patterns. This is a fundamental step to achieve global contract law in states' contracts, in the respective jurisdictions, which is consistent with international commercial contracts' principles. The interaction between administrative law on

2 *Milton Friedman on Economics: Selected Papers*, University of Chicago Press Journal, 2008.

one hand and private law principles[3] on the other, is presented in comparative and transnational contexts.

This monograph envisages being a unique point of reference for academics and academic researchers on all issues pertinent to harmonizing and unification of international contract law in the MENA region in particular, Egypt, the Gulf States of Saudi Arabia, United Arab Emirates, Qatar, Bahrain, Kuwait, and Oman, to achieve a global contract law. The Maghreb countries of Tunisia, Algeria, and Morocco are also important sources to cover when they are relevant. It is worth noting that Egyptian legislation and case law are the fundamental influential factors and legal foundations to the procedural and substantive law and policy regimes of the relevant Gulf States and other MENA countries.

The substantive scope is an attempt to explore the interaction between global principles of contract law and states' contracts on one hand and Egypt and the MENA countries' similar principles on the other. This monograph explores how global contract law has influenced contract law and states' contracts principles in Egypt and the MENA countries' legal systems. It is clear that standardization and unification of globally accepted contract law principles will remove barriers between both common law and civil law legal cultures, in public and private contracts. Further, unification of contract law to achieve global contract law principles is a step to removing public law barriers in the MENA region.

3 Private law extends to cover international contract law, common law principles in contract law (English case law), UNIDROIT various instruments, UNCITRAL instruments, international arbitration law and practice, and Civil Codes in Egypt and MENA countries, etc.

Acknowledgments

I would especially like to express my sincere gratitude to Professor Louise Gullifer QC (hon), FBA, Rouse Ball Professor of English Law, University of Cambridge and Fellow of Gonville and Caius College, for writing a foreword to this monograph, which is a remarkable addition to the academic value of the monograph. Many thanks to Alison Kirk, Senior Commissioning Editor, Routledge, Taylor & Francis Group, for her considerable support during the past years that positively influenced my work in this book. Special thanks and gratitude go to Nicola Sharp, Law Editor, Routledge, Taylor & Francis Group, to whom I address my deepest appreciation for her continual support, help, fruitful cooperation, and constructive coordination. I strongly believe that without her continual and faithful support, this book would not have appeared. I would especially like to express my appreciation to Diksha Bhugra, Editorial Assistant, Routledge, Taylor & Francis Group, for her cooperation and successful coordination.

I also wish to express my deep appreciation to the UNIDROIT staff in Rome, in particular Professor Anna Veneziano, the Deputy Secretary General and Alexandra Logue from the UNIDROIT Secretariat.

List of Abbreviations

AAA	American Arbitration Association
AC	Law Reports, House of Lords (Appeal Cases)
AI	Artificial intelligence
All ER	All England Law Reports
ARE	Arab Republic of Egypt
BITs	Bilateral Investment Treaties
BOO	Build, Own, Operate
BOOT	Build, Own, Operate, Transfer
BOT	Build, Own, Transfer
CA	Court of Appeal of England and Wales
CAPM	Capital Asset Pricing Model
CIA	Chartered Institute of Arbitrators
CIL	Customary International Law
CISG	United Nations Convention on Contracts for the International Sales of Goods
CRCICA	Cairo Regional Centre for International Commercial Arbitration
DCFR	Draft Common Frame of Reference
DEPP	Directorate for State Enterprises and Privatization
DGASGP	Direction générale d'audit et de suivi des grands projets
DGPPP	Direction générale des partenariats public-privé
DRM	Dispute Resolution Mechanism
EC	European Community
EPC	Engineering, Procurement, Construction
EPPPL	European Procurement and Public Private Partnership Law Review
EU	European Union
FDI	Foreign Direct Investment
FIDIC	Fédération International des Ingénieurs Conseils
GCC	Gulf Cooperation Council
GPL	General Principles of Law
HCCH	Hague Conference on Private International Law
HL	House of Lords
ICC Institute	ICC's Institute of World Business Law

ICLR	International Construction Law Review
ICC	The International Chamber of Commerce
ICSID Convention	Washington Convention on the Settlement of the Investment Disputes between States and Nationals of Other States, 1965
ICSID	International Centre for Settlement of Investment Disputes
IFDI	Inward of Foreign Direct Investments
IICs	International Investment Contracts
ISDS	Investor-State Dispute Settlement
IWPP	Independent Water and Power Producer
KAPP	Kuwait Authority for Partnership Projects
LDs	Liquidated Damages
LNG	Liquefied Natural Gas
MENA	Middle East and North Africa
MITs	Multilateral Investment Treaties
Model Law	UNCITRAL Model Law on International Commercial Arbitration adopted in June 1985 and amended in 2006
OECD	Organization for Economic Co-operation and Development
OHADA	Organization for the Harmonization of Business Law in Africa
PC	Privy Council
PECL	Principles of European Contract Law
PPP	Public-Private Partnership
PPPCU	Public-Private Partnership Central Unit
RCADI	Recueil des Cours de l'Académie de Droit International de la Haye
Rev Arb	Revue de l'arbitrage
SDGs	Sustainable Development Goals
SPV	Special Purpose Vehicle
State Council	Conseil d'État
STPR	Social Time Preference Rate
UAE	United Arab Emirates
UNCITRAL RULES	UNCITRAL Arbitration Rules as Amended 2010
UNCITRAL	United Nations Commission on International Trade Law
UNCTAD	United Nations Conference on Trade and Development
UNIDROIT	International Institute for the Unification of Private Law
UPICC	UNIDROIT Principles of International Commercial Contracts
Washington Convention	Washington Convention on the Settlement of the Investment Disputes between States and Nationals of Other States, 1965

Introduction

The influence of the cultural and legal globalization phenomena on the Egyptian and MENA countries' legal systems is clear upon the enhancements to and modernization of administrative contracts' traditional theory and practice.[1] New patterns of administrative contracts have appeared in Egypt and MENA countries such as PPP contracts, which have *hybrid* legal nature. States in Egypt and MENA countries may enter into administrative contracts or private contracts to achieve public interests.

The current Constitution of 2014 in Egypt adopts liberal ideology as it did not adopt specific economic ideology and left the door open for the presidential and parliamentary elections to determine the economic pattern, and economic ideology and policies, for each electoral term. Therefore, Egypt, in light of the amendments to the 1971 previous constitution and the following constitutions with new liberal economic ideology, could promulgate PPP law. Many MENA countries followed Egypt and promulgated PPP laws.[2]

The Egyptian judicial system is unique as it has a *dual* judicial structure; the first is the ordinary courts for civil, commercial, criminal, and all other disputes

1 Legal globalization is a cultural socio-economic phenomenon. Culture is influenced to a great extent by globalization and it represents a set of practices, values, beliefs, and customs acquired by individuals as members of a distinctive society and resulting from interaction among people. With respect to the economic dimension of globalization, Stiglitz has highlighted the problems caused by globalization in some parts of the world, as it generates unbalanced outcomes, both between and within countries. See: Joseph Stiglitz, *Globalization and its Discontents* (W.W. Norton, 2004); Joseph Stiglitz, *Making Globalization Work* (W.W. Norton, 2007); Brian Snowdon, *Globalisation, Development and Transition* (Edward Elgar, 2007). Nowadays, globalization plays a significant role in enhancing comprehension between legal cultures. '*Le contrat administratif*' theory and practice were directly influenced by cultural and legal globalization. Further, the influence of the Anglo-American legal culture is remarkable upon Arab civil law legal culture, particularly in legislation, case law, and the rise of new contractual patterns in state contracts such Private-Public Partnerships (PPP) and Built Operate Transfer (BOT) agreements. See: Mohamed A.M. Ismail, *Globalization and New International Public Works Agreements in Developing Countries, An Analytical Perspective* (Routledge, 2016 and 2011, pp. 1–8) with a foreword by HH Humphrey Lloyd QC and for the same author see: *Public Private Partnership Contracts: The Middle East and North Africa* (Routledge, 2020).

2 Egypt has promulgated PPP Law No. 67 of 2010; Kuwait PPP Law No. 116 of 2014, and Jordan PPP Law No. 31 of 2014 as amended in 2020, Morocco PPP Law No. 86-12 of 2014, Dubai PPP Law No. 22 of 2015 and Tunisia PPP Law No. 45 of 2015.

DOI: 10.4324/9781003466352-1

and the second, which is the Conseil D'État courts, is specialized in administrative disputes. The Egyptian Conseil D'État is an independent judicial organ, pursuant to the Egyptian Constitutions of 1971, 2012, and 2014.[3]

State contracts' principles in Egypt and in MENA countries have been established through the Egyptian Conseil D'État decisions, in particular the Supreme Administrative Court decisions, which were influenced to a great extent by the decisions of the French Conseil D'État.[4] Procedural and substantive principles of states' contracts have flown from Egypt to MENA countries' legal systems. Administrative law is not yet codified (written) in Egypt and MENA countries.

This monograph answers many crucial questions, which are raised in the international sphere. This answer constitutes a coherent theme, as follows:

- How can cultural and legal globalization phenomena affect contract law, in particular state contracts, in Egypt and MENA countries, to achieve global contract law principles?[5]
- Has the legal globalization phenomenon created coherent private law, in particular contract law, in Egypt and MENA countries? Do state contracts have special significance in this context?
- What is the role of Supreme Courts in Egypt, as the leading jurisdiction in the MENA region, to create unified contract law in state contracts?
- Why may courts intervene in state contracts' disputes? To what extent may courts intervene? What are the boundaries and limitations of courts' intervention?
- How do the national courts resolve contract law issues? What is argued in legal doctrine on how the courts deal – or ought to deal – with them? What is the situation in Egypt and MENA countries? To what extent is courts' intervention feasible to create global contract law principles in states' contracts?
- In general, what is the courts' intervention role in shaping state contracts' legal order in Egypt and MENA countries, to be consistent with international commercial contracts' principles?
- What is the extent of the influence of global administrative law on the legal framework of states' contracts in Egypt and the MENA countries? What is the

3 It is worth noting that previous Egyptian Constitutions of 1971 and the current constitution of 2014 as well as MENA countries' constitutions were inspired by the French Constitution of the Fifth Republic promulgated in 1958. In addition, Egyptian Civil Code and MENA countries' civil codes were greatly inspired by the French civil code.

4 Sarwat Badawi, *Administrative Law* (Dar El Nahdah El Arabia, 1985 and 2010 editions, in Arabic); see also: Atef Al Bana, *Al Wassit in Administrative Law*. Cairo (Dar Al Nahda Al Arabia, 1992, in Arabic).

5 It is worth noting that the controversial theory of Clash of Civilizations which was adopted by Samuel Huntington in international relations is not valid in the international legal sphere. There is an integration in the international legal order rather than a clash. For more elaboration on Samuel Huntington's views, see his famous thesis: *The Clash of Civilization and the Remaking of World Order* (Free Press, London, 1996). Henry Kissinger described the book as 'one of the most important books to have emerged since the end of the cold war.'

extent of the coexistence between the core principles of contract law in state contracts in Egypt and the MENA region on one hand and the huge global diversity of international contracts principles on the other hand? To what extent are courts in Egypt and MENA countries influenced by international commercial contracts' principles?

- Is there an innovative role for new types of state contracts such as PPP contracts to create global contract law in the respective jurisdictions?
- How can PPP contracts in Egypt and MENA countries, as they introduce the latest types of states' contracts which do not have a purely administrative legal nature, play a significant role to create unified contract law principles, which are consistent with international commercial contracts' substantive principles?
- Is there a unified contract law in Egypt and MENA countries which is consistent with the global diversity of contract law principles? How can such unification be achieved?
- How can unified contract law of states' contracts be achieved in light of international standards? How can global and unified principles of contract law be achieved in the respective jurisdictions?
- To what extent is private law in light of international standards consistent with the traditional theory of '*Le contrat administratif*' in Egypt and the MENA countries?
- How far are Egypt and MENA countries' legal systems adopting the UN Sustainable Development Goals (SDGs) in states' contracts, in particular PPP contracts? What is the role of the latter goals to create coherence and consistency between contract law in states' contracts in Egypt and MENA countries on one hand and international commercial contracts on the other?
- How far are states' contracts in Egypt and in the MENA countries adopting socio-economic dimensions? To what extent do socio-economic approaches, in states' contracts, affect the unemployment rate and crime rate (in particular terrorism)? How can global contract law principles, if achieved, improve the socio-economic lifestyle in the respected jurisdictions?
- Digitalization and Artificial Intelligence (AI) are tools to achieve unified contract law principles in international states' contracts and private contracts as unification of substantive principles is needed. To what extent do such principles have to be consistent with global principles of contract law?
- Is codification of administrative law principles in Egypt and MENA countries a tool to achieve unification of contract law in international states' contracts to be consistent with international commercial contracts substantive principles?
- To what extent does private-public arbitration create unification in contract law principles in international states' contracts, in particular through creating a global and unified set of substantive principles in international contract law? Has such unification of international contract law, through private-public arbitration, affected international states' contracts principles in the MENA countries?
- What is the role of international organs such as the UNIDROIT and UNCITRAL to create coherent set of substantive principles in private law contracts? How

far this approach affects international states' contracts in Egypt and the MENA region?

- What is the impact of unification of private law principles, convention law and other instruments of law, adopted by the international organs such as the UNCITRAL and UNIDROIT, on contract law in Egypt and MENA countries?
- How can global contracts law principles, if achieved, maintain the legitimate expectations of foreign investors in Egypt and MENA countries?

The answer to the above-mentioned questions constitutes a coherent sharp focus of this monograph.

Analyzing courts' intervention through analyzing Egyptian Supreme Administrative Courts' decisions is an innovative step in the English legal literature. This monograph is a comprehensive study which can add an in-depth analysis to the pulse and dynamics of states' contracts, in light of international contract law principles. It introduces critical analysis to the interplay between private law and public law in state contracts in the respective jurisdictions.

Courts' intervention is an important judicial tool in states' contracts theory and practice as, from a technical point of view, there are some differences in practice, for instance, between national courts' power and arbitral tribunals' power. Both aim at creating unified contract law principles in states' contracts that shall not violate the economic expectations of foreign investors in Egypt and MENA countries.

The extent of courts' intervention and its powers while intervening without a legislative provision is of great significance because if courts' intervention has wide powers without any limitations, such intervention is a threat to investors, in particular foreign investors, who inject FDI in the respective jurisdictions. Foreign investors expect judicial resolution that may achieve their financial and economic expectations which they have illustrated in their feasibility study upon entering into any project with the state. Encouraging the inward of FDI is a fundamental policy adopted in Egypt and MENA countries' constitutions, legislation, and regulatory framework. It is worth noting that the increase of FDI is one of the 2030 vision goals in Egypt and in MENA countries. As the majority of developing economies are characterized by their low productivity, it is assumed that adopting global contract law principles in states' contracts should be a factor behind the increase of productivity in developing countries. Other tools to create unified private law contracts in states' contracts such as digitalization of public contracts and judiciary; new types of states' contracts in the MENA countries, such as PPPs; and codification of administrative law are the pillars to introduce the interplay between contract law/private law on one hand and states' contracts principles in Egypt and MENA countries on the other. Such tools to achieve global contract law principles in states' contracts are the motive behind the increase of FDI to Egypt and MENA countries in states' contracts in huge infrastructure and services projects. Achieving global coherent contract law/private law principles in states' contracts is a remarkable step towards transnational understanding of private law and unified contract law in states' international transactions in Egypt and MENA countries, which shall not violate economic expectations of foreign investors. Coherent contract law in states' contracts in Egypt and the MENA region, which is consistent with global contract law, shall increase the inward of FDI to respective jurisdictions.

It is important to highlight the legal framework of administrative contracts, differences and similarities with some types of public and private contracts, in Egypt and the MENA region.

Administrative Contract ('*Le contrat administratif*') in the Egyptian and MENA Countries' Legal Systems

The administrative contract (*Le contrat administratif*) in the respective jurisdictions is a contract between a public juristic person on one hand, and private person whether the latter is a natural or a juristic person on the other hand. The administrative contract must have three conditions, together, to qualify as an administrative and not private contract. Those conditions[6] are:

a) Public juristic person must be party to the contract.
b) Contract must concern the running and/or the management of any of the public utilities.
c) The contract must contain excessive/exorbitant clauses (*clauses exorbitantes*) which aim to achieve public interests.[7]

Administrative contract aims to achieve public interests. Therefore, the substantive nature of the administrative contract requires that the contracting state is not in an equal bargaining power with the private person. The contracting state can achieve public interests through containing the administrative contract exorbitant clauses. The justification of the substantive legal nature of administrative contracts is that the contracting state aims to achieve public interests.

6 Those three conditions are called in the Egyptian doctrine 'administrative contract criterion,' see: Soliman El Tamawy, *General Principles of Administrative Contracts* (5th edn, Ain Shams University Press, 1991, in Arabic); Atef Al Bana, *Administrative Contracts* (Dar Al Nahda Al Arabia, 1984, in Arabic); Sarwat Badawi, *The General Theory of Administrative Law*. (5th edn, Cairo, Dar Al Nahda Al Arabia, 1994, in Arabic); O. Helmy, *Criterion for Distinguishing Administrative Contracts* (Dar Al Nahda Al Arabia, 1993, in Arabic); Gaber Gad Nassar, *Administrative Contracts* (Dar Al Nahda Al Arabia, 2005, in Arabic). In French doctrine see: Laurent Richer and François Lichère, *Droit des Contrats Administratifs* (10th edn, LGDJ, 2016 and 11th edn, 2019).

7 In exorbitant clauses in the Egyptian and MENA countries' legal system see: Soliman El Tamawy, *General Principles of Administrative Contracts* (5th edn, Ain Shams University Press, 1991, in Arabic); Abdel Badie Mohamed Salah, '*The Power of the Authority to Terminate Administrative Contract*' (PhD, Faculty of Law, Ain Shams University, Cairo, 1993, in Arabic); H.A. Elgamal, '*Legal System for the Sanctions in Public Construction Contracts*,' PhD thesis (Ain Shams University, 1979, in Arabic). In French doctrine see: G. Vedel, 1956, 'Remarques sur la Notion de Clause Exorbitante,' *L'évolution du droit public: études en l'honneur d'Achille Mestre*, Sirey; L. Richer and F. Lichère, *Droits des Contrats Administratifs* (11th edn, LGDJ, 2019).

Private Law Contracts and Adhesion Contracts in the Egyptian and MENA Countries' Legal Systems

It is worth noting that administrative contracts in the Egyptian and MENA countries' legal systems are different from adhesion contracts. Substantive rights in adhesion contracts are governed only by the Egyptian Civil Code provisions and their disputes are subject to the jurisdiction of ordinary civil courts in the Egyptian judiciary, as they are characterized as private law contracts. The legal framework of administrative contract is different and they are subject to the jurisdiction of the Conseil D'État courts.

In Egypt, the state can enter into an administrative contract and/or a civil contract (civil or commercial contract).[8] It has been decided that the administration can enter into either administrative contracts or private law contracts[9] to achieve public interests.

Contracts with Hybrid/Mixed Legal Nature

In addition, the influence of the cultural and legal globalization phenomena to the Egyptian legal system was clear upon the enhancements to and modernization of administrative contracts' traditional theory and practice.[10] New patterns of administrative contracts have appeared in Egypt and MENA countries such as BOT/BOOT and PPP contracts.

The current Constitution of 2014 in Egypt adopts liberal ideology as it did not adopt specific economic ideology as it left the door open for the presidential and

8 Mohamed A.M. Ismail, *Globalization and New International Public Works Agreements in Developing Countries, An Analytical Perspective* (Routledge, 2016 and 2011, PP. 1–8 with a foreword by HH Humphrey Lloyd QC).

9 See the Egyptian Supreme Administrative Court decision, Case No. 41354/ 56, session 11/2/2017 and the Egyptian Supreme Constitutional Court Decision, Case No. 7/22, session 5/5/2001 and SCC Case No. 3 of 39, session 2 June 2018. For more elaboration in doctrine see: Soliman El Tamawy, *General Principles of Administrative Contracts* (5th edn, Ain Shams University Press, 1991, in Arabic), and Sarwat Badawi, *Administrative Contracts* (Dar Al Nahda Al Arabia, 1992, in Arabic). In the English legal text see: Mohamed A.M. Ismail, *Globalization and New International Public Works Agreements in Developing Countries, An Analytical Perspective* (Routledge 2016 and 2011, ch. 2).

10 In the legal and cultural globalization generally see: Joseph Stiglitz, *Globalization and its Discontents* (W.W. Norton 2004); Joseph Stiglitz, *Making Globalization Work* (W.W. Norton 2007); Brian Snowdon, *Globalisation, Development and Transition* (Edward Elgar, 2007). The influence of the Anglo-American legal culture is remarkable upon Arab civil law legal culture, particularly in legislation, case law, and the rise of new contractual patterns in state contracts. See: Mohamed A.M. Ismail, *Globalization and New International Public Works Agreements in Developing Countries, An Analytical Perspective* (Routledge 2016 and 2011, pp. 1–8 with a foreword by HH Humphrey Lloyd QC) and for the same author see: *Public Private Partnership Contracts: The Middle East and North Africa* (Routledge, 2020). In new types of states' contracts in the MENA region see: H. Elhaddad, *Contracts Concluded between States and Private Foreign Persons* (1st edn, Dar El Nahda Al Arabia, 1996, in Arabic) and in the international sphere see: J.F. Lalive, *Contrats entre État ou éntreprises étatiques et personnes privées* (Vol. II, *Académie de droit international*, 1983); P. Leboulanger, *Les contrats entre états et entreprises étrangères* (Economica, 1985).

parliamentary elections to determine the economic pattern and economic policies for each electoral term. Therefore, Egypt, in light of the amendments to the 1971 Constitution and the new constitutions with new liberal ideology, could promulgate PPP law. Many MENA countries followed Egypt and promulgated PPP laws.[11]

The Legal Framework of Contracts of Mixed Legal Nature

Contracts of mixed nature such as PPPs and BOT/BOOT are governed with special legislation. For instance, PPP law 67 of 2010 and its executive regulations, govern the procedural phase and contain some other legislative provisions to govern the substantive phase (performance phase) in addition to basic substantive principles stipulated in Egyptian Civil Code provisions. Therefore, awarding PPP contracts is not subject to ordinary public procurement law.[12] The same legal framework exists in other MENA countries which promulgated PPP laws.

Conversely, BOT/BOOT contracts are subject during the procedural phase to ordinary public procurement law. They are subject to some substantive provisions stipulated in some laws which relate to some public utilities' sectors (i.e. electricity, public roads, specialized ports, civil aviation, etc.),[13] in addition to Egyptian Civil Codes legislative provisions which govern substantive rights.

Egypt has been a leading jurisdiction in the MENA region since the 19th century. The Egyptian legal system has greatly influenced MENA countries' legal systems and transferred French civil law legal culture to MENA countries, as most of these legal systems were relying before only on *Sharia'a* law. Administrative law principles are not yet codified (written) in Egypt or in MENA countries and the substantive principles of administrative law (administrative contracts and administrative decrees) were created by the Egyptian Conseil D'État case law through decades. Therefore, the substantive principles of administrative decrees and administrative contracts were flown from Egypt to all MENA countries since the establishment of the Egyptian Conseil D'État in 1946 and until the present.

The previous Egyptian Constitution of 1971 which adopted Marxist ideology has significant importance in economic life and in particular states' contracts. The constitutional amendments in 2007 relinquished Marxist theory and opened doors for more participation of the private sector in all economic sectors. The constitutional framework of state contracts in Egypt and the MENA countries, and the influence of the economic ideologies in the MENA countries' constitutions on state contracting is of fundamental importance. As the Egyptian legal system has influenced MENA countries' legal systems to a great extent, the developments of the

11 Egypt has promulgated PPP Law No. 67 of 2010; Kuwait PPP Law No. 116 of 2014, and Jordan PPP Law No. 31 of 2014 as amended in 2020, Morocco PPP Law No. 86-12 of 2014, Dubai PPP Law No. 22 of 2015 and Tunisia PPP Law No. 45 of 2015.

12 See Article 1 of the promulgation articles of the Egyptian PPP Law No. 67 of 2010.

13 In Egypt, there is no coherent BOT/BOOT legislation but a partial legislative reform was adopted by the Egyptian government in the late 1990s. Egyptian government has promulgated some BOT/BOOT legislation relating to some economic sectors.

legal framework of state contracts in the MENA countries in legislation, regulation, polices, and contractual patterns is clear. Egypt and MENA countries' constitutions currently are not adopting specific static economic ideology whether socialist or free market economy. It opens the door to the elections, whether parliamentary or presidential, to determine the right economic dynamic ideology for each presidential or parliamentary term. The economic ideology has special significance in state contracts legislation. Further, the current constitutions of the MENA countries do not prohibit new patterns of administrative contracts such as PPP techniques. In light of the current constitutional dynamics in the MENA countries, particularly the amendments to the 1971 Egyptian Constitution in 2007, there were rapid legislative and regulatory changes. The current constitution of Egypt, promulgated in 2014, adopts a liberal economic ideology, which permits the government to conclude PPP contracts and other new types of states' contracts. These new types of states contracts inject foreign investments and increase the inward of FDI to Egypt and MENA countries.

The Legal and Judicial Frameworks of Administrative Contracts, in Egypt and MENA Countries

Administrative contracts are subject during the procedural phase to public procurement law. During the execution (performance) phase, substantive rights (conclusion, performance, termination, etc.) are governed by Egyptian Civil Code legislative provisions in addition to substantive principles established by the Egyptian Supreme Administrative Court since 1955, the date of establishment of the court. The case law principles established by the Egyptian Conseil D'État courts play a fundamental role in administrative contracts' law and practice since the administrative law is not codified (written) in Egypt and in MENA countries.

The Egyptian judicial system in Egypt is unique as it has a *dual* judicial system; the first is the ordinary courts for civil, commercial, criminal and all other disputes and the second, which is the Conseil D'État, is specialized in administrative disputes. The Egyptian Conseil D'État is an independent judicial organ, pursuant to the Egyptian Constitutions of 1971, 2012 and 2014, specialized in the settlement of administrative disputes which arise between public juristic entities and private persons whether the latter persons are natural or juristic persons. Pursuant to the Conseil D'État Law No. 47/1972, the Conseil D'État is composed of three sections. Firstly, the Judicial Section which contains the Supreme Administrative Court at the top, and below it the Appeal Administrative Courts and then the Administrative Courts are the lowest step in the judicial hierarchy. The Conseil D'État courts are responsible for the settlement of disputes between public juristic persons and private persons. Secondly, the Legal Opinion Section which contains at the top the General Assembly for Legal Opinion and Legislation and the three committees for legal opinion below the Assembly, and then departments for legal opinion as the lowest step at the hierarchy. The Legal Opinion Section is responsible for submitting opinion in legal matters for public juristic persons and in addition, pursuant to Article 66/d of the Conseil D'État Law No. 47 of 1972, the General Assembly is responsible for settlement of the disputes which arise between two or more public juristic entities with a binding decision. Thirdly, the Legislation Section which is responsible for reviewing legislation before promulgation by the parliament. The Egyptian Conseil D'État was established in 1946 and is tasked with creating a sensible balance between safeguarding public interests, on one hand, and protecting private liberties on the other as one of the democracy guarantees in Egypt.

The Egyptian Constitution of 1971 was of great significance to administrative contract theory and practice in Egypt, since the Egyptian previous public procurement laws No. 9 of 1983 and No. 89 of 1989 respectively were promulgated during the validity of the 1971 Constitution. The 1971 Constitution provides in Article 172, the Egyptian Conseil d'État exclusive jurisdiction, which is concerned exclusively with administrative disputes. The Egyptian Conseil D'État has built on the principles of the administrative contracts' theory through decades, because administrative law in MENA countries is not yet codified through legislation.[14] Administrative law and administrative contracts' principles in Egypt and in MENA countries have been established through the Egyptian Conseil D'État decisions, in particular the Supreme Administrative Court decisions, which were influenced to a great extent by the decisions of the French Conseil D'État.[15] The substantive legal nature of the administrative contract has a special significance to this study, as these contracts' disputes fall in light of their substantive legal nature, within the jurisdiction of the Egyptian Conseil D'État courts.[16] The administrative contracts thus are unique with their special substantive nature through implementing excessive/exorbitant clauses (i.e. liquidated damages as a penalty for delay, unilateral termination of the contract by the contracting state, forfeiture of the performance bond by the contracting state, etc.). Those exorbitant clauses aim at achieving public interests and protecting public funds. Further, Egypt and MENA countries' legal systems have been considerably influenced by the French legal culture through the Egyptian Conseil D'État decisions of the excessive/exorbitant clauses, '*Les Clauses Exorbitantes*' of administrative contracts, which were transferred from France to the Egyptian Conseil D'État jurisprudence, and which aim to promote public interests of the contracting State.[17]

14 Sarwat Badawi, *Administrative Law* (Dar Al Nahda Al Arabia, 1985, in Arabic), and for the same author see: *Administrative Contracts* (Dar Al Nahda Al Arabia, 1992, in Arabic); Raslaan Anwar, *Administrative Law* (Dar Al Nahda Al Arabia, 1994, in Arabic); Soliman El Tamawy, *General Principles of Administrative Contracts* (5th edn, Ain Shams University Press, 1991, in Arabic). In French doctrine see: A. de Laubadère, J-C. Venezia, and Y.Gaudemet, *Traité de droit administratif* (Tome 2, 10th edn, LGDJ, 1995); J. Rivero and J. Waline, *Droit Administratif*, (15th edn, Dalloz, 1994).

15 Sarwat Badawi, *Administrative Law* (Dar El Nahda El Arabia, 1985 and 2010 editions, in Arabic).

16 Mohamed A.M. Ismail, *International Construction Contracts Arbitration* (Al Halabi Publishing Co., Beirut, 2003, in Arabic); and for the same author see: Ismail, *Public Economic Law and the New International Administrative Contract* (Al Halabi Publishing Co., Beirut, 2010, in Arabic). The latter book was awarded the State Prize in Academic Legal Research in Egypt, 2011.

17 Sarwat Badawi, *Administrative Law* (Dar Al Nahda Al Arabia, 2010, in Arabic); and for the same author see: *Administrative Contracts* (Dar Al Nahda Al Arabia, 1992, in Arabic).

Procedural Phase

Previous Public Procurement Laws Nos. 9 of 1983 and 89 of 1989 and their executive regulations respectively were promulgated in Egypt to govern the procedural phase and awarding public contracts.

The new promulgated Public Procurement Law (State Contracting Law No. 182 of 2018) was promulgated and came into force on 3 November 2018.[18] The new law has a modern approach which is consistent with international standards in public procurement and the UN SDGs. It reflects innovation in public procurements in the Egyptian legal system. The Conseil D'État courts' decisions through decades illustrate the procedural principles of administrative contracts in Egypt and MENA countries while interpreting public procurement legislation. The role of the Conseil D'État courts to create rules is limited as there is a valid written legislation. However, this role has wider scope in the absence of written legislation as there is a duty upon the administrative judge to create rules which are applicable to administrative contracts.

Performance Phase

The Egyptian Civil Code is applicable to both the conclusion, the execution, and performance until final completion of administrative contracts and also applicable to private contracts. Similar to private law contracts, substantive rights of the administrative contracts are governed by the Egyptian Civil Code provisions.

In administrative contracts, parties to these contracts, a public body, and a private entity, have the same contractual obligations and can seek the same remedies as the two private parties to a private contract of a private nature. In addition, administrative contracts are unique with their exorbitant clauses which do not exist in private contracts. The justification for adopting exorbitant clauses in administrative contracts is to achieve public interests.[19] In the absence of written legislation in most cases, the Conseil D'État courts' decisions, through decades, created a set of the substantive principles of administrative contracts in Egypt and MENA countries (exorbitant clauses, contract performance, the prohibition of *Exceptio non-adimpleti contractus* in administrative contracts as a general rule subject to minor exceptions, unilateral termination by the contracting state, etc.).

18 Article 5 of the promulgation articles of Law No. 182 of 2018 stipulates that law has to come into force after 30 days from the date of its publication in the *Official Gazette*. The Law was published in the *Official Gazette* on 3 October 2018.

19 For the aims of administrative contracts (*Le contrat administratif*) in France see: André de Laubadère, Frank Moderne, and Pierre Delvolvé, *Traité des contrats administratifs* (LGDJ, 1983, Tome I, p. 210 et seq.); see also ibid., Tome II; Laurent Richer, *Droits des Contracts Administratifs* (LGDJ, 1995, p. 85 et seq.); and for the same author see: 6th edn (LGDJ, 2008, p. 90). In public works agreements see: D. Chabanol and J-P. Jouguelet, 1994, *Marchés publics de travaux*, 2nd edn. See the same aims in Egyptian and Arab doctrine, Soliman El Tamawy, *General Principles of Administrative Contracts* (5th edn, Ain Shams University Press, 1991, in Arabic), and Sarwat Badawi, *Administrative Contracts* (Dar Al Nahda Al Arabia, 1992, in Arabic).

1 Courts' Intervention in Case of Mandatory Legislative Provision

Introduction

In this chapter, the legal framework of respective states in Egypt and the Gulf region is explored, in an attempt to position the case law covering jurisdictional competences, in addressing practical cases, and legal examples in the relevant jurisdictions. An anatomy is provided to specific cases, which are significant to international contract law theory and practice. It is important to analyze *force majeure* in legislation. In addition, Article 147 of the Egyptian Civil Code provides for '*l'imprévision*' theory, which is a mandatory rule in the Egyptian legal system, and stipulates that contracting parties cannot avoid the application of the theory of '*l'imprévision*.' Accordingly, if contracting parties wish to exclude the application of the principle, courts (or an arbitrator) can interfere and declare the exclusion 'unfair' deeming the contractual agreement null and void, seeing as it is contrary to public policy. Similar provisions exist in several MENA jurisdictions.[1] Such provisions aim to maintain the financial equilibrium of the contract and to protect the weaker party in the contractual relationship. Further, Article 224/3 of the Egyptian Civil Code stipulates that the contracting parties cannot deprive courts (or arbitrators) from exercising judicial review over an agreed amount of *quantum* for compensation in contracts. Similar legislative provisions in the MENA countries' civil codes are scrutinized. It is fundamental to analyze some substantive principles of contract law in Egypt and MENA countries which are significant to achieve global contract law.

1 *L'imprévision* theory exists in MENA countries' civil codes, for instance see: Article 130 of the Bahrain Civil Code, Article 198 of the Kuwaiti Civil Code, Article 107 of the Algerian Civil Code, Article 249 of the UAE Civil Code, Article 146/2 of the Iraqi Civil Code, Article 171/2 of the Qatar Civil Code, Article 159 of the Omani Civil Code, Article 205 of the Jordanian Civil Code, Article 148 of the Syrian Civil Code, and Article 147/2 of the Libyan Civil Code. Generally, the Egyptian Civil Code was influenced by the French Civil Code and all Arab civil codes were influenced by the Egyptian Civil Code. Such influence reflects the legal globalization phenomenon implications in the MENA countries. In *l'imprévision* in the Egyptian Civil Code see: Abdel Baki, Abdel Fatah (1984), *The Encyclopedia of Egyptian Civil Law, Contract and Unilateral Acts Theory, a Comparative Study with Islamic Doctrine*; Abdel Wadood Yehia, *Brief in the General Theory of Obligations, Sources of Obligations* (Dar Al Nahda Al Arabia Part I, 1989).

DOI: 10.4324/9781003466352-2

Changing of Circumstances and Financial Equilibrium

Contract determines the limits of the right of the contracting parties to amend such contracts by adding provisions related to compensation in case the cost of performing the contract increases significantly or if the value of the revenues from such performance is significantly reduced compared to the performance costs.[2] Contract value may be changed and performance may be onerous as a result of:

1. Changes in economic or financial conditions.
2. Amendments to laws and/or regulations that affect financial equilibrium of the contract.

In the cases provided for in paragraphs (1) and (2), the following conditions shall be met:

1. The changes in economic or financial conditions and/or the amendments to laws and/or regulations occurred after the conclusion of the contract.
2. The above-mentioned changes and amendments were unpredictable when the contract was concluded.
3. The above-mentioned changes and amendments are beyond the control of the parties.

The Impossibility of Performing the Contractual Obligations: *Force Majeure* and Its Effect upon Exemption from Liability

A fundamental concept to raise contractual liability in MENA countries' legal systems is the existence of a contractual breach; damage and the causality (*lien de causalité*) between them.

The impossible performance of an obligation can be factual or legal. An external cause is a hardship, *force majeure*, the debtor's breach or a third party's tort. The *force majeure* or the accidental event must be impossible to prevent, such as an earthquake, flood, volcanic eruption, or an outbreak of war, all of which make the contract performance impossible.

2 It is important to differentiate between contract price and contract value. Contract price, generally, has become nowadays a dynamic process rather than a static process as in the past and in light of the traditional theory of administrative contracts. It is suggested that review should be on a monthly basis in order to update the value of payments with the same contract price and to face the rapid change in raw materials prices. In the first month of performance, the first certificate equals £E100,000, meanwhile, the true value of the 19th or the 20th certificate (assuming that each certificate equals £E100,000) is £E118,000. Despite the fact that inflation and currency depreciation are domestic factors, change in materials prices is a regular international phenomenon. Following this concept, it is clear that there is an essential need to update the value not the price. Price will remain the same (i.e., the true value of the Egyptian pound in month zero equals £1, while it equals £0.78 in month 36). It is suggested that currency units at the time of contracting should equal the same units at the final completion date.

The *force majeure* must be warranted by two conditions: The first condition is that the event is accidental; the second condition is that the event cannot be prevented. The external cause eliminates the causality link (*lien de causalité*) between the breach and the damage and can be a *force majeure*, an accidental event, a breach by the debtor, or an act by a third party.[3]

Force majeure is a purely legal concept forged by the lawmaker as a preventive measure against any matter that may cause a breach of contractual obligations where it becomes impossible to perform them.[4]

Article 165 of the Egyptian Civil Code stipulates that: 'If a person proves that the damage has occurred due to an external cause beyond his control, such as an accidental event, a *force majeure*, or a tort by a third party, he is not obligated to compensate for such damage unless otherwise specified in a legislative provision or an agreement.'

In light of the above Article, the external cause can be a *force majeure* or an accidental event. A *force majeure* or an accidental event must be unpreventable and unforeseeable.

The Egyptian Court of Cassation ruled that a *force majeure* must be unforeseeable and unpreventable. These two conditions are drawn from precedents exclusively examined by the courts; the cassation courts of all MENA countries concluded the same approach.[5]

The unforeseeable nature of the event is the first condition that must be established in this respect; a person is deemed negligent if he or she could foresee the event and did not take the necessary precautions to avoid the consequential effects. The criteria of unforeseeable must be an objective one, where the event cannot be

3 Abdel Wadood Yehia, *Brief in the General Theory of Obligations, Sources of Obligations* (Part I, 1989, in Arabic), p. 256 and see generally: Abdel Baki Abdel Fatah, *The Encyclopedia of Egyptian Civil Law, Contract and Unilateral Acts Theory, a Comparative Study with Islamic Doctrine,* (1984, in Arabic). In English law see: G.H. Trietle, *Frustration and Force Majeure* (Sweet & Maxwell, 1994, ch. 5, p. 191); Hugh Beale, *Chitty on Contracts, General Principles* (30th edn, Vol. 1, 2008, p, 1479); Ewan McKendrick, *Force Majeure and Frustration of Contract* (2nd edn, Routledge, 1995, pp. 3–19 and 21–31); Richard Stone and James Devenney (eds), *Texts, Cases and Materials on Contract Law* (Routledge, 2014); I.D. Wallace, *Hudson's in Building and Engineering Contracts* (11th edn, Vol. 1, Sweet & Maxwell, 1995, p. 655). In French doctrine see: Laurent Richer, *Droits de Contrats Administratifs* (LGDG, 2008, p. 214); A. de Laubadère, F. Moderne, et P. Delvolvé, *Traite de Contrats Administratifs* (Tome 2, Paris, LGDJ, p. 727). In building contracts in comparative jurisprudence and international customs, see: Christopher S. Thomas, '*Aspects of Building Contracts: A Comparative View of English and French Law in the Light of Potential Harmonization*' (PhD thesis, School of Law, Kings College, London, 1995); Philippe Lane Bruner, 'Force Majeure under International Law and International Construction Contract Model Forms' (*ICLR*, Part 2, April 1995, p. 274); Douglas Jones, '*Force Majeure* in Australian Construction Law' (*ICLR*, Part 2, April 1995, p. 295); Stanley Jeremiah, 'Insurability of *Force Majeure* Events in Construction Contracts' (*ICLR*, Part 2, April 1995, p. 319); John C. Chen, '*Force Majeure* in Construction Contracts, Taiwan' (*ICLR*, Part 2, April 1995, p. 328).

4 Pronchai Wiwatpattarakul, 'A Critical Examination of the Concept of *Force Majeure* at Thai Law and Its Impact in the Context of Construction Contracts' (*ICLR* 1, 174).

5 Egyptian Cassation Court, Civil Circuit, Session of 27 March 1980, Case No. 979 of 47, *The Collection of the Technical Bureau*, Judicial Year 31, Rule 183, 930.

foreseen by even the most prudent person, which makes it absolutely – and therefore not relatively – impossible.[6]

The second condition to be established is related to the unpreventable nature of the event. *Impossible* means absolute impossibility, whereupon there is an absolute impossibility of performing the obligation.

If both conditions are established, the debtor is exempted from the contractual liability, and the causality link (*lien de causalité*) between the breach and damage is then ruled out; hence, there is no ground for compensation in either case.[7]

The concept of *force majeure* has great significance in all legal systems. In the English system, *force majeure* topic is characterized as 'frustration of contract.'[8] The Egyptian judiciary has applied an objective criterion/approach whereupon it is absolutely impossible to perform the obligations, and the *force majeure* or the accidental event is unpreventable, which makes such performance absolutely impossible, not only to the debtor but also to any other person in the same position as the debtor.[9]

Force Majeure in the Egyptian Conseil D'État Case Law

The Egyptian administrative judiciary confirmed the established approaches adopted by Egyptian jurisprudence with regard to *force majeure*. The Supreme Administrative Court decided that where the impossibility to perform an obligation was attributed to an external cause, 'the obligation to perform is then lifted, whether performance in kind or by way of compensation.' An external cause is an accidental event, *force majeure*, debtor's breach, or a third party's tort. A *force majeure* or an accidental event must be unforeseeable and unpreventable; if these two provisions exist, such an event is then unpredictable and beyond the control of not only the debtor but also the most prudent person. The criterion is objective and not subject to the ordinary individual; nevertheless, it requires absolute impossibility. The *force majeure* or accidental event must be unpreventable; thus, if it is preventable, though unforeseeable, it is not a *force majeure* or accidental event. It must also render the execution absolutely impossible, not only for the debtor but also for any person who is in the position of the debtor. This point makes the distinct difference between a *force majeure* and an accidental event that renders the execution onerous but not impossible. The effect of a *force majeure* or an

6 Abdel Wadood Yehia, *Brief in the General Theory of Obligations, Sources of Obligations* (Part I, 1989, pp. 256–8, in Arabic).

7 Egyptian Cassation Court, Civil Circuit, session of 29 January 1976, *The Collection of the Technical Bureau*, Judicial Year 46, Rule 243, 27.

8 Hugh Beale, *Chitty on Contracts, General Principles* (30th edn, Vol. 1, 2008, p. 1479); Treitel, *Frustration and Force Majeure* (1994 and 2nd edn, 2004, Sweet & Maxwell); Ewan McKendrick, *Force Majeure and Frustration of Contract* (2nd edn, 1995), and for the same author see generally in contract law theory in English law: *Contract Law* (11th edn, Palgrave Law Master, 2015, p. 254).

9 The Supreme Administrative Court, Judgment No. 689 – 4, 12 December 1969, 5/15/106 – *Forty Years Collection of Court Judgments*, p. 473.

accidental event varies according to the circumstances; if it was the sole cause for the damage that occurred, the causal link is then ruled out, which, in turn, provides an exemption from responsibility. The consequence can be the suspension of the execution and not the exemption from performing the obligation, until such event has ended. Both parties may modify their agreement in accordance with the effect of the *force majeure* or accidental event; for example, they may agree that the debtor shall not be exempted from the obligation and shall be responsible for the consequence of any external cause. Hence, although it is impossible to perform the obligation due to an external cause, such performance is not lifted but is replaced by compensation, where the debtor is like an insurance entity, and the creditor is the insurer against any event attributed to a *force majeure*. The aforementioned principles were codified in the MENA countries' civil codes. While these principles are applied within the context of relationships under private law, the administrative judiciary has consistently taken them into consideration as a general principle to be applied in determining the administrative contractual relations under public law, as long as it is in conformity with the functioning of the public utility and ensures the reconcilement of this latter with the individual interests.[10].

The Supreme Administrative Court at the Egyptian Conseil D'État also held that where an event was foreseeable though unpreventable, or vice versa, it was not deemed a *force majeure* and did not give rise to an exemption from responsibility. The Supreme Administrative Court also mentioned in one of its leading judgments that the intervention made by the Supreme Council of Antiquities was foreseeable and cannot be deemed an external cause or a *force majeure*, since it was expected – when concluding a contract – to suspend the work when there were archeological finds on site.[11]

The Supreme Administrative Court added that the contracting parties might not modify their agreement to change the effect of *force majeure*, for example, by agreeing that the debtor would bear the consequential effect.[12]

Difficulty of Performing Contractual Obligations in Contracts

The concept of the contract's financial equilibrium[13] is one of the most important topics in contract frustration theory and practice. It is important to analyze the

10 The Supreme Administrative Court, Judgment No. 689 – 4 (12 December 1969, 5/15/106) – *Forty Years Collection of Court Judgments*, p. 473.

11 The Supreme Administrative Court, Judgments Nos. 1320 and 1340 – 12 (15 February 1969, 14/48/373) – *Forty Years Collection of Court Judgments*, p. 474.

12 Ibid.

13 For elaboration on this concept, see: Al Tamawy, *The General Principle of Administrative Contracts* (5th edn, 1991, p. 61, in Arabic). In Egyptian and MENA countries' civil codes see: Abdel Baki Abdel Fatah, *The Encyclopedia of Egyptian Civil Law, Contract and Unilateral Acts Theory, a Comparative Study with Islamic Doctrine,* (1984, in Arabic); Yehia, Abdel Wadood, *Brief in the General Theory of Obligations, Sources of Obligations* (Dar Al Nahda Al Arabia Part I, 1989, in Arabic).

theory of unforeseen circumstances ('*l'imprévision*') in the Egyptian and MENA countries' legal systems.

Theory of Unforeseen Circumstances ('L'imprévision')

The theory of unforeseen circumstances, '*l'imprévision*' was established within the provisions of the Egyptian and MENA countries' civil codes, considering that the change in circumstances – during the contract performance – is the most important cause for the contract's financial equilibrium, which requires restoring the contract's economic balance to meet the contracting parties' financial expectations.[14]

The theory of unforeseen circumstances in MENA countries' civil codes is a mandatory legislative rule which is a matter of public policy as the contracting parties cannot avoid the theory application by their contractual agreement.[15]

Since this theory is founded within the provisions of the civil codes, it is appropriate to refer to the general literature related to the Egyptian Civil Code construing this theory in administrative contracts.[16]

The basis of this theory was founded in the administrative contracts in the French Conseil D'État where it was set forth to address the accidental economic

14 For instance, Article 147/2 of the Egyptian Civil Code, Article 130 of the Bahrain Civil Code, Article 198 of the Kuwaiti Civil Code, Article 107 of Algerian Civil Code, Article 249 of the UAE Civil Code, Article 146/2 of the Iraqi Civil Code, Article 171/2 of the Qatar Civil Code, Article 159 of the Omani Civil Code, Article 205 of the Jordanian Civil Code, Article 148 of the Syrian Civil Code, and Article 147/2 of the Libyan Civil Code. Generally, the Egyptian Civil Code was influenced by the French Civil Code and all Arab civil codes were influenced by the Egyptian Civil Code. Such influence reflects the legal globalization phenomenon implications in the MENA countries.

15 For instance, see: Article 147/2 of the Egyptian Civil Code, Article 198 of the Kuwaiti Civil Code, Article 130 of the Bahrain Civil Code, Article 107 of the Algerian Civil Code, Article 249 of the UAE Civil Code, Article 146/2 of the Iraqi Civil Code, Article 171/2 of the Qatar Civil Code, Article 159 of the Omani Civil Code, Article 205 of the Jordanian Civil Code, Article 148 of the Syrian Civil Code, and Article 147/2 of the Libyan Civil Code. All these Arab civil codes consider the application of the theory of unforeseen circumstances as a mandatory rule which is a matter of public policy. Contracting parties cannot ignore or avoid the application of such theory by their contractual agreement and any contractual clause which contains an exemption from the application of such theory is null and void pursuant to these legislative provisions. It is clear that most Arab countries' legislation is following the Egyptian legislation.

16 See the Arab jurisprudence: Abdel Wadood Yehia, *Brief in the General Theory of Obligations, Sources of Obligations*, (Part I, 1989, in Arabic); Abdel Baki, Abdel Fatah, *The Encyclopedia of Egyptian Civil Law, Contract and Unilateral Acts Theory, a Comparative Study with Islamic Doctrine*, 1984 (in Arabic); Ga'far, Anas and Ga'far, Ashraf Anas, *Administrative Contracts* (Dar Al Nahda Al Arabia, 2021, p. 163, in Arabic); Abdel Azim Abdelsalaam, *The Unforeseen Circumstances and Physical Difficulties upon the Performance of Administrative Contracts*, 1990 (in Arabic). In the French doctrine, see: A. de Laubadère, F. Moderne, et P. Delvolvé, *Traite de Contrats Administratifs* (Tome 2, Paris, LGDJ, p. 559); Jacques Clément et Daniel Richer, *Les Marchés Publics de Travaux des Collectivités Territoriales* (2nd edn, Economica, 1993, 208 et seq.); Laurent Richer, *Droits de Contrats Administratifs* (LGDJ, 2008, p. 210); and see generally R. Chapus, *Droit Administratif Général* (8th edn, Tome 2, Montchrestien, 1995); R. Chapus, *Droit administrative general* (15th edn, Tome 1, Paris: Montchrestien, 2001); P. Delvolvé, *Droit Administratif* (12th edn, 1992).

circumstances during World War I and recognized the right of the contracting party to compensation in case of those unforeseen circumstances. The purpose of this compensation was to sustain the functioning of the public utilities that provided citizens with services.[17]

The French Conseil D'État stipulated that in order to fulfill the condition of compensation entitlement, an unforeseen circumstance must be unexpected;[18] however, it ruled out the claim for compensation if the price increases were expected, which did not destabilize so much the contract's economies.[19]

The Theory of Unforeseen Circumstances in State Contracts in MENA Countries' Jurisprudence

The Egyptian Conseil D'État established the foundations for the application of the theory of unforeseen circumstances in general, following the model of the French administrative judiciary, which was the founder of this theory.

The Supreme Administrative Court at the Egyptian Conseil D'État confirmed that the application of the theory of unforeseen circumstances in jurisprudence and administrative judiciary was subject to the occurrence of incidents or circumstances, which are natural or economic, during the contract performance or an act committed by a third party other than the contracting authority. The court stipulated that the contracting party could neither expect nor prevent these circumstances when concluding the contract and that they caused individual serious injuries giving rise to grave destabilization of the contract's financial equilibrium. The rationale behind the application of such a theory, after fulfilling its conditions, was to obligate the administration to bear jointly the loss occurred during such unforeseen circumstances, so as to ensure the contract performance and the public utility's sustainability. The role of the administrative judge was limited to rule for a suitable compensation without modifying the contractual obligations.[20]

The Supreme Administrative Court confirmed in another judgment that in order to apply the theory of unforeseen circumstances, the contract's financial equilibrium must be gravely destabilized as this theory was based upon the concept of

17 Jacques Clément et Daniel Richer, *Les Marchés Publics de Travaux des Collectivités Territoriales* (Economica, 2nd edn, 1993, p. 208); see also: J. Dufau, *Le droit des travaux public* (Tome 1, Editions du Moniteur, 1988.)

18 C.E., 30 Mai 1916, *Compagnie générale d'eclairage de Bordeaux*, leb. 125.

19 C.E., 7 Juillet 1976, *Societé demongeot, inedit*; C.E., 17 Juin 1981, *Commune de Papeete;* see: Jacques Clément et Daniel Richer, *Les Marchés Publics de Travaux des Collectivités Territoriales* (Economica, 2nd edn, 1993, p. 208).

20 The Supreme Administrative Court, Judgment No. 1562 – 10, 67 – 11, 11 May 1968, 13/117/874 – *Forty Years Collection of Court Judgments*, p. 440. This theory was established by virtue of a judgment issued by the French Conseil D'État on 30 March 1916 – C.E., 20 March 1916, *Compagnie générale d'éclairage de Bordeaux,* Leb, 125. In Egyptian and MENA countries' doctrine see: Al Tamawy, *The General Principle of Administrative Contracts* (5th edn, 1991, p. 61, in Arabic); Anas Ga'far and Ashraf Anas Ga'far, *Administrative Contracts* (Dar Al Nahda Al Arabia, 2021, p. 163, in Arabic); Sarwat Badawi, *Administrative Contracts* (Dar Al Nahda Al Arabia, 1992, in Arabic).

absolute justice – a mainstay of the administrative law. In addition, the purpose of this theory is to realize the public interest by ensuring the systematic, regularity, and consistent functioning of the public utility and prompt services delivered to the public. The contracting party's intent was to help realize the public interest by fulfilling the obligation in an honest and adequate manner in consideration of a profit and fair revenues. This required understanding and collaboration to overcome the difficulties and impediments to perform the contract.

The court explained in this judgment the theory's purpose and essence and confirmed that the occurrence of unforeseen circumstances did not render the execution impossible, but cumbersome to carry out, destabilizing the contract's financial equilibrium and causing losses to the contracting party exceeding the normal and logical losses that any contracting party might have sustained.

In this regard, the court held that the purport of the theory of unforeseen circumstances is that, where circumstances or events take place during the administrative contract performance and were not expected when concluding the contract, by which the contract's economies are destabilized, and where such circumstances or events do not render the contract performance impossible but rather more onerous and more costly than reasonably estimated by both contracting parties, and where the loss resulting therefrom is grave, exceptional and unexpected, exceeding the normal loss that any contracting party may sustain, the injured party has the right to request the other party to bear jointly the loss by partly compensating therein. As such, a new obligation is added to the contracting party's obligations that were not included in the contract, which means imposing an obligation upon the debtor in the administrative contract to pay the creditor a compensation to ensure the proper execution of the contract, so long as these unforeseen circumstances or events cause a loss to the debtor, which can be deemed as destabilizing the contract's economies.

It is evident that the Supreme Administrative Court imposed an obligation upon the administration to pay compensation to ensure the proper contract performance as long as these unforeseen circumstances or events caused a loss to the debtor, which could be deemed as destabilizing the contract's financial equilibrium. Nevertheless, the court asserted that the compensation paid by the creditor must be a part of the compensation (partial compensation and not full compensation)[21] for the loss sustained by the debtor who was not entitled to claim for compensation based on loss of profits or unrealized gains.

The court added that to estimate the destabilization of the contract's financial equilibrium, considering its occurrence, all losses affecting the contract's economies must be taken into account. The contract must be considered, not as individual elements as some elements could be compensated, thereby offsetting other elements

21 The Supreme Administrative Court judgment on 27 October 2020, Case No. 58619 Judicial Year 62, which distinguishes between the unforeseen circumstances theory where the Court orders for partial compensation in favor of the injured contracting party, however, the Court orders for full compensation in favor of the injured contracting party if the Prince Theory required conditions are met.

that caused a loss. As such, the contract's economies' destabilization could not be noticed or ascertained unless all the work related to the contract was completed.[22]

The Supreme Administrative Court held that the application of the theory of unforeseen circumstances in administrative contracts, and other matters related to the public law, was subject to the occurrence of such unforeseen circumstances during the contract performance and not after the contract completion.[23]

The Supreme Administrative Court distinguished between the accidental event and *force majeure*, describing that the unexpected price increases during the performance of administrative contracts, which gave rise to an increase of the contracting party's burdens by the grave losses that individual would sustain to the extent of gravely destabilizing the contract's economies, was an accidental circumstance and not a *force majeure*.[24]

Two crucial points are worth considering as unforeseen circumstances namely: the effect of legislation and foreign currency exchange rates upon the contract performance.

The Impact of Legislation and the Exchange Rate of the Foreign Currency Upon the Contract Performance[25]

The General Assembly of the Legal Opinion and Legislation in the Egyptian Conseil D'État issued an opinion that the application of a new legislation, such as the Law of General Tax on Sale promulgated under Law No. 11 of 1991, affected the sales prices set forth in contracts concluded before the enforcement of the said law, as the contracting companies agreed in the contracts with the pharmaceutical

22 The Supreme Administrative Court, Judgment No. 46 – 14, 17 June 1972, 17/83/576 – *Forty Years Collection of Court Judgments*, p. 442; The Supreme Administrative Court, Judgment Nos. 1223 and 1224–27, 18 December 1984, 30/45/250 – *Forty Years Collection of Court Judgments*, p. 446.

23 The Supreme Administrative Court, Judgment Nos. 843 and 922–26, 20 November 1982, 28/18/86 – *Forty Years Collection of Court Judgments*, pp. 458–9.

24 Administrative Court Judgment No. 2150–6, 9 June 1962, 7/96/1024 – *Forty Years Collection of Court Judgments*, p. 458.

25 Depreciation of the currency in developing countries is clear as inflation rate and increase in materials prices play a considerable role in determining the contract value during works progress. Some of these factors are related to internal market mechanisms while others are influenced by international market prices and their fluctuations. All these factors play a significant role in the industrial process and in the international demand for exported cement, for instance, which consequently affects prices of construction materials in the Egyptian market. Following this concept, it is clear that there is an essential need to update the value not the price. Price will remain the same (i.e., the true value of the Egyptian pound in month zero equals £1, while it equals £0.78 in month 36). It is suggested that currency units at the time of contracting should equal the same units at the final completion date. Having a clear contractual regime is of fundamental importance to achieve financial equilibrium and to avoid uncertainties and unpredictability. This will lead to the right application of legal provisions and clear interpretation of the contract clauses and parties' intentions, upon contracting, to some extent to maintain a balanced relationship with the administration in the domain of the administrative contract. Financial equilibrium mechanisms and principles of administrative contracts have to be consistent with international commercial contracts' principles and standards.

company that the value of the contracting work was total and final. As such, pursuant to the Civil Code provisions, the company might not claim for price increases resulting from the application of the Law of General Tax on the basis that it would have rendered the contract performance difficult. It was not apparent from the documents that the application of the said law would affect only the contracting company by sustaining grave loss destabilizing the contract's economies; thus, one of the conditions of the theory of unforeseen circumstances was not fulfilled, and the General Assembly ruled against compensation on this basis.[26] In such a case, the General Assembly restricted the application of the theory and did not consider the successive tax legislation as causing financial burdens on the party or grounds for compensation on the basis of the theory of unforeseen circumstances since it did not give rise to grave losses.

In another opinion, the General Assembly concluded that the Prime Minister's decree to devalue the Egyptian pound against the US dollar was a general exceptional event, pursuant to Article 147/2 of the Civil Code, where both parties could not expect it when concluding the contract. If the party should have expected that the government might seek to devalue the Egyptian currency, the contracting party could not predict how far this devaluation would be; thus, the results and effect of this procedure upon the contract's financial equilibrium must exceed what the party would have expected when concluding the contract. In both cases, if the loss sustained by the party with the obligation to perform the contract rendered the fulfillment of the obligation onerous and gave rise to serious loss, the other party should jointly bear such loss, to make it reasonably bearable for that party. This means that the expected loss should be borne by the party with the obligation to perform the contract, whereas the unexpected loss should be jointly borne by both parties, to mitigate its gravity.[27]

In another opinion, the General Assembly concluded that the tender's general conditions, pursuant to Article 20, stipulated that the tenders must be submitted for the supply of goods based upon the tax rate, production duties and any other duties applicable at the time. In case the above-mentioned rates and duties changed in the period between submitting the tender and the deadline for the supply of goods, and the supply took place within the specified period, the difference should be settled accordingly, on condition that the contractor had proofs of paying the duties on the supplied goods based upon the modified increased rates. If the modification required reducing the rates, the difference should be deducted from the contract's value unless the contractor had proofs that he or she paid the duties based on the original rates before the modification. Article 62 of the general conditions provides that 'the final statement shall apply the rates included in the price tables, regardless

26 The General Assembly's legal opinion No. 328 on 24 April 1993, session, 28 March 1993, 47, Opinion No. 127 on 31/ January 1993 – Session 31January 1993, 47 – *Forty Years Collection of Court Judgments*, pp. 461–2.

27 Legal Opinion No. 360 of 17 July 1954, *Modern Administrative Encyclopedia* (1st edn, Vol. 18, 1986/1987, 796, Rule No. 568).

of any price changes or currencies fluctuation.' It also stated that 'the contractor shall bear all price increases for the materials, freight, shipping, all types of insurance, and labor costs during the work's period, and may not request any increase or change the prices he accepted.'

The Supreme Administrative Court approach varies according to the accidental reason affecting the tender's value. If the reason is attributed to market volatility and currency fluctuation, the contractor must bear the consequences, whether it is an increase or decrease in prices; if the reason is attributed to modification in taxes and duties, the contracting authority (the ministry) must bear the consequences as provided in Article 20, whether the reason affecting the tender's value has taken place before or after the contract's conclusion.[28]

The Egyptian Conseil D'État was hesitant to consider the market volatility and currency fluctuation as unforeseen circumstances, as the General Assembly had – in its opinion – considered it to be unforeseen circumstances on one occasion, and the Supreme Administrative Court denied such approach on another.

The same applies to the tax and customs legislation. In a judgment issued by the Supreme Administrative Court in the 1960s,[29] the court considered the modification of taxes and customs duties as unforeseen circumstances, which would not be valid without legislation. In the 1990s,[30] the General Assembly refused to consider the Law of General Tax on Sale as unforeseen circumstances unless – as expressed by the court – it rendered the contract performance difficult. Following the Egyptian Conseil D'État jurisprudence, the above-mentioned principles were well established, decades ago, in the MENA countries' jurisprudence.

The Unforeseen Circumstances in PPP Contracts

PPP techniques aim to encourage greater inward investments and are a significant boost for the economy. Egypt and MENA countries aim to enhance its investment ecosystem by implementing PPP legislation and incorporate it into their legislative and regulatory frameworks. PPP techniques in the MENA region provide a vision which is eager to continue ramping up inward of FDI by creating legislative and regulatory frameworks for PPPs which strengthen the business environment and promote better threshold of protection to foreign investors.[31]

Egypt and MENA countries' PPP legislation is part of a package of legal reforms intended to strengthen the legislative climate for current and prospective investors in the MENA region and shore up the economy as a result. This legal approach is

28 The Supreme Administrative Court – Case No. 1186, Judicial Year 10, session of 25 November 1967, *Modern Administrative Encyclopedia* (Vol. 18, 797–898), Rule No. 570.

29 Ibid.

30 The General Assembly's legal opinion No. 328 on 24 April 1993, session (28 March 1993) 47, Opinion No. 127 on 31 January 1993 – Session (31 January 1993) 47 – *Forty Years Collection of Court Judgments*, pp. 461–2.

31 Mohamed A.M. Ismail, *Public Private Partnership Contracts, The Middle East and North Africa* (Routledge, 2020).

also consistent with the UN SDGs as it increases the ranking of the MENA countries, as host countries which have good business environment, in the international financial institutions' classifications. It is an attempt to achieve a real implementation of the vision of 2030. The PPP approach is part of a wider and diversified program of ongoing reforms designed to create new opportunities for investors looking for access to the MENA countries' market. Reforms implemented in recent years have helped to increase the inward of FDI. PPPs techniques in the MENA region enable experimentation and innovation by businesses and improve the outcomes of public services for end-users.

PPPs are now being used in many countries in the MENA region to develop infrastructure and services projects. Typically, PPP transactions are based on a network of complex legal agreements, however, at the center of each transaction there is normally a PPP contract, in the form of a modernized concession agreement or similar document, between a government or other public juristic entity (the Contracting Authority) and a private company or a consortium of companies (the Private Partner). The complexity and sophistication of PPP transactions, and the fact that they are often heavily negotiated to reflect the characteristics of a given infrastructure project, frequently means that considerable time and expenses are involved in preparing and finalizing PPP contracts. This has led many interested parties to ask if it is possible to reduce the costs, and speed the process, by standardizing the provisions found in such contracts. It is of fundamental importance to note that there is significant improvement and innovation in award profile during the procedural phase in selecting the private partner with the contracting authority as most PPP legislation in the MENA countries provide for a new legislative framework for the selection of the private partner which is different from the traditional public procurement legislation that is still used in traditional administrative contracts and not for PPP contracts.[32]

PPP legislation in the MENA region provides significant improvements to the traditional theory of contract price in administrative contracts. Innovation in contract price is one of the main features of the current PPP legislation in the MENA countries. The Egyptian PPP legislation in Article 8 permits the contracting parties to stipulate in the contract that they can amend this contract to maintain financial equilibrium (the law pointed out the unforeseen circumstances and if there is any new legislation which may violate financial equilibrium). Article 31 of the PPP legislation of Dubai provides that in case of unforeseen circumstances, the contract can be amended to promote financial equilibrium. Article 36 of the PPP legislation of Kuwait pointed out that the amendment of the Partnership Agreement may

32 Mohamed Am Ismail, *Innovation in Public Procurements in the Egyptian PPPs Legislation, (With Reference to PPPs Legislation in Dubai and Kuwait)* (Book chapter on Joint Public Procurement and Innovation, Lessons Across Borders, edited by Gabriella Racca and Christopher Yukins, Bruylant, 2019, p. 565). It is worth noting that most MENA countries' PPP legislation contains procedural provisions for private partner selection during the procedural phase and substantive provisions for the performance phase of the PPP contract, for instance Egyptian PPP legislation 2010, Kuwaiti PPP legislation 2014, Morocco PPP legislation 2014, Dubai PPP legislation 2015.

be agreed upon in accordance with the principle and the rules provided for under the agreement, if unforeseen circumstances occurred after the conclusion of the Partnership Agreement, including amendments to the laws in force at the time of conclusion of this agreement and leading to a financial imbalance of the agreement. PPP legislation in Egypt, Dubai, and Kuwait contains provisions to maintain financial equilibrium during performance and until the final completion of the contract through contractual mechanisms and without the need to start litigation or arbitration. PPP legislation in Egypt and Kuwait contains provisions to maintain stabilization for the price against change of laws during contract performance and until final completion. It is appropriate to refer, briefly, to the profile of innovation in contract price and the new mechanisms by which contractors can guarantee that the contract price shall not violate their economic expectations during performance and until the end of the project. PPP agreements are complex long-term agreements and price value must be stable during the contract's duration and until the end of performance. Contract price, generally, has become nowadays a dynamic process rather than a static process as in the past in light of the traditional theory of *Le contrat administratif*. In public works agreements as in most traditional administrative contracts, it is suggested that review to contract price should be on a monthly basis in order to update the value of payments and to face the rapid change in raw materials prices in the Egyptian markets. For instance, in the first month of performance, the first certificate equals £E100,000, meanwhile, the true value of the 19th or the 20th certificate (assuming that each certificate equals £E100,000) is £E118,000. The current depreciation of the Egyptian Pound caused fundamental unpredictability to contractors with the state. Following this concept, it is clear that there is an essential need to update the value not the price (i.e. the true value of the Egyptian pound in month zero equals £E1, while it equals £E0.80 in month 36). It is suggested that currency units at the time of contracting should equal the same units at the final completion date of the project.

PPP legislation in Egypt and the MENA countries has unique innovations in many substantive aspects which differ from the traditional concession exorbitant clauses. Contract price is one of the new main substantive aspects as contract price in PPP contracts is not subject to unilateral amendments by the contracting authority. Further, contract price can be amended by the contracting parties without reliance on financial equilibrium theories (such as *l'imprévision*) and without recourse to litigation or arbitration.

The Egyptian PPP law provides that in case of the occurrence of unforeseen circumstances after starting performance of the PPP contract, including amendments to laws or regulations that were enforceable at the time of performance of the PPP contract, it may be agreed to amend the PPP contract in accordance with the conditions and rules stipulated in such contract.[33]

PPP law in Dubai stipulates that a PPP contract may be amended according to the basis and rules of the unforeseen circumstances; administrative decrees which

33 The Egyptian PPP law, 2010, Article 8.

are issued to implement this law shall clarify the rules to apply the unforeseen circumstances theory, how to compensate the private partner and how to amend the PPP contract.[34]

Kuwaiti PPP law pointed out that the amendment of the partnership agreement may be agreed upon in accordance with the principle and the rules provided for under the agreement, if unforeseen circumstances occurred after the conclusion of the Partnership Agreement, including amendments to the laws in force at the time of conclusion of this agreement and leading to a financial imbalance of the agreement.[35]

Morocco PPP law provides that the contracting parties have the right to maintain the financial equilibrium of the contract in case of *force majeure* or unforeseen circumstances.[36]

The Tunisian PPP law stipulates that the partnership contract is concluded between the public person and the project company for a duration, taking into account in particular the depreciation period of the investments to be made and the financing methods selected. The contract of partnership is not renewable. Exceptionally, the contract may be extended for a maximum of three years in cases of emergency to ensure the continuity of the public service, in the case of *force majeure* or during the occurrence of unpredictable events, after the notice conformity of the General Public Partnership Authority referred to in Article 38 of this Law.[37]

It is clear that the approach of Egyptian and MENA countries' legislation to maintain the financial equilibrium of the PPP contract is unique. The encouragement of the flow of FDI into the MENA countries is of a great significance in the views of PPP legislation as it is one of the main targets to adopt PPP techniques.

It is worth noting that the Supreme Administrative Court in Egypt supersedes the party autonomy principle and its leading judgments, on many occasions, decided that state contract clauses prevail if these contractual clauses contradict any legislation or regulation.[38] However, it is suggested that contractual clauses

34 Dubai PPP law, 2015, Article 31.

35 Kuwaiti PPP law, 2014, Article 36.

36 Morocco PPP law, 2014, Article 17, '*Droit au maintien de l'équilibre du contrat en cas d'évènements imprévus ou de force majeure.*'

37 Tunisian PPP law, 2015, Article 17 reads as follows '*Art. 17 – Le contrat de partenariat est conclu entre la personne publique et la société du projet pour une durée déterminée en tenant compte notamment de la durée d'amortissement des investissements à réaliser et des modalités de financement retenues. Le contrat de partenariat n'est pas renouvelable. Exceptionnellement, le contrat peut être prorogé pour une durée maximale de trois ans dans les cas d'urgence pour assurer la continuité du service public, dans le cas de force majeure ou lors de la survenance d'évènements imprévisibles, et ce, après l'avis conforme de l'instance générale de partenariat public privé mentionnée à l'article 38 de la présente loi.' Journal Officiel de la République Tunisienne — 1er décembre 2015*, No. 96, p. 2857.

38 The Supreme Administrative Court, Case No. 9559 of the Judicial Year 47, session 20 December 2005.

may not contradict any mandatory rule in any valid legislation of the host state as mandatory legislative rules relate to public policy.

It is suggested that PPP techniques, as adopted by PPP legislation in Egypt and the MENA countries, in dealing with unforeseen circumstances without recourse to litigation or arbitration, are a consistent approach with international commercial contracts' principles. Such techniques are a considerable step to achieve global contract law principles in the respective jurisdictions, whether public or private contracts.

The *quantum* of Compensation and Courts/Arbitrators' Authority to Exercise Judicial Review: Civil Codes Mandatory Rules

Article 224/3 of the Egyptian Civil Code stipulates that the contracting parties cannot deprive courts (or arbitrators) from exercising judicial review over an agreed amount of *quantum* for compensation in contracts. This is a mandatory rule in the Egyptian legal system and a matter of public policy. For example, if the contracting parties agree on a fixed *quantum* for compensation in the event of any contractual breach, and in turn state that the courts cannot review this agreed sum as a *quantum*, this provision would be deemed an 'unfair' null and void contractual term. The courts always reserve their rights to exercise review in relation to due compensation.[39]

1. Article (224) of the Egyptian Civil Code stipulates that: 'the agreed compensation is not due if the debtor proved that the creditor did not suffer any damages (loss).
2. A judge (or arbitrator) can reduce the amount of compensation if the debtor proved that there is an exaggeration in that amount to a great extent or that the original obligation was partially executed.
3. Any agreement contrary to the abovementioned provisions 224/1 and 224/2 is null and void.'

Pursuant to Article 225, if 'the damages exceeded the agreed compensation value, the creditor cannot claim more than the stipulated amount unless the debtor is accused of committing fraud or a fundamental mistake.'

The Egyptian doctrine[40] explains this pre-estimated compensation as being agreed upon and stipulated between the contracting parties under the agreement or any of its appendices. This compensation is not due in the absence of loss or dam-

39 Article 227 of Bahrini Civil Code; Article 227 of Libya Civil Code; Article 266 of Qatar Civil Code; Article 179 Saudi Civil Code; Article 303 of Kuwaiti Civil Code; Article 390 of UAE Civil Code; Article 267 of Omani Civil Code; Article 225 of Syria Civil Code; Article 184 of Algerian Civil Code.

40 Abdel Wadood Yehia, *Obligation Stipulations at Egyptian Civil Law* (Dar Al Nahda Al Arabia, 1987, pp. 52–5, in Arabic); and Egyptian Cassation Court, decision No. 227, Civil circuit, year 19, session 25 December 1968.

ages to the creditor. The court or arbitral tribunal can reduce the compensation if it is not adequate to the damages or 'the contractor executed the contract partially, partial execution,' to create a contractual balance between the due compensation amount and the damages. This dimension in the Egyptian Civil Code is to maintain fairness and balance of the contractual relationship. These rules are mandatory pursuant to the Egyptian Civil Code.

Decisions of the Egyptian Cassation Court (Civil and Commercial Circuits)

The civil and commercial circuits of the Egyptian Cassation Court directly applied stipulations of Article 224 of the civil law. The court held in some of the leading cases that 'in the light of article (224) of the Egyptian civil law if there is a penalty clause in the contract, damages are presumed unless the debtor proved the opposite or that stipulated compensation at the contract exceeded the actual loss.' [41,42]

The Court held in recent cases that 'the contracting parties can fix a pre-estimated compensation for damages as a result for non-performance of any of the stipulated obligations [...] If the debtor proved that the pre-estimated compensation exceeded the actual loss or that he performed some of his obligations, the Court shall reduce compensation to be adequate to actual loss.'[43]

The Egyptian Cassation Court held currently that 'fixed compensation, in accordance with Article 224 of the Egyptian Civil Code, is subject to the Judge's assessment. It is permissible [for the judge] to reduce [the compensation fixed by agreement] if the debtor proves that the estimate was exaggerated to a great extent [...].'[44]

Conclusions

- Frustration of contract, whether public or private (commercial) contracts, in Egypt and MENA countries' legislation clarify how far such legislation, in Egypt and MENA countries, is consistent with international standards.
- It is suggested that the established theories in contracts' financial equilibrium, whether in public or private (commercial) contracts, and whether such theories are established in legislation or by the Egyptian and MENA countries' case law, are paving the way to the unification of contract law substantive principles towards a global contract law. Such global contract law assumes that the substantive principles of contract law, whether public or private (commercial) contracts, in Egypt and MENA countries, are consistent with the global diversity of contract law principles and with international commercial law theory and practice.

41 Egyptian Cassation Court, Case 415, year 46, 13 February 1980.
42 Egyptian Cassation Court, Case 26, year 38, 18 December 1973.
43 Egyptian Cassation Court, Cases 1859, 2444, 2447, year (70), 12 June 2001.
44 Cassation No. 8258 of Judicial Year 85, hearing dated 27 June 2021.

- It is clear how unification of PPP legislation in Egypt and MENA countries, and unification of Egyptian and MENA countries' civil codes in *'l'imprévision'* theory, established a coherent and integrated set of substantive principles of contract law in both private (commercial) contracts and public contracts. Therefore, a unification of contract law principles is underway to achieve global contract law principles.
- Egyptian and MENA countries' civil codes are influenced by the French Civil Code and the Egyptian Cassation Court and Egyptian Conseil D'État jurisprudence are influenced, to a great extent, by the French Jurisprudence. Such influence reflects the civilized approaches by the Egyptian and MENA legislature and the developments of the case law in Egypt and MENA countries.
- Civilized legislation and developed case law in Egypt and MENA countries will lead to a rapid and easy integration of the contract law of the respective jurisdictions into the global contract law order.

2 Courts' Intervention in Light of Non-Mandatory Legislative Provision or in Absence of Legislative Provision

Introduction

This chapter identifies the principles which underpin contract law, whether public contracts or private contracts (commercial contracts), in the relevant jurisdictions, namely in the absence of mandatory legislative rules, or in the absence of a legislative provision in the Egyptian and MENA countries' legal systems. This chapter aims to explore and evaluate the case law in public contracts and private contracts in the relevant jurisdictions, trace their evolution, assess their impact on law and policy making, and evaluate their effects. This chapter answers the question on how the perceived lack of standardization appears as a deterrent in developing public contractual interfaces in the MENA region through analyzing case law in specific topics in the respective jurisdictions. Is unification of contract law principles in international states' contracts, which is consistent with international commercial contract law principles, a tool to achieve standardization of public contractual interfaces in the relevant jurisdiction?

This chapter deals, from a critical analysis perspective, with the following topics which have special significance in international contract law and international states' contracts:

- As a general principle, the right of *Exceptio non-adimpleti contractus* (Article 161 of the Egyptian Civil Code) exists in civil and commercial contracts. This right, however, does not extend to administrative contracts, due to the principle of regularity and continuity of public utilities. That being said, this principle is subject to several derogations as a contractor can withhold or suspend (and not terminate) performance, in the event the contracting authority does not pay its dues. This is not termination of the obligation (i.e., set-off for instance). It should be noted that the Egyptian courts have issued controversial judgments which reflect controversial approaches relating to this matter.
- Courts' intervention in light of Articles 452 and 453 of the Egyptian Civil Code, and similar provisions in Arab Civil Codes. Articles 452 and 453, regulate the right to file a case against commodities' defect in sales contracts as civil and commercial contracts. These articles of the Egyptian Civil Code do not have a mandatory nature. In supply agreements to the state, the Egyptian Supreme Administrative Court considered these agreements as sales contracts.

DOI: 10.4324/9781003466352-3

However, the general provisions of sales contracts, as civil and commercial contracts, in the Egyptian Civil Code do not apply to supply agreements as such because these contracts have the administrative legal nature as they are relating to public interests. Therefore, the Egyptian Supreme Administrative Court rejected the time-bar for the one-year duration to file a case against commodities' defects which are supplied to state, as this time-bar in the Egyptian Civil Code is not a mandatory rule. The state can file a case within the long prescription period of 15 years and not be obliged by Article 452 of Egyptian Civil Code.

- Prince Theory was established by the French and Egyptian Conseil d'État jurisprudence, and does not exist either in the Egyptian legislation or in the MENA countries' legislation. It is one of the important mechanisms to maintain the administrative contracts' financial equilibrium. Egyptian Conseil d'État case law created the Prince Theory substantive principles as an inspiration by the French Conseil d'État jurisprudence. MENA countries' case law is influenced by the Egyptian Conseil d'État decisions in this context.

Principle of Termination of Performance (performance suspension) *Exceptio non-adimpleti contractus*

The General Principle in the Egyptian Civil Code

The Egyptian Civil Code provides in Article (161) that 'in contracts that are obligatory for both parties, if mutual obligations are due, it is optional for any of the contracting parties to terminate performance if the other party has not performed its obligation.'[1] In Egypt, the doctrine affirms that this principle is an application of the general rules of contract in civil law.[2] The basis of this concept in civil and commercial transactions is that, where two mutual obligations are due at the same time and reciprocity in executing obligations is not sufficient, the obligations are also conditional on each other. In civil and commercial contracts concluded by and between private entities, and in particular in construction contracts, it is an obligation by the employer to deliver the construction site to the contractor without any obstacles that might prevent performance. That obligation is a precondition to performance by the contractor. Moreover, the obligation to pay the contractor is a precondition to the contractor continuing performance. Consequently, if the employer stops paying, the contractor has the right to terminate performance until payment is received from the employer. It can be argued[3] that this concept is a self-defense

1 For MENA countries' civil codes, see for instance: Bahrini Civil Code Article 150; Kuwaiti Civil Code Article 219; UAE Civil Code Articles 414–419; Qatar Civil Code Articles 280–284.

2 Abdel Baki Abdel Fatah, *The Encyclopedia of Egyptian Civil Law, Contract and Unilateral Acts Theory, Comparative Study with Islamic Doctrine* (1984, p.667, in Arabic).

3 Said Aly, *Principle of Not Executing Contract* (2006, p. 16, in Arabic); and Abdel Baki Abdel Fatah, *The Encyclopedia of Egyptian Civil Law, Contract and Unilateral Acts Theory, Comparative Study with Islamic Doctrine* (1984, p. 667, in Arabic).

mechanism in favor of contractors to get their rights promptly instead of starting litigation or arbitral proceedings to claim payments as such measures would take a long time and incur heavy costs.[4] In case of termination, or suspension of performance, the contract is still valid and is not rescinded. It is a form of suspension of mutual obligations until the party in default resumes its contractual undertakings.[5]

The Administrative Contracts' Exception in the Egyptian Conseil D'État Decisions

Administrative contracts have special exceptions by the Egyptian Conseil D'État decisions. In one of the leading cases concerning a contract concluded by and between a public juristic entity and a private company for the maintenance of elevators, the Administrative Appeal Court, after consolidation of the procedure of the two cases, dismissed the contractor's claims and held that the contractor was obliged to pay a penalty for delay as it was in breach of its contractual obligations.[6]

After the case was referred to the Supreme Administrative Court, that court held that 'it is not permitted for the contracting company to terminate works or to suspend performance at any stage of the contract performance, even if the public juristic entity is in breach of its obligations to make payments to the contractor. This contract is related to the management and operation of one of the public utilities.'[7] In a recent case, the Supreme Administrative Court held that:

> All contracts must be performed *bona fide* whether the contracts are concluded between private entities or between the state and private entities. Accordingly, if the state delays delivery of the construction site to contractor, the contractor does not have the right to claim not performing his contractual obligations. The contractor cannot argue that the state terminated or delayed in any of its contractual obligations. The principle of terminating contractual obligations by the contractor is not permitted, at any circumstances, under administrative contracts as they have their unique characteristics in addition to the fact that they are connected to public utilities which must run regularly and in a disciplinary manner. The contractor only has the right to claim compensation.[8]

4 Mohamed A.M. Ismail, *Public Economic Law and the New International Administrative Contract* (Beirut: El Halabi Publishing Co., 2010, pp. 277–8, in Arabic).

5 Termination of performance, as mentioned above, is a totally different concept from 'set-off' in the Egyptian legal system. Set-off is a cause or mechanism by which the financial obligation is totally paid and the obligation is settled (Article (362) of the Egyptian Civil Code). Similar provisions exist in MENA countries' civil codes.

6 Supreme Administrative Court, Case No. 2606, 24 April 1990, Judicial Year 31. See also Supreme Administrative Court, Case No. 3177, 12 May 1998, Judicial Year 41.

7 Ibid.

8 Supreme Administrative Court, Case No. 6337, 16 March 2004, Judicial Year 46; see also Supreme Administrative Court, Case No. 834, 18 October 2005, Judicial Year 46 and Supreme Administrative Court, Case No. 9689, 17 January 2006, Judicial Year 49.

The General Assembly for Legal Opinion and Legislation upheld all legal opinions that the principle of termination of the contractual obligation and suspension of performance is not permitted in administrative contracts.[9]

Legal Globalization and New Trends in the Conseil D'État Decisions

Cultural and legal globalization have, to some extent, influenced the Egyptian Conseil D'État decisions in rejecting the principle in some exceptional cases, in which the Supreme Administrative Court has held[10] that:

> The breach of contractual obligations by the administration and terminating contractors' payments is a considerable reason for termination of performance by the contractor. As the project financing by the state in Public Works Agreements is the fundamental element in executing works, there is an essential obligation upon the administration to deliver to the contractor his payments promptly, otherwise, it will be impossible for him to continue to perform his contractual obligations. The well-established principle in administrative contracts in the *Conseil D'État* decisions and in the Egyptian administrative doctrine, rejecting granting the right to the contractor to terminate or suspend performance upon getting his payments from the state, is not applicable in this case before the court. It could be applicable in suspending some contractual obligations by the state but not one of the fundamental contractual obligations such as payments. The obligation to pay the contractor is a fundamental obligation, by which the contract cannot continue without payments on due date, especially if it is a great sum that substantially affects performance. The contract must be executed by the administration in a *bona fide* manner. Moreover, the administration delayed in delivering designs for the contractor in the preliminary stages of the contractual process.

The court accepted that the contractor could suspend performance until such time as payments were made by the state. A clear example of violating such substantial obligations is not paying large sums to the contractor without any reason where the absence of such payment would substantially affect performance. In another leading decision, the Supreme Administrative Court held that

> Project financing by the administration is the crucial factor that directly affects performance by the contractor. Suspending or terminating administrations' obligation for payments shall affect contractor's creditworthiness and performance of the contractual obligations to execute works until final completion. The court found that the fundamental principle of rejecting contractor's

9 For example, General Assembly for Legal Opinion and Legislation, No. 453, 8 June 1995, session 31, May 1995, file 32/2/2545; and see also No. 137, 20 February 2008, session 15 March 2008, file No. 32/2/3808.

10 Supreme Administrative Court, Case No. 4483, 6 May 1997, Judicial Year 41.

> right to suspend works is not applicable in the current case before the court. Suspending works by the contractor is a legal right as he did not get paid. The latter is a default by the contracting public juristic entity.[11]

The General Assembly for Legal Opinion and Legislation has held the same views (but in rare decisions) and has granted the contractor the right to suspend performance in case of delay in obtaining payments from the administration.[12]

The decisions were a real revolution in the basic and fundamental principle of rejecting principles of termination of performance. Despite the fact that they were in 1997 and that other decisions rejecting the principle were in 2004, this marks a new trend in Conseil D'État decisions since the end of the last decade. It is a new era of modernization of the traditional concepts of the administrative contract. The latter enhancements are as a direct result of globalization and liberalization of the traditional theory of the administrative contract (*Le contrat administratif*). In 2004,[13] the Supreme Administrative Court stated that

> The basic and fundamental principle in implementing administrative contracts is that the contractor cannot stop or terminate performance in contracts with the state, concerning public utilities, but there are exceptions to this principle when there is a serious violation by the administration (a violation of substantial obligation) in order that the contractor can continue performance, there is no reason to affirm the old principle. In some cases, when the administration did not submit drawings to the contractor or terminated his payments as it is the source which enables contractor to finance the public works project, especially when it is a large sum of money, it is the right of the contractor to suspend or terminate performance until the administration fulfils its contractual obligations. However, the administration cannot impose penalty for delay upon the contractor because the latter's fault was a result of the administration's default in one of its substantial obligations.

This approach is a direct result of cultural and legal globalization upon the case law of Egypt and MENA countries' supreme courts.

Further, the Egyptian Supreme Administrative Court held in one of its current decisions that 'the principle of *Exceptio non-adimpleti contractus* is permissible in administrative contracts in two exceptional cases: 1) if there is impossibility of performance as a result to the contractual default from the contracting authority;

11 Supreme Administrative Court, Cases Nos. 4697 and 4717, 24 June 1997, Judicial Year 39; see: Said Aly, *Principle of Not Executing Contract* (2006, pp.89-90, in Arabic). See also recent cases, e.g., Case No. 291, 14 March 2000, Judicial Year 43.

12 E.g., General Assembly for Legal Opinion, opinion No. 541, 8 July 1993, session 16 May 1993, *The General Principles of the General Assembly*, Judicial Years 47 and 48 (1999).

13 Supreme Administrative Court, Case No. 10572, 30 November 2004, Judicial Year 47; see also, e.g., No. 291, session 14 March 2000, Judicial Year 43.

and 2) if the parties agreed in the contract that the contractor can suspend performance as a result to the contractual breach by the contracting authority.'[14]

The Egyptian Supreme Administrative Court added in another case that 'the principle of *Exceptio non-adimpleti contractus* is permissible in administrative contracts if the contractual breach by the contracting authority is greater than the breach by the contractor, and such breach by the contracting authority is a reason to impossibility of the administrative contract performance.'[15]

There is, however, an essential need for a legislative reform to add an extension of time to the contract duration if the state delays contractor's payments, and to avoid payment of liquidated damages.

Conclusions

In conclusion, despite the fact that the Conseil D'État decisions have begun a new era, in a few cases more than a decade ago, in trying to apply the principle in favor of the contractor, the decisions do not have a specific judicial methodology. In order to achieve fairness in the contractual relationship and to maintain equal bargaining power for the contracting parties, it is suggested that the principle should be applied in the domain of the administrative contracts and it will maintain contractual equilibrium, as the contractor usually has project financing from lending banks and assigns his payments to the lenders. If the state suspended the payments, the contractor would pay a higher interest rate during a longer period of time. The latter scenario would violate the financial expectations and feasibility studies made by the contractor before the tender and before concluding the contract with the state.

Unification of contract law principles between administrative contracts and international commercial contracts in accepting suspension of performance in case of any contractual breach by the contracting state would create coherent contract law principles in both public and private contracts. It is a considerable step to achieve global contract law principles despite public law constraints.

Courts' Intervention in Light of Articles 452 and 453 of the Egyptian Civil Code, as Not Mandatory Rules

In supply agreements to the contracting state, the Egyptian Supreme Administrative Court considered these agreements as sales contracts. However, the general provisions of sales contracts in the Egyptian Civil Code do not apply to supply agreements as such because these contracts have the administrative legal nature. Supply agreements relate to public interests. Therefore, the Egyptian Supreme Administrative Court has rejected the time-bar for the one-year duration to file a case against commodities' defects which are supplied to the state. The state can file

14 The Supreme Administrative Court, Case No. 3028 of Judicial Year 58, session 24 December 2019.
15 The Supreme Administrative Court, Case No. 57849 of Judicial Year 62, session 27 October 2020.

a case within the long prescription period of 15 years and is not obliged by Article 452 of Egyptian Civil Code.

Article 452 of the Egyptian Civil Code provides that: '1 – filing a case for defective commodity is subject to prescription time-bar of one year from time of delivery of commodity, even if the buyer did not discover the defect after the time of delivery, unless the seller accepts to extend the prescription period for a longer time. 2 – Seller cannot defend that the prescription period is only one year if he deliberately hid the commodity defect by way of fraud.'

Article 453 provides that 'contracting parties (buyer and seller) by their agreement may extend the prescription period; or reduce it; or cancel such prescription. Every agreement which cancels such guarantee (prescription period) or reduces its period is null and void if the seller has deliberately hid the commodity defect by way of fraud.'

The Egyptian Supreme Administrative Court held that in administrative contracts, filing a case against commodities' defects which are supplied to the state is not within one year from supplying the commodities to the contracting authority as the plaintiff alleges that this supply agreement is subject to Article (452) from the Egyptian Civil Code. It is clear from analyzing the legal nature of this time-bar of one year provided in Article (452) that this Article is a rule *normes facultatives or normes supplétives* and not mandatory. The contracting parties can agree upon a different time-bar from that provided in Article (452). This vision is confirmed in Article (453) from Egyptian Civil Code which provides that the contracting parties (buyer and seller) may agree upon a different time-bar; they may increase the duration of the time-bar; reduce it; or even cancel such a time-bar unless a defect is hidden in the commodity as a deliberately fraud by the seller. The Supreme Administrative Court elaborated that the contract in dispute is an administrative contract which is a public law contract and is connected to the administration and public utilities' running and management which are totally different from other private law contracts (civil and commercial contracts). The Court added that administrative contracts have a unique legal system which contains special legal principles such as running the public utilities in regularity and continuity. As a result, the administrative contract has its legal nature as it is regulating public interests; and therefore, administrative contracts are not subject to the legislative time-bar provided in Article (452) of the Egyptian Civil Code for the prescription of filing the case for commodities' defects. Such an Article which has the legal nature as *normes facultatives* or *normes supplétives* and does not have the mandatory rule nature, regulates commercial and civil contracts and is not regulating commodities' defects in administrative contracts.[16]

16 Case No. 7308 of Judicial Year 55, session 26 October 2021.

Courts' Intervention in the Absence of Legislative Provisions: The Prince Theory (*'Le Fait du Prince'*) in Administrative Contracts[17]

Prince Theory was established by the French and Egyptian Conseil D'État jurisprudence, and does not exist either in the Egyptian legislation or in the MENA countries' legislation. Egyptian Conseil D'État case law created the Prince Theory substantive principles as an inspiration by the French Conseil D'État jurisprudence. MENA countries' case law has been influenced by the Egyptian Conseil D'État decisions.

While the administration in an administrative contract has the right to unilaterally modify the undertakings of the contracting party with direct decisions, such a right is met with a corresponding right: to maintain the contract's financial equilibrium.[18]

The jurisprudence in the MENA countries recognizes the right of the administration to unilaterally modify the contracts, based on public interest constraints. To apply such theory, several conditions must be fulfilled as follows:

> Jurisprudence defines the Prince Theory's application as a special procedure whereby the contract's clauses can be directly modified, having an effect upon the contract performance and imposing upon the contracting party new unexpected financial burdens.

The French judiciary provided the example of police procedures that led to an increase of the contracting party's obligations, such as the decision issued by the administration – the police in this case – requesting the contracting party to relocate the electric wires for public safety reasons,[19] as well as the decision issued by the administrative authority to the contracting party, upon which new burdens were imposed, by virtue of its power of supervision and direction. Another example was public works or physical works carried out by the administration causing injuries to the contracting party with regard to contract performance or increasing contractual obligations.

17 The Prince Theory in the MENA countries' legal systems is not codified in a written legislation, therefore, in the absence of such legislation, the Supreme Administrative Court at the Egyptian Conseil D'État has created the judicial principles of this theory. The Supreme Administrative Court was influenced to a great extent by the French Conseil D'État case law. For more elaboration see: Mohamed A.M. Ismail, *Globalization and New International Public Works Agreements in Developing Countries, An Analytical Perspective* (Routledge, 2016 and 2011, with a foreword by HH Humphrey Lloyd QC); and for the same author also see: *International Public Works Agreements Arbitration* (Al Halabi, 2003, in Arabic).

18 Ibid., p. 631. In the French doctrine, see: De Laubadère, Moderne, and Delvolvé, *Traité des contrats administratifs* (Tome 2, LGDJ, p. 515 et seq.); Sarwat Badawi, *Le fait du Prince dans les contrats administratifs* (LGDJ, 1954). In the Arab doctrine, see: Abdel Azim Abdelsalaam, *The Effect of the Prince Theory upon the Performance of Administrative Contracts* (1989, in Arabic); Anas Ga'far and Ashraf Anas Ga'far, *Administrative Contracts* (Dar Al Nahda Al Arabia, 2021, p. 170, in Arabic).

19 Sarwat Badawi, *Le fait du Prince dans les contrats administratifs* (LGDJ, 1954, p. 104 et seq.)

Jurisprudence also considers that the promulgation of laws or regulations would increase the contracting party's obligations towards the administration, as a general procedure, according to the Prince Theory in administrative contracts. The French Conseil D'État was of the opinion that the general procedure that was not directly addressed to the contracting party would not be compensated, except in two cases: first, where the contract explicitly stated such a clause and second, where such a procedure was unexpected; hence, the Prince Theory was not applied, but rather the theory of unforeseen circumstances. Where the general procedure results in a direct modification of the contract terms, whether by stopping their implementation, or by modifying them, or by prematurely terminating the contract, the contracting party must be compensated on the basis of the Prince Theory, regardless of the legitimacy of these laws.[20]

The general procedure must also modify the external conditions for the execution, which would be more difficult for the contracting party to carry out. According to the French Conseil D'État, the rule is that the contracting party may not be indemnified for the damage sustained in such circumstances, except for extremely particular cases; as such, it can be said that the rule is to rule out the compensation, and the exception is to rule for it.[21]

The Egyptian judiciary adopted the same approach. In its judgment issued on 16 June 1953, the Appeal Administrative Court ruled out the compensation of a company claiming for injuries sustained due to having been levied with a council tax for electricity although it was not a burden added to the company's obligations or destabilizing the contract's financial equilibrium. On 28 October 1964, the General Assembly of the Legal Opinion and Legislation, the Egyptian Conseil D'État, ruled out the compensation of the Technical Company for Public Works for price differences for the supply of materials due to the 1956 war, a commission for Misr Company for Foreign Trade, an export bonus, a logistic duty and a maritime duty. The grounds for such a ruling were that these sums of money were not in direct connection with the contracting administrative authority, where there must have been a special or general procedure issued by the administration to apply the Prince Theory, leading to a special injury incurred upon the contracting party, where he or she was the sole injured party by such general decision.[22]

20 Judgment of the French Conseil D'État issued on 23 March 1994 in the case of *Ste Energie electrique de la Basse-Loire*. The Conseil D'État ruled out the compensation in certain cases for different reasons. See the thesis of Badawi, *Le fait du Prince dans les contrats administratifs* (LGDJ, 1954, p. 167 et seq.)

21 See the thesis of Badawi, ibid., 207 et seq. and the judgment of the French Conseil D'État issued in January 1945 in the case of *Ste anonyme motobloc*, where it ruled out the compensation on the basis of the Prince Theory in the area of taxes and duties that rendered the performance difficult. See also: the Egyptian Appeal Administrative Court – 16 June 1953 – *Forty Years Collection of Court Judgments*, Judicial Year 7, 1578.

22 Legal opinions issued by the General Assembly of the Counsel Department, Judicial Year 19, 51.

The Conseil D'État in Egypt summarized the provisions for the application of the Prince Theory in administrative contracts as follows:[23]

1. That there is an administrative contract.
2. That the injury is committed by the contracting authority.
3. That the injury affects the contracting party regardless of how grave the injury is.
4. That it is assumed that the contracting authority was not wrongful when taking such a harmful decision since it has a contractual obligation without a breach.
5. That the procedure taken by the authority is not expected.
6. That the contracting party has sustained a personal injury where he or she is the sole injured party by such general decision.

The Harmful Act is Committed by the Contracting Authority

The act must be committed by the contracting authority and not by any juristic entity other than the entity that concluded the contract; otherwise, the condition of the Prince Theory is not fulfilled,[24] and the theory of unforeseen circumstances may be applicable where appropriate.

The Injury Sustained by the Contracting Party is a Personal Unexpected Injury

The General Assembly of the Legal Opinion and Legislation at the Egyptian Conseil D'État confirmed that it was necessary to have this condition, that the injury sustained by the contracting party was a personal injury where no third party was affected by the general decision. The claim of the contracting companies for price increases to the contracts concluded with the Ministry of Housing before applying Law No. 63 of 1964 of Social Security had no legal grounds. The said law obligated all companies and not only the contracting companies to increase their social security contributions for seasonal laborers; hence, the Prince Theory could not be applied as the promulgation of such a law was an expected procedure. The lawmaker declared in Law No. 92 of 1959 that the plan was to extend the social insurance benefits to cover all laborers, which rebuts that such increases were not expected.[25]

23 The Supreme Administrative Court – Judgment No. 56 – 12, 20 May 1961, 6/141/1133 – Damascus, *Forty Years Collection of Court Judgments*, p. 42. The Supreme Administrative Court in Egypt distinguished between the required conditions to apply the Prince Theory and the required conditions to apply the theory of unforeseen circumstances in the leading judgment issued on 27 November 2020, Case No. 58619, Judicial Year 62.

24 The Supreme Administrative Court – Judgment No. 1562 – 10 and 67 – 11, 11 May 1968, 13/117/874 – *Forty Years Collection of Court Judgments*, p. 424.

25 Legal Opinion No. 297 on 11 March 1965, session 24 February 1965, 19/88/309 – *Forty Years Collection of Court Judgments*, p. 426.

The Procedure is Issued by the Contracting Administrative Authority

The Supreme Administrative Court at the Egyptian Conseil D'État confirmed that the intervention of the Administrative Courts to realize the administrative contract's financial equilibrium, in application of the Prince Theory, would be possible when its conditions were fulfilled, including the condition that the harmful act was committed by the contracting administrative authority. In case such an act was taken by a juristic entity that did not conclude the contract, one of the Prince Theory's conditions was not then fulfilled and thus the theory could not be applied. However, this did not stop the application of the theory of unforeseen circumstances where appropriate.[26]

The General Assembly for the Legal Opinion and Legislation, the Egyptian Conseil D'État, concluded that the contract between the Ministry of Irrigation and a number of contractors for the execution of certain works in the Ministry's departments and Inspection Offices during the financial year 1969/1970 did not grant those contractors any rights to address the Ministry with a claim for price differences, as a result of an increase of the price tariffs of steel and cement or due to receiving quantities of imported steel in lieu of local steel, whether such price increases took place subsequent to concluding the contract or during the contract performance. These procedures were taken by an authority other than the contracting authority (Ministry of Irrigation), which meant that a fundamental condition for the application of the Prince Theory was not fulfilled.[27]

The Effect of Fixing the Tender Prices Upon the Application of the Prince Theory

The administrative judiciary decided to fix the tender prices of the agreement concluded between the supplier and the administration as from the date of submitting the tender until the handover of the work, subject to the contract. These prices were not subject to any changes that might occur during the contract term, whether the reasons for such changes were related to foreign currency fluctuation, price increases, or change in import, production, or any other duties. The contracting party might not refer to the Prince Theory or the theory of unforeseen circumstances to rest the claim for damages for injuries sustained due to any of the aforementioned changes.[28]

26 Case No. 562, Judicial Year 10 – session 11 May 1968 and see also the leading judgment of the Supreme Administrative Court in Egypt which distinguishes between the required conditions to apply the Prince Theory and the required conditions to apply the theory of unforeseen circumstances in the leading judgment issued on 27 November 2020, Case No. 58619, Judicial Year 62.

27 File No. 78/1/46 – session 11 July 1971, *Modern Administrative Encyclopedia* (1st edn, Vol. 18, 873).

28 The General Assembly of Legal Opinion and Legislation, File 78/1/29, session 28 October 1964, *Modern Administrative Encyclopedia* (1st edn, Vol. 18, p. 882).

The Consequences of Applying the Prince Theory

Upon the fulfillment of the theory's conditions and as a consequence of the act committed by the public authorities, the injured party was granted full compensation, in addition to possible exemption of delay fines (penalty for delay), if it was established that such an act made it difficult for the party to perform the work on time; it might even exempt the contracting party from the performance of the contract if the Prince Theory resulted in the impossible performance. The contracting party had the right to terminate the contract in case the Prince Theory resulted in an excessive increase of that party's obligations.[29]

Jurisprudence had divergent opinions in establishing a compensation for the contracting party in the case of fulfilling the Prince Theory's conditions. The Egyptian Conseil D'État decided that the contract's financial equilibrium was the grounds for entitlement for compensation. The administration must restore such equilibrium every time it was destabilized, as a result of an act committed by the authority.[30]

Doctrine supports the notion of financial equilibrium as a general rule, which was to obligate the administration to ensure the contract's financial equilibrium every time it was destabilized, whether it was the result of an act committed by the contracting authority or caused by an external factor beyond its control. It has been suggested that this notion is as dangerous and inexact as it is generalized, giving rise to compensation to the contracting party even if the financial equilibrium is not caused by the administration.[31]

However, it is not a correct notion as the compensation ruled for the contracting party, due to a breach committed by the authority to the contract's economies, does not always correspond with the contract's financial equilibrium that was taken into consideration when the contract was concluded. MENA countries' doctrine provides two examples for such a case: The contracting party may wrongly accept unfavorable prices when concluding the contract. If the authority intervenes in the contract performance afterwards, the court shall rule for full compensation, not based on the price accepted by the party at the time of concluding the contract but based on the real price at the time of the authority's intervention in the contract performance. This theory also applies in the case of price increases after concluding the contract, as the judge, when issuing a judgment, takes account of the new prices for compensation and not those specified at the time of concluding the contract.

29 El Tamawy, *The General Principle of Administrative Contracts* (5th edn, 1991, 653, in Arabic). See the effect of the Prince Theory and the theory of unforeseen physical circumstances in restoring the administrative contract's financial equilibrium under unforeseen circumstances: Amin Mohamed Said, *General Principles for the Performance of Administrative Contracts* (Dar Al Thakafa Al Gameya, 1991, 302 et seq., in Arabic); Jean-Quentin De Cayper, Le fait du prince libère-t-il une entreprise public, *Revue de droit des affaires internationals* (No. 8, 1993, p. 959).

30 The Supreme Administrative Court, Case No. 1562, Judicial Year 10, 67 of Judicial Year 11, on session 11 May 1968.

31 Mohamed A.M. Ismail, *International Public Works Agreements Arbitration* (Al Halabi, 2003, in Arabic); Badawi, *Le fait du prince dans les contrats administratifs* (LGDJ, 1954, p. 24).

The second example is the case of terminating the contract by the administration without any breach committed. The notion of financial equilibrium cannot warrant the compensation ruled by the Administrative Court, as the financial equilibrium cannot be hypothetically discussed for a non–existing contract.[32]

Another jurisprudential opinion was that the second rule for compensation was the administration's contractual responsibility. As such, the administration had a contractual responsibility without a breach as the Prince Theory assumed that the authority was not wrongful when committing such an act; however, the responsibility had different grounds. Contract's financial equilibrium complements the administration's contractual responsibility without a breach, but it is a responsibility to maintain the contract's financial equilibrium. Professor De Laubadère was of the opinion that there was no difference between both notions, as according to the Prince Theory it was a contractual responsibility based upon the contract's financial equilibrium.[33]

This construes the condition currently imposed by the French Conseil D'État that the Prince Theory is applied when the act is committed by the administration, and the compensation is denied where the act is performed by a public authority other than the contracting authority, which distinguishes between state responsibility in the case of applying the Prince Theory or unforeseen circumstances. This approach is in line with sound legal logic as the contractual liability is due to the application of the Prince Theory that causes an injury to the contracting party and destabilizes the contract's financial equilibrium, although such injury is not grave. If during the contract performance, the authority commits an act that requires the application of the Prince Theory, it has a contractual liability based upon the need to restore the contract's financial equilibrium.

Conclusions

- The Principle of Termination or suspension of Performance (*Exceptio non adimpleti contractus*), needs to be codified in the Egyptian and MENA countries' legislation. There is an essential need for a legislative reform to add an extension of time to the contract duration, if the state delays a contractor's payments or any substantial obligation, and to avoid payment of liquidated damages as penalty for delay. If legislation grants the contractor the right to suspend performance, where there is a contractual breach by the state, legislative and contractual approaches in both commercial and administrative contracts would be unified.
- This chapter answers the question of how the perceived lack of standardization appears as a deterrent in developing public contractual interfaces in the MENA region through analyzing case law in specific topics in the respective jurisdictions. Is unification of contract law principles in international states'

32 Badawi, *Le fait du prince dans les contrats administratifs* (LGDJ, 1954, p. 25).
33 De Laubadère, Moderne, and Delvolvé, *Traité des contrats administratifs* (Tome 2, LGDJ).

contracts, which have to be consistent with international contract law principles, a tool to achieve standardization of public contractual interfaces in the relevant jurisdiction? It is important to achieve unified principles in case law in Egypt and MENA countries and to achieve unification in contract law legislation in Egypt and MENA countries. Such unification of both legislation and case law, in Egypt and MENA countries, is the first step to achieve unification in contract law principles, whether public contracts or commercial contracts. Global contract law can be achieved if such unification in legislation and case law is adopted in the respective jurisdictions.

- In the absence of mandatory rules regulating the time-bar to file a case against defective commodities supplied to the state, the Egyptian Conseil D'État Courts[34] considered such a contract as an administrative contract and not a sales contract which has a commercial or civil nature. The result is that administrative contract as such is not subject to the time-bar provided in Article 452 of the Egyptian Civil Code. This current approach by the Egyptian Supreme Administrative Court creates unpredictability as deviation between sales contracts' rules in commercial activities and in administrative contracts is a challenge against unification of contract law principles. Companies concluding sales contracts (supply agreements) with the state need certainty and fairness as they are commercial companies and such judicial approaches by the Supreme Administrative Courts violate their legitimate expectations.
- In the absence of a legislative provision, frustration of contract, whether public or private (commercial) contracts, in Egypt and the MENA countries, case law in the respective jurisdictions reflects the liberalization and modernization of contract law substantive principles, as such principles are consistent with the international contract law theory and practice. The Prince Theory reflects the developed approaches of the Egyptian Conseil D'État Courts which adapt the French Conseil D'État case law approaches. This is a fundamental step towards the unification of contract law principles to achieve global contract law.
- It is suggested that the established theories in contract financial equilibrium, whether in public or private (commercial) contracts, and whether such theories are established in legislation or by the Egyptian and MENA countries' case law, are paving the way to the unification of contract law substantive principles towards a global contract law. Such global contract law assumes that the substantive principles of contract law, whether public or private (commercial) contracts, in Egypt and the MENA countries, are consistent with the global diversity of contract law principles and with international commercial law theory and practice. Global contract law is underway despite public law constraints.

34 Case No. 7308 of Judicial Year 55, session 26 October 2021.

3 Courts' Intervention in the Light of Contractual Provisions

Introduction

Unification of substantive contract law principles can be achieved through courts' intervention in many aspects, as the legal globalization phenomenon has inspired courts' approaches in Egypt and the MENA countries. Among these aspects is the role of the Egyptian Supreme Administrative Court, and Cassation Court, in light of the existence of an unfair contractual provision. What are the Egyptian Supreme Administrative Court and Cassation Court approaches in case of the existence of an unfair contract term? How can such an approach play a significant role in the unification of the substantive principles of public contracts and private contracts in Egypt and MENA countries? How can such principles, of both types of contracts, be consistent with the international contract law principles? What is the role of the constitutional and legislative provisions in light of the existence of contractual clauses? What are public law constraints?

The Egyptian Supreme Administrative Court and Cassation Court are the oldest and most eminent leading supreme courts in Egypt and the MENA region. Among supreme courts in the MENA countries, the Egyptian Supreme Administrative Court played a crucial role, through decades, in transferring judicial principles, not only in administrative contracts' principles, but also other substantive principles of administrative law, to other MENA countries' supreme courts. Therefore, most MENA countries' supreme courts are inspired, to a great extent, by the jurisprudence of the Egyptian Supreme Administrative Courts, and also the jurisprudence of the Egyptian Cassation Court.

This chapter provides a taxonomy of the international states' contracts case law by reference to the source of the litigation process and to Egyptian case law as the leading jurisdiction in the MENA region. This chapter aims to identify the key characteristics of courts' intervention, in light of contractual provisions, and the extent to which courts can intervene if there is an 'unfair' contract term. The chapter highlights case law in specific topics, which have special significance in international practice and in the MENA countries' international state contracts. Further, the chapter explores, in depth, Egyptian Cassation Court case law, as the latter court approaches constitute the leading principles in private contracts (commercial and civil contracts) in the MENA region.

DOI: 10.4324/9781003466352-4

The question is: How can courts' intervention be considered a fundamental tool to achieve coherent contract law in international states' contracts which is consistent with international commercial contracts principles? It is important to explore the interplay between international contract law, and public law principles of international states' contracts, in particular administrative contracts. Further, how can courts intervene in the latter case without violating the principle of '*pacta sunt servanda*'? Is courts' intervention consistent with the international contract law substantive principles? To what extent is there coexistence between the core principles of contract law in state contracts in Egypt and the MENA region courts on one hand, and the huge global diversity of international contracts' principles on the other hand? To what extent are courts in Egypt and MENA countries influenced by global contract law principles?

This chapter deals with three case studies as follows.

Case Study No. 1: International Arbitration and Egyptian Court of Cassation Approaches: Can Arbitral Tribunals Enforce the Principle of Legality in Egypt and MENA Countries? A Case Study from An International State Contract

- A BOT contract contains ICC arbitration clause.
- The contracting authority decides to abandon a project, after the contract award decision, and before the final completion of the project. Is such an administrative decree connected to the contract or not? The Egyptian Supreme Administrative Court has created the theory of connected administrative decrees to administrative contracts and the unconnected decrees to the administrative contracts. What are the legal effects? To what extent can the court intervene, in the case of illegal administrative decrees, which are connected to the administrative contract (and considered part of the contractual process) and administrative decrees which are not connected to the administrative contract? Is there a difference between the scope of judicial review between national courts and arbitral tribunals? Can arbitral tribunals exercise judicial review upon administrative decrees, whether they are connected to the contract or not?
- How can unification of substantive contract law principles, in state contracts, to be consistent with international commercial contracts, be achieved, when the matter relates to public policy? What is the approach of the Egyptian Cassation Court? What are public law constraints?

Arbitrability of administrative decrees in the Egyptian legal system is a legal and technical issue which needs an in-depth analysis of the current situation in litigation and arbitration. However, arbitrability of administrative contracts is well recognized in the Egyptian legal system since 1997 pursuant to Article 1/2 of the Egyptian Arbitration Act No. 27 of 1994 as amended by Law No. 9 of 1997. Before

1997, arbitrability of administrative contracts was controversial as there were various contradictory legal opinions issued by the General Assembly for Legal Opinion and Legislation of the Egyptian Conseil D'État; some of these opinions permit arbitration in administrative contracts[1] and one opinion prohibits arbitration in such contracts.[2] The Egyptian Arbitration Act 1994, as amended, expressly permits arbitration in administrative contracts and this is conditional on the consent of the concerned minister to recourse to arbitration.[3] However, arbitration of administrative decrees has not been yet scrutinized in the Egyptian and MENA countries' doctrine in the absence of any legislative approach regulating such a topic. It is not clear, at present, whether administrative decrees' legality falls within the jurisdiction of the arbitral tribunals in international or domestic commercial arbitration or not. In other technical words: Can arbitral tribunals exercise judicial review upon the legality of administrative decrees? Can arbitral tribunals exercise judicial review to apply the principle of legality ('*principe de légalite*') upon administrative decrees? Similar to state courts, arbitration is a form of justice, but to what extent can arbitral tribunals exercise judicial review upon administrative decrees, in the absence of a legislative approach, dealing with the arbitral tribunal's powers in this regard?

It is true that the Egyptian Cassation Court adopts very narrow perspective in setting aside arbitration awards, as arbitration award in the Egyptian legal system is final, binding and enforceable. The approach of the Egyptian Cassation Court is to minimize setting aside arbitral awards as, in the view of the Cassation Court, the legislative policy in the Egyptian Arbitration Act 1994 is to restrict and minimize challenging arbitral awards. The Egyptian Cassation Court rarely issues a judgment to set aside an arbitral award as setting aside an arbitral award is an exception in the Egyptian legal system.

Arbitrability of administrative decrees, if not understood clearly, is dangerous and unpredictable, as it may open doors to unjustified fears by foreign investors, who wish to exercise economic activities in Egypt and MENA countries. Further, it may open doors to inconsistent findings by different arbitral tribunals.

The analysis in this case study is an attempt to answer the following question: Are administrative decrees arbitrable in the Egyptian legal system? Can arbitral tribunals exercise judicial review and apply the principle of legality upon administrative decrees? And, consequently, does this topic create unpredictability to foreign investors when they try to inject Foreign Direct Investments (FDI) into Egypt and MENA countries to start any economic activity? Is arbitrability of administrative

1 The General Assembly for Legal Opinion and Legislation, opinion issued on 17 May 1989; and opinion issued on 10 March 1993.

2 The General Assembly for Legal Opinion and Legislation, opinion issued on 18 December 1996.

3 Following the legislative approach in Article 2060 of the French Civil Code and Article 1 of the Egyptian Arbitration Act No. 27 of 1994, Qatar Arbitration Act No. 2 of 2017 provides in Article 2/2 that arbitration in administrative contracts is permitted with the consent of the Prime Minister. It is also worth noting that Saudi Arbitration Act No. 34 of 2012 provides in Article 10/2 that any public juristic entity may not enter into arbitration, in any dispute, whether contractual or otherwise, without the consent of the Prime Minister, unless otherwise provided in another private legislation.

decrees in Egypt and MENA countries consistent with legitimate expectations of foreign investors in the respective jurisdictions?

The Egyptian Cassation Court adopted an innovative approach in one of its leading judgments in the famous case of *Dipco*.[4] The judgement in the *Dipco* case dealt with arbitrability of administrative decrees, and the constitutional and legislative mandatory rules in the Egyptian legal system, in light of public policy constraints. Therefore, it is important to analyze the Egyptian Cassation Court judgment in the *Dipco* case. Before analyzing the judicial approach of the *Dipco* case, an overview of the situation in the Egyptian legal system regarding arbitrability of administrative contracts is necessary.

Arbitrability of Administrative Contracts in the Egyptian and MENA Countries' Legal Systems

Similar to many legal systems, arbitration in the Egyptian and MENA countries' legal systems can be in any contractual dispute or otherwise. Non-arbitrable matters are defined in an exhaustive list as an exception.[5] Administrative law is regulating the activities of the administration during the daily performance of the government. In any legal system, governments exercise the management of public utilities through administrative decrees and administrative contracts. Arbitration is more important when administrative decrees or contracts are involved, as it normally aims to settle disputes of infrastructure projects and services, which states inject billions of US Dollars, or the private partner injects huge investments, when the contract is one of the new patterns of states' contracts, such as Public Private Partnership (PPP) contracts between states and any private partner.

Arbitrability of administrative contracts is confirmed in the Egyptian legal system by Article 1 of the Egyptian Arbitration Act No. 27 of 1994 as amended by Law No. 9 of 1997. It is also confirmed in the Oman Arbitration Act 1997, Saudi Arbitration Act 2012, Qatar Arbitration Act 2017, and UAE Arbitration Act 2018.

Unlike many legal systems, the Egyptian Arbitration Act stipulates in Article 1 that arbitration in administrative contracts is permitted, as a general principle, but with the consent of the competent minister before recourse to arbitration.

4 The Egyptian Cassation Court Judgment, Civil and Commercial Circuits, on consolidated Cases Nos. 1964 and 1968 of the Judicial Year No. 91, session 8 July 2021.

5 Article 2 of the Egyptian Arbitration Act No. 27 of 1994 provides: 'Arbitration is commercial within the scope of this Law when the dispute arises over a legal relationship of an economic nature, whether contractual or non-contractual. This comprises, for instance, the supply of goods or services, commercial agencies, construction and engineering or technical knowhow contracts, the granting of industrial, touristic and other licenses, transfer of technology, investment and development contracts, banking, insurance and transport operations, and operations relating to the exploration and extraction of natural wealth, energy supply, laying of gas or oil pipelines, building of roads and tunnels, reclamation of agricultural land, protection of the environment and establishment of nuclear reactors. Article 11 of same Law provides: 'Arbitration agreements may only be concluded by natural or juridical persons having the capacity to dispose of their rights. Arbitration is not permitted in matters which cannot be subject to compromise.'

Arbitration in any dispute involving the administration, other than administrative contracts disputes, is permitted without any legislative or regulatory prohibition.

When scrutinizing the French legal system, for instance, Article 2060 of the French Civil Code prohibits recourse to arbitration, as a general legislative prohibition, in disputes[6] concerning public bodies and institutions and more generally in all matters in which public policy is concerned. Such prohibition is not absolute as, in many cases, the French legislature codified many exceptions to this legislative prohibition. Due to the rule of *Parallélisme des Normes* in public law, French legislature promulgated laws that permit the administration to enter into arbitration to settle disputes in some economic sectors and some cultural sectors such as the Paris Opera and the *Comédie Française.* In addition, and among some other French legislation permitting arbitration, the French PPP legislation No. 735 of 2008 permits arbitration in PPP disputes when the administration is a party to the dispute.

In light of the legal globalization phenomenon in Egypt and the MENA region, Saudi Arbitration Act No. 34 of 2012 was inspired by Article 2060 of the French Civil Code. Saudi Arbitration Act provides in Article 10/2 a legislative prohibition by which public juristic entities cannot recourse to arbitration to settle its disputes, whether contractual or otherwise, unless a consent of the Saudi Prime Minister is obtained.[7] However, Qatar Arbitration Act No. 2 of 2017 is inspired by the Egyptian Arbitration Act No. 27 0f 1994 and stipulates in Article 2/2 that the Prime Minister's consent is required before recourse to arbitration in administrative contracts.[8]

It is worth noting an analytical perspective to Article 2060 of the French Civil Code: Article 1 of the Egyptian Arbitration Act 1994 as amended by Law No. 9 of 1997; Article 10/2 of the Saudi Arbitration Act 2012; and Article 2/2 of Qatar Arbitration Act 2017, shows that two legal facts are concluded:

- Firstly; due to the special nature of administrative contracts which deal with public funds and due to public interests' constraints, many legal systems around the world have promulgated legislative frameworks that contain some restrictions aiming to protect public funds and public interests, and in general, trying to offer higher threshold of protection to states' transactions, whether domestic or international. Such transactions differ, to some extent, from

6 Article 2060 of the French Civil Code provides: 'One may not enter into arbitration agreements in matters of status and capacity of the persons, in those relating to divorce and judicial separation or on controversies concerning public bodies and institutions and more generally in all matters in which public policy is concerned. However, categories of public entities of an industrial and commercial character (*Etablissements publics à caractère industriel et commercial*) may be authorized by decree to enter into arbitration agreements.'

7 Article 10/2 of the Saudi Arbitration Act No. 34 of 2012 provides that: 'Public juristic entities are not permitted to enter into arbitration agreements without the consent of the Prime Minster, unless otherwise provided in another private legislation.'

8 Article 2/2 of the Qatar Arbitration Act No. 2 of 2017 provides that: 'It is obligatory to obtain the Prime Minister's consent or the consent of any person delegated from the Prime Minister before arbitration in administrative contracts.'

private law transactions where civil and commercial contracts are involved. Legislative restrictions are different from one country to another, as each legal system represents the constitutional and legislative ideology of each country. Therefore, legislative restrictions are different from one country to another. The legislative policy of general prohibition, which is not absolute, in the French and Saudi legislation is more onerous than partial restrictions adopted by the Egyptian and Qatar legislation, which confined restrictions to the prior consent from either the competent minster as in Egyptian legislation or the Prime Minister as in Qatar legislation, before recourse to arbitration in administrative contracts. Other states' disputes in Egypt and Qatar are arbitrable without any restrictions whether legislative or regulatory. The legislative policy behind the previous legislation in France, Saudia Arabia, Egypt, and Qatar is to protect public interests which is a matter of public policy. The flow of the legal culture to Egypt and MENA countries is clear.

- Secondly; in light of legal and cultural globalization phenomena, and the efforts made by many countries to increase the inward of FDI and indirect investments, and as many countries are keen to be a global seat of arbitration and mediation, there is in every legal system, some basic constitutional and legislative requirements which are necessary, as these basic requirements reflect the static ideology of any country.[9] Such ideology reflects the social, political, economic, and moral beliefs of the society, and are normally contained as mandatory rules in the constitution and legislation, and not in a regulatory framework, due to these rules' imperative nature. These rules have a mandatory nature and are a matter of public policy. Those mandatory rules are different from other legislative rules which, in many cases, do not have such mandatory nature (*normes facultatives* or *normes supplétives*). The basic rules which constitute the social, political and economic structure of any state, are

9 The static ideology in any constitution or legislation of any state normally relates to political ideology, organization and structure of the state; state's security, and other matters which constitute the higher national interests for any nation. However, the economic ideology in the constitution and legislation in any state is normally dynamic, flexible, and not static as it changes after parliamentary or presidential elections due to state's needs and national economy requirements. Therefore, the constitution left the presidential and parliamentary elections to determine the political and economic ideology to be adopted for each period. One may refer to the French experience when President Valéry Giscard d'Estaing adopted free market economy policies, and after a certain period of time and due to some domestic changes, President François Mitterrand changed to socialist policies. It is also clear that the economic ideologies to be adopted in the USA before the economic crises in 2008 are completely different from those to be adopted after the crises. These polices directly affect the international infrastructure agreements, concession agreements, arbitration in developing states, and the relevant mechanisms whether legislative or contractual. New patterns of states' contracts began to appear such as PPP techniques. Further, such economic ideology directly affects the inflow of FDI to developing states, and the new creative policies to be adopted in order not to lose FDI in the field of infrastructure sector, services, and state contracts. For more elaboration see: Mohamed A.M. Ismail, *Globalization and New International Public Works Agreements in Developing Countries* (Routledge, 2011 and 2016, with a foreword by HH Humphrey Lloyd QC). And see for the same author, 'Legal Globalization and PPPs in Egypt' (EPPPL,1/ 2010, Berlin, p. 62).

contained in the constitution and legislation, as these rules concern any state or any government during exercising public powers of the state. These rules constitute the ideology and the structure of any state which are represented in the beliefs of the nation. Constitution and legislation, in any state, has to codify such rules as mandatory rules, which are a matter of public policy. Among these mandatory rules, are constitutional and legislative rules, that regulate all matters relating to public interests' constraints, public funds and in general some rare rules relating to administrative contracts.

Since many decades, it is confirmed in the Egyptian and MENA countries' legal systems that administrative contracts' disputes are arbitrable, conversely, arbitrability of administrative decrees still needs more analysis, as there are no legislation or judicial precedents in the Egyptian legal system to deal with such crucial topic. Further, there are no academic studies in the Arabic literature to deal with the topic. The question is: Are administrative decrees arbitrable in the Egyptian and MENA countries' legal systems? Can arbitral tribunals exercise judicial review, and apply the principle of legality '*principe de légalite*', upon administrative decrees?

The Egyptian Cassation Court judgment in the *Dipco* case established a new judicial principle in the Egyptian and MENA countries' legal systems regarding the doctrine of arbitrability of administrative decrees.

Factual Background of *Dipco* Case

A BOT contract was concluded on 8 May 2006 between Damietta Port Authority (the Contracting Authority) and *Dipco* Company (the Company). Pursuant to concession and to Contract clauses, the Company undertakes to design, finance, construct, commission, and provide maintenance for new Damietta Port Container Terminal (the Project). The concession contract shall occupy one million square meters. The Egyptian Prime Minster issued decree No. 1119 of 2006 to approve the contract and to grant a licence to the Company for 40 years as the Project shall be transferred to the government by the end of the concession period. After starting works performance, disputes started between the contracting parties regarding contractual undertakings in addition to many controversial views about financial and technical issues, which were interrelated. On 5 May 2009, under the auspices of the Egyptian government, a settlement agreement, which contained many amendments to the Contract, was concluded. As a result of negotiations, and due to the change of some circumstances, the parties have concluded two annexes to the settlement agreement; the first was dated 15 September 2009; and the second was dated 4 October 2010. The settlement agreement and its annexes constitute new undertakings, such as agreed compensation in favor of the Contracting Authority, to be paid by the Company as the latter didn't respect the stipulated time for works' completion and, consequently, there was a delay to start commissioning for the Project. New conflicts between the contracting parties arose, regarding the undertakings imposed by the settlement agreement and regarding project finance and stipulated time for works' completion. Due to the failure of amicable settlement between the parties, on 30 August 2015, the Contracting Authority unilaterally terminated the Contract on the grounds that there was a contractual breach from the Company. On 29 October 2015, the Egyptian Prime Minster issued decree No. 2799 of 2015, to approve the unilateral termination of the Contract, and to cancel the concession licence granted to the Company. Pursuant to the arbitration clause in the Contract, *Dipco* started ICC arbitration proceedings based in Cairo, claiming that the Contracting Authority shall pay the Company various compensations as a result to the unlawful unilateral termination of the Contract, and as the latter termination caused the Company loss, in addition to the loss of profit expected to the Company for the whole Project duration. The Company further claimed that it has injected considerable amounts of money at the Project, and claimed to be reimbursed. Conversely, the Contracting Authority started arbitration proceedings against the Company, claiming that the Company shall pay the Authority compensation as a result of the Company's breach of the Contract. An arbitral tribunal was constituted, and started by consolidation of procedures for the two arbitrations in one arbitral dispute. The Arbitral tribunal issued its award on 9 February 2020 in favor of the Company. The Contracting Authority challenged the award before the Cairo Court of Appeal on the grounds that there was a violation of the award to Article 53 of the Egyptian Arbitration Act No. 27 of 1994. Cairo Court of Appeal dismissed the challenge, on the grounds that the award didn't violate Article 53 of the Egyptian Arbitration Act. The Contracting Authority filed an appeal before the Egyptian Cassation Court, as Cairo Court of Appeal judgment was violating Egyptian Law, and Egyptian public policy, when it refused to set aside the arbitral award. The Egyptian Cassation Court issued its judgment on the arbitral award challenge on 8 July 2021, and decided that the award is null and void.

The Egyptian Cassation Court Decision[10]

The Cassation Court found that the decree of the Egyptian Cabinet is an administrative decree, which falls within the exclusive jurisdiction of the Egyptian Conseil D'État courts. Any violation to such exclusive jurisdiction mandatory rules is considered null and void, as this jurisdiction is a matter of public policy in the Egyptian legal system. The Egyptian Cassation Court concluded that the arbitral award in *Dipco* case is null and void, because the arbitral tribunal didn't apply administrative law rules, which was established by the Egyptian Conseil D'État courts in administrative contracts, as the disputing parties have chosen the Egyptian law to be applicable law to the dispute. Therefore, the arbitral tribunal didn't apply, to the merits of the dispute, the choice of applicable law made by the disputing parties. The Cassation Court added that the contracting parties in administrative contracts

10 The Egyptian Cassation Court Judgment, Civil and Commercial Circuits, on consolidated Cases Nos. 1964 and 1968 of the Judicial Year No. 91, session 8 July 2021.

are not regulated only by the contractual clauses, but also by the regulatory rules of the public utilities, as the public interests prevail over personal and individual interests. The Cassation Court added that this exceptional nature of administrative contracts shall not affect the parties' contractual and financial obligations which are protected from any violation by the contracting authority (the administration).[11] The Cassation Court, when dealing with financial clauses of the contract in dispute, respected the party autonomy by the contracting parties. Further, the exceptional nature of the administrative contract prevails, even if the contract in dispute is a new modernized type of international public works agreements, or a new pattern of the concession of public utilities. The contract in dispute is an administrative contract, and is governed by the established substantive principles of administrative contracts in the Egyptian legal system.

Further, the Cassation Court referred to the legal fact that any resolution issued by the Egyptian Cabinet constitutes a final administrative decree, pursuant to Article 171 of the Egyptian Constitution of 2014,[12] and any attempt to annul any final administrative decree issued by any public juristic entity (the administration) in the Egyptian legal system falls within the exclusive jurisdiction of the Egyptian Conseil D'État courts. Such exclusive jurisdiction is confirmed by Article 190 of the Egyptian Constitution of 2014.[13]. The Cassation Court referred to Articles 10/5, 10/11 and 10/14 of the Egyptian Conseil D'État Law No. 47 of 1972, as these legislative provisions stipulate for the exclusive jurisdiction of the Conseil D'État courts, to adjudicate in all administrative disputes (mainly administrative decrees and administrative contracts),[14] The Cassation Court referred to Article 109 of the Egyptian Code of Civil Procedures[15] which provides that non-competence of courts is a matter of public policy. The above-mentioned constitutional and legislative

11 The Cassation Court confirmed that the administration cannot take any unilateral action (decree) against the financial obligations of the contracting parties in *Dipco* dispute. It is clear that the Cassation Court supersedes party autonomy.

12 Article 171 of the Egyptian Constitution of 2014 provides: 'Regulations to create and organize public utilities: The Prime Minister issues the regulations necessary for the creation and organization of public utilities and interests upon the approval of the government.'

13 Article 190 of the Egyptian Constitution of 2014 provides: 'The State Council, Mandate: The State Council is an independent judicial body that is exclusively competent to adjudicate in administrative disputes, disciplinary cases and appeals, and disputes pertaining to its decisions. It is also solely competent to issue opinions on the legal issues of bodies to be determined by law, review and draft bills and resolutions of a legislative character, and review draft contracts to which the state or any public entity is a party. Other competencies are to be determined by law.'

14 Article 10 of the Egyptian Conseil D'État Law No. 47 of 1972 provides: 'State Council Courts have the exclusive competence to adjudicate in: [...] 10/5: appeals submitted by individuals challenging final administrative decrees; [...] 10/11: disputes concerning concession contracts, public works contracts, supply contracts or any other administrative contract [...] and 10/14: all other administrative disputes.'

15 Article 109 of the Egyptian Code of Civil Procedures provides: 'In case of challenge of court's competence for lack of jurisdiction or due to the subject-matter of the dispute or due to case value, the court shall *ipso jure* decide on the case. It is permitted to raise such challenge at any stage of litigation.'

provisions are of a mandatory nature in the Egyptian legal system, as they relate to public policy, and in particular judicial public policy. These constitutional and legislative mandatory rules draw the line between ordinary courts' (civil and commercial courts) jurisdiction and Conseil D'État administrative courts' jurisdiction. The contracting parties cannot agree upon any contractual provision which may contradict with such mandatory rules.

The Cassation Court elaborated to conclude that the Egyptian Cabinet's approval to the settlement agreement between the disputing parties is a final administrative decree. Such decree annulment or judicial review to monitor its legality, falls within the exclusive jurisdiction of the Egyptian Conseil D'État courts. The arbitral award in the *Dipco* case exercised judicial review upon the legality of the Egyptian Cabinet's approval to the settlement agreement between the disputing parties dated 5 July 2009 (and its annexes 1 and 2), and the arbitral award exercised judicial review upon the legality of such decree. Such a decree is a final administrative decree, and the judicial review as such can only be exercised by the Egyptian Conseil D'État courts. Unlike the Egyptian Conseil D'État courts, the arbitral tribunal cannot exercise judicial review upon the legality of administrative decrees, and cannot apply the principle of legality. The arbitral tribunal, further, elaborated to conclude that the cabinet's administrative decree is null and void, and has no legal effect. As a matter of fact, such conclusion by the arbitral tribunal, is in its substance, a judicial review upon the Cabinet's administrative decree existence, form and legality, and is an implied judgment in the legality of such administrative decree, which violates the substantive principles of courts' jurisdiction in the Egyptian legal system. Courts' jurisdiction in the Egyptian legal system, is regulated through constitutional and legislative provisions, which have mandatory nature, and these provisions are a matter of public policy in the Egyptian legal system. The arbitral award approach is clear and explicit, that there is considerable violation to the substantial and basic rules relating to the judiciary jurisdiction in the Egyptian judicial system, which is violation to the public policy in the Egyptian legal system.

The Cassation Court found that public contracts are different from private law contracts, as public law contracts have a main objective, which is the better management and regularity of public utilities. This main objective justifies the exceptional nature, and the special rules, which regulate administrative contracts. Public law rules grant the administration, as the contracting authority is always a party to administrative contracts, some exceptional privileges which aim to achieve public interests.

The Cassation Court analyzed the Cairo Court of Appeal judgment in challenge and found that the Cairo Court of Appeal concluded that the contract in dispute is a BOT agreement which is directly relating to public interests, public juristic entities, and social infrastructure. The contract is mixed of a construction contract on one hand, and granting a concession of public utilities from the state to the private company on the other hand. The contract in dispute is linked to the public interest concept, and connected to the state's role, as it has organizational powers and exercises supervision. The Cassation Court found that Cairo Court of Appeal's analysis of the award in challenge leads to the conclusion that the contract in dispute is concession of public works and concession of public utilities. The Cassation Court elaborated that, in administrative contracts, the administration (the contracting authority), can exercise wide powers and privileges such as supervision, direction, organization, amendments to contract, and unilateral termination of the contract, as these powers and privileges are not granted to the private party to the administrative contract. Nevertheless, the Cassation Court added that financial terms and obligations in administrative contracts cannot be amended without the consent of the contracting parties. The legal justification of such powers and privileges granted to the administration is the public interests' constraints, and the aim to achieve the best management to public utilities. The private party to the administrative contract cannot deny such exceptional powers and privileges granted to the administration, as any private entity that enters into an administrative contract, with the state, accepts in advance such exceptional privileges and powers, therefore, the private party cannot allege that private interests may prevail over public interests. The contracting state cannot waive such exceptional powers and privileges, as these powers and privileges are not of a financial nature, and consequently, cannot be compromised. Such exceptional powers and privileges are a matter of public policy in the Egyptian legal system, and cannot be waived by the administration's consent.

The Cairo Court of Appeal judgment in challenge considered the contract in dispute as private law contract, didn't apply Article 53/2 of the Egyptian Arbitration Act No. 27 of 1994,[16] and didn't set aside the arbitral award in the *Dipco* case, despite the fact that the latter has violated the public policy in the Egyptian legal system. Therefore, the Cassation Court annulled the Cairo Court of Appeal judgment as it violates the Egyptian law.

The Egyptian Cassation Court confirmed that the arbitral award in challenge exercised judicial review upon the legality of the Cabinet's administrative decree of amicable settlement of the disputing parties and concluded that such a decree has not fulfilled the legal requirements stipulated in Article 4/*bis* of Law No. (1) of 1996.[17] The arbitral award further decided upon the existence and legal formalities of the Cabinet's decree, and such an approach falls outside of the jurisdiction of the arbitral tribunal, and is considered part of the exclusive jurisdiction of the Conseil D'État courts. The Cassation Court added that the arbitral tribunal should have suspended arbitration proceedings, and referred the matter of legality of the Cabinet's administrative decree to the Conseil D'État competent court, pursuant to Article 46 of the Egyptian Arbitration Act No. 27 of 1994 and Article 129 of the Egyptian Code of Civil Procedures.[18] The principle of equal bargaining powers of

16 Article 53/2 of the Egyptian Arbitration Act No. 27 of 1994 provides that: '2. the court adjudicating the action for annulment shall *ipso jure* annul the arbitral award if it is in conflict with the public policy in the Arab Republic of Egypt.'

17 Law of Specialized Ports No. 1 of 1996 and its amendments.

18 Article 46 of the Egyptian Arbitration Act No. 27 of 1994 provides that: 'If, in the course of the arbitral proceedings, a matter falling outside the scope of the arbitral tribunal's jurisdiction is raised, or if a document submitted to it is challenged for forgery, or if criminal proceedings are undertaken regarding the alleged forgery or for any other criminal act, the arbitral tribunal may decide to proceed with the subject-matter of the dispute without any reliance on the incidental matter raised or

the disputing parties, which is the main argument that the Cairo Court of Appeal's judgment in challenge relied on, eliminates the exceptional powers and privileges of the administration as the contract in dispute relates to public utilities which is a matter of public policy in the Egyptian legal system.

The Egyptian Cassation Court finally decided that the arbitral award in the *Dipco* case, issued on 9 February 2020, is totally null and void in all its parts, as the award parts and sections are directly coherent, interrelated, and cannot be separated.

International Commentary

Following the annulment of the arbitral award in *Dipco* case by the Egyptian Court of Cassation, some scholars pointed out the negative impact upon arbitration as a feasible process of disputes settlement in Egypt. Further, it is argued that such an outcome by the Egyptian Cassation Court adds to the uncertainties associated with administrative approvals, and may render arbitration involving such approvals practically unfeasible. Given the influence of Egyptian jurisprudence, courts elsewhere in the Arab world may be inspired to take a similar stance. It will also disappoint those hoping that the introduction of BOT legislation and other regulations relating to PPPs would set investors on an equal footing with government entities.[19]

It is suggested that public policy is an important feature of any legal system in any country. Arbitrable matters and non-arbitrable matters exist in all legal systems around the world. For instance, the French Cassation Court, which is one of the leading Cassation Courts in the world, issued over decades, many judgments to annul arbitral awards, which violate the French Republic Public Policy. The latter approach by the French Cassation Court was not a reason to reduce the attractiveness of Paris as a favorable seat of arbitration to all investors from different regions around the world.[20]

In addition, the French Cassation Court, in some recent judgments, approved Paris Court of Appeal judgments, and set aside arbitral awards which violated public policy in France, and violated international public policy.[21]

---

on the document alleged to be a forgery or on the other criminal act. Otherwise, the arbitral tribunal shall suspend the proceedings until a final judgment is rendered in this respect. Such measure shall entail suspension of the period for making of the arbitral award.' Further, Article 129 of the Egyptian Code of Civil Procedures provides that '[...] the court may order suspension of the case proceedings, if such suspension is necessary and conditioned to the outcome of another case.'

19 Alexander Hiller, Arbitrating Government Contracts in Egypt, Observations on *DIPCO v. Damietta Port Authority, Association Suisse de l'arbitrage* (ASA) Bulletin, Kluwer, March 2022, p. 82 and p. 90.

20 For instance, see: *Dutco* Case, French Cassation Court judgment issued on 7 January 1992, see also in *Dutco* Case: Christopher R. Sepalla, 'French Supreme Court Nullifies ICC Practice for Appointment of Arbitrators in Multi-Party Arbitration Cases,' *ICLR*, 1993, pp. 222–7.

21 For instance, see: *Belokon* v. *Republic of Kyrgyztan* Case, Paris Court of Appeal judgment on 21 February 2017 which was approved by the French Cassation Court on 23 March 2022; *MK Group* Case, Paris Court of Appeal judgment on 16 January/2018; and *Libya* v.. *Sorelec* Case, Paris Court of Appeal judgment on 17 November 2020 which was approved by the French Cassation Court on 7 September 2022.

In many leading legal systems such as the English legal system, English case law was clear when it established some substantive principles of contract law that relate to principles of contractual justice between the contracting parties. English courts, for many decades, annulled some contractual clauses which have a punitive nature and which are extravagant to the other contracting party, such as in liquidated damages clauses, which English courts refused to enforce in many occasions, as these clauses were punitive in nature, and do not represent a real compensation that was equal and adequate to the actual loss suffered by the other contracting party. [22]

Further, English courts annulled arbitration awards, in rare cases, when it violates public policy.[23]

The Egyptian legislature in the Egyptian Civil Code[24] and the Code of Commerce has adopted similar approaches as mandatory rules in these codes which regulate private law transactions are minimal. The legislative policy of the Egyptian legislature is to supersede party autonomy in private law transactions, and any legislation regulating private law transaction contains very few mandatory rules, as the legal nature of the majority of legislative rules in such legislation is that these rules are *normes facultatives* or *normes supplétives* and not mandatory.

It is true that legislation in MENA countries has followed the steps of the Egyptian legislature, as MENA civil codes and codes of commerce were inspired by the Egyptian legislature, and adopted the same legislative policy to minimize mandatory legislative provisions in private law; civil and commercial transactions. In the Egyptian and MENA countries' legislation, mandatory rules in any legislation that regulate private law transactions are very rare. The party autonomy principle prevails, as Egyptian and MENA countries' legislation adopts, in private law transactions, party autonomy, particularly in contract law. Contracting parties are free to agree upon any contractual clauses, which may achieve their financial and economic expectations, and to maintain contractual justice as a general principle. This is conditional on such contractual clauses not violating any mandatory rule which is considered a matter of public policy.

22 See the leading Case in English case law: *Dunlop Pneumatic Tyre Company Ltd* v. *New Garage & Motor Company Ltd* (1915) AC 79. This approach of English Courts has been updated in other cases such as: *Philips Hong Kong Ltd* v. *Attorney General of Hong Kong* (1993), 61 BLR 41. For the new approach by English Courts in LDs see: *Cavendish Square Holding BV* v. *El Makdessi; ParkingEye Ltd* v. *Beavis* [2016] 2 All ER 519, 533.

23 *Soleimany* v. *Soleimany* [1999] Q.B. 785 19 February 1998, and [1999] 3 All ER 847; and the recent case of *Payward Inc* v. *Chechetkin* [2023] EWHC 1780 (Comm) represent a rare example of English courts refusing to enforce an arbitral award on public policy grounds. The award in question was rendered against Mr, Chechetkin, a UK-domiciled lawyer, who suffered significant losses trading on the Claimant's cryptocurrency platform. The English Commercial Court declined enforcement primarily because the arbitrator had not considered or applied English consumer rights and financial services laws.

24 Contract law substantive principles are codified in Egypt in the Egyptian Civil Code as 'The Contract' as one of the main sources of obligations in the Egyptian Civil Code. The same approach is adopted by MENA countries' legal systems.

Following the same approach of English case law on many occasions, legislation in Egypt and MENA countries, while codifying some rare mandatory rules, aims to protect the weaker party in the contract and to achieve contractual justice between the contracting parties. An example of some rare mandatory rules in Egyptian and MENA countries' legislation is the theory of unexpected circumstances ('*L'imprévision*') that occur during contract performance and due to such circumstances, performance becomes onerous, and the financial equilibrium of the contract is negatively affected.[25] Further, another mandatory rule in the Egyptian and MENA countries' civil codes is that the contracting parties cannot deprive the judge/arbitrator from exercising judicial review upon the compensation *quantum* which is agreed by the contracting parties if such *quantum* is unfair or extravagant.[26]

The legislative policy behind such mandatory provisions is to protect the weaker party in the contract, and to achieve contractual justice and fairness between the contracting parties. Such legislative mandatory provisions reflect the ideology of the Egyptian and MENA countries' legislation, which aims to achieve fairness and contractual justice in economic, business, and legal transactions.

Unification of theories relating to frustration of contract which aim to maintain financial equilibrium of the contract is a fundamental tool to achieve global contract law and to mitigate public law constraints.

Unification of the Public Policy Concept in the Egyptian and MENA Countries' Legal Systems

In any legal system, whether a civil law legal system or a common law jurisdiction, it is true that as there is a state, it has its independent and unique political, economic, and social ideologies. The latter ideologies constitute the public policy regime, borders, and frontiers in every state. The constitution and legislation codify these ideologies in the constitutional and legislative provisions, which in some cases, have an imperative and mandatory nature, as these provisions in most cases relate to public security; public health; public tranquility; the imperative principles of justice, and the judicial public policy of any state.

25 See: Article 147/2 of the Egyptian Civil Code, Article 198 of the Kuwaiti Civil Code, Article 130 of the Bahrini Civil Code, Article 107 of the Algerian Civil Code, Article 249 of the UAE Civil Code, Article 146/2 of the Iraqi Civil Code, Article 171/2 of the Qatar Civil Code, Article 159 of the Omani Civil Code, Article 205 of the Jordanian Civil Code, Article 148 of the Syrian Civil Code, and Article 147/2 of the Libyan Civil Code. All these Arab civil codes consider the application of the theory of unforeseen circumstances ('*L'imprévision*') as a mandatory rule which is a matter of public policy. Contracting parties cannot ignore or avoid the application of such a theory by their contractual agreement, and any contractual clause which contains an exemption from the application of such a theory is null and void, pursuant to these legislative provisions. It is clear that most Arab countries' legislation is following the Egyptian legislation. Generally, the Egyptian Civil Code was inspired by the French Civil Code and all Arab civil codes were influenced and inspired by the Egyptian Civil Code. Such influence reflects the legal globalization phenomenon implications in the MENA countries.

26 Article 224 of the Egyptian Civil Code and Article 227 of the Civil Code of the Kingdom of Bahrain.

Public policy, in any state, represents the basic political, social, economic, and moral rules which constitute the structural values of the state,[27] as drawn up by the constitution and legislation. These values are of fundamental importance to the state rather than individuals, and legislature, whether in the constitution or legislation, codifies these imperative rules in the form of mandatory rules. In addition, mandatory rules reflect the culture of every society. Cultural interaction is the main outcome of the flow of ideas and values in each country. Culture represents a set of practices, values, beliefs, and customs acquired by individuals as members of a distinctive society, and resulting from interaction among people. States aim to keep public policy through regulating legislation, that maintains the culture and values of each society. Imperative legislative rules codified in legislation represent the culture and values of any society that states aim to protect, and these imperative mandatory rules are rare in every legal system.

Political and economic ideologies of any constitution of every state are important factors behind codifying basic and substantive principles of each society. It is worth noting that the Egyptian Constitution of 2014 has not adopted a certain economic ideology, to ensure that the electoral process – whether parliamentary or presidential – shall impose the proposed ideology chosen by the nation. This ideology will be changed from one decade to another, according to the economic situation; the economic and social requirements of the society. For instance, in the USA, the ideology adopted before the 2008 economic crisis is certainly different from the one that is being adopted after the crisis. It is also important to refer to the French experience, when President Valéry Giscard d'Estaing adopted free market economic policies, and after a certain period of time and due to some domestic changes, President François Mitterrand changed to socialist policies. It is worth mentioning that this flexibility, which currently is codified in the Egyptian Constitution of 2014, reflects a huge growth in the Egyptian infrastructure legislation and consequently, an increase of the inward of FDI in several economic sectors. These polices directly affect the international states' agreements in developing countries and affect mechanisms whether legislative or contractual.

In Egypt and MENA countries, where culture is a dynamic value changing from one country to another and from time to time, governments represent the nation in managing and operating public utilities.[28]

As public policy reflects values, culture, morals, and ideology that represent the philosophical and ideological beliefs of the society, public policy has a *dual* role as follows:

- It represents the values, cultural, social, moral, economic, and political ideology of the society in the form of mandatory rules which are a matter of public policy in constitution and legislation. These rules are imperative in nature and have a compulsory power more than other legislative provisions;

27 Emad Tarek Al Bishry, *Public Policy Concept in Theory and Practice, A Comparative Study between Legislation and Sharia'a Law Doctrine* (Shorouk International Library, 2011, in Arabic).

28 The General Assembly for Legal Opinion and Legislation, the Egyptian Conseil D'État, opinion in session 18 December 1996.

- The public policy concept protects the imperative nature which is the substance of the mandatory rules, as they represent a higher public interest of the society: a) from any violation by the administration that may constitute any infringement to individuals' liberties or human rights; b) from individuals if they violate mandatory rules through contractual clauses which are against public policy; c) or from an external threat through using *Renvoi*, as a conflict of laws technique, that may lead to the application of a foreign law which violates a mandatory rule in the national law *lex fori*.[29]

The general principle in the Egyptian Civil Code and MENA countries civil codes[30] is that party autonomy prevails because the contract, as a source of obligation, constitutes the law of the parties. In very rare cases, any contractual clause, if it violates a mandatory rule, is null and void.

The Egyptian Supreme Administrative Court, as the highest step in litigation at the Egyptian Conseil D'État, decided in many leading judgments that:

> '[…] if the contract provisions contradict with legislative or regulatory provisions, the contractual provisions prevail. Rights and obligations of the contracting entity with the administration are totally governed by the administrative contract, not with the decisions of the administration. Similar to civil contract, the administrative contract constitutes the law of the contracting parties […].' [31]

It is understood that any contractual clause prevails over legislation and regulations, and if it is not contradicting a mandatory rule which is a matter of public policy.

It is true that the public policy concept is mitigated, to some extent, by the cultural and legal globalization phenomena forces. Judicial principles established by the Egyptian Supreme Administrative Court in administrative contracts are mitigated, such as the prohibition of *Exceptio non-adempleti contractus* when the administration failed in some of its obligations (in particular delay of payment to contractors), the contractor cannot suspend contract performance to exercise pressure upon the administration, until he receives payments. It is prohibited to suspend performance of the administrative contract, as these contracts are connected with the public utilities, and the real application of principle of regularity of public utilities implies that an administrative contract cannot be suspended, even if there is a contractual breach from the contracting authority. There are current trends in new judgments, permitting contractors to suspend performance, in some exceptional

29 In conflict of laws basic concepts such as *Renvoi* see generally: Dicy, Morris and Collins, *The Conflict of Laws* (Sweet and Maxwell, 2022); Paul Lagarde and Henri Battifol, *Droit International Privé* (LGDJ, 1981). In Arab doctrine see: F. Riad and S. Rashed, *A Concise Guide to the Conflict of Laws and International Judicial Jurisdiction,*(1988, in Arabic); Fouad Riad, *Conflict of Laws, Conflict of Forum and the Effects of Foreign Judgments* (Dar Al Nahda Al Arabia, 1999, in Arabic).

30 Article 147 of the Egyptian Civil Code and Article 130 of the Civil Code of the Kingdom of Bahrain.

31 The Egyptian Supreme Administrative Court, Case No. 9559 of Judicial Year 47, session 20 December 2005.

cases. This approach by the Court reflects the influence of the cultural and legal globalization phenomena on the substantive principles of the administrative contracts in the Egyptian legal system.[32]

Administrative Decrees Connected to the Administrative Contract (Actes non-détachables) and other Decrees Which Are Not Connected (Actes détachables)

An administrative Decree may be connected to the administrative contract and may not be connected. An administrative decree which is not connected to the contract (separated from the contract) is not part of the arbitration agreement. The Egyptian Conseil D'État courts established the doctrine of administrative decrees which are connected to the contract, or which are separated from the contract.

During the contractual process, decrees which are connected to the contract are considered part of the contractual process,[33] therefore, arbitral tribunals may arbitrate and compensate all financial consequences, if any. Conversely, decrees separated from the contract fall within the exclusive jurisdiction of the Conseil D'État courts, to exercise judicial review upon the principle of legality, pursuant to Article 190 of the Egyptian Constitution of 2014 and Articles 10/5, 10/11 and 10/14 of the Egyptian Conseil D'État Law No. 47 of 1972. Disputes concerning separated administrative decrees and applying the principle of legality are non-arbitrable, as they fall within the exclusive jurisdiction of the Conseil D'État courts.

In applying the above-mentioned principles to the *Dipco* case and reviewing the legality of the administrative decrees issued by the Egyptian Cabinet, it is clear that two legal facts are concluded:

- The Cabinet's administrative decree is separated from the administrative contract concluded between the *Dipco* company and Damietta Port Authority (the contracting authority), as the Cabinet's decree is an administrative decree issued from another authority (the Egyptian Cabinet) which is different from the contracting authority (Damietta Port Authority).
- The Cabinet's separated decree, as such, is not part of the contract and consequently, not part of the arbitration agreement. If the arbitral award decided

32 The Egyptian Supreme Administrative Court, Case No. 3028 of Judicial Year 58, session 24 December 2019. It is worth noting that the right to suspend performance in contracts as a pressure upon the other contractor '*Exceptio non-adempleti contractus*' exists in Article 161 of the Egyptian Civil Code and is an optional right of the contractor, subject to some conditions, in civil and commercial contracts.

33 For instance: see the judgment issued by the Egyptian Supreme Administrative Court on consolidated Cases Nos. 456 and 320 of the Judicial Year 20, session 5 April 1975, p. 307. The Supreme Administrative Court held that a separated administrative decree is independent from the contractual process whether the contract is an administrative contract or a civil contract, therefore, such an administrative decree may be challenged separately before the Conseil D'État courts which have the exclusive jurisdiction to exercise the judicial review as such. The legal definition of such an administrative decree is important as jurisdiction of the Conseil D'État courts is a matter of public policy. In the same meaning see: The Egyptian Supreme Administrative Court, Case No. 10211 of the Judicial Year 49, session 13 June 2006 and Case No. 2784 of the Judicial year 49, session 13 June 2006.

upon the legality of the Cabinet's administrative decree, in addition to the violation of the mandatory rules in the Egyptian judicial system of the jurisdiction of the Conseil D'État courts, the arbitral award would have decided on matters which are not contained in the contract and not contained in the arbitration agreement, as such matters are not arbitrable.[34] The arbitral award went far beyond the jurisdiction of the arbitral tribunal.

The Egyptian Cassation Court in the *Dipco* case achieved a sensible balance between respecting party autonomy regarding financial contractual clauses on one hand, and on the other hand applying public policy constraints, of the mandatory constitutional and legislative rules of the Egyptian legal and judicial systems.

International Instruments: United Nations Convention on the Recognition and Enforcement of Foreign Arbitral Awards (New York Convention 1958)[35]

The New York Convention 1958 dealt with public policy constraints as one of the most important reasons which render foreign arbitral awards unenforceable.

Article 5/2/a of the Convention provides that recognition and enforcement of an arbitral award may be refused if the competent authority in the country where recognition and enforcement is sought finds that the subject-matter of the dispute is not capable of settlement by arbitration (non-arbitrable) under the law of that country. The law of the country, where enforcement is sought, is significant in this context, as pursuant to the law of the country of enforcement the subject-matter of the dispute has to be arbitrable. Further, Article 5/2/b of the Convention assures the public policy significance as any arbitral award must comply with the public policy mandatory rules of the state of recognition and enforcement. Article 5/2/b pointed out that recognition and enforcement of an arbitral award may also be refused if the competent authority in the country where recognition and enforcement is sought finds that the recognition or enforcement of the award would be contrary to the public policy of that country. [36]

The scope of application of the New York Convention is not confined to foreign arbitral awards, but it extends to contain arbitral awards which are not considered as domestic awards in the state where their recognition and enforcement are sought. The arbitral award in the *Dipco* case falls within this category of awards, as it is an award rendered in an international commercial arbitration dispute, pursuant to

34 Hamdy Yassin Okasha, *The Encyclopedia of Practical Problems in Administrative Contracts Disputes* (fourth volume, 2016, p. 839, in Arabic). The author refers to the legal fact that judicial review to an administrative decree separated from the contract has to rely upon the violation of the principle of legality and not the violation of contractual obligation relating to the administrative contract.

35 United Nations Convention on the Recognition and Enforcement of Foreign Arbitral Awards (New York, 10 June 1958), ratified by A.R.E on 9 March 1959.

36 Article V of the New York Convention 1958 provides: '2– Recognition and enforcement of an arbitral award may also be refused if the competent authority in the country where recognition and enforcement is sought finds that: (a) The subject matter of the difference is not capable of settlement by arbitration under the law of that country; or (b) The recognition or enforcement of the award would be contrary to the public policy of that country.'

Article 3 of the Egyptian Arbitration Act.[37] Unification of the principles of enforcement is clear through the New York Convention as an international instrument. The international community in the New York Convention agreed to the fact that an arbitral award is not enforceable if the subject-matter of the dispute is non-arbitrable, or if the recognition or enforcement of the award would be contrary to the public policy of that country where recognition or enforcement is sought.

Finally, the Egyptian Cassation Court decision in the *Dipco* case has to be understood and interpreted in a very narrow scope as it is only confined to the dispute between the *Dipco* Company and Damietta Port Authority. Arbitral tribunals in the Egyptian legal system, normally, have very wide powers when dealing with an arbitral tribunal's jurisdiction. Arbitrability of administrative decrees separated from the administrative contract, and the non-arbitrable nature of a separated administrative decree when reviewing its legality is an exception in the Egyptian legal system.

It is true that public policy constraints in the Egyptian and MENA countries' legal systems are very rare in civil and commercial transactions. In addition, public policy constraints in the Egyptian and MENA countries' legal systems are very rare in administrative contracts, as in the latter contracts party autonomy principle prevails.[38]

The Egyptian Cassation Court rarely nullifies an arbitration award, as the understanding of the Egyptian Cassation Court of the legislative policy behind the Egyptian Arbitration Act 1994, in challenging arbitration awards, is that such a challenge is an exception. An arbitration award, in the view of the Egyptian Cassation Court, is final, binding, and enforceable. Setting aside an arbitral award is an exception in the Egyptian legal system, as the list of cases to challenge an arbitral award, as mentioned in Article 53 of the Egyptian Arbitration Act, is exhaustive and not subject to any analogy or addition by Egyptian courts.[39] Due

37 Article I of the New York Convention 1958 Provides: 'The Convention shall also apply to arbitral awards not considered as domestic awards in the State where their recognition and enforcement are sought.'

38 The Egyptian Supreme Administrative Court, Case No. 9559 of Judicial Year 47, session 20 December 2005.

39 Article 53 of the Egyptian Arbitration Act No. 27 of 1994 provides that: '1. An arbitral award may be annulled only: a) If there is no arbitration agreement, if it was void, voidable or its duration had elapsed; b) If either party to the arbitration agreement was at the time of the conclusion of the arbitration agreement fully or partially incapacitated according to the law governing its legal capacity; c) If either party to the arbitration was unable to present its case as a result of not being given proper notice of the appointment of an arbitrator or of the arbitral proceedings, or for any other reason beyond its control; d) If the arbitral award failed to apply the law agreed upon by the parties to govern the subject matter in dispute; e) If the composition of the arbitral tribunal or the appointment of the arbitrators was in conflict with this Law or the parties' agreement; f) If the arbitral award dealt with matters not falling within the scope of the arbitration agreement or exceeding the limits of this agreement. However, in the case when matters falling within the scope of the arbitration can be separated from the part of the award which contains matters not included within the scope of the arbitration, the nullity affects exclusively the latter parts only; g) If the arbitral award itself or the arbitration procedures affecting the award contain a legal violation that causes nullity. 2. The court adjudicating the action for annulment shall *ipso jure* annul the arbitral award if it is in conflict with the public policy in the Arab Republic of Egypt.'

to this list's exceptional nature, exceptional cases in Article 53 of the Egyptian Arbitration Act have to be very narrow interpreted by Egyptian courts.

The Egyptian Court of Cassation judgment in the *Dipco* case is consistent with international standards, as is the case in the New York Convention 1958, and consistent with the judicial approaches of the French Court of Cassation as it applies and respects public policy constraints on many occasions. The same principle exists in English case law, even if the English courts set aside arbitral awards for public policy violation in very rare cases. Such an approach shouldn't create any fears for foreign investors, as public policy matters are very rare in arbitral disputes, whether domestic or international. Public policy is an exception from the party autonomy principle as the latter principle prevails in state contracts and commercial contracts in Egypt and the MENA region.

It is very clear that the principles relating to public policy are unified in the Egyptian and MENA countries' legal systems. National courts play a fundamental role to achieve the unification of contract law principles, and to maintain the unification of approaches setting aside arbitral awards in the respective jurisdictions.

The decision of the Egyptian Cassation Court in *Dipco* is not a threat to the unification of contract law principles as such a decision has a very narrow interpretation in the Egyptian and MENA countries' legal systems. Global contract law is underway in the region, whether in public or private contracts, despite public law constraints.

Case Study No. 2: Liquidated Damages' Contractual Clauses, How Can Courts' Intervention Creates Unification in Substantive Contract Law Principles in the Case of Unfair Contract Terms?

Liquidated damages clauses are common clauses in international contracts, whether public or private (commercial) contracts. How can courts intervene to maintain a fair contractual relationship, through protecting contractual justice, and offering a high threshold of protection to the weaker party in the contract?

English Case Law

English case law has a unique perspective regarding the liquidated damages clause stipulated in contracts. It is important to scrutinize some of the most important cases in English case law, as they represent an advanced approach in the doctrine of LDs.

Kemble v. *Farren* (1829)[40] was one of the leading cases that came before the court during the 19th century. A contract was entered into by and between the defendant (actor) and the contractor, stipulating the appearance of the former as a principal comedian at the Covent Garden Theatre against a remuneration of £3.6 per night for four seasons. The contract also contained a provision specifying that

40 *Kemble v. Farren* (1829) 6 Bing 141.

if either party failed to fulfill the terms of the contract, or any part thereof, such party would be subject to the payment of a sum of £1,000 in liquidated damages.

During the second season, the defendant refused to act because of failure of the contractor to meet a single payment of £3.6. The court held that, the sum of £1,000 shall be made to the defendant (actor) as recompense, for the failure of the plaintiff (contractor) to make payment. Since the sum of £3.6 is very trivial in comparison to that of £1,000, the clause has thus been rendered into a penalty clause, rather than liquidated damages.

In the 1906 *Public Works Commissioner* v. *Hills* case[41] – the fourth of its kind to be held under a railway construction contract – the indefinite sum ruled by the court could not be a genuine pre-estimate of loss, and was therefore regarded as a penalty clause.

In the *Ford Motor Company* v. *Armstrong* case (1915),[42] Armstrong, a retailer, agreed not to sell any Ford car, or any part thereof, below the set price list; he also agreed to pay £250 in liquidated damages for every act of breach. The court held that the sum of £250 was a penalty since it is not equal to the damages encountered.

In the leading case of *Dunlop Pneumatic Tyre* v. *New Garage* (1914)[43] the House of Lords stated: 'The essence of liquidated damages is a genuine covenanted pre-estimate of loss.' Lord Dunedin elaborated, 'Though the parties to a contract who use the words "Penalty" or "Liquidated damages" may *prima facie* be supposed to mean what they say, yet the expression is not conclusive. The court must find out whether the payment stipulated is in truth a penalty or liquidated damages.'

In other words, 'a penalty clause [...] was a term designed to punish the party in breach rather than compensate the innocent party for its loss.'[44] For parties wishing to incorporate LDs into their agreement, it is essential to tread the line between LDs, and penalty clauses carefully.

As Eggleston[45] pointed out, the terminology itself is not decisive, and if, as a matter of construction, the courts find that liquidated damages are penalties or *vice versa*, they will award accordingly.

Lord Dunedin's judgment in the Dunlop case remains the objective test on which following judgments have relied. In addition to the above-mentioned phrases, Lord Dunedin stated:

'The essence of a penalty is the payment of money stipulated as a threat to the offending party; meanwhile, the essence of liquidated damages is a genuine covenanted pre-estimate of damage.'

41 *Public Works Commissioner* v. *Hills*, (1906) AC 368.

42 *Ford Motor Company Ltd (England)* v. *Armstrong* (1915). Brian Eggleston, *Liquidated Damages and Extensions of Time: In Construction Contracts* (2nd edn, Blackwell Science, 1997, pp. 59, 60).

43 *Dunlop Pneumatic Tyre Company Ltd* v. New *Garage & Motor Company Ltd* (1915) AC 79.

44 Ewan McKendrick, *Contract Law* (14th edn, Macmillan Law Masters, 2021, p. 428). And for LDs in the MENA countries see: Joseph Chedrawe, LDs for Delay in the Middle East: Not Etched in Stone, *BCDR International Arbitration Review*, 4, 2017, p. 105.

45 Brain Eggleston, *Liquidated Damages and Extension of Time in Construction Contracts* (2nd edn, Blackwell Science, 1997, p. 56).

Whether a stipulated sum is regarded as a penalty or a liquidated damage is a question of construction to be decided upon the terms and inherent circumstances of each particular contract and should be determined as at the time of making the contract, not the time of breach. To assist this task of construction, various tests have been suggested which, if applicable to the case under consideration, may prove helpful or even conducive. Such are:

1 The stipulated sum will be held to be a penalty if it is extravagant and unconscionable, in amount in comparison with the greatest loss, that could conceivably be proved to have followed from the breach.
2 The stipulated sum will be held as a penalty if the breach is represented only in the failure to pay a sum of money that is less than the stipulated sum.
3 There is a presumption (but no more) that the stipulated sum is a penalty when 'a single sum is made payable by way of compensation as a consequence of the occurrence of one or more events, some of which may occasion serious and other trifling damage.'
4 The stipulated sum, being a genuine pre-estimate of the expected damage as a consequence of the breach, should not render price pre-estimation an obstacle or an impossibility. On the contrary, that is just the situation where it is probable that the pre-estimated damage is the true bargain between the parties.

It is clear that during that period, and up till the last decade of the 20th century, English courts did not validate penalty clauses.

The sum stipulated by the parties must reflect the 'genuine pre-estimated loss' and must be reasonably adequate to the actual loss. This should be determined by the contracting parties.

The burden of proving that the stipulated sum (clause) is actually a penalty lies on the party challenging the clause. It is the duty of the said party to prove the punitive nature.

In a recent case famous for applying new principles, English courts had different perspectives. This is evident as follows:

Philips Hong Kong Ltd v. *Attorney General of Hong Kong* (1993)[46]

In the leading case of Philips Hong Kong, Philips entered into a contract with the Hong Kong government to design, supply, install, and commission a computerized supervisory system for a new route to the approach roads and twin tunnels. The contract was one of seven contracts, six of which contained a flow chart setting out a program for the progress of work. In addition, there were other flow charts setting out the work of five different contracts. The flow charts identified key dates on which the work performed by Philips interfaced with the programs of other contracts. Clause 27 of the Philips contract imposed an obligation on Philips to meet its

46 *Philips Hong Kong Ltd* v. *Attorney General of Hong Kong* (1993), 61 BLR 41.

key dates; simultaneously, clause 29 provided that failure to meet key dates shall entail the payment of liquidated damages.

The Privy Council held that the provision stipulating liquidated damages under the contract entered into between the parties was a genuine pre-estimate and was thus enforceable, since the parties were able to estimate with a reasonable degree of certainty the extent of their liability and the potential risk. The court applied the party autonomy and freedom of contract principles. It adopted an objective assessment that will not normally identify situations where the application of the provision could result in a larger sum being recovered by the injured party as compared to the actual loss sustained. The court concluded that if the liquidated damages clause is a genuine pre-estimate of what the loss is likely to be, thus, it is not a penalty clause.

The fact remains that the issue has to be determined objectively and that judgment must be made on the date the contract was entered into.

The court held that in the case of a governmental body, the nature of the loss is especially difficult to evaluate because the government reasonably adopted a formula that reflected the loss of returns on the capital involved on a daily basis.[47]

The following two cases are recent English cases that illustrate the application of these rules as influenced by the Philips case:

1 *M & J Polymers Ltd* v. *Imerys Minerals Ltd*[48]

In 1991, Imerys (the defendant) had received supplies of chemical products from Polymers (the appellant). In July 2003, both parties entered into a new contract effective until December 2004.

Pursuant to the latter agreement, Polymers was to supply Imerys with chemicals to be used in producing high quality printings; nevertheless, there was a shortage in acrylic acid, one of the ingredients to be supplied, that would last till the end of 2004. Pursuant to the terms of agreement, the defendant terminated the contract. The claimant alleged that the contract termination was illegal.

The court held that the take or pay clause stipulated under the contract held by and between the parties is not a penalty; it is a liquidated damage clause for damages that are a genuine pre-estimate of loss.

The court confirmed that English courts had never before held a take or pay clause to be a penalty clause. Furthermore, the court rejected the counterclaim made by Imerys (defendant).

2 *Liberty Mercian Limited* v. *Dean & Dyball Construction Limited* (2008)[49]

In the latest case of liquidated damages, the English court held that the liquidated damages clause is a genuine pre-estimate of the specific loss of the incomplete part.

47 Brain Eggleston, *Liquidated Damages and Extension of Time in Construction Contracts* (2nd edn, Blackwell Science, 1997, pp. 61–2).

48 *M & J Polymers Ltd* v. *Imerys Minerals Ltd* (2008) I All ER (COMM 893).

49 *Liberty Mercian Limited* v. *Dean & Dyball Construction Limited* (2008) BLR 29.

The dispute concerned a construction contract. The question before the court was whether or not there was a sectional completion of works, and whether the liquidated damages clause was applicable at this stage, or was it considered an unenforceable penalty clause?

The court applied the choice made by the parties and enforced the liquidated damages clause.

Nonetheless, the *Dunlop* criterion required reform, and the court in *Cavendish Square Holding BV* v. *Talal El Makdessi* and *ParkingEye Ltd* v. *Beavis* (two cases heard in the same appeal) found that the tests placed by Lord Dunedin are unfit for complex agreements.[50] In *Cavendish* and *ParkingEye*, Lord Neuberger and Lord Sumption held that the question that should be asked is if the fixed damages are penal, not whether they are a pre-estimate of loss.[51] Lord Neuberger and Lord Sumption found that the 'law relating to penalties has become the prisoner of artificial consideration.'[52] Accordingly, in *Cavendish* and *ParkingEye*, the Lords found that 'the real question when a contractual provision is challenged as a penalty is whether it is penal, not whether it is a pre-estimate of loss. These are not natural opposites or mutually exclusive categories. A damages clause may be neither or both. The fact that a clause is not a pre-estimate or loss does not therefore, at any rate without more, mean that it is penal.'[53] In their analysis, the Lords held that a challenged clause could fall outside the ambit of a 'genuine pre-estimation of loss' and still not be penal in nature. They further drew reference to the fact that a clause being a deterrent does not add much to the argument as 'it is no different from contractual inducement'[54] – which is not penal in nature. The Lords guided themselves by the following standard in determining whether contractual inducement can be viewed as penal: 'whether the means by which the contracting party's conduct is to be influenced are "unconscionable" or "extravagant" by reference to some norm.'[55]

Compiling their definition of a penalty clause, and their view on the pre-estimate test, the Lords set the following new test in assessing LDs: 'The true test of a penalty was whether the impugned provision was a secondary obligation which imposed a detriment on the contract-breaker out of all proportion to any legitimate interest of the innocent party in the enforcement of the primary obligation. The innocent party could have no proper interest in simply punishing the defaulter. His interest was in performance or in some appropriate alternative to performance. In the case of a straightforward damages clause, that interest would rarely extend beyond compensation for the breach. However, compensation was not necessarily

50 *Cavendish Square Holding BV* v. *El Makdessi; ParkingEye Ltd* v. *Beavis* [2016] 2 All ER 519, 533.

51 Ibid., 538. And see also: Youssef Ismail, *Enforceability of Liquidated Damages Clauses and the Extent of Judicial and Arbitral Intervention, a comparative study Between the English and Egyptian Jurisdictions,* 'Arbitration,' *The International Journal of Arbitration, Mediation and Dispute Management,* Kluwer Law International, 2023, 89(4), pp. 516–35.

52 Ibid., p. 537.

53 Ibid., p. 538.

54 Ibid.

55 Ibid.

the only legitimate interest that the innocent party might have in the performance of the defaulter's primary obligations. [...] Deterrence was not penal if there was a legitimate interest in influencing the conduct of the contracting party which was not satisfied by the mere right to recover damages for breach of contract.'[56]

Considering the above, the English courts now apply a legitimate interest test, in determining whether a liquidated damages clause is valid. This legitimate interest test is coupled with a 'proportionality' test.[57]

Penalty Clauses or Liquidated Damages in the Egyptian Legislation

As a matter of general principle, the Egyptian Civil Code enshrines the notion of *pacta sunt servanda*.[58] A contract shall be enforceable unless otherwise agreed to by the parties. In that regard, parties are free to agree on the terms of their obligations, and any consequences resulting therefrom. This is confirmed by Article 223 of the Egyptian Civil Code, in the case of predetermining the amount of due relief in the event of a contractual breach. Article 223 reads as follows: 'The contracting parties are entitled to determine in advance the amount of damages either in the contract or in a subsequent agreement [...]'

Whilst the Egyptian legislator has provided for freedom of contract, leaving the parties to choose whatever damages they would be entitled to, such freedom is not without its limitations. The Egyptian Civil Code provides that damages are not due in the following cases, pursuant to Article 224, '(1) Damages fixed by agreement are not due if the debtor proves that the creditor has not suffered any prejudice. (2) The judge may reduce the amount of damages if the debtor proves that the evaluation has been extremely excessive or that the obligation has been partially performed. (3) Any agreement contravening the two previous sub-clauses is void.'

In public contracts, liquidated damages in the Egyptian legal system are penalty clauses applicable for the delay in works performance. The penalty is *dual* in nature; it acts as a punitive clause and exercises pressure upon the contractor.[59]

56 Ibid.

57 Youssef Ismail, Enforceability of Liquidated Damages Clauses and the Extent of Judicial and Arbitral Intervention, A Comparative Study Between the English and Egyptian Jurisdictions,, 'Arbitration: The International Journal of Arbitration, Mediation and Dispute Management,' Kluwer Law International, 2023, 89(4), pp. 516–35.

58 The Egyptian Civil Code, Article 147 /1.

59 Article (23) of the previous State Procurement Law promulgated by Law No. 89 of 1998 provides for: 'If the contracting party delayed the work after the set completion date, the authority concerned, can, for public interest, grant the contractor an extension of time for total completion and it can impose a penalty (fine) pursuant to percentages and rules stipulated by executive regulations. The total (fine) shall not exceed (3%) of the total contract value in purchasing immovables, receiving services, consultation studies and technical works, and shall not exceed (10%) in public works and transportation.' Article 48 of the current State Contracting Law No. 182 of 2018 provides: 'If the contractor has delayed in performance than the schedule of perofrmance or the performance duration stipulated in the contract, the contracting authority may grant him an extension of time, without applying penalty for delay, due to public interests considerations, if delay is out of his control. If the

The administration (state) shall collect the penalty for delay (fine) *ipso facto* without prior notice or any preliminary (or Judicial) procedures. The contracting party can be exempted from the penalty, after a legal opinion from the Conseil D'État, if the delay was out of the control thereof. The contracting authority accepts in this case, after consulting with the Conseil D'État, to exempt the contracting party from the fine, if the delay did not cause any damage. The penalty imposed and collected from the contracting party will not violate the right of the authority concerned to reclaim compensation from the contractor for delay in performance.

The penalty or fine shall be calculated and deducted from the value of total works (take-over certificate shall be considered), if the concerned authority decided that the delayed part of works of the project will directly or indirectly prevent the state from the utilization of public utility thereof at the stipulated time. If the contracting authority decided that the delayed part of the works will not cause such prevention, the fine calculation will be pursuant to stipulated percentages and conditions from the value of the delayed part of works only.

The trend with the 1998 legislation and the executive regulations there of was that a contractor can be exempt from the penalty if the legal opinion department at the Conseil D'État approved the exemption. Otherwise the contractor is obliged to pay the fine up to the cap (ceiling) stipulated under article (23) of the 1998 legislation. If there is a delay, the penalty should be paid *ipso facto* regardless of the fact that no damage or loss was suffered by the state.

Despite the fact that there are some enhancements in the new trend adopted by the current legislation No. 182 of 2018, the fine still has its exorbitant nature. The penalty is due, in any circumstances, when there is a delay even in light of the current

---

delay is due to the contractor's fault, a penalty for delay is applicable, calculated from the date of delay, without any alert, notice or otherwise, according to the following: 1) In public works agreements, the penalty of delay is 10% of the total value of the contract price if the delay does not exceed 10% of the total duration of the contract. However, the penalty of delay cap is 15% of the total value of the contract, if the delay is more than 10% of the total duration of the contract. The penalty of delay is calculated only from the delayed part of the project, if the contracting authority found that the delayed part shall not prevent it from exploiting the other completed parts of the project, whether directly or indirectly, if these completed parts were executed corectly at the stipulated time. If the delayed parts of the project render the exploitations of the other parts of the project impossible, the calculation of the penalty of delay will be from the final certificate of the project. [...] 2) in other contracts, the penalty of delay is 3% of the total value of the contract price if the delay does not exceed 10% of the total duration of the contrcat. However, the penalty of delay cap is 5% of the total value of the contract, if the delay is more than 10% of the total duration of the contract. The penalty of delay is calculated only from the delayed part of the contract performance, if the contracting authority found that the delayed part shall not prevent it from exploiting the other completed parts of the contract, whether directly or indirectly, if these completed parts were executed correctly at the stipulated time. If the delayed parts of the project render the exploitations of the other parts of the project impossible, the calculation of the penalty of delay will be from the total value of the contract. The contracting authority may exempt the contractor from the penalty of delay value if the delay is beyond his control or in other cases, a contracotr may be exempted from the penalty of delay, totally or partially, if there is no loss occurred to the contracting authority. The contracting authority may ask for a legal opinion from the competent department at the Conseil D'État. [...]'.

legislation stipulations. There are some enhancements in the penalty of delay legal nature due to Article 48 of the new State Contacting Law No. 182 of 2018. The contracting authority may exempt the contractor from the penalty of delay value if the delay is beyond his control or in other cases, a contracotr may be exempted from the penalty of delay, totally or partially, if no loss occurred to the contracting authority. The contracting authority may ask for a legal opinion from the competent department at the Conseil D'Etat. Enhancements to legislation in State Contracting Law No. 182 of 2018 are a result of the legal globalization phenomenon.

Pursuant to Article 225 of the Egyptian Civil Code, if 'the damages exceeded the agreed compensation value, the creditor cannot claim more than the stipulated amount unless the debtor is accused of committing fraud or a fundamental mistake.'

The Egyptian doctrine[60] explains this pre-estimated compensation as being agreed upon and stipulated between the contracting parties under the agreement or any of its appendices. This compensation is not due in the absence of loss or damages to the creditor. The court or arbitral tribunal can reduce the compensation if it is not adequate to the damages or 'the contractor executed the contract partially, partial execution' to create a contractual balance between the due compensation amount and the damages. This dimension in the Egyptian Civil Code is to maintain fairness and balance of the contractual relationship. These rules are mandatory pursuant to the Egyptian Civil Code.

The question is to compare the legal nature of the pre-estimated and agreed compensation on one hand, and penalties stipulated pursuant to previous Egyptian State Procurement Law of 1998, and the current State Contracting Law 182 of 2018 on the other.

According to the legal nature of the penalties (fines) under Article (23) of previous Law No. 89 of 1998, these penalties resemble a fine on the contractor in public construction contracts (domestic and international) up to 10% of the total value of the contract price, even if no damages occurred to the state contracting entity.[61]

This is a mandatory rule in the Egyptian legal system under an administrative contract. Consequently, the state must take this action of a punitive nature pursuant to the law and exorbitant clauses in the administrative contract in light of this legislation without a need for any judicial action.

Conversely, the agreed compensation (Liquidated Damages) in the Egyptian Civil Code applies to civil and commercial contracts which fall in the scope of private law. First, the compensation aims to compensate the creditor in case of damages only. Second, this compensation should be fair and adequate to the actual loss. Third, the national court or arbitral tribunal can exercise its power to review

60 Abdel Wadood Yehia, *Obligation Stipulations at Egyptian Civil Law* (Dar Al Nahda Al Arabia, 1987, pp. 52–5, in Arabic); and Egyptian Cassation Court, decision No. 227, Civil circuit, year 19, session 25 December 1968.

61 It is worth mentioning that parties to the contract can stipulate a different percentage or cap and this can supersede caps or percentages stipulated by law (this very rarely happens). See opinion from The General Assembly for Legal Opinion and Legislation, No. (800) dated 13 December 1999, session 20 October 1999 file No 54/1/358.

the amount of compensation to assure that it is fair and adequate. These rules are mandatory in the domain of civil and commercial agreements.

Pursuant to Article 48 of the new State Contacting Law No. 182 of 2018, a contracotr may be exempted from the penalty of delay, totally or partially, if no loss occurred to the contracting authority. This is an enhancment to the legal nature of penalty of delay in the Egyptian new legislation, when the matter relates to administrative contracts. Developments in the doctrine of penalty of delay in administative contracts are narrwing the gap between civil and commercial contracts on one hand and administaive contracts on the other, particularly if the matter relates to contrcat substantive principles.

Decisions of Egyptian Courts: Egyptian Conseil D'État Courts:

The Egyptian Supreme Administrative Court distinguishes between penalties in administrative contracts and liquidated damages which are pre-estimated and agreed upon in civil and commercial transactions as private law (commercial) contracts.

The court pointed out that: 'Penalties in administrative contracts differ in nature from pre-estimated compensation in civil and commercial contracts. The latter is a pre-estimated compensation agreed upon between the parties and payable upon breach of contract by any of the contracting parties. This compensation is conditioned to be paid in all stipulations of the Egyptian law for compensation in general, such as the necessity of damages to the other contractor, notification to the party who caused the breach and a court judgment which can reduce compensation if one of the parties proved that compensation exceeds damages or loss. [...] It is not acceptable from the contractor to prove that no damages occurred, as the administration (state) has stipulated, under the contract, a certain time for completion of works, taking into consideration the essential need to public utility to execute works at the stipulated time without delay. Damages are always presumed.'[62]

The Court confirmed in one of the leading cases that 'the penalty (fine) is applicable in case of delay, without a need to notify the contractor or to prove that damages occurred. If the Appeal Administrative Court stipulated that there must be damages to the state to apply the penalty, this judgment by the Appeal Court should be annulled.' The Supreme Administrative Court exempted the contractor in some occasions from the penalty, despite the fact that it has confirmed the punitive nature of the penalty, as a penalty clause in the public works agreement imposed by the state upon contractors, without a need to prove that damages occurred to the state. In this case, there is a presumption that damages exist promptly when there is a delay. If the contractor failed to obtain a legal opinion in his favor from the Conseil

62 Supreme Administrative Court, Egyptian Conseil D'État, principles of Supreme Administrative Court and the General Assembly for Legal Opinion, Collection of Forty Years on Administrative Contracts, decision 1772-29, 5 February 1985 and decision 741-27, 28 May1985. In the same meaning, decision 612-2, 21 September 1960.

D'État to exempt him from the penalty, he has to start either arbitration or litigation for some years. During these years, the value of the currency may possibly depreciate causing the inflation rate to increase in developing countries, in particular, and the contractor can only reclaim the fine deducted from his payments plus an interest rate of 5% from the date of reclaiming the amount until the actual payment by the state through either an enforceable court judgment (Appeal Court Judgment) or an arbitral award pursuant to the Egyptian Arbitration Act No. 27 of 1994 and its amendments.

Moreover, it is very difficult to deny the loss to a contractor, and the consequential loss or indirect damages that he could not recover. At that stage, the significance of arbitration appears as, in most cases, damages are prompt and adequate to the actual loss, because of the vast authority entrusted to arbitrators, and the flexibility to apply different rules of law in various cases. The parties can achieve a rapid resolution through a final, binding and enforceable arbitral award.

The Egyptian Supreme Administrative Court in some recent decisions[63] confirmed an extravagant and exorbitant clause of the fines as a penalty for delay.

It is appropriate to refer to the fact that there is a new approach in the Egyptian Conseil D'État courts reflecting the extent to which cultural and legal globalization phenomena affect the application and interpretation of the legislative clauses even if it is punitive in nature. It is clear to what extent judges are trying to achieve fairness in the contractual relationship between state and contractor. They are obliged to apply the legislation as stipulated by the legislature and adopted by the contracting parties. However, these new trends do not reflect a complete new methodology or approach adopted by the Conseil D'État in Egypt. It is clear that there is an essential need to adopt new approaches by the Egyptian legislature which do not exist even in the current legislation No. 182 of 2018.[64]

Decisions of the Egyptian Cassation Court (Civil and Commercial Circuits):

The civil and commercial circuits of the Egyptian Cassation Court directly applied stipulations of Article 224 of the civil law. The court held in some of the leading cases that 'in the light of article (224) of the Egyptian civil law, if there is a penalty clause in the contract, damages are presumed unless the debtor proved the opposite or that stipulated compensation at the contract exceeded the actual loss.'[65,66]

The court held in recent cases that 'the contracting parties can fix a pre-estimated compensation for damages as a result for non performance of any of the stipulated obligations [...] If the debtor proved that the pre-estimated compensation exceeded

63 Supreme Administrative Court decision in Case 10834, year (47), 30 May 2006, Third Circuit; and Case 11986, year (48), 16 January 2007, Third Circuit (*unpublished decisions*).

64 Mohamed A.M. Ismail, Globalization and Liquidated Damages in the International Public Works Agreements, An Analytical Perspective for the Penalty of Delay Clause in Infrastructure Agreements, *International Construction Law Review*, 26, Part 4, 2009.

65 Egyptian Cassation Court, Case 415, year 46, 13 February1980.

66 Egyptian Cassation Court, Case 26, year 38, 18 December 1973.

the actual loss or that he performed some of his obligations court shall reduce compensation to be adequate to actual loss.'[67]

The Egyptian Court of Cassation has confirmed the above-mentioned principles in many of its rulings. It has long been held that 'fixed compensation, in accordance with Article 224 of the Egyptian Civil Code, is subject to the Judge's assessment. It is permissible [for the judge] to reduce [the compensation fixed by agreement] if the debtor proves that the estimate was exaggerated to a great extent [...].'[68] In this case, the lower courts failed to assess the real damage caused to the Defendant, and whether the amount of compensation awarded is proportional to that damage or not. Accordingly, the Cassation Court annulled the Court of Appeal's judgment upholding the liquidated damages.[69]

Conclusion

The Conseil D'État courts, while excercising judicial review, can exempt the contractor in certain cases stipulated in Egyptian Conseil D'État practices. The contractor can be exempted from the penalty for delay in case of *force majeure*, or fundamental default by the state which exempts the contractor from his obligations and, consequently, from the penalty for delay. This is not contrary to the punitive nature of the penalty for delay clause as this clause is always a penalty clause. Egyptian administrative courts recognize penalty clauses in administrative contracts, whether national or international, and consider them legal.

If there is no loss, consequently, there is no damages; the contractor can be exempt from the pre-estimated sum stipulated by the State Contracting Law of (2018) or the contract, in certain cases such as the partial completion of the project, if the administartion can use part of the public utility, and the delay cannot prohibit the partial usage of the public utility. Further, the contractor may be exempted from the penalty for delay if the delay was beyong his control. Finally, the contactor can be exempted from the penalty for dealy (totally or partially) if there is no loss suffered by the contracting authority. The contracting authority may seek a legal opinion from the Conseil D'État. These current changes in the last decade are a direct result of cultural and legal globalization phenomena.

Transfer and flow of the legal culture from common law jurisdictions to civil law legal systems is of great importance, as the administrative contract theory

67 Egyptian Cassation Court, Cases 1859, 2444, 2447, year (70), 12 June 2001.

68 Cassation No. 8258 of Judicial Year 85, hearing dated 27 June 2021. See also: Youssef Ismail, *Enforceability of Liquidated Damages Clauses and the Extent of Judicial and Arbitral Intervention, A Comparative Study Between the English and Egyptian Jurisdictions,* Arbitration: The International Journal of Arbitration, Mediation and Dispute Management, Kluwer Law International, 2023, Volume 89, Issue 4, pp. 516–35.

69 Ibid. See also: Youssef Ismail, *Enforceability of Liquidated Damages Clauses and the Extent of Judicial and Arbitral Intervention, A comparative study between the English and Egyptian jurisdictions,*, Arbitration: The International Journal of Arbitration, Mediation and Dispute Management, Kluwer Law International, 89(4), 2023, pp. 516–35.

needs more modifications and enhancements. Globalization plays a significant role in changing some of the main features of this theory, to be adopted through drafting international administarive agreements with private foreign entities. This is a new trend in civil law legal culture. The reform to administrative contracts theory and practice is underway, in Egypt and the MENA countries.

Despite the modern approaches adopted by the new State Contracting Law No. 182 of 2018, it is strongly recommended that there is an essential need for a legislative reform of Article (48) of the State Contracting Law of (2018) to reduce the cap of the fine which is high comparing to the actual loss sufered by the contracting state. Article (48) provides that the fine is 10% of the total value of the contract price in public works contracts if the delay does not exceed 10% of the total duration of the contract. However, the fine cap is 15% of the total value of the contract, if the delay is more than 10% of the total duration of the contract. It is fundamental to propose that the penalty shall be calculated according to the actual loss and not a pre-estimated and fixed sum by legislation and regulations. Conseil D'État Courts have to apply proportionality test. The penalty can even reflect the substantial loss to the state public utility and be calculated pursuant to the substantial loss, which may be less than the actual loss in many cases.

In common law jurisdictions, courts consider, in many cases, liquidated damages to be genuine pre-estimated compensation that should be estimated according to the actual loss. In some cases, the contractor can be exempted from the penalty if the substantial completion was achieved in a reasonable time, and the state can start utilization of the completed part of the public utility. Despite the fact that some recent cases applied a liquidated damages clause, and considered it valid, the latter view considered the stipulated sum adequate to the actual loss. The clause was not applied as a penalty clause in any circumstances.

Another difficulty that needs to be considered is that in accordance with the principles of the administrative courts of the Egyptian Conseil D'État[70] a contractor, in certain cases, cannot suspend or terminate works if the administration terminates his payments. He cannot claim to stop performance until he gets his payments from the state. In that case, the administration applies Article (48) of State Contracting Law 2018 on the penalty for delay if he does not achieve final completion at the stipulated date, despite the fact that he is not paid his payments by the administration.

70 A contractor cannot stop or suspend performance of works in any circumstances even if the contracting state fails to make payments, in which case the penalty for delay is applicable (Supreme Administrative Court, case 5959, year (44), 26 January 2001). On very rare occasions the court allowed the contractor to stop performance if the state delayed his payments (i.e. case 4483, year (41), session 6 May1997). In some other rare cases the contractor stipulates at the contract that the period of late payments shall be added to the completion date (contract term). This clause is valid as it is not contrary to mandatory rules of the state procurement law. An old legal opinion confirms that in some cases the contract provisions can supersede procurement law. Legal opinion for the General Assembly *fatwa* No (100), session 20 March 1985, file(47/2/350).

This critical situation needs a legislative reform of the State Contracting Law No. 182 of 2018, as termination of payments is an example of a fundamental default (breach of contract), by the state, pursuant to the Egyptian Civil Code. Few exceptions to this principle by Egyptian Conseil D'État courts are considered to be the direct result of legal globalization.

Contrary to this concept, in civil and commercial transactions, pursuant to Article (161) of the Egyptian civil legislation, if one party to a contract failed to fulfill his obligations, the other party can suspend or terminate performance.

Moreover, the proposed legislative reform must consider the dynamic relationship in some contracts such as international public works agreements, which differ from static relationships in other transactions. This dynamic relationship is related to many factors such as contract price, total sum stipulated as a penalty, the extent to which it is adequate to the loss, currency depreciation, inflation rate, contractual relations with lending banks, insurance institutions, and the change in raw material prices in developing countries, which may change contract price under different circumstances.

Finally, such legislative reform shall assist arbitral processes in international contract, in particular construction contracts arbitration between Egypt and MENA countries, and foreign contractors. The arbitral tribunal in applying substantive law to facts has to determine first if the contract is an administrative contract and the fixed sum is a penalty and is applicable regardless of any existing loss, or if it is a commercial contract and consequently the pre-estimated compensation is, subject to the arbitral tribunal review, to be adequate to the actual loss. This is the current situation at the Egyptian and MENA countries' legal systems where a legislative reform shall establish new concepts to be applied in both arbitration and litigation.

It is suggested that unification of contract law principles in liquidated damages between public contracts and private contracts is underway. The new State Contracting Law in Egypt is a considerable step to achieve global contract law in Egypt and MENA countries which is underway in the region. The new approach adopted by the Egyptian legislature in Article (48) of the new State Contracting Law is a step towards the deterioration of public law constraints, to achieve global contract law principles, in the respective jurisdictions. States' international contracts' principles in Egypt and MENA countries are nowadays more consistent with international commercial contracts principles. The gap between public contracts principles in the region and international commercial contracts practice is becoming narrow as a result of the legal globalization phenomenon.

Case Study No. 3: The Interpretation of an Ambiguous Term in the Contract: Parties Hold Different Meanings as to the Interpretation of an Ambiguous Term in the Contract

The Problem

Contracting authority, A undertakes a tendering procedure. Subsequently, A concludes a contract with B. In the course of the performance of the contract, it becomes clear that A and B hold differing meanings as to the interpretation of an ambiguous term in the contract.

A dispute arises between A and B on the question whether the contract is to be performed by the parties in accordance with A's interpretation. If so, the result would be that B will suffer financial loss. In the event that the contract is to be performed according to B's interpretation, this would be detrimental to A. Does interpretation of the contract term have to be consistent with public interests' constraints?

General Contract Law: Overview of the Law on Interpretation of Contracts

When interpreting an ambiguous or unclear term in a contract, the Egyptian Civil Code requires a court to do so by applying rules of interpretation. These rules are different from one case to another. The rules that are to be applied in a particular case depend mainly on the intention of the contracting parties and the nature of the transaction (the contract) of the case. In practice, in the case of administrative contracts and concession contracts, the contracting authority has the power, in most cases, to unilaterally interpret the ambiguous or unclear terms of the contract. Thus, when a contract term is unclear or ambiguous, the contracting authority has to provide the right interpretation of such term. Such an interpretation has to be consistent with public interests' constraints. However, in many cases the contracting authority and the private entity may negotiate the interpretation of an ambiguous term. In fact, both parties do not re-negotiate the contract, but they are trying to achieve an interpretation of the ambiguous term of the contract, and such interpretation has to be consistent with the common and real intention of the contracting parties. The absence of specific provisions in public procurement law and other relevant laws means that the contracting authority has to conduct this interpretive task pursuant to the criteria established in the Egyptian Civil Code whilst taking into account the public interests' constraints and the Supreme Administrative Court principles.

Article 150 of the Egyptian Civil Code provides that: '(1) If the term of the contract is clear, it is not permissible to deviate from it by interpreting it to identify the intention of the contracting parties. (2) If there is a need to interpret the contract, then the common intention of the contracting parties must be discovered without considering the literal meaning of the words, in light of the nature of the transaction, and what is assumed to be available of integrity and confidence of the contracting parties, according to the current custom in transactions.'

Article 151/1 provides that: '(1) Doubt is interpreted in favor of the interest of the debtor.' The term 'doubt' means when the courts have doubts regarding controversial interpretation of an ambiguous contract term, not doubts about the disputing parties to the said term.

Interpretation has to be exercised in a *bona fide* manner and in light of the customs of the transaction. Article 148 of the Egyptian Civil Code provides that: '(1) A contract must be performed in accordance with what it contains (contractual provisions) and in a manner that is consistent with good faith (*bona fide* manner).'

While explaining the nature of a contract, obligations and the transaction's nature, customs, and contract supplements according to law and justice principles,

Article 148/2 provides: '(2) The contract is not limited to obligating the contracting party to what is stated on its provisions, but also deals with what is required of it, in accordance with the law, custom, and justice according to the nature of the obligation.'

It is worth noting that Article 90 of the Egyptian Civil Code, while explaining contract rules as a source of obligations, sets the general principle that the parties may express their intention in a contract implicitly as it provides that: '(1) Expressing the intention is done either verbally or in writing. It can be done with a common sign, as well as by taking a position that does not raise any doubts that the circumstances are evident of the real (specific) intention. (2) The expression of the intention may be implicit, if the law does not provide or the parties did not agree that it should be expressed.'[71]

Application of General Contract Law to the Case Study

The Supreme Administrative Court has to apply Egyptian Civil Code legislative provisions, public procurement law, in addition to judicial principles established by the Court itself in the absence of a mandatory rule in legislation. The public procurement law provisions are procedural rules dealing with procedural phase of the contractual process; it does not directly deal with interpretation of the contract terms which are dealt with in Article 150 the Egyptian Civil Code. The Supreme Administrative Court has considered the legal context of the competitive tendering procedure preceding the conclusion of the contract and the factual background of each case. The Court considers factual background and competitive tendering process on a case-by-case scenario. It is important to assure that Court has interpreted ambiguous or unclear terms considering previous factors but in light of public interest principle constraints. Over decades, the Court reasoning and decisions were influenced to a great extent by the public interest principle as a governing principle to all state contracts whether administrative, private, or contracts of mixed/hybrid legal nature. The test adopted by the Court in interpreting ambiguous or unclear contract terms is a *dual* test in its nature as it is a mix of subjective and objective tests. The test and methodology adopted by the Court are different from some cases to another.

While analyzing the Court's decisions through decades, it is clear that it has considered the following factual and legal points:

- If the contract terms are clear, there is no point to interpret those terms far beyond the contract term's direct meaning.
- The Court focuses, as a start, on the customary linguistic meaning of the wording of the term in normal language.

71 For more elaboration in doctrine see the leading authority in the Egyptian and MENA doctrine: Abdelrazak Al Sanhory, *Al Wassit in Civil Law, Sources of Obligation* (First Part, Dar Al Shourouk, 2010, p. 143, in Arabic); see also: Abdelwadood Yehia, *Sources of Obligation* (Dar Al Nahda Al Arabia, 1989, p.30, in Arabic); Abdel Baki Abdel Fatah, *The Encyclopedia of Egyptian Civil Law, Contract and Unilateral Acts Theory, a Comparative Study with Islamic Doctrine*, (1984 in Arabic).

- If the contract terms are not clear or are ambiguous, the Court has considered parties' intention within the nature of the transaction, and assumed integrity and confidence between the contracting parties in light of the customs adopted in such transactions.
- Sentences and phrases of the contract have to be clear to reflect parties' intention, but if the contractual circumstances provide that the contracting parties have used misleading phrases, in the latter case the Court will not follow the wrong direct interpretation but it has to reach the common and real intention of the contracting parties.
- Where the literalness of the terms of the contract seems to be contrary to the real intention of the parties, the latter shall prevail over the former.
- The Court in many reasonings refers to objective criterion in discovering the common and real intention of the contracting parties.[72]
- The intention of the contracting parties prevails over the typological and linguistic errors as parties' intention reflects party autonomy principle.[73]
- The Court has adopted the party autonomy principle in reasoning its decisions in all cases.
- Contract sentences and phrases are interrelated while interpreting parties' intention to discover the real intention of the contracting parties. While interpreting contract terms' meaning, the Court did not isolate one single phrase from the contractual context. As the term is part of a contract, it must be interpreted in accordance with the contract as a whole.[74]
- Contract performance technique is one of the factors that lead to the parties' intention.
- Contract obligations have to be performed in light of *bona fide* principles in Article 148 of the Egyptian Civil Code and therefore, contract terms' interpretation has to follow *bona fide* principle in the Egyptian Civil Code and contract law in particular.[75]
- Clear terms mean clear intention of the contracting parties. If the contracting parties misuse sentences, phrases, and terms of the contract, and therefore interpretation of contract terms is not clear, the Court shall not follow such misleading interpretation and it shall search for the real intention of the contracting parties in light of objective criterion of the contract circumstances, nature of the contract, and the customs of such transaction.[76]
- If the contract stipulates that pre-contractual documents are an integral part of the contract terms and provisions, the Court has to scrutinize and analyze

72 Supreme Administrative Court, Case No. 3364/27, session 15 December1985.

73 Supreme Administrative Court, Case No. 31525/55, session 22 May 2016 and Case No. 34646/56, session 6 March 2016.

74 Supreme Administrative Court, Case No. 16621/52, session 26 May 2009.

75 Ibid.

76 Supreme Administrative Court, Case No. 2348/36, session 7 March 1995 and Case No. 4708/41, session 5 January 1999.

pre-contractual documents to discover the real intention of the contracting parties. This is a real adoption of the party autonomy principle.[77]

It is important to refer to the following findings reached from analyzing the Court reasoning to its judgments:

- Public interest principle constraints have special significance as they are important factors behind any interpretation adopted by the Court.
- Parties' intentions have to be interpreted not only in light of public interest principles but also within the fundamental principle of how to promote public fund protection.
- The factual and legal contexts of competitive tendering were of fundamental importance during reasoning of the Court decisions.
- Despite the fact that the administration can unilaterally amend or terminate the administrative contract due to specific mandatory legislative provisions or specific contractual provisions, it is not possible to introduce any unilateral modifications by either party, or to re-negotiate the contract without the consent of the contracting parties.
- The factual background of the case is an important factor for the Court to rely on upon interpreting the contract terms.
- The Court supersedes the party autonomy principle in all its judgments' reasoning within public interest principle constraints.
- The Court has applied the correct rule of interpretation by considering the customary linguistic meaning of the wording of the term in *bona fide* manner, if the contract terms are clear and straightforward.
- The execution of the contract may also have an impact on the interests of the other tenderers (third party rights) that participated in the preceding tendering procedures. If the interpretation of contract terms will result in financial consequences that may affect the financial priority of tenderers upon entering into the tender and before awarding the contract, the Court shall reject such interpretation as it means that the financial offers will be different in priority and the lowest bidder in price will not be in the same position. Despite the fact that the priority of the financial offer (the lowest bidder has to remain the lowest during contract performance as a general rule) was stipulated in the previous executive regulations and not in the legislation itself,[78] this rule is of

77 Supreme Administrative Court, Case No. 5997/58, session 28 February 2015.

78 There were fundamental concerns to stipulate the priority of the financial offer (lowest bid stipulation) in the executive regulation of the previous Public Procurement Law No. 89 of 1989 and not in the legislation itself. This approach raises concerns of unconstitutionality of this provision in the executive regulations, as the latter regulations cannot impose stipulations but can only provide details of how to implement legislation. Stipulations have to be provided only by legislative provision, not regulatory provision. The lowest bid stipulation is to promote fair competition between tenderers and is one of the guarantees of competitive tendering, therefore it has to be stipulated by legislative provision as it is a mandatory rule. Executive regulations cannot contain mandatory rules.

a fundamental importance to promote fair competition and equality between bidders and maintain the lowest bidder as it is the lowest price during contract performance.

- The Court takes into account the public procurement law provisions and the legislative policy behind such law when interpreting contracts concluded following competitive tendering procedures.
- The Court adopts reasonable justification to its approaches in many judgments which means that the Court while interpreting contract terms cannot violate the legitimate economic expectations of the contracting parties. Such legitimate economic expectations were expressed during the competitive tendering process.
- The Court considers both the factual and legal contexts of the competitive tendering procedures when interpreting an ambiguous term in the contract.
- In addition to interpretation rules, the Court considers on its reasoning, in implied words, the principle of transparency under public procurement law, international standards, and the established principles the Court itself.

Supreme Administrative Court principles through decades have established substantive coherent and solid frameworks of judicial principles in administrative contracts in general. For the purposes of this case study, the Court has established remarkable principles based on the interpretation of the Egyptian Civil Code provisions, the competitive tendering process, and the contract terms itself which have to reflect contracting parties' intentions. The Court has adopted both objective tests and subjective tests. The Court approaches are consistent, to a great extent, with the international practice whether in the comparative law or the international standards illustrated by international organizations (OECD and The World Bank). Nevertheless, judicial approaches of the Egyptian Conseil D'État courts, in general, need more developments to adopt the latest international standards and innovation in public procurement. The new State Contracting Law 182 of 2018 is expected to enhance the practice of state contracting from many aspects as this new law is following international organizations' standards. This new law shall be a fundamental factor to modernize and develop judicial approaches as the Court creates substantive rules only at the absence of legislative mandatory provisions. In addition, during the procedural phase and during contract drafting, it is fundamental that the contracting authority realizes the importance of the proper drafting of the contract to define the obligations of each contracting party precisely and sharply to avoid any future unpredictability.

In conclusion, in each contract, there is no one authentic interpretation of the terms of the contract or no one specific meaning. The right interpretation of the contract terms has to be in line with the documents during the procedural phase, contract documents whether pre-contractual documents or the contract document itself, documents and correspondences which are relevant to contract performance and exchanged by the parties during contract performance, and other relevant documents (documents which parties may exchange upon contract completion or upon the starting of a dispute whether in litigation or arbitration). Courts have to consider the existing mandatory legislative framework, the Supreme Administrative Court principles, and regulatory framework. It is clear from analyzing Supreme Administrative Court judgments that there is a need for an objective interpretation to the contract, instead of the ordinary subjective-objective interpretation which has a *dual* nature as an interpretation of contract terms. When interpreting the terms 'objective test' and 'subjective test,' it is suggested that objective has the sense that the linguistic meaning of the ambiguous term as it is understood in relevant legislation, Supreme Administrative Court principles, and relevant regulations. The linguistic meaning of the term has to be interpreted in light of an objective rule that is relevant to the term use in the contractual context (transaction nature and customs). Subjective has the sense that relevance will be attached to the parties' subjective intentions that can be derived from their conduct and statements before and after entering into the contract.

An objective interpretation of the contract terms paves the way to the unification of states' contracts; substantive principles to be consistent with international commercial contracts; substantive principles. The approaches adopted by Egyptian Supreme Administrative Court are fundamental to achieve global contract law principles in public and private contracts in the MENA countries. Such approaches need modernization and developments to be adopted by the Egyptian Supreme Administrative Court. The objective interpretation to contract terms has to understand the linguistic meaning of the ambiguous term as it is understood in relevant legislation, Supreme Administrative Court principles and relevant regulatory framework. The linguistic meaning of the term has to be interpreted in light of an objective test that is relevant to the term use in the contractual context. The contractual context can be understood and interpreted through analyzing transaction nature and customs. In addition, parties' subjective intentions can be derived from their conduct and statements before and after entering into the contract, and are fundamental to reach a proper interpretation of contract ambiguous terms. Parties' intentions have to be interpreted mutually in light of the nature of the subject-matter of the dispute.[79]

Conclusions

Courts' intervention is a fundamental tool to achieve global substantive contact law, in public and private (commercial) contracts. The legal globalization phenomenon has influenced Courts' decisions in Egypt and MENA countries, as follows:

- In a more general sense, the Egyptian Supreme Administrative Court, Egyptian Cassation Court and MENA countries' supreme courts, are usually bound by the confines of the law, and its statutory provisions. That being said, courts are bound by constitutional and legislative provisions which have a mandatory nature. Meanwhile, in some circumstances, courts may rule outside of

79 Supreme Administrative Court, Case No. 16621/52, session 26 May 2009.

legislative provisions when the matter relates to public policy, and there is no legislative provision to govern the case, or there are legislative provisions which do not have the mandatory nature, and allow courts to intervene in a wider scope.

- It is clear that courts' intervention is significant to achieve coherent contract law in international states' contracts and international commercial contracts. The interplay between international commercial contract law and public law principles of international states' contracts, in particular administrative contracts, is explored.
- Courts' intervention is usually bound by the *pacta sunt servanda* principle in Egypt and MENA countries. It is clear that MENA courts supersede the party autonomy principle.
- In most cases, and in particular in commercial contracts, courts' intervention in Egypt and the MENA countries is consistent with the international contract law substantive principles, as is clear from the Egyptian Cassation Court case law. Courts' intervention is inspired by the legal globalization phenomenon.
- The coexistence between the core principles of contract law in state contracts, international commercial contracts in Egypt and the MENA region, on one hand and the huge global diversity of international contracts principles on the other hand, is a reality. Courts in Egypt and MENA countries are influenced by global contract law principles which supersede party autonomy and *pacta sunt servanda* principles.
- Courts' intervention in Egypt and MENA countries, if it is consistent with the global diversity of international contracts' principles, shall create a suitable environment for investments in the respective jurisdictions and raise the threshold of protection granted to foreign investors.
- Courts' intervention in Egypt and MENA countries, if it is consistent with the global diversity of international contracts' principles, shall increase the inward of FDI to the respective jurisdictions. Consequently, it shall enhance the socio-economic life of the ordinary citizens in Egypt and MENA countries.
- The decision of the Egyptian Cassation Court in *Dipco* is not a threat to the unification of contract law principles as such a decision has a very narrow interpretation in the Egyptian and MENA countries' legal systems. Global contract law is underway in the region, whether in public or private contracts, despite public law constraints.
- It is suggested that unification of contract law principles in liquidated damages between public contracts and private contracts is underway. The new State Contracting Law in Egypt No. 182 of 2018 is a considerable step to achieve global contract law in Egypt and MENA countries, which is underway in the region. The new approach adopted by the Egyptian legislature in Article (48) of the new State Contracting Law is a step towards the deterioration of public law constraints, to achieve global contract law principles, in the respective jurisdictions. States' international contracts' principles in Egypt and MENA countries are nowadays more consistent with international commercial contracts

principles. The gap between public contracts principles in the region and international commercial contracts' practice, is becoming narrow as a result of the legal globalization phenomenon. However, a partial reform is needed to legislation and courts' approaches in administrative contracts, when the matter relates to liquidated damages, which have to be consistent with international contract law practices, and in particular, English case law principles.[80]

- Egyptian Conseil D'État Courts have to adopt proportionality test when assessing penalty for delay. Proportionality test is a fundamental tool to achieve fair contractual relationship as the *quantum* of damages has to be calculated to be adequate to the actual loss suffered by the administration.
- In the case of unfair contract terms, courts' intervention needs a further in-depth approach to maintain priority for both the objective tests and party autonomy principle. Courts' approaches have to be consistent with international commercial contracts principles, despite public law constraints.

80 *Cavendish Square Holding BV* v. *El Makdessi; ParkingEye Ltd* v. *Beavis* [2016] 2 All ER 519, 533.

4 New Types of International States' Contracts

PPPs and Energy Concessions as Tools to Achieve Global Contract Law in the MENA Countries

Introduction

The objective of this chapter is to explore how PPP contracts in Egypt and MENA countries, as they introduce the latest types of international states' contracts which do not have pure administrative legal nature, play significant role to create coherent contract law principles, which are consistent with global principles of contract law?

PPP contracts have a *hybrid* legal nature as excessive/exorbitant clauses are minimized during the performance phase of the contract. Private law substantive clauses are very clear in PPP contracts because private foreign entities to PPP contracts may not accept excessive/exorbitant clauses, as the latter clause are well recognized in traditional concessions.[1] PPP contracts in Egypt and MENA countries, in most cases, are adopting private law substantive clauses and techniques. PPP contracts in Egypt and the MENA region represent a clear example of the interplay between global contract law principles and international states' contracts. Coherent contract law is needed to achieve harmonization of substantive clauses in transnational contractual transactions where states are party to the contract. Is adopting PPP techniques in the MENA countries consistent with international standards and international contract law principles?

This chapter aims to elaborate on the unification of states' contracts principles and PPP techniques as well as the thrust of the relevant legislation. PPP techniques involve private foreign entities and they contain an understanding of global contract law standards. The chapter provides an in-depth analysis of the relevant developments in jurisprudence and their effect on policy and law making. In particular, this chapter assesses the applicability of the rules of international contract law to international states' contracts in the MENA countries. This chapter represents a genuine innovation in international contract law (whether public or private contracts) literature, as it provides a comprehensive set of the assessment tests deployed by Egypt, the Gulf States and North African countries' legislation to ascertain the applicability of international and global contract law principles to

1 For more elaboration, generally see: Mohamed A.M. Ismail, *Public Private Partnership Contracts: The Middle East and North Africa* (Routledge, 2020).

DOI: 10.4324/9781003466352-5

international states contracts in the MENA region. Such applicability will create unification in international states' contracts principles which results in the increase of inward of FDI to the MENA countries.

The influence of the cultural and legal globalization phenomena on the Egyptian and MENA countries' legal systems was clear upon the enhancements to and modernization of administrative contracts' traditional theory and practice.[2] New patterns of administrative contracts have appeared in Egypt and the MENA countries such as PPP contracts which have *hybrid* legal nature. States in Egypt and the MENA countries may enter into administrative contracts or private contracts to achieve public interests.

The current Constitution of 2014 in Egypt[3] adopts liberal ideology which permits legislation in Egypt to regulate PPP techniques. Egypt, in light of the amendments to the 1971 previous constitution and the following constitutions with new liberal ideology, could promulgate PPP legislation. Many MENA countries followed Egypt and promulgated PPP legislation.[4]

State contracts' principles in Egypt and in MENA countries have been established through the Egyptian Conseil D'État decisions, in particular the Supreme Administrative Court decisions, which were influenced to a great extent by the decisions of the French Conseil D'État.[5] Procedural and substantive principles of states' contracts have flown from Egypt to MENA countries' legal systems. It is worth noting that administrative law is not yet codified (written) in Egypt and MENA countries, therefore, the Egyptian Conseil D'État decisions constitute a formal and main source of administrative law in the MENA region.

PPPs in Egypt and the MENA Countries, Why?

The leading schools in economics such as the Chicago school reduce state intervention in economic activities to the minimum, however, state intervention to permit

2 See: Joseph Stiglitz, *Globalization and its Discontents* (W.W. Norton, 2004); Joseph Stiglitz, *Making Globalization Work* (W.W. Norton, 2007); Brian Snowdon, *Globalisation, Development and Transition* (Edward Elgar, 2007). Nowadays, globalization plays a significant role in enhancing comprehension between legal cultures. '*Le contrat administratif*' theory and practice were directly influenced by cultural and legal globalization. Further, the influence of the Anglo-American legal culture is remarkable upon MENA countries' Civil Law Legal Culture, particularly in legislation, case law, and the rise of new contractual patterns in state contracts such as Private-Public Partnerships (PPP) and Build Own Operate (BOT) agreements. See: Mohamed A.M. Ismail, *Globalization and New International Public Works Agreements in Developing Countries, An Analytical Perspective* (Routledge, 2011 and 2016, pp. 1–8 with a foreword by HH Humphrey Lloyd QC) and for the same author see: *Public Private Partnership Contracts: The Middle East and North Africa* (Routledge, 2020).

3 It is worth noting that previous Egyptian Constitution of 1971 and the current Constitution of 2014 as well as MENA countries' constitutions were inspired by the French Constitution of the Fifth Republic promulgated in 1958. In addition, the Egyptian Civil Code and MENA countries' Arab Civil Codes were greatly inspired by the French Civil Code.

4 Egypt has promulgated PPP Law No. 67 of 2010; Kuwait PPP Law No. 116 of 2014, and Jordan PPP Law No. 31 of 2014 (as amended in 2020), Morocco PPP Law No. 86-12 of 2014, Dubai PPP Law No. 22 of 2015 and Tunisia PPP Law No. 45 of 2015.

5 Sarwat Badawi, *Administrative Law* (Dar Al Nahda Al Arabia, 1985, and 2010 editions, in Arabic).

PPP techniques through legislation and regulatory frameworks is necessary in the MENA countries as the permissibility of PPP contracts was controversial in some MENA countries.

PPP techniques have been exercised in practice, as there were many PPP projects in reality before promulgating PPP legislation in many MENA countries. This situation happened in Egypt and many other MENA countries before promulgating PPP legislation.

PPP legislation in MENA countries is a codification of PPP techniques. Further, it creates a new procedural framework to select the private entity in PPP transactions different from the traditional Public Procurement law which is convenient for traditional concessions but not for PPPs.[6]

MENA governments' intervention to create legislative and regulatory frameworks to govern procedural and substantive issues was necessary for PPP contracts, providing that the party autonomy concept is the base for contractual transactions in PPP techniques. The source for obligations in PPP techniques and projects is the contract between the contracting parties. The necessity for MENA governments' intervention has legal and factual justifications, as the main concept for state transactions is to enter into administrative contracts, which contain excessive clauses in traditional concessions and other administrative contracts.[7] The trajectory of the legislative and regulatory intervention from the MENA countries to permit new PPP patterns has historical developments, particularly in Egypt, Kuwait, and some other MENA countries. For instance, in Egypt the General Assembly for Legal Opinion and Legislation in the Egyptian Conseil D'État issued a legal opinion to decide that Build, Own, Operate, Transfer (BOOT) agreements are subject to the previous State Procurement Law which was promulgated by Law No. 89 of 1998 as a result of the absence of a specialized legislation regulating procedural matters for BOT or PPPs techniques.[8] State intervention was necessary particularly since there is no constitutional ban in MENA constitutions.

Morocco and Tunisia as of 1 October 2014 indicated that many changes and transitions are taking place as governments improve the institutional framework for PPP.

6 There are several international instruments towards the unification of PPP contracts, such as the UNCITRAL Model Legislative Provisions on Public-Private Partnerships, 2020; the UNCITRAL Legislative Guide on Public-Private Partnership, 2020; the UNCITRAL Guide Privately Financed Infrastructure Projects (2000); European Union concession-related materials including the Concession Directive of 2014; the UNECE Guidebook on promoting good governance in Public-Private Partnership (2008) and various World Bank and PPIAF initiatives dealing with PPP, including the latest World Bank Benchmarking PPP Procurement, 2017. See: Bruno De Cazalet, The expected benefit of CIS PPP Model Law, *International Business Law Journal* (I.B.L.J. 2017, 2, pp. 97–114).

7 Ragab Mahmoud, *Public-Private Partnership Contracts* (Dar Al Nahda Al Arabia, 2007, in Arabic) and for the same author see: *Partnership Contracts Between Public and Private Sectors* (Dar Al Nahda Al Arabia, 2010, in Arabic); Sarwat Badawi, *General Theory of Administrative Contracts* (Dar Al Nahda Al Arabia, 1994, in Arabic); Soad Al Sharkawi, *Administrative Contracts* (Dar Al Nahda Al Arabia, 1998, in Arabic); Gaber Gad Nassar, *Administrative Contracts* (Dar Al Nahda Al Arabia, 2005, in Arabic).

8 The General Assembly for Legal Opinion and Legislation, legal opinion no. 602, 4 June 2003, file no. 100/2/14.

The main findings for some MENA countries include:

- **Egypt:** Has enacted specific PPP legislation No. 67 of 2010 as the first PPP legislation in the MENA region and has created an active PPP Central Unit. However, there remains scope for concessions under several sector-specific laws.
- **Jordan:** Has a good track record of successful infrastructure projects which have largely been procured under the existing Privatization Law. A PPP Law, which is the exclusive legal regime for PPPs, was promulgated by Law No. 31 of 2014 and amended in 2020.
- **Morocco:** Has a tradition of public involvement in infrastructure through concession arrangements. A PPP Central Unit was created in 2011. The Central Unit was also largely responsible for a new PPP Law, which was adopted by the House of Representatives in February 2014.[9]

PPP Legal Framework in Egypt

PPP legislation is promulgated by Law No. 67 of 2010 and its executive regulations to regulate partnership with the private sector in infrastructure projects, services, and public utilities which are the basis of the PPP legal framework. This PPP Law is a comprehensive and reasonably workable legal framework for PPPs, but the same cannot be said for the granting of concessions in general; these can still be undertaken under numerous pieces of older legislation. The PPP Law only applies to projects procured on a PPP basis with a minimum investment value of EGP 100 million. There are no legal restrictions on the sectors eligible for PPP. Projects can be concluded in commercial sectors, such as energy, transport, water, and oil and gas. Projects can be also concluded in non-commercial government services such as schools, hospitals, and housing. If any of the criteria for dealing with a project under the PPP Law are not met, the relevant sectors' specific law applies. For instance, the Egyptian Electricity Law No. 87 for year 2015 plays a significant role as the legislation regulating the electricity sector in Egypt.[10]

PPP Institutional Framework in Egypt

A PPP Central Unit was established by the Ministry of Finance in 2006, as the main entity responsible for the initiation and implementation of PPP projects in Egypt. It provides that the Minister of Finance designs the structure of the unit, while the executive regulations of the PPP Law determine the administrative and financial

9 For PPPs in Dubai also see: Adrian Creed, Dubai's new PPP Law, *Construction Law Journal* (Const. L.J. 2016, 32(7), pp. 808–10). In the procedural phase of PPP contracts in the MENA region see: Mohamed AM Ismail '*Innovation in Public Procurements in the Egyptian PPP Legislation*' (with reference to PPP Legislation in Dubai and Kuwait), in Gabriella M. Racca and, Christopher R. Yukins, *Public Contracting and Innovation, Lessons across Borders* (Bruylant 2019, p. 567).

10 Mohamed A.M. Ismail, *Public Private Partnership Contracts: The Middle East and North Africa* (Routledge, 2020).

framework for operations. This includes the Unit's relationship with other public organizations, its operational system, and employee remuneration. In practice, the unit is increasingly involved in the negotiation and execution levels of PPP bids and contracts. The law also provides that PPP 'satellite units' are to be established, whenever necessary, within the different administrative authorities.[11]

The PPP Law provides that a Supreme Committee for Public Private Partnership Affairs shall be formed and chaired by the Prime Minister. The PPP Supreme Committee is notably responsible for setting an integrated national PPP policy, endorsing use of the PPP structure for administrative authority projects, monitoring the financial resources allocation to meet obligations resulting from PPP contracts, issuing rules and general criteria for PPPs, and endorsing standard PPP contracts for use in different sectors.

The PPP Central Unit provides technical, financial and legal expertise to the PPP Supreme Committee as well as to the PPP satellite units. It is responsible for setting and following up on procedures for the tendering and conclusion of PPP contracts, as well as their execution. The consent of the PPP Unit is necessary for the development and granting of PPP projects in Egypt, and the Supreme Committee for PPP Affairs must approve PPP tenders.

Kuwait, PPP Legislation in 2014

The Kuwait PPP Law No. 116 of 2014 establishes a legislative framework to promote PPPs in public infrastructure and services in Kuwait, based on the principles of transparency and competitiveness. A PPP is defined in the PPP Law as:

'a project to implement an activity through which the State targets to provide a public service of economic, social or service importance, or to improve an existing public service or to develop, reduce the costs or increase the efficiency of any such service, procured by the Authority in cooperation with the Public Entity and in accordance with the PPP Model after the approval of the Higher Committee, provided it does not contradict with the provisions of Articles 152 and 153 of the Constitution.'[12] The main features of the Kuwaiti PPP Law No. 116 of 2014 may be underscored in some major points. PPPs must follow the 'PPP Model' which, in Article (1) of the PPP Law, is defined as

> a model whereby a private investor invests in State-owned real property – if required – in one of the projects procured by the Authority in collaboration with one of the Public Entities after signing an agreement with the investor to implement or build or develop or operate or rehabilitate a service or an

11 OECD, *Public-Private Partnerships in the Middle East and North Africa, A Handbook for Policy Makers*, p. 39.

12 Article 1 of the Kuwaiti PPP legislation. It worth noting that Articles 152 and 153 of the Kuwaiti Constitution deal with granting natural resources and public utilities' concessions or any monopoly which has to be granted by legislation and for a certain period of time, *PPP Guidebook, Kuwait Authority for Partnership Projects*, pp. 11–13 (in Arabic).

infrastructure project, and to provide financing thereto and operate or manage and develop the project, for a specified term, after which the project shall be transferred to the State; the foregoing shall be carried out in one of two forms: 1) the implementation of the project in consideration for fees – for services or works performed – to be paid to the investor by the end-users or by the public entities who have entered into an agreement with the investor, and whose objectives are in compliance with the project or by both the beneficiaries and the public entities; and 2) the purpose of the project is for the investor to implement a project with strategic importance to the national economy and to exploit it for a specified term. In both cases, the investor shall pay a fee for the use of any state-owned real property allocated for the project.

In accordance with this definition, the PPP Model in Kuwait therefore requires the following criteria to be met:

- A private investor to invest in a project on state-owned property (if required).
- Procurement of the project by KAPP,[13] in collaboration with a public entity.
- The signing of an agreement with the investor to implement or build or develop or operate or rehabilitate a service or an infrastructure project, to provide financing to this end, and to operate or manage and develop the project, for a specific period; and
- Following the end of the agreement, the transfer of the infrastructure facilities to the State.

The salient features of the PPP Law include:[14]

- In general, no public body may enter into a PPP contract without first obtaining the approval of the Higher Committee for PPPs.[15]
- KAPP provides advisory support to the Higher Committee in its decision making.
- A time limit for PPP projects of 50 years[16] (if a project's bid documents do not contain a certain term, its lifespan will be deemed to be 25 years).
- Restrictions on the sale or mortgage of state land/public property in PPP projects, although security over the 'private assets' is permitted, which includes revenues of the project and shares in the project company.
- Provisions allowing the state to collect a fee from the project for use of state land.

13 The PPP Law 2014 creates a new PPP governing authority, the Kuwait Authority for Partnership Projects (KAPP).

14 PPP Guidebook, *Kuwaiti Authority for Partnership Projects*, pp. 11–13 (in Arabic).

15 There are a few exceptions to this general rule, such as is the case with the Public Authority for Housing Welfare established under Law No. (47) of 1993, which may tender PPPs within its scope of work.

16 Under the IWPP Law and the IWPP Regulations the time limit for PPP Projects is capped at 40 years.

- Projects exceeding KWD 60 million in value must be carried out by a PPP project company which will be a Special Purpose Vehicle (SPV) formed as a Kuwaiti joint stock company, in which no less than 26% and up to 44% of shares would be offered to an investor, with the majority of the remainder of the shares being offered to the Kuwaiti citizens and public entities allowed to invest in the project (subject to these shares being held temporarily by KAPP until full operation of the project).
- Provisions allowing for unsolicited proposals of two types: (i) initiative projects and (ii) distinguished projects.
- Possibility of settlement of disputes through arbitration; and
- Grievance mechanism for violations of the PPP Law and the executive regulations.

The Kuwaiti PPP Law of 2014 provides for transition arrangements. Projects existing before the entry into force of the PPP Law shall continue until the expiry of the term in the agreement or until termination. Upon the entry of the PPP Law into force, no amendments, renewals, or extensions may be given on such projects, and such projects shall be handed back to the state for re-tendering or for operating and managing the project itself (in accordance with Article 30 of the PPP Law). Further transitional arrangements are in place for projects whose term has expired at the time the PPP Law came into force. These may be granted a one-time extension for a maximum period of one year pursuant to their respective contractual provisions and subject to the approval of the Higher Committee.[17]

It is worth noting that PPP executive regulations[18] were issued to set out further details on the project flow process, procurement, and implementation of PPPs in Kuwait.

Institutional Structure for PPPs in Kuwait

The institutional structure for the implementation of PPP Projects, as introduced in the PPP Law and the executive regulations, consists of the following institutions:

The Higher Committee (HC)[19]

The Higher Committee has the powers and authorities of acting as KAPP's board of directors. It is chaired by the Minister of Finance and consists of:

- The Minister of Municipalities.
- The Minister of Public Works.
- The Minister of Trade and Industry.
- The Minister of Electricity and Water.

17 Article 7 of the Kuwaiti PPP Law. PPP Guidebook, *Kuwaiti Authority for Partnership Projects*, p. 13 (in Arabic).
18 Decree No. 78 of 2015.
19 PPP Guidebook, *Kuwaiti Authority for Partnership Projects*, p. 17 (in Arabic).

- The Director General of the Kuwait Environment Public Authority.
- The Director General of KAPP.
- Three experienced specialists to be named by the Council of Ministers from civil servants; and
- A representative of the public entity responsible for the project under consideration, who shall be invited to the concerned meeting but will not have a right to vote.

The responsibilities of the Higher Committee include:

- Setting the general policies for projects and initiatives of strategic importance to the national economy, identifying priorities and approving detailed documentation related thereto.
- Approving the requests of the Public Entities for the procurement of PPP Projects.
- Proposing PPP projects to Public Entities.
- Approving KAPP's proposed budget and final accounts.
- Approving the financial and administrative statutes as well as KAPP's employees' regulations and its organizational structure.
- Identifying the relevant Public Entity which will participate in the procurement of a project with KAPP and which will countersign the PPP Agreement and be responsible for its implementation and monitoring.
- Approving requests for allocation of land necessary for the implementation of PPP Projects, in coordination with the competent authorities.
- Approving the studies and concepts of PPP Projects and approving the procurement thereof.
- Approving the successful investor for a project, on the recommendation of KAPP.
- Approving PPP contracts to be executed by public entities.
- Deciding upon the requests of public entities for contract cancellation/termination (including for public interest); and
- Examining the semi-annual report of PPP Projects.

The PPP Law provides that the decisions of the Higher Committee will only have effect after they have been approved by the Minister of Finance.[20]

PPP Legal Framework in Morocco

In Morocco, public-private partnerships were ruled by laws governing specific sectors. In the motorway sector, Decree no.2-89-189 dated 2 February 1993 applying Law No. 4-89 pertaining to motorways authorized the state to grant motorway concessions with the right for the concessionaire to collect fees from the motorway users. More than ten motorway concessions have been granted to the *Société*

20 Article 2 of the PPP Law. PPP Guidebook, *Kuwaiti Authority for Partnership Projects*, p. 18 (in Arabic).

Nationale des Autoroutes du Maroc for the design, financing, building, operation, and maintenance of the motorway links between Rabat and Tangier, Tetouan and Fnideq, Casablanca and El Jadida or Rabat and Fes.[21]

In the port sector, the Decree-Law No. 2-02-644 dated 10 September 2002 creating the Tanger-Med special area and the Law No.15-02 pertaining to ports respectively entitled TMSA and ANP to launch bidding processes, within which there were in some instances of competing dialogue with the public body, for the concessions of container terminals, RoRo terminals, tug and rescue services, and oil terminals. The concessionaire brought the financing and know-how, designed and built the terminals, operated them, and collected fees in consideration for the services provided.[22]

In energy, a bidding process has been launched for the financing, design, construction, operation, and maintenance of electricity production capacities against energy fees payable by the public off-taker.

The public work concession is also possible under Moroccan law even if this formula has not been used very often. This concept consists of the public body in granting the right for a private partner to occupy the public domain, to build a public construction work, to operate it, and to collect fees from the users. There is no legal framework for such a concept, which is only mentioned briefly in the code of public procurement (to exclude it from the public procurement regime).[23]

To promote the increase of the participation of the private sector in infrastructure projects, the Kingdom of Morocco created in 2014 new types of state contract[24] implemented through the enactment of the PPP Law No. 86-12.[25] The purpose of this law is to establish a coherent legislative framework, which introduces innovation in award procedures for PPP projects, as these procedures must be consistent with sustainable development goals. Further, the PPP Law creates substantive incentives to private sector to participate in the development of infrastructures in Morocco. For the purposes of the implementation of the PPP law, the PPP Decree no. 2-15-45 of 13 May 2015 was issued.[26] In the law preamble, the lawmaker indicates that the Law and, also, the PPP contract targets to meet at best the citizen's expectations for infrastructure and public services of good quality and the services rendered must comply with the equality and continuity principles.[27]

21 Philippe De Richoufftz, The Moroccan PPP Contract, *International Business Law Journal* (I.B.L.J. 2015, 5, p.390).

22 Philippe De Richoufftz, The Moroccan PPP Contract, *International Business Law Journal* (I.B.L.J. 2015, 5, p.390).

23 Philippe De Richoufftz, The Moroccan PPP Contract, *International Business Law Journal* (I.B.L.J., 2015, 5, p.390).

24 Philippe De Richoufftz, The Moroccan PPP Contract, *International Business Law Journal* (I.B.L.J. 2015, 5, pp.389–98).

25 Published on the Official Gazette no. 6332 of 5 February 2015.

26 Published on the Official Gazette no. 6365 of 1 October 2015.

27 Philippe De Richoufftz, The Moroccan PPP Contract, *International Business Law Journal* (I.B.L.J. 2015, 5, p.395).

An inter-ministerial commission for PPP contracts has been established and mainly composed of representatives of various Moroccan ministries, under the auspices of the Ministry of Economy and Finance. The purpose of this commission is to issue opinions on PPP contracts entered into with the state, preliminary assessments, and the award of the contract.

Articles 1 and 3 of the PPP Law define PPPs and ensure that principles of equal access and treatment, objectiveness, competitiveness, transparency, and respecting best practices shall be upheld in the PPP procurement process. Nonetheless, a delegated management of public services (the 'DM') in accordance to the provisions of Law No. 54-05 of 14 February 2006[28] and Decree No. 2-06-362 of 9 August 2006[29] preceded the 2015 regulatory framework on PPPs. Furthermore, there are specific sectoral laws on concessions, which include: i) Law No. 4-89 relating to motorways promulgated in August 1992; ii) Law No. 15-02 relating to ports and creating the Ports National Agency and the Ports Operating Company promulgated on November 2005; iii) Law No. 52-02 relating to the organization and the operation of the national railway network promulgated in January 2005; and iv) Law No. 25-79 creating the Airports National Office as amended by Law No. 14-89 and Law No. 1-93-140. The previous legislative and regulatory instruments form the legal framework on PPPs in Morocco for the purposes of PPP procurement.

The PPP procuring authorities in Morocco include: public law entities or public juristic entities (*Etablissements publics de l'État*) excluding Local Authorities; and public law companies (*entreprises publiques*): pursuant, to the provisions of Law No. 69-00 relating to State Financial Control of the Public Companies and other Entities. The public law companies who may enter into a PPP contract are (i) state companies whose share capital is wholly owned by public entities; (ii) public subsidiaries whose share capital is held more than half by public bodies and (iii) mixed company whose share capital is owned up to 50% by public entities.

The approval of the Minister in Charge of Finances is necessary with regards to the feasibility of conducting the contracts under a PPP structure pursuant to Article 4 of the PPP Decree.

In addition, the approval of the Inter-ministerial Commission on PPPs is necessary. Pursuant to Article (5/1) of the PPP Decree, the latter commission provides its opinion on the pre-feasibility evaluation report prepared by the procuring authority, to assure the opportunity to realize the project under the PPP contract.

The PPP law provides that PPP contracts can be subject to three different tender procedures: competitive dialogue, call for tenders, and a negotiated procedure. The PPP law requires that the public authority carry out a preliminary assessment which must include a comparative analysis with the other frameworks of implementation of the project. In addition, the preliminary assessment considers the complexity of the project, the financial arrangement, and the means of financing. However, contrary to what was implemented in France, the entering into of this

28 The Official Gazette no. 5404 of 16 March 2006.

29 The Official Gazette no. 5454 of 7 September 2006.

contract is not strictly delimited. Indeed, the PPP Law does not solely apply to contracts characterized by a trait of urgency or complexity, thus diminishing the risk of litigation. The PPP Law also provides, following the example of the relevant French framework, that candidates can present a spontaneous offer to the public authorities considered under the PPP Law. Consequently, the public authority can be presented with an innovative project by an operator, and, if the project addresses the public authority's needs and presents technical and financial innovations, it can decide to proceed to the necessary preliminary assessment of the project and initiate a competitive dialogue.[30]

The PPP Law also provides that the public authority can conduct a negotiated procedure, without advertising or calling for competition, with the operator when the spontaneous offer addresses an innovative and urgent need, while at the same time being financially competitive.

The PPP Law in Morocco introduces a significant step in the MENA countries to avoid the pitfalls in other countries' PPP legislation. The award of the PPP contracts aims to achieve a criteria of national preference, that could be taken into account, in order to support the national economy.

Legislative Progress in PPP Law in Morocco

The PPP law provides for a list of mandatory clauses which must be included in the PPP contract. These mandatory clauses concern some substantive issues such as the financial conditions of the PPP contract, as well as the contract performance. According to the financial clauses pursuant to PPP Law, the remuneration of the private partner will be paid, in its entirety or partially, by the public authority. In the event where the public authority does not pay the entirety of the remuneration of the private partner, it may be remunerated by the end-users (the public) through the cash flow generated by the project. This remuneration is linked to performance objectives, thus guaranteeing the compliant carrying out of the PPP contract. The corollary of these objectives is the possibility for the public authority to impose penalties on the private partner, in the event where the latter does not fulfill its contractual obligations.[31]

The PPP Law provides that the private partner may, for the benefit of the lending institutions, create security interests over its assets acquired or carried out under the performance of the PPP contract.[32] The type of security interests that can be granted is quite large since the PPP law considers 'all security interests.' Furthermore, the assignment of receivables by way of security does not appear to be confined in the sense that the number of claims which can receive an act of acceptance from the public party, as assigned debtor, is not limited to 80% of the investment and financing costs. The maximum contract duration which is permitted pursuant to the

30 White & Case, Client Alert Energy, Infrastructure, Project and Asset Finance.
31 White & Case, ClientAlert Energy, Infrastructure, Project and Asset Finance.
32 White & Case, ClientAlert Energy, Infrastructure, Project and Asset Finance.

PPP Law is up to a maximum of 50 years. It also imposes the inclusion of a clause in the PPP contract pertaining to the allocation of risks between the parties, which is subject to the contractual practice of optimal risk sharing. Furthermore, the PPP law establishes a substitution right, whereby the public authority can replace the private partner with a substituted entity, notably in the event of a serious breach of its obligations. It should be noted that the PPP Law also enables the lending institutions to ask the public authority to substitute the private partner with a new entity, in the case of a serious breach of its obligations.

In conclusion, the PPP Law takes into consideration standard market practices, which are implemented in international project finance and should permit the avoidance of the main pitfalls observed in countries with similar frameworks.[33]

The PPP Law in Morocco draws heavily on French law. It allows the use of PPPs in sectors where it is not appropriate to allocate operating risks to the private party including non-commercial sectors of a social infrastructure nature such as hospitals.[34]

PPP Institutional Framework in Morocco:

The PPP Unit or the *Commission de Partenariat Public-Privé* has been established at the Ministry of Economy and Finance within the Directorate for State Enterprises and Privatization (DEPP). The PPP Unit is a cell dedicated to PPPs, in order to establish a structured framework for the development of PPPs and broaden their fields of action.

The PPP Central Unit was established in September 2011 and has cooperated closely with a number of international institutions such as the European Investment Bank and the International Finance Corporation. This unit was notably in charge of the drafting and scoping of the new PPP Law. It may also play a significant role in the development of PPP pilot projects.

In Morocco, the decision-making process for major infrastructure projects involves many sectors of the government. Projects are likely to involve a wide range of stakeholders, including decision-making committees across ministries for centrally procured projects.

PPP Legal Framework in Tunisia[35]

Tunisia has currently promulgated PPP Law which is Law No. 45/2015. The PPP Law in Tunisia was promulgated in November 2015. Decree no. 771/2016 was issued in June 2016 to establish the Strategic Council for PPPs and Decree no. 772/2016, issued in June 2016, created the procedural framework for awarding

33 White & Case, Client Alert Energy, Infrastructure, Project and Asset Finance.

34 OECD, *Public-Private Partnerships in the Middle East and North Africa, A Handbook for Policy Makers*, p. 37.

35 The African Legal Support Facility (ALSF), PPP country Profile, Tunisia.

PPP contracts. Further, Decree no. 782/2016 was issued in June 2016, which permits the registration of real rights over the buildings, enterprises, and fixed equipment under PPP contracts. The other applicable sectoral laws are Law No. 12 of 11 May 2015 on the production of electricity from renewable energies.[36]

PPP Institutional Framework in Tunisia

The Ministry of Economy and Finance also houses a body tasked with PPPs, the *Direction générale des partenariats public-privé* (DGPPP) whose main role is to monitor the fiscal and financial risks of public spending on PPP projects. The DGPPP has also contributed to developing the draft legislation on PPPs, and will remain involved in the preparation and negotiation of PPP projects once the new PPP regime is in place. The *Direction générale d'audit et de suivi des grands projets* (DGASGP), also within the Ministry of Economy and Finance, is responsible for the audit and the OECD, in cooperation with the USC and the African Development Bank, has been engaged with the Government of Tunisia as it reforms its institutional framework for PPPs. As part of the 'Operationalising PPPs in Tunisia' project, funded by the Deauville Partnership Transition Fund, the OECD expects to publish reports in the second quarter of 2015 that examine the legal, institutional, and budgetary frameworks for PPPs in the country.

It is important to note that the concessions and PPP regime in Tunisia are separate from the public procurement regime (*régime des marchés publics*), which is governed by the 2014 Decree on Public Procurement (no. 2014-1039 of 13 March 2014). Accordingly, public procurement that does not involve concessions or PPPs is managed by a separate set of institutions.[37]

PPP Legal Framework in Algeria[38]

The legal framework in Algeria consists of the Presidential Decree no. 15/247 of 2 Dhou El Hidja 1436, corresponding to 16 September 2015, on the regulation of public contracts and public service delegations. It also consists of:

- Law No. 99-09 of 28 July 1999 on the control of energy.
- Law No. 02-01 of 5 February 2002, on Electricity and Public Distribution of Gas by Pipeline.
- Law No. 04-09 of 14 August 2004 on the promotion of renewable energies in the context of sustainable development.
- Law No. 12-2005 of 4 August 2005 on water.
- Executive Decree No. 05-495 of 26 December 2005 concerning the energy audit of major energy-consuming establishments.

36 The African Legal Support Facility (ALSF), PPP country Profile, Tunisia.

37 The African Legal Support Facility (ALSF), PPP country Profile, Tunisia.

38 The World Bank Group, PPP Legal Resource Centre (PPPLRC), available at: https://ppp.worldbank.org/public-private-partnership/ppp-legal-framework-snapshots-0#A, last seen on 7 January 2024.

- Ministerial Decrees of 2 February 2014 fixing the guaranteed purchase rates for the production of electricity from installations using the photovoltaic industry and the conditions of their application.
- Ministerial Decrees of 2 February 2014 fixing the guaranteed purchase rates for the production of electricity from installations using the wind energy industry and the conditions of their application.

PPPs International Dynamics

An important question arises, how are the international dynamics of PPPs in Egypt and MENA countries subjected to achieving the unification of contract law principles, for public and private contracts, and to achieving coherent and substantive global contract law principles?

When an analogy is made to the MENA countries' PPPs legislation and regulation on one hand, and the international standards stipulated by international organs such as the UNECE, OECD, and the World Bank on the other, the case study of Egypt, Kuwait, and Dubai is of a fundamental importance. To what extent are PPPs' procedural techniques in the above-mentioned countries compatible with international standards? It is important to compare the current situation of PPPs in the MENA countries, and if they are consistent with the UN SDGs or not. Factual economic statistics, which are necessary to understand the international dynamics of PPP, show how far the MENA countries' legal regimes are compatible with international standards. Further, an introduction to the UN 2030 Agenda and the UN SDGs, and how PPPs can be subjected to serve such goals in light of the international organs' practice?

Finally, it is suggested that compatibility of PPP legislation and regulatory frameworks with the international standards, is a pillar towards achieving global substantive contract law, in Egypt and MENA countries, in both public and private (commercial) contracts.

Factual Economic Statistics

The World Investment Report[39] highlights the fact that after a strong rebound in 2021, global FDI fell by 12% in 2022 to $1.3 trillion, due mainly to overlapping global crises – the war in Ukraine, high food and energy prices, and soaring public debt.

The decline was felt mostly in developed economies, where FDI fell by 37% to $378 billion. But flows to developing countries grew by 4% – albeit unevenly, with a few large emerging countries attracting most of the investment while flows to the least developed countries declined.

On a positive note, greenfield investment project announcements were up 15% in 2022, growing in most regions and sectors. Industries struggling with

39 The UNCTAD, The World Investment Report 2023, available at: https://unctad.org/publication/world-investment-report-2023, last accessed 11 November 2023.

supply chain challenges, including electronics, semiconductors, automotive, and machinery, saw a surge in projects, while investment in digital economy sectors slowed. International investment in renewable energy generation, including solar and wind, also continued to grow – but at a slower 8% than the 50% growth recorded in 2021. Notably, projects announced in battery manufacturing tripled to more than $100 billion in 2022.

The report also notes that major oil companies are gradually selling fossil fuel assets – at a rate of about $15 billion per year – mostly to unlisted private equity firms and smaller operators with lower disclosure requirements.

The 2030 Agenda to achieve the SDGs provides an opportunity for the development of traditional patterns of administrative contracts, to attract investment in PPPs-relevant activities, and adopt the highest levels of PPPs standards and compliance. The achievement of shifting from the total reliance on oil and gas economy to digital economy is one of the main goals in the Gulf countries. Such development of administrative contracts is a significant step, which paves the way to create unified substantive principles of contract law, in both public and private contracts. A global contract law is underway.

UNCITRAL's PPP Legislative Guide[40]

The United Nations Commission on International Trade Law (UNCITRAL) has adopted the UNCITRAL Model Legislative Provisions on Public-Private Partnerships, 2020; the UNCITRAL Legislative Guide on Public-Private Partnership, 2020; and previously, the UNCITRAL Guide on Privately Financed Infrastructure Projects 2000.

There is an essential need worldwide for a tested recipe book on infrastructure investment. In many cases, governments look to long-term PPPs with private companies to help to achieve their infrastructure objectives. Risk management and benefits in these relationships is challenging and the proper balance often elusive, even in developed countries that are well-equipped to structure and oversee them. Ideally, an infrastructure recipe would call for a number of recognizable ingredients to attract private capital, and straightforward methods to process it.

Achievement of the SDGs requires quality infrastructure, not just quantity, addressed specifically by SDG No. 9, which aims at building resilient infrastructure, promoting inclusive and sustainable industrialization, and fostering innovation.

Countries need infrastructure that promotes economic development, jobs, and widespread public benefit. The finance ministers of Francophone low-income countries, for example, have articulated their needs in infrastructure PPPs, and they make it clear that they will not accept just any PPP – they want public investment projects which target universal access to services in sectors such as education, health, water, and energy, with reduced costs and risks of PPPs. While '*value for*

40 Available at: https://uncitral.un.org/en/working_groups/1/pfip?utm_source=CCSI+Mailing+List&utm_campaign=d3e76b1335April_newsletter_2019&utm_medium=email&utm_term=0_a61bf1d34a-d3e76b1335-57387505, last accessed on 7 January, 2024.

money' and management of fiscal and financial risks are essential, so is management of the nonfinancial risks of PPPs, such as environmental, social, and governance risks.

This means that countries cannot focus solely on facilitating and strengthening processes and legal frameworks around procurement, and contract negotiation, implementation, and termination. They must also select and advance infrastructure projects in a way that minimizes all material risks, including sustainability risks, and maximizes economic, environmental, and social sustainable development objectives, all of which must be supported and advanced by the PPP regulatory framework.[41]

PPP contractual relationships often last for decades so it is incumbent on governments to foresee these risks and benefits, to anticipate them, and to integrate them early in any project. Any regulatory framework for PPPs must equip countries to do this.

Considering the appetite for PPPs, a legislative guide to PPPs intended for use by governments must take a more holistic approach to better describe and help address the recurrent sustainability challenges that PPPs face. Any UN instrument that helps to enable PPPs must explicitly place PPPs in today's world and not the world of 20 years ago. It must do its part to help countries manage the environmental and social risks and realize the sustainable development benefits of PPPs.[42]

An enabling provision for the conclusion of PPP projects requires a definition of the projects covered.[43] These projects are always developed in accordance with a contract setting out the mutual obligations of the parties and providing often for related contractual arrangements. For instance, financing, building, or rehabilitating the infrastructure, operating the service, supplying, off taking, etc. PPPs can be described as mutually beneficial contractual arrangements, trying to achieve a *win-win* situation as a contractual target for both parties. The *win-win* situation is not recognized in administrative contracts in civil law countries, such as France and MENA countries, where states do not have an equal bargaining power with the private investor. In PPP contracts, resources are contributed by both the public and private partners (including provision of private finance, professional and other knowledge, expertise, and skills on the one hand, and granting of rights, such as rights over land and to exclusive operation of infrastructure on the other).[44]

41 Motoko Aizawa and Brooke Guven, *UNCITRAL's PPP Legislative Guide Must be Fit for Today's PPPs*, Columbia Center on Sustainable Development, Columbia University, 2019, available at: https://ccsi.columbia.edu/news/uncitrals-ppp-legislative-guide-must-be-fit-todays-ppps, last accessed on 7 January, 2024.

42 Ibid.

43 Available at: https://uncitral.un.org/en/working_groups/1/pfip?utm_source=CCSI+Mailing+List&utm_campaign=d3e76b1335April_newsletter_2019&utm_medium=email&utm_term=0_a61bf1d34a-d3e76b1335-57387505, last accessed on 7 January, 2024.

44 Available at: https://uncitral.un.org/en/working_groups/1/pfip?utm_source=CCSI+Mailing+List&utm_campaign=d3e76b1335April_newsletter_2019&utm_medium=email&utm_term=0_a61bf1d34a-d3e76b1335-57387505, last accessed on 7 January, 2024.

The UNCITRAL Model Legislative Provisions on Public-Private Partnerships, 2020 and the UNCITRAL Legislative Guide on Public-Private Partnership, 2020 are significant steps towards the unification of global contractual principles for PPPs, which are adopted, to a great extent, by Egypt and MENA countries.

Transforming Our World: the 2030 Agenda for Sustainable Development[45]

This Agenda is a plan of action for people, planet, and prosperity. It also seeks to strengthen universal peace in larger freedom. It is recognized that eradicating poverty in all its forms and dimensions, including extreme poverty, is the greatest global challenge and an indispensable requirement for sustainable development.[46] The 17 SDGs and 169 targets which we are announcing today demonstrate the scale and ambition of this new universal Agenda. They seek to build on the Millennium Development Goals and complete what these did not achieve. They seek to realize the human rights of all and to achieve gender equality and the empowerment of all women and girls. They are integrated and indivisible and balance the three dimensions of sustainable development: the economic, social, and environmental.

The Goals and targets will stimulate action over the next 15 years in areas of critical importance for humanity and the planet. The SDGs determined to protect the planet from degradation, including through sustainable consumption and production, sustainably managing its natural resources, and taking urgent action on climate change, so that it can support the needs of the present and future generations.

The SDGs determined to ensure that all human beings can enjoy prosperous and fulfilling lives and that economic, social, and technological progress occurs in harmony with nature.

The interlinkages and integrated nature of the SDGs are of crucial importance in ensuring that the purpose of the new Agenda is realized. If we realize our ambitions across the full extent of the Agenda, the lives of all will be profoundly improved and our world will be transformed for the better.[47]

The UN has adopted a historic decision on a comprehensive, far-reaching and people-centered set of universal and transformative goals and targets. The UN is committed to work tirelessly for the full implementation of this Agenda by 2030. The UN recognizes that eradicating poverty in all its forms and dimensions, including extreme poverty, is the greatest global challenge and an indispensable requirement for sustainable development. The UN is committed to achieving sustainable development in its three dimensions – economic, social, and environmental – in a balanced and integrated manner.

45 Available at: https://sustainabledevelopment.un.org/post2015/transformingourworld. Last accessed on 7 January 2024.

46 The UN Sustainable Development Agenda is available at: www.un.org/sustainabledevelopment/development-agenda/, last accessed on 7 January 2024.

47 The High-level Political Forum on Sustainable Development is the central UN platform for the follow-up and review of the 2030 Agenda for Sustainable Development adopted at the United Nations Sustainable Development Summit on 25 September 2015.

It is a fundamental target to resolve between now and 2030, to end poverty and hunger everywhere; to combat inequalities within and among countries; to build peaceful, just and inclusive societies; to protect human rights and promote gender equality and the empowerment of women and girls; and to ensure the lasting protection of the planet and its natural resources. The UN resolves also to create conditions for sustainable, inclusive, and sustained economic growth, shared prosperity and decent work for all, taking into account different levels of national development and capacities.

This is an Agenda of unprecedented scope and significance. It is accepted by all countries and is applicable to all, taking into account different national realities, capacities, and levels of development and respecting national policies and priorities. These are universal goals and targets which involve the entire world, developed and developing countries alike. They are integrated and indivisible and balance the three dimensions of sustainable development.

The Goals and targets are the result of over two years of intensive public consultation and engagement with civil society and other stakeholders around the world, which paid particular attention to the voices of the poorest and most vulnerable. This consultation included valuable work done by the General Assembly Open Working Group on SDGs and by the United Nations, whose Secretary-General provided a synthesis report in December 2014.

In these Goals and targets, the UN is setting out a supremely ambitious and transformational vision that envisages a world free of poverty, hunger, disease, and want, where all life can thrive. The UN vision envisages a world free of fear and violence. A world with equitable and universal access to quality education at all levels, to health care and social protection, where physical, mental, and social well-being are assured. A world where we reaffirm our commitments regarding the human right to safe drinking water and sanitation and where there is improved hygiene; and where food is sufficient, safe, affordable, and nutritious. A world where human habitats are safe, resilient, and sustainable and where there is universal access to affordable, reliable, and sustainable energy.

The vision envisages a world of universal respect for human rights and human dignity, the rule of law, justice, equality, and non-discrimination; of respect for race, ethnicity and cultural diversity; and of equal opportunity, permitting the full realization of human potential and contributing to shared prosperity.

The vision envisages a world in which every country enjoys sustained, inclusive, and sustainable economic growth and decent work for all. A world in which consumption and production patterns and use of all natural resources – from air to land, from rivers, lakes, and aquifers to oceans and seas – are sustainable. One in which democracy, good governance, and the rule of law as well as an enabling environment at national and international levels, are essential for sustainable development, including sustained and inclusive economic growth, social development, environmental protection, and the eradication of poverty and hunger. One in which development and the application of technology are climate-sensitive, respect biodiversity, and are resilient.

The new Agenda is guided by the purposes and principles of the Charter of the United Nations, including full respect for international law. It is grounded in the Universal Declaration of Human Rights, international human rights treaties, the Millennium Declaration, and the 2005 World Summit Outcome Document. It is informed by other instruments such as the Declaration on the Right to Development.

The UN reaffirms the outcomes of all major UN conferences and summits which have laid a solid foundation for sustainable development and have helped to shape the new Agenda. These include the Rio Declaration on Environment and Development; the World Summit on Sustainable Development; the World Summit for Social Development; the Programme of Action of the International Conference on Population and Development; the Beijing Platform for Action; and the United Nations Conference on Sustainable Development ('Rio+ 20').

The UN reaffirm all the principles of the Rio Declaration on Environment and Development, including, *inter alia*, the principle of common but differentiated responsibilities, as set out in principle 7 thereof.

The challenges and commitments contained in these major conferences and summits are interrelated and call for integrated solutions. To address them effectively, a new approach is needed. Sustainable development recognizes that eradicating poverty in all its forms and dimensions, combating inequality within and among countries, preserving the planet, creating sustained, inclusive and sustainable economic growth and fostering social inclusion are linked to each other and are interdependent.

The world today is at a time of immense challenges to sustainable development. Billions of our citizens continue to live in poverty and are denied a life of dignity. There are rising inequalities within and among countries. There are enormous disparities of opportunity, wealth, and power. Gender inequality remains a key challenge. Unemployment, particularly youth unemployment, is a major concern. Global health threats, more frequent and intense natural disasters, spiraling conflict, violent extremism, terrorism, and related humanitarian crises and forced displacement of people threaten to reverse much of the development progress made in recent decades. Natural resource depletion and adverse impacts of environmental degradation, including desertification, drought, land degradation, freshwater scarcity, and loss of biodiversity, add to and exacerbate the list of challenges which humanity faces. Climate change is one of the greatest challenges of our time and its adverse impacts undermine the ability of all countries to achieve sustainable development. Increases in global temperature, sea level rise, ocean acidification, and other climate change impacts are seriously affecting coastal areas and low-lying coastal countries, including many least developed countries and small island developing states. The survival of many societies, and of the biological support systems of the planet, is at risk.

It is also, however, a time of immense opportunity. Significant progress has been made in meeting many development challenges. Within the past generation, hundreds of millions of people have emerged from extreme poverty. Access to education has greatly increased for both boys and girls. The spread of information and communications technology and global interconnectedness has great potential to accelerate human progress, to bridge the digital divide and to develop knowledge societies, as does scientific and technological innovation across areas as diverse as medicine and energy.

The UN announced 17 SDGs with 169 associated targets which are integrated and indivisible. Those targets are setting out on the path towards sustainable development, devoting ourselves collectively to the pursuit of global development and of '*win-win*' cooperation that can bring huge gains to all countries and all parts of the world.[48]

The sustainable development goals reaffirm the importance of the Universal Declaration of Human Rights, as well as other international instruments relating to human rights and international law. Further, the goals emphasize the responsibilities of all states, in conformity with the Charter of the United Nations, to respect, protect, and promote human rights and fundamental freedoms for all, without distinction of any kind as to race, color, sex, language, religion, political or other opinion, national or social origin, property, birth, disability, or other status.[49]

The new Goals and targets came into effect on 1 January 2016 and will guide the decisions we take over the next 15 years. Those Goals are committed to ending poverty in all its forms and dimensions, including by eradicating extreme poverty by 2030.[50]

States are strongly urged to refrain from promulgating and applying any unilateral economic, financial, or trade measures not in accordance with international law and the Charter of the United Nations that impede the full achievement of economic and social development, particularly in developing countries.[51]

How can PPPs be subjected to serving sustainable development goals in light of the international organs' practice? How can PPPs subjected to achieving coherent contract law through implementing a set of unified principles towards a global contract law?

International Organizations' Standards

PPP award procedures in Egypt, Kuwait, and Dubai are fundamental tools in implementing the basic principles adopted by OECD MAPS and OECD

48 The UN Sustainable Development Agenda, Department of Economic and Social Affairs, Sustainable Development, is available at: www.un.org/sustainabledevelopment/development-agenda/, last accessed on 7 January 2024 and Available at: https://sustainabledevelopment.un.org/post2015/transformingourworld. Last accessed on 7 January 2024.

49 Available at: https://sustainabledevelopment.un.org/post2015/transformingourworld, last accessed on 7 January 2024 and the UN Sustainable Development Agenda is available at: www.un.org/sustainabledevelopment/development-agenda/, last accessed on 7 January 2024.

50 Marco Ceruti, Sustainable Development and Smart Technological Innovation within PPPs: the Strategic Use of Public Procurement, *European Procurement & Public Private Partnership Law Review* (EPPPL 2017, 12(2), pp. 183–91).

51 Available at: https://sustainabledevelopment.un.org/post2015/transformingourworld. Last accessed on 7 January 2024 and the UN Sustainable Development Agenda is available at: www.un.org/sustainabledevelopment/development-agenda/, last accessed on 7 January 2024.

Recommendations on Public Procurement 2015.[52] For instance, the Egyptian legislation develops effective, accountable, and transparent administrative organs such as the PPP Central Unit (PPPCU) at the Egyptian Ministry of Finance. PPP legislation aims at promoting public procurement practices that are sustainable, in accordance with national polices and priorities. The award process is a very crucial stage in the government procurement chain. Efforts in promoting competition, transparency, equal treatment, and objectivity, on one hand, while preventing corruption, on the other hand, play a fundamental role in the public procurement process.

In Egypt, Kuwait, and Dubai, PPP legislation and its executive regulations require the procuring entity to have objective awarding criteria that aim to protect public interests and public funds.

There are various mechanisms and guarantees to prevent corruption and bureaucracy in PPP legislation in Egypt, Kuwait, and Dubai. An on-line bidding system exists (to some extent) in some Arab countries as one of the mechanisms to maintain objectivity, fight corruption, and avoid bureaucracy. Arab countries have not yet implemented a full on-line bidding system.

Generally, the type of legal system and whether it is a common law or civil law weigh heavily on the type of PPP legislative and regulatory frameworks that exists in a particular jurisdiction. Jurisdictions with 'common law' legal systems tend to rely on policy documents and administrative guidance materials, whereas jurisdictions with 'civil law' legal systems are more likely to set up a detailed PPP framework in a binding legal document or statute or legislation.[53] Egypt, Kuwait, and Dubai have civil law legal systems.[54] The selection of the private partner is usually carried out through a public tendering process, applying either general public procurement legislative and regulatory rules, or procurement legislative and regulatory rules specially adapted for PPP.

It is of fundamental importance that award procedures in PPP legislation achieve the agreed standards recognized by the international organizations. The sub-indicator adopted by the OECD is significant in the PPP award procedures context in Egypt, Kuwait, and Dubai. The purpose of the sub-indicator, as it is stipulated by the OECD, is to determine: a) the structure of the regulatory framework covering

52 OECD, *Methodology for Assessment Procurement Systems 2018*, available at: www.mapsinitiative.org/methodology/MAPS-methodology-for-assessing-procurement-systems.pdf, last accessed on 7 January 2024.

53 Benchmarking Public-Private Partnerships Procurement, Benchmarking PPP Procurement: Assessing Government Capability to Prepare, Procure and Manage PPPs (2017, 22), available at: https://ppp.worldbank.org/public-private-partnership/sites/ppp.worldbank.org/files/documents/Benchmarking_PPPs_2017_ENpdf.pdf; The World Bank Group, Procuring Infrastructure PPPs (2018); available at: https://ppp.worldbank.org/public-private-partnership/library/procuring-infrastructure-ppps-2018, last accessed on 7 January, 2024.

54 The World Bank, Benchmarking Public-Private Partnerships Procurement, Benchmarking PPP Procurement: Assessing Government Capability to Prepare, Procure and Manage PPPs 2017, 22, available at: https://ppp.worldbank.org/public-private-partnership/sites/ppp.worldbank.org/files/documents/Benchmarking_PPPs_2017_ENpdf.pdf; The World Bank Group, Procuring Infrastructure PPPs 2018, last accessed on 7 January 2024 and available at: https://ppp.worldbank.org/public-private-partnership/library/procuring-infrastructure-ppps-2018, last accessed on 7 January 2024.

public procurement; b) the extent of its coverage; and c) the public access to the laws and regulations.[55]

It is important to underscore the following legal facts:

1. The profile of innovation in award procedures in Egypt, Kuwait, and Dubai in PPP projects is significant in PPP legislation and regulation. A fair assessment of the quality and effectiveness of the PPP procurement system in Egypt, Dubai, and Kuwait, the OECD MAPS is of special significance as in most cases, PPP MENA legislation has implemented OECD principles in award procedures. The review of the legislative and regulatory frameworks in MENA countries as well as the World Bank Benchmarking Report on PPP Procurement 2017, shows that MENA legislation and regulations have implemented the internationally accepted good practices. Such practices reflect the trend to achieve unification of contract law principles, whether public or private (commercial) contracts. Further, the developments of PPP award procedures in MENA countries have direct positive impact on the inward of foreign investments to MENA countries as well as the potential significant improvements on the socio-economic life of citizens.
2. OECD Recommendation of the Council on Public Procurement, advises to harmonize public procurement principles across the spectrum of public services delivery, as appropriate, including for public works, public-private partnerships, and concessions. When delivering services under a wide array of arrangements with private-sector partners, adherents should ensure as much consistency as possible among the frameworks and institutions that govern public services delivery to foster efficiency for the government and predictability for private-sector partners. It is clear that Arab PPP legislation, as a unified legislative approach, eliminates the application of the states' procurement legislation in Egypt, Kuwait, and Dubai and applies the current promulgated PPP legislation.[56]

   The World Bank Benchmarking Public-Private Partnership Procurement Report 2017 pointed out that:

'The PPP Procurement thematic area explores a range of elements that spread throughout the procurement process, such as bidders' access to procurement-related information, the clarity and comprehensiveness of the procurement documents, the qualification of bid evaluation committee members, the bid selection criteria used, the way governments deal with cases of sole proposals, and the restriction on negotiation during the award phase. The recognized good practices that could be drawn from the areas covered in the procurement of PPP projects are summarized in Box 3

55 OECD MAPS, 2016, sub-indicator 1 (a), the scope of application and coverage of the legislative and regulatory framework, pp.10–11.

56 OECD, *Recommendation of the Council on Public Procurement*, p. 13.

Box 3 Good practices in the procurement of PPPs, which help to ensure fair competition and transparency during the PPP procurement process, are:

- The bid evaluation committee members meet minimum technical qualifications.
- The procuring authority publishes the public procurement notice on-line.
- The procuring authority grants at least 30 calendar days to potential bidders to submit their proposals.
- The tender documents detail all the stages of the procurement process: Assessing Government Capability to Prepare, Procure and Manage PPPs.
- Potential bidders can submit questions to clarify the public procurement notice and/or the request for proposals and the answers are disclosed to all potential bidders.
- Bidders prepare and present a financial model with their proposal.
- The procuring authority evaluates the proposals strictly and solely in accordance with the evaluation criteria stated in the tender documents.
- The procuring authority follows a specific procedure in the case that only one proposal is submitted to guarantee '*value for money*.'
- The procuring authority publishes the award notice on-line.
- The procuring authority provides all bidders with the results of the PPP procurement process including the grounds for the selection of the winning bid.
- Any negotiations between the selected bidder and the procuring authority after the award and before the signature of the PPPs contract are restricted and regulated to ensure transparency.
- The procuring authority publishes the signed PPPs contract online.[57]

It is clear that PPP legislation in Egypt, Kuwait, and Dubai has implemented most of the above-mentioned procedures suggested by the World Bank PPPs Benchmarking Report in 2017. It is suggested that most of the MENA countries who are progressing with the promulgation of new PPP legislation have to adopt the above-mentioned procedures. This is the sign of unification of PPP contract law principles in Egypt and the MENA countries. Such unification is consistent with the global principles of contact law.

4. In some economies, procuring authorities can also use a 'competitive dialogue' procedure, which involves more extensive engagements with two or more bidders as they prepare their proposals. In this procedure, bidders submit technical proposals, which are then subject to feedback and discussion with the procuring authority. These discussions allow them to align their proposals with the

57 The World Bank, *Benchmarking Public-Private Partnership Procurement*, p. 32: Assessing Government Capability to Prepare, Procure and Manage PPPs 2017, op. cit., available at: https://ppp.worldbank.org/public-private-partnership/sites/ppp.worldbank.org/files/documents/Benchmarking_PPPs_2017_ENpdf.pdf., last accessed on 7 January 2024.

authority's needs before they submit a final proposal. In 45% of the surveyed economies, competitive dialogue either is allowed by law or takes place in practice. The latter case can be seen in Bangladesh, Canada, Jamaica, Myanmar, and the United States. Even where competitive dialogue is possible, its content and results are not always disclosed to all potential bidders, as in Egypt, where there are no requirements for such disclosure of information.[58] The OECD Recommendation of the Council on Public Procurement pointed out that the government should engage in transparent and regular dialogues with suppliers and business associations to present public procurement objectives and to assure a correct understanding of markets. Effective communication should be conducted to provide potential vendors with a better understanding of the country's needs, and government buyers with information to develop more realistic and effective tender specifications by better understanding market capabilities. Such interactions should be subject to due fairness, transparency, and integrity safeguards, which vary depending on whether an active procurement process is ongoing. Such interactions should also be adapted to ensure that foreign companies participating in tenders receive transparent and effective information.[59]

5. It is suggested that in PPP MENA legislation, award procedures should insist upon using technologies which are friendly to the environment. The transfer of technology during recent decades is playing a significant role in facilitating the cultural and legal globalization process. It allows the application of new techniques in public procurements in PPP. Furthermore, international public works agreements, nowadays, play an important role in spreading environmentally friendly technologies from developed states to developing nations.[60] Environmental legislation stipulations currently tend to be an integral and compulsory part of tender documents. Hamilton pointed out an example in Canada (Vancouver city efforts to reduce emissions in 2001) where there was a private partner who financed, designed, built, owned, and operated a landfill and a 2.9 km pipeline to take gas from the landfill to a nearby agricultural complex, where they built a common power generating plant. The latter plant

58 The World Bank, Benchmarking Public-Private Partnerships Procurement, Benchmarking PPP Procurement: Assessing Government Capability to Prepare, Procure and Manage PPPs 2017, 37, available at: https://ppp.worldbank.org/public-private-partnership/sites/ppp.worldbank.org/files/documents/Benchmarking_PPPs_2017_ENpdf.pdf., last accessed on 7 January 2024.

59 OECD, *Recommendation of the Council on Public Procurement*, p. 9.

60 Methane is of special concern since it generates a global warming effect 23 times that of CO_2. For details on the role of PPPs in mitigating climate change and increasing FDI, *see* Geoffrey Hamilton, *FDI – the Global Crisis and Sustainable Recovery,* Working Paper for Public Private Partnerships, and *FDI as a Means of Securing a Sustainable Recovery* (paper submitted to the Fourth Columbia International Investment Conference, Vale Columbia Centre, Columbia Law School, Columbia University, 5–6 November 2009). For more information, see also: J.D. Sachs, *Common Wealth 'Economics for a Crowded Planet'* (Penguin Books, 2008, ch. 4, 'Global Solutions to Climate Change', pp. 84–114). *See* also: C. Bovis, 'Editorial', in EPPPL, 1/2010; and for the same author, *EC Public Procurement: Case Law and Regulation* (OUP, 2006) and also *The Law of EU Public Procurement* (2nd edn, OUP, 2015); M.A.M. Ismail, *Legal Globalisation and PPPs in Egypt* (EPPPL, 1/2010); Ismail, *Globalization and New International Public Works Agreements in Developing Countries* (Routledge, 2011, ch. 4).

was built by the private partner to generate electricity to supply 5000 homes and to reduce carbon dioxide emission by approximately 200,000 tons per year (emission of about 40,000 cars).

Advanced technologies are a step towards unification of contract law principles to achieve global contract law.

6. An on-line bidding system is not fully existing in Arab countries, however, using technology and Artificial Intelligence (AI) in award procedures is growing as it is one of the tools of the current legal globalization phenomenon in MENA countries. It is suggested that using a fully automated system in on-line bidding is one of the guarantees to achieve best practices in award procedures, particularly maintaining objectivity, integrity, and avoiding bureaucracy. Further, a fully automated bidding process guarantees the transnational character of PPP transactions which is a significant step towards the unification of contract law principles.
7. Only about 15% of the world economies have an issue of sole bidders being regulated with greater detail. In those economies, the law mandates a special procedure that needs to be followed before awarding PPP projects. This is the case, for example, in Egypt, where the regulatory framework specifies the conditions and process for accepting sole bids. A single bid may be accepted through a decision by the competent authority based on the recommendation of the bid evaluation committee, after the approval of the Supreme Committee for PPP affairs, if the public interest does not allow for re-tendering procedures, or if re-tendering would be futile, and if the sole bid is technically acceptable and meets the specifications of the tender.[61] As OECD recommendations state, governments should use competitive tendering and limit the use of exceptions and single-source procurement. Competitive procedures should be the standard method for conducting procurement as a means of driving efficiencies, fighting corruption, obtaining fair and reasonable pricing and ensuring competitive outcomes. If exceptional circumstances justify limitations to competitive tendering and the use of single-source procurement, such exceptions should be limited, predefined and should require appropriate justification when employed, subject to adequate oversight taking into account the increased risk of corruption, including by foreign suppliers.[62]

61 The World Bank, Benchmarking Public-Private Partnerships Procurement, Benchmarking PPP Procurement: Assessing Government Capability to Prepare, Procure and Manage PPPs (2017, pp. 35 and 36) available at: https://ppp.worldbank.org/public-private-partnership/sites/ppp.worldbank.org/files/documents/Benchmarking_PPPs_2017_ENpdf.pdf., last accessed on 7 January 2024. The report refers to the situation in Nigeria: 'Similarly, in Nigeria, although the regulatory framework allows for direct negotiation with a sole bidder, it requires the procuring authority to ensure that the bid is technically and financially advantageous compared with market prices and to include, in the record of procurement proceedings, a statement of the grounds for its decision and the circumstances justifying the single-source procurement.'

62 OECD, *Recommendation of the Council on Public Procurement*, Directorate for Public Governance and Territorial Development, p. 8.

The same situation exists in Dubai PPP legislation.

Conclusions

MENA countries which have PPP legislation and regulation have developed public procurement legal instruments and practice comparing it with the traditional public procurement in administrative contracts. PPPs' legislation and regulation in MENA countries have been considerably influenced by the international organizations' recommendations and methodologies in establishing proper legal framework in PPPs' public procurement, which aims at maintaining transparency, accountability, objectivity, equality, fair competition, and integrity. As a result, the profile of innovation in award procedures has significant developments.

Government procurement has considerable economic relevance for the high percentage of the Gross Domestic Product (GDP) in developed and developing countries in both domestic and international levels accounting.[63] Government procurement provisions also play a central role in international trade agreements.[64] As efficiency is one of the main goals for government procurement, the MENA legislatures in Egypt, Kuwait, and Dubai play a significant role in incorporating provisions that promote innovation in the award procedures in their respective PPP legislations. To achieve many targets for MENA governments, PPP legislation in MENA countries has created a new procedural framework for the award of PPP contracts to private sector entities. The new rules are clear in the Egyptian PPP legislation No. 67 of 2010 and its executive regulations, the Kuwaiti PPP Legislation No. 116 of 2014 and its executive regulations, and the Dubai PPP legislation No. 22 of 2015.

Innovation in public procurements in PPP legislation in Egypt, Kuwait, and Dubai, shows the unification of PPP contracts in the procedural phase. It is important to note that many MENA countries have already initiated the promulgation of their respective PPP legislation, which are similar to Egypt, Kuwait, and Dubai. For instance, the Kingdom of Bahrain is about to enact its PPP legislation to encourage the inflow of FDI to various economic sectors as well as many other MENA countries.

It is clear that there are unified PPP contract law principles in Egypt and MENA countries, which are consistent with international commercial contracts' principles. Establishing global contract law theory and practice is underway despite public law contracts' constraints.

The Financial Equilibrium of PPP Contracts and the Current PPP Legislation in the MENA Countries: A Sign for Unification!

MENA countries' PPP legislation have adopted new ideologies in state contracts which were not known in traditional concessions and administrative contracts. These ideologies represent an increasing approach towards the liberalization of

63 G.M. Racca, R.C. Perin, and G.L. Albano, Competition in the Execution Phase of Public Procurement, *Public Contract Law Journal*, 41(1), fall 2011, p. 92.

64 G.M. Racca, ibid, p. 93, et seq.

the administrative contracts' traditional theory, and represent an attempt to maintain the financial equilibrium of the PPP contract through new mechanisms which allow the contracting authority to re-adjust contract price through direct negotiations and to avoid litigation or arbitration as a dispute settlement mechanism, to try to achieve financial equilibrium. Direct negotiations with the contracting authority are more rapid and flexible processes than litigation and arbitration. The process of negotiations process is less costly. It is worth noting that a comparison between the civil codes' approach in the MENA countries and the administrative judiciary approach on one hand and the PPP legislation approach on the other hand, shows the significant progress in the legislature approach in dealing with the unforeseen circumstances as legislative tool, and the Prince Theory as judicial tool, to maintain financial equilibrium in state contracts. The contracting authority maintains financial equilibrium without recourse to any disputes' settlement mechanisms.

The Egyptian PPP Law pointed out that in case of the occurrence of unforeseen circumstances, after starting performance of the PPP contract, including amendments to laws or regulations that were enforceable at the time of performance of the PPP contract, it may be agreed to amend the PPP contract in accordance with the conditions and rules stipulated in such a contract. [65]

PPP law in Dubai stipulates that a PPP contract may be amended according to the basis and rules of unforeseen circumstances; administrative decrees which issued to implement this law shall clarify the rules to apply the unforeseen circumstances theory, how to compensate the private partner, and how to amend the PPP contract.[66]

The Kuwaiti PPP law pointed out that the amendment of the partnership agreement may be agreed upon in accordance with the principle and the rules provided for under the agreement, if unforeseen circumstances occurred after the conclusion of the Partnership Agreement, including amendments to the laws in force at the time of conclusion of this agreement, and leading to a financial imbalance of the agreement.[67]

The Morocco PPP law provides that the contracting parties have the right to maintain the financial equilibrium of the contract in case of *force majeure* or unforeseen circumstances.[68]

The Tunisian PPP law stipulates that the partnership contract is concluded between a public person and a project company for a duration, taking into account in particular the depreciation period of the investments to be made, and the financing methods selected. The contract of partnership is not renewable. Exceptionally, the contract may be extended for a maximum of three years in cases of emergency, to ensure the continuity of the public service, in the case of *force majeure*, or during

65 The Egyptian PPP Law, 2010, Article 8.

66 Dubai PPP Law, 2015, Article 31.

67 Kuwaiti PPP Law, 2014, Article 36.

68 Morocco PPP Law, 2014, Article 17: '*Droit au maintien de l'équilibre du contrat en cas d'évènements imprévus ou de force majeure.*'

the occurrence of unpredictable events, after the notice conformity of the General Public Partnership Authority referred to in Article 38 of this Law.[69]

The legislative policy behind the above-mentioned provisions contained in PPP legislation in the MENA countries, which shows unification of legislative approaches of substantive principles relating to frustration of contract, is to achieve the following:

- Maintain the financial equilibrium of the PPP contract regarding the fact that the implementation of the contractual undertakings is usually for a long duration.
- In such long duration, unpredictability many occur, in particular the local currency depreciation, raw material price change, in addition to many other economic and financial factors.
- The main outcome of this new legislative approach, which is different from the traditional approach of the unforeseen circumstances' theory in the MENA countries' civil codes, is how the private partner can achieve the contractual equilibrium without recourse to litigation or arbitration. The contractual equilibrium may be achieved through direct negotiations between the contracting parties.
- The target of the direct negotiations between the contracting parties is to readjust contract price, to maintain the regularity of public utilities and services, which aims to achieve the best practice of the legal principle of running the public utility with regularity and continuity.
- The encouragement of the flow of FDI into the MENA countries is of great significance in the views of PPP legislation, as it is one of the main targets to adopt PPP techniques in legislation, and to subject them in practice for many years even before the promulgation of the PPP legislation in the MENA countries.
- It is important to note that financial equilibrium must be maintained for both contracting parties; the contracting authority and the private partner. If the financial equilibrium is maintained for the private partner and not for contracting authority this may be described as a positive discrimination in favor of the private partner. In a PPP contract, which is a long-term agreement, the financial equilibrium has to be maintained in favor of both the private partner and the contracting authority, in order not to violate the financial and economic

69 Tunisian PPP Law, 2015, Article 17 reads as follows '*Art. 17 - Le contrat de partenariat est conclu entre la personne publique et la société du projet pour une durée déterminée en tenant compte notamment de la durée d'amortissement des investissements à réaliser et des modalités de financement retenues. Le contrat de partenariat n'est pas renouvelable. Exceptionnellement, le contrat peut être prorogé pour une durée maximale de trois ans dans les cas d'urgence pour assurer la continuité du service public, dans le cas de force majeure ou lors de la survenance d'évènements imprévisibles, et ce, après l'avis conforme de l'instance générale de partenariat public privé mentionnée à l'article 38 de la présente loi.' Journal Officiel de la République Tunisienne – 1er décembre 2015*, no. 96, p. 2857.

expectations of the private entity, and it has to be maintained for the contracting authority to achieve public interests.

- PPP legislation in the MENA countries maintains an easy, flexible, and rapid process for the modifications to the PPP contracts, which aim at achieving financial equilibrium and the fair economic expectations of both contracting parties.[70]
- It is worth noting that the Egyptian Supreme Administrative Court supersedes party autonomy principle and its leading judgments, on many occasions, decided that state contract clauses prevail if these contractual clauses contradict any legislation or regulation.[71] However, it is understood, in any legal system, that contractual clauses may not contradict any mandatory rule in any valid legislation of the host state, as mandatory legislative rules are relating to public policy.
- PPP legislation when regulating the unforeseen circumstances theory, in a way which is different to MENA countries' civil codes, introduces a sign of unification of PPP contract substantive clauses. Such a sign assures that the dynamics and substantive clauses of the PPP contract are similar to international commercial contracts' principles.
- It is suggested that PPP rules, whether procedural or substantive, pave the way for the integration of states' international contracts into the global system of international commercial contract law, to achieve global substantive contract law for both public and private law contracts.

Conclusions

The trajectory of the states' intervention in PPP legislation and regulation shows an increasing trend by the MENA countries in the current years to intervene towards the codification of PPP techniques in the MENA countries' legal systems. Even though this intervention contradicts the principles of the Chicago school in economics which minimizes state intervention, this intervention from MENA states through legislation and regulation is clear evidence that, unlike traditional concessions, MENA states relinquish the role of the employer in favor of being only a regulator. This is a unified approach by Egypt and all MENA countries.

70 In contract modifications in the UK see: Katie Smith, A risk worth taking? Practical application of the law on contract modifications in the context of PPP accommodation projects, *Public Procurement Law Review, P.P.L.R.* (2019, pp.1, 16–25); and S. Arrowsmith, *The Law of Public and Utilities Procurement* (3rd edn, Vol.1, Sweet & Maxwell, 2014, pp. 597–604); K. Hartlev and M.W. Liljenbol, Changes to existing contracts under the EU Public Procurement Rules and the drafting of review clauses to avoid the need for a new tender (PPLR 22 (2013),pp. 51–73 on review clauses); S.T. Poulsen, The possibilities of amending a public contract without a new competitive tendering procedure under EU law' (PPLR (2012) 21, pp. 167–87).

71 The Egyptian Supreme Administrative Court, Case No. 9559 of the Judicial Year 47, session 20 December 2005.

Unification of PPP procedural and substantive rules, through legislation and regulations, is a significant step towards the unification of substantive principles of states' contracts, to be consistent with international commercial contracts, and to create global contract law. Therefore, the following remarks are concluded:

- Many MENA countries have codified PPP legislation such as Egypt 2010, Kuwait, Morocco 2014, Jordan 2014 as amended in 2020, Dubai 2015, and Tunisia 2015. This trajectory by legislative intervention is supported by a detailed regulatory framework and new modified polices in many MENA countries, which reflect the profile of innovation in award procedures in PPPs on the procedural grounds and how far PPP techniques are consistent with the socio-economic targets and the UN SDGs in practice.
- It is worth noting that PPP legislation in Egypt 2010, Kuwait 2014, Morocco 2014, Jordan 2014 as amended 2020, Dubai 2015, and Tunisia 2015 that is currently promulgated by MENA countries' parliaments, is the direct result of legal globalization phenomenon.[72]
- Innovation in the award procedures shows how PPPs can improve life, infrastructure, and public services in MENA countries.
- The new PPP legislation supports the innovation in substantive rules in the PPP contracts, which represent a considerable step towards the liberalization of the administrative contract, in particular traditional concessions from the rigid excessive clauses (*'Les clauses exorbitantes'*). There is an increasing trend towards unification of contract law principles, in particular PPP contracts, not only in the event of unforeseen circumstances, but also in other substantive aspects.
- MENA states' intervention reflects the high degree of flexibility in the economic ideology and legislative policy behind promulgating economic legislation, as PPP legislation is one of the most significant steps from the economic angle, because it represents the increasing trend for MENA countries to permit private sector participation in the public utilities and infrastructure projects. The economic ideology behind promulgating such liberal economic legislation is clear in the MENA constitutions and it has been implemented in the current MENA PPP legislation. This is a unified approach by Egypt and other MENA governments.
- States' intervention through legislation and regulation to permit PPP techniques and to formulate new policies in public utilities, services and infrastructure projects plays a considerable role to enhance the MENA countries' ranking in the international financial institutions' reports. MENA countries

72 Latin American states have remarkable legislative policies towards encouraging Foreign Direct Investment (FDI) in the infrastructure and services sectors, particularly through PPP techniques. FDI has significantly increased in Latin America, particularly before the economic crises of 2008, in Brazil and many Latin America developing states in infrastructure projects and after promulgation of the 2004 PPP Brazilian Act. For details, see: Cecilia Vidigal Monteira De Barros, PPPs in Brazil, *International Construction Law Review* 26, Part 2 (2009), pp. 180–1.

are exercising new polices to create a new environment that promotes high threshold of protection to foreign investments, and maintain better investments' atmosphere which facilitates the increase of inflow of FDI to MENA countries.

- MENA states' intervention through legislation and regulation to permit the participation of the private sector in public utilities, services, and infrastructure projects, through PPP techniques, is a remarkable step towards the implementation of 2030 vision goals in MENA countries. Many countries at the MENA region have established legal and economic frameworks and a chronology to achieve the 2030 vision goals. The role of states' intervention in economic life has been considerably reduced. The interplay between the international dynamics and the unification of PPP contracts' principles in Egypt and the MENA countries is a reality.
- It is important to refer to the fact that many MENA countries are underway to promulgate new PPPs legislation. The Kingdom of Bahrain is on the way to promulgate new PPP legislation to encourage the inflow of FDI to various economic sectors, and to subject PPP techniques to achieve the UN SDGs, towards the implementation of 2030 economic vision. PPP started in practice in the Kingdom of Bahrain many years ago and yet legislation has not been promulgated.
- In light of the above-mentioned remarks, unification of procedural and substantive principles of PPP contracts, to be consistent with international commercial contracts' principles, is a fundamental step underway to achieve global contract law principles, in theory and in practice.
- It is clear that there are unified PPP contract law principles in Egypt and MENA countries, which are consistent with international commercial contracts' principles and dynamics. Establishing global contract law theory and practice, in public and private contracts, is underway in the MENA countries, despite public law constraints in the respective jurisdictions.

Energy Concessions in Egypt

Oil and Gas Industry in Egypt, an Overview

Oil and gas are one of the most dynamic industries in Egypt as they represented around 13.6% of total GDP in 2018. Egypt has significant energy resources, both in traditional fossil fuels and in renewable energy. Egypt's proven hydrocarbon reserves stood at 3.3 billion barrels of oil and 77.2 trillion cubic feet of natural gas at the end of 2018. The Egyptian government encourages international oil companies ('multinational oil companies') to participate in the oil and gas sector, and currently more than 50 international oil companies are operating in Egypt. Egypt plays a vital role in international energy markets through the operations of the two Suez Canal transit points and the Suez-Mediterranean (SUMED) pipeline. Expanded in 2015, the Suez Canal is an important transit route for oil and Liquefied Natural Gas (LNG) shipments traveling southbound from North Africa and along the Mediterranean Sea to Asia. Egypt plans to invest around $38 billion developing its petrochemicals sector over the next four years. The petrochemical sector represents about 12% of industrial production and generates revenues totaling USD 7 billion, equivalent to nearly 3% of GDP. Egypt has the largest refinery capacity in Africa at a nominal 840,000 barrels per day, although it operates well below this capacity, with 508,000 barrels per day processed in 2017. Currently, the government is updating existing refineries, and a new private sector refinery is also set to begin production.

Egypt has discovered large gas reserves in the Eastern Mediterranean, including its Zohr field, to consolidate its position as a regional energy hub. In a deal estimated to be $20 billion, a consortium of Houston-based Noble Energy, Israel's Delek Drilling, and Egypt's Dolphinus Holdings Ltd, has started pumping natural gas from the Tamar and Leviathan fields in Israel to Egypt in early 2020. In addition, Egypt has concluded an agreement with Cyprus to build a subsea pipeline between the two countries. Egypt plans to use imported gas for domestic use and re-export to global markets through its LNG facilities on the Mediterranean coast. In December 2017, Egypt's Zohr gas field started production. The Zohr field is considered the largest discovery ever made in the Mediterranean Sea. Production is estimated at 30 trillion cubic feet. There is also the Nooros Gas Field in the Nile Delta that produces 32 million cubic meters per day. Atoll is another gas field in the East Delta that produces 350 million cubic meters per day and 10,000 barrels of condensate.[73]

It is worth noting that Egypt has signed around 83 oil and gas exploration deals with international oil companies between November 2013 and February 2020, worth about USD 15.5 billion. It has also offered signing bonuses of more than USD 1 billion for the drilling of 319 wells. In 2020, nine petroleum agreements were signed for oil and natural gas exploration with a minimum investment of around $452.3 million in the Mediterranean and Western Desert regions. U.S. energy giants like ExxonMobil and Chevron entered Egypt's dynamic upstream sector in 2019 and won additional concessions in early 2020. The Egyptian government's investment in natural gas was expanded by 25% in the fiscal year of 2017, adding to an expansion of 33% from the previous fiscal year. Crude oil projects did not see a similar favorable return on investment, but several multinational firms announced commitments to increase their investment to total USD 10 billion in fiscal year 2018/2019.[74]

Developments in State Contracts' Legal Framework in Egypt

It can be said that the rigid patterns of administrative contracts as well as their substance and exorbitant features have significantly changed in the last decades in the civil law legal culture, particularly in Egypt and the MENA countries, especially in oil and/or gas agreements with foreign private entities. These new legal patterns such as

73 Department of Commerce, United States of America, the official website of the International Trade Administration, available at: www.trade.gov/energy-resource-guide-egypt-oil-and-gas, last accessed on 24 December 2023.

74 Please visit: www.trade.gov/energy-resource-guide-egypt-oil-and-gas, last accessed on 24 December 2023.

the introduction of the new International Public Works Agreements; Build, Operate, Transfer (BOT); Build, Own, Operate and Transfer (BOOT); and PPP transactions represented the start of a new era in Egyptian legal culture – one with unique, liberal mechanisms and stipulations. Further, oil and gas agreements concluded between Egypt and private foreign entities have developed remarkably regarding the substantive contractual clauses and mechanisms which aim to offer a higher threshold of protection to foreign investors. Such mechanisms are consistent with global developments in contract law, whether public or private contracts. Legal and cultural globalization phenomena have had their influence on legislation, litigation, and the contractual regime of the administrative contract, in both developed countries and in developing countries.

Egypt and MENA countries' constitutions have adopted significant developments and interpretations regarding state tools and mechanisms of contracting, whether through domestic or international contracts. As Adam Smith pointed out, the state role has to be confined to its basic functions. In light of Adam Smith's views, MENA countries' constitutions have not adopted a specific economic ideology. MENA countries' constitutions have adopted a dynamic economic ideology which enables states to change their economic model from a socialist model to a free market economy model to adapt the international market's dynamic theories and practices, as was the case in Egypt. Meanwhile, the political ideology in the MENA countries' constitutions is static. The legal framework of state contracts in the MENA countries has significantly developed whether in legislation, regulation, polices, or in contractual patterns.[75] This is an attempt to explore the new developments in the constitutional framework of oil and gas concession contracts in light of the Egyptian and MENA countries' constitutions, and how such developments play a vital role towards achieving coherent global contract law.

The Constitutional Framework of Administrative Contracts in Egypt and the MENA Countries: Historical Background

The influence of the French Constitution of the Fifth Republic 1958 upon the previous Egyptian Permanent Constitution of 1971 was clear, in particular the fundamental (core) rights and liberties in the latter Constitution.[76]

The current Egyptian Constitution of 2014 has not adopted a specific economic ideology and has left the door open to the parliamentary and presidential elections

75 Egypt and MENA governments may enter into administrative contracts and private law contracts to achieve public interests. State contracts' term extends to include both types of contracts. See Sarwat Badawi, *Administrative Contracts* (Dar Al Nahda Al Arabia, 1988, in Arabic).

76 Fathy Fekry, *Constitutional Law* (Dar Al Nahda Al Arabia, 2009, in Arabic). For more elaboration see: Mohamed A.M. Ismail, *Arab Constitutions Facts and Prospects* (Al Halabi Publishing, Beirut, 2015, in Arabic); Sarwat Badawi, *Administrative Law* (Dar El Nahdah El Arabia, 1985, in Arabic) and for the same author see: *Administrative Contracts* (Dar El Nahdah El Arabia, 1988, in Arabic). See also: Soliman El Tamawy, *General Principles of Administrative Contracts* (5th edn, 1991, in Arabic).

to determine the economic pattern which governs economic life in Egypt during the presidential or parliamentary term.[77]

The Egyptian constitutional system has greatly influenced MENA countries' legal systems and transferred French civil law legal culture to MENA countries. Further, MENA countries' legal systems have been considerably indirectly influenced by the French legal culture in particular the French Constitution of 1958 and the French Napoleonic Codes through the flow of French legal culture from Egypt to MENA countries. The Egyptian Civil Code was influenced by the French Civil Code. MENA countries' civil codes were greatly influenced by the Egyptian Civil Code.

The economic ideology in Egypt and MENA countries' constitutions governs the concept of state contracting, particularly how the state can enter into administrative contracts with domestic or international entities. The question arises in both kinds of contracts; private contracts and administrative contracts, as the latter contracts' constraints and exorbitant clauses exist in the Egyptian and MENA countries' legal culture. In Egyptian and the MENA countries' legal culture, public contracts, which are in the majority of cases administrative contracts, contain excessive clauses. The purpose of the excessive clauses in administrative contracts is to achieve public interest.

The Constitutional Framework of Natural Resources' Concessions in Egypt and the MENA Countries

It is important to differentiate between natural resources particularly oil and/or gas concessions on one hand and PPPs on the other hand, in light of MENA countries' constitutional perspective. The previous Egyptian Constitution of 1971 stipulated that all natural resources concessions must be granted by law in each concession (not pursuant to law).[78] Each concession of oil and/or gas or any concession concerning natural resources (such as mining concessions), must be granted by law (legislation) promulgated by the parliament in each case, and not by any regulatory tool which may be issued pursuant to law. The current Constitution of 2014 stipulates the same.[79] Therefore, oil and/or gas concessions in the Egyptian legal system have to

77 In Gulf countries, and through decades, constitutions have not adopted socialists' ideology but left the door open to a wide role for the private sector participation in all economic activities and all economic sectors. This applies to the Kuwait Constitution of 1962, UAE Constitution of 1996, Oman Constitution of 1996, and the Kingdom of Bahrain Constitution of 2002 as amended in 2012. The same vision exists in the Morocco Constitution 2011, Tunisia Constitution 2014, and Algeria Constitution 2016. Gulf countries' constitutions left the door open to a wide role for the private sector participation in all economic activities and all economic sectors. MENA countries' constitutions adopted free market economy concepts which open doors to private sector participation in all economic sectors.

78 Article 123 of the previous Egyptian Constitution of 1971.

79 Article 32 of the 2014 Constitution reads as follows: 'Natural resources belong to the people. The state commits to preserving such resources, to their sound exploitation, to preventing their depletion, and to take into consideration the rights of future generations to them. The state commits to making the best use of renewable energy resources, motivating investment, and encouraging relevant

be granted by legislation in each case.[80] The constitutional requirement to grant each oil and/or gas concession by law in each case 'not pursuant to law' is justified by the object of the natural resources as they are the property of the nation and also justified by the essential need to promote the right procedures and the proper contractual substantive clauses which achieve public interests and protect the nation's wealth. Promulgating legislation for each concession by the parliament, whether oil and/or gas concession, guarantees that the private party (contractor) selection shall be made through the proper procedures pursuant to public procurement law until the final contract is drafted and promulgated as final legislation (including publication at the Official Gazette). The role of the parliament in promulgating the final contract as a valid legislation is an effective tool to maintain that the best selection of the private party was made by the administration, and the best contractual substantive provisions were drafted to achieve the best contract performance. Oil and/or gas concessions are long-term agreements and the proper performance of the contract depends mainly on the right selection of a highly qualified contractor during the procedural phase and the proper drafting of the contractual clauses throughout the legislative process until the promulgation of the contract as a valid legislation and finally the publication of this legislation at the Official Gazette. Publication of all legislation at the Official Gazette is mandatory requirement in the Egyptian legal system as it is a constitutional requirement for any legislation to be valid after publication.[81]

---

scientific research. The state works on encouraging the manufacture of raw materials, and increasing their added value according to economic feasibility. Disposing of the state's public property is forbidden. Granting the right to exploit natural resources or a concession to a public utility shall take place by law for a period not exceeding 30 years.' It is worth noting that the Kuwaiti Constitution 1962, Article 152 stipulates that 'Any obligation to invest in natural resources or public utilities shall be granted by law and for a limited period of time.' The Omani Constitution 1996, Article 11,'Economic principles,' provides that 'Natural resources and its income are owned by the state which maintains to keep it and offer the best exploitation for it taking into consideration state security constraints and the national economy interests. Granting any concession or investment to any of the country natural resources must be by law, for a certain period of time and consistent with national interests.' The Kingdom of Bahrain's Constitution 2002, as amended in 2012, Article 116 stipulates that 'Any concession to invest a natural resource or a public utility shall be granted by law and for a limited period of time. The preliminary procedures for granting such concession shall facilitate research, disclosure, publicity and competition.' The Tunisian Constitution 2014, Article 13, provides that 'Natural wealth belongs to the Tunisian people, and the state exercises sovereignty over it in its name. Related investment contracts are presented by the competent committee of the parliament. The agreements to be concluded shall be submitted to the parliament for approval.' The Algerian Constitution 2016, Article 19, pointed out that the 'State shall ensure the rational use and conservation of natural resources for the benefit of the coming generations. Legislation shall determine the modalities of application of this article.'

80 In 1958, and before the 1971 Constitution, the Egyptian parliament promulgated law No. 61 of 1958 concerning Natural Resources Concessions stipulating that granting natural resources concessions has to be by presidential decree after the parliament approval.

81 Article 225 of the Egyptian Constitution of 2014 provides that: 'Laws are published in the Official Gazette within 15 days from the date of their issuance, to be effective 30 days from the day following the date of publication, unless the law specifies a different date. Provisions of the laws apply only from the date of their entry into force.' There was a similar constitutional provision in the 1971 Constitution in Article 188.

Promulgating concessions' legislation is subject to the 'procedural criterion' of promulgating any legislation in the Egyptian legal system as promulgating concession agreements has to pass through all procedural steps which are required to promulgate any other legislation.[82] Amendments to concession legislation such as price formula ('contract price') have to be done by legislation in each case. Each amendment by legislation is considered a new legislation which has to follow all procedural steps that are required to promulgate any other legislation.[83] One of the important substantive clauses in oil and/or gas concessions is a stabilization clause which protects the private contractor from the change of legislation and/or regulations risk, performance cost changes relating to host state intervention that may increase the production costs during contract performance. This costs change may occur in raw material or the increase of the US Dollar's exchange rates against the Egyptian Pound or the change of legislation, if any of these changes affected the financial equilibrium of the concession contract. Unlike other states' contracts,[84] stabilization of contract price in oil and/or gas can be maintained by legislation amendment and not by contract price amendment or separate invoice. Contract price is still a dynamic clause in an oil and/or gas concession contract but any amendment has to be by legislation in each case and with respect to the 'procedural criterion' of the legislation promulgation in the Egyptian legal system. This is the rule of *Parallèlisme des normes* in public law in the Egyptian legal system.

It is settled in the Egyptian legal system that a concession contract, whether it concerns natural resources or not, is an administrative contract.[85] The direct result is that the procedural phase of the contract is subject to the State Contracting legislation No. 182 of 2018. In addition, the contract shall have some exorbitant substantive clauses which do not exist in private law contracts. The aim of exorbitant clauses is to achieve public interests and to protect public funds.

The legal result of this administrative nature of the natural resources' concession contract is that the competent judiciary (if there is no arbitration agreement in the contract) is the Egyptian Conseil D'État administrative courts not the ordinary civil judiciary courts. Secondly, if the parties to the contract agreed to refer their dispute to arbitration, the consent of the competent minister is required before recourse to arbitration, as it is a legislative stipulation in the Egyptian Arbitration Law.[86] Failure to obtain such consent from the competent minister may result that the arbitral tribunal has no jurisdiction to hear the case.

82 In Egypt and MENA countries' legal systems see: M.M. Abul'enein, *Legislative deviation and the Oversight on its Constitutionality* (Dar Al Nahda Al Arabia, 1987, in Arabic).

83 Unlike other state contracts which can amend contract price by contract amendment.

84 Such as public works agreements which contain a stabilization clause that avoids the increase in contract performance costs. Stabilization can be achieved through contract amendments or separate invoice.

85 The Egyptian Supreme Administrative Court, session on 19 March 2007, Case No. 17254 of Judicial Year 52.

86 Article 1 of the Egyptian Arbitration Law No. 27 of 1994 as amended by Law No. 9 of 1997.

Procedural Phase

The procedural phase is of fundamental importance to oil and/or gas concession agreements as the proper selection to the private party (the contractor) in such concession agreements is a fundamental factor to achieve the best contract performance. The best contract performance has a direct impact upon the revenues which the contracting authority earns from concession contracts. In addition, the better contract performance has direct positive results to the national budget.

The award is governed by State Contracting Law No. 182 of 2018 and its executive regulations. This is the valid public procurement legislation in Egypt.[87] There is an innovation in award profile adopted by this new legislation as one of its targets is to achieve objectivity, transparency, fair competition, equal opportunity, equality before law, and non-discrimination. Among many targets, State Contracting legislation aims to achieve UN SDGs. The role of these principles is to select the right private contractor with the state for the best contract performance. The best contract performance assures that the public interest is maintained and the nation's public wealth (oil and gas as natural resources) is protected through offering the best revenues formula to the contracting state.

To select the best private party as a contractor to enter into a concession agreement with the state, the contracting authority follows a strict process through adopting an auction for candidates to submit the best contract price for the contracting authority. This process aims to achieve the highest revenues for the contracting authority. The contracting authority awards the contract to the best technical offer which offers the best contract price (the highest price)[88] to assure that the best contract price formula shall maintain the best revenues to the contracting authority during the contract term. Oil and/or gas concessions are long-term contracts and following an auction process is one of the fundamental procedural guarantees to achieve public interests and protect public funds through better exploitation of natural resources which are the nation's wealth pursuant to the Egyptian constitutions.

87 The previous public procurement legislation in Egypt were: Public Procurement Law No. 9 of 1983 and Public Procurement Law No. 89 of 1998, respectively.

88 The contracting authority (in oil and/or gas sector/s) announces a bid round to all the companies interested in exercising the exploration and exploitation activities in the Egyptian territory. The bidding companies are required to submit to the contracting authority two separate sealed envelopes. The first envelope contains the technical offer and technical qualifications of the bidding company (i.e., the previous exploration experience and activities of the company all over the world including development projects, gas or petroleum production, reserves and the latest technology used, along with the bidding company's annual report). The second envelope contains the financial offer based on which the bidding company, if successful, shall undertake the exploration and exploitation activities. The second envelope will not be opened unless the first envelope, which contains the technical offer of the bidding contractor, is accepted. Pursuant to State Contracting Law (and previous public procurement laws), unlike tenders, the contracting authority in auction awards the contract to the technically accepted offer with the highest price, meanwhile in tenders the contracting authority awards the contract to the technically accepted offer with the lowest price.

This process assures the highest revenues to the contracting authority and national budget throughout the contract term.[89]

The Threshold of Protection Granted to Private Party during Procedural Phase and during Performance Phase

Threshold of Protection during Procedural Phase

The high threshold of protection granted to the private party can be achieved in two ways:

- Investment promotion in Egypt can offer a higher threshold of protection to both domestic and foreign investors.
- How can innovation in award procedures in the Egyptian State Contracting legislation offer a high threshold of protection to both domestic and foreign investors through enhancing the socio-economic life of the citizens?

How Investment Promotion in Egypt Can Offer a Higher Threshold of Protection to Both Domestic and Foreign Investors

With the Egyptian government objectives of (i) fostering an open, transparent and conducive national policy environment for investment, and (ii) promoting inclusive economic growth and sustainable development, the aim of the Egyptian government is:

- Recognizing the critical role of investment as an engine of economic growth in the national economy, investment policies establish open, non-discriminatory, transparent, and predictable conditions for investment.
- Investment policies should provide legal certainty and strong protection to investors and investments, tangible and intangible, including access to effective mechanisms for the prevention and settlement of disputes, as well as to enforcement procedures. Dispute settlement procedures should be fair, open and transparent, with appropriate safeguards to prevent abuse.
- Regulation relating to investment is developed in a transparent manner with the opportunity for all stakeholders to participate, and embedded in an institutional framework based on the rule of law.
- Investment policies and other policies that impact on investment are coherent at both the national and international levels and aim at fostering investment, consistent with the objectives of the UN SDGs and inclusive growth.
- Cooperation between the Egyptian government and the international community should continue to engage in dialogue with a view to maintaining an open and conducive policy environment for investment, and to address shared investment policy challenges.

89 Egypt has signed around 83 oil and gas exploration deals with international oil companies between November 2013 and February 2020, worth about USD 15.5 billion. Please visit: www.trade.gov/energy-resource-guide-egypt-oil-and-gas, last accessed on 24 December 2023.

Oil and/or gas concessions' legislative and regulatory frameworks are fundamental pillars and determining factors in any legal system which can be described as incentives to attract and increase the inward of FDI. There is a direct causality link between the existence of advanced concession contracts' legislative and regulatory frameworks on one hand and the increase of the inward of FDI and the improvement of life of the ordinary citizens in Egypt on the other. The aim to offer higher protection to a private party, in particular if it is a foreign investor, is to encourage and increase the inward of FDI in the energy (natural resources) sector and to enhance the socio-economic pattern of the ordinary citizens.

It is clear that oil and/or gas agreements in Egypt, as well as other MENA countries, have developed to be consistent with the targets of oil and/or gas agreements in the international sphere, and such agreements in Egypt and MENA countries have the same targets and the same impact on the socio-economic aspects, similar to these agreements in the developed countries. This consistency is a considerable step towards achieving global contract law.

How Can Innovation in Award Procedures in The Egyptian State Contracting Legislation Offer a High Threshold of Protection to Both Domestic and Foreign Investors Through Enhancing the Socio-Economic Life of Citizens?

Oil and/or gas concessions' award procedures in the Egyptian State Contracting legislation 2018 aim to create better environment which increases the threshold of protection granted to foreign investors through fighting corruption, and aims consequently to increase incentives for foreign investments which raise the inward of FDI to Egypt. Principles of achieving public interests, integrity, objectivity, equality, equal opportunity, free competition, fair competition, publicity, and transparency are pivotal mechanisms to fight corruption and they are the same principles which procure a better environment to increase the inward of FDI to Egypt. In the Egyptian State Contracting legislation 2018, the Egyptian legislature assures the fundamental importance of the abovementioned principles. It is true that there is an overlapping between the principles which govern award procedures in oil and/or gas legislation in Egypt and principles which attract FDI to Egypt as they are similar principles which are required to maintain clean environment to various economic sectors. Principles for both targets may cooperate to encourage oil and/or gas concessions, socioeconomic developments, increasing productivity, and developing Egyptian economy in various ways.

As award procedures aim to achieve objectivity, integrity, equal opportunity, fair competition, and many other principles, it aims to enhance the life of ordinary citizens in Egypt. Award procedures aim to attain properly structured concession contracts that are more likely to provide better revenues to the national budget and be commercially viable for the private party.

The innovation in award procedures is a pivotal tool to provide a higher threshold of protection to the private party, in particular foreign investors, and enhance the life of Egyptian ordinary citizens as follows:

- Awarding oil and/or gas projects aims to the increase the inward of FDI to Egypt. Increasing the inward of FDI to various economic sectors in Egypt, in particular the oil and/or gas sector, is a fundamental factor to fight unemployment and decrease the unemployment rate. The increase of the unemployment rate in Egypt is a fundamental factor behind the increase of crime and terrorism in the Middle East region. Oil and/or gas projects create hundreds of thousands of job opportunities in Egypt.
- The increase of oil and/or gas projects in Egypt enhances the quality of products and services as in most cases the private party is a huge multinational company which has a unique profile and distinguished experience in the oil and/or gas sector/s worldwide. The private party injects its technological input and modern techniques to achieve the best standards for the running and management of public utilities as these inputs and techniques have direct positive impact to the country.
- The increase of oil and/or gas projects in Egypt maintains sustainable developments in the country which has direct impact to ordinary citizens' lives and standard of living, education, health, and other crucial services offered by Egyptian government.
- The increase of oil and/or gas projects transfers modern and advanced technologies to Egypt through awarding many of these projects to multinational companies.
- Transfer of technology is a pivotal factor to create highly qualified trained expertise and labor in Egypt, as Egyptian citizens will have more job opportunities in oil and/or gas advanced technology projects.
- Egypt will have the opportunity to export qualified and trained labor and expertise to the surrounding MENA countries and to other regions of the world, as a result of awarding oil and/or gas projects in Egypt and its leading role in the MENA region to create highly qualified expertise.
- Awarding oil and/or gas projects would inject billions of hard currencies to Egypt which maintain the stability of the currency exchange rate of the Egyptian Pound against US Dollar in the country as it increases the supply of hard currency in the Egyptian markets against the demand.

The new State Contracting legislation of 2018 is evidence that the quality and effectiveness of the public procurement system in Egypt is maintained. The OECD MAPS[90] is of special significance as in most cases, Egyptian legislation has implemented OECD principles in award procedures. Further, it is concluded that the developments of oil and/or gas concession contracts award procedures in Egypt have direct positive impact on the inward of FDI to Egypt as well as the potentially significant improvements on the socio-economic life of citizens. Further, the Egyptian legal system has many contractual and legislative instruments that offer the private party high threshold of protection.

90 Methodology for Assessing Procurement Systems, 2018, adopted by the OECD.

As a step towards unification of contract law to achieve global contract law, it is clear how innovation in award procedures in the Egyptian State Contracting legislation can offer a high threshold of protection to both domestic and foreign investors through enhancing the socio-economic life of the citizens. Such protection and enhancement are goals of oil and/or gas agreements in Egypt and MENA countries and both goals clarify the extent of unification which is achieved by Egypt and MENA countries. Unification of contract law principles to achieve global contract law is guaranteed as the Egyptian legal system and MENA countries' legal systems are adopting international standards of protection to foreign investors. Egypt and MENA countries are achieving unification of contract law substantive principles in oil and/or gas agreements to be consistent with international commercial contracts. Such unification will not violate the economic expectations of foreign investors as it offers a high threshold of protection to those investors. Adopting international commercial contracts principles in state oil and/or gas contracts provides for a higher threshold of protection to foreign investors as there is a direct causality link between achieving global contract law principles and protecting foreign investors. Both targets of achieving global contract law and protecting foreign investors are interrelated.

Threshold of Protection during Performance Phase (Substantive Protection)

The transfer of risk from the government to the private party does not exceed the 'normal' risk of doing business as various risk factors, if any, are clear to the private party during the auction and public procurement process and before concluding the contract. The Egyptian legal system considers the financial equilibrium of the oil and/or gas concession contract as well as other public and private contracts. The Egyptian Civil Code stipulates that the theory of unexpected circumstances ('*l'imprévision*') is a mandatory rule in the Egyptian legal system.[91] There is no obligation upon the private party to perform even in the situation when performance is onerous or there is no profit. The contractual clauses in all oil and/or gas concession contracts provide a high threshold of protection to foreign investors. One of the most important contractual clauses is a stabilization clause which maintains the financial equilibrium during performance and assures that the private party is covered by a contractual mechanism which aims to reimburse the private party in case of price change in crude material or the increase of the US Dollar's exchange rates against the Egyptian Pound or the change of legislation which may increase the contract performance costs. Whether

91 Article 147/2 of the Egyptian Civil Code stipulates that the contracting parties cannot avoid the application of the theory of unexpected circumstances by their agreement. For instance, see: Article 130 of the Bahrain Civil Code, Article 198 of the Kuwaiti Civil Code, Article 107 of the Algerian Civil Code, Article 249 of the UAE Civil Code, Article 146/2 of the Iraqi Civil Code, Article 171/2 of the Qatar Civil Code, Article 159 of the Omani Civil Code, Article 205 of the Jordanian Civil Code, Article 148 of the Syrian Civil Code, and Article 147/2 of the Libyan Civil Code. All these Arab civil codes consider the application of the theory of unforeseen circumstances as a mandatory rule which is a matter of public policy. Contracting parties cannot ignore or avoid the application of such theory by their contractual agreement and any contractual clause which contains an exemption from the application of such theory is null and void pursuant to these legislative provisions. It is clear that most Arab countries' legislation is following the Egyptian legislation.

the risk which may occur during performance is *de facto* risk or *de jure* risk, the private party is protected by various contractual and legal mechanisms (contractual, legislative or the Conseil D'État case law) as follows:

- One of the most important contractual clauses is the stabilization clause which maintains the financial equilibrium during performance and assures that the private party is covered by a contractual mechanism which aims to reimburse the private party in case of price change in crude material or the increase of the US Dollar's exchange rates against the Egyptian Pound or the change of legislation and/or regulations which may increase the contract performance costs.
- Article 147/2 of the Egyptian Civil Code stipulates that the contracting parties cannot avoid the application of the theory of unexpected circumstances. The administration has to compensate the private party if the contract performance becomes onerous. The compensation has to be awarded through a court final judgment or an arbitral award. The civil law is applicable because the 'contract theory' in the civil code (as a source of obligation in the Egyptian and MENA countries' civil codes) is the base and source of administrative contracts' theory as the latter substantive principles exist in the Egyptian and MENA countries civil codes with some exceptional rules which belong to the administrative contracts, and consistent with the nature and aims of such contracts as these contracts deal with public interests and public utilities.
- Investment legislation[92] and its executive regulations: Egyptian investment law offers many incentives and guarantees to investments whether domestic or foreign investments.
- Egyptian Arbitration Law No. 27 of 1994 as it constitutes the legislative framework for commercial arbitration whether domestic or international.
- Multilateral legislative instruments (multilateral treaties): 1) Washington Convention, Convention on the Settlement of Investment Disputes Between States and Nationals of Other States, 1965, as one of the most important international instruments which offers high threshold of protection to foreign investors in Egypt.[93] 2) New York Convention on the Recognition and Enforcement of Foreign Arbitral Awards, also known as the 'New York Arbitration Convention' or the 'New York Convention,' 1958.[94]
- Bilateral Investment Treaties (BITs): Egypt has ratified more than 115 BITs.[95] BITs offer a high threshold of protection to foreign investors as they can recourse to ICSID[96] arbitration (investment arbitration) in case of any investment dispute.

92 Law No. 72 of 2017.

93 Egypt has ratified the Washington Convention on 3 May 1972 and the Convention entered into force in Egypt as a valid legislation on 2 June 1972. Please visit: https://treaties.un.org/pages/showDetails.aspx?objid=080000028012a925, last accessed on 24 December 2023.

94 Egypt has ratified the New York Convention 1958 on 9 March 1959. Please visit: www.newyorkconvention.org/list+of+contracting+states, last accessed on 24 December 2023.

95 https://investmentpolicy.unctad.org/international-investment-agreements/countries/62/egypt, last accessed on 24 December 2023.

96 The International Center for the Settlement of Investment Disputes.

- Case law of the Egyptian Supreme Administrative Court[97] in frustration of contract. The Court applies the theory of '*le fait du prince dans les contrats administratifs*' and the theory of unexpected circumstances. Principles of both theories are well established since the establishment of the Court in 1955.[98] Egyptian Courts award full compensation in the case of '*le fait du prince dans les contrats administratifs* ' and partial compensation in the case of unexpected circumstances.[99]

It is important to note that Article 32 of the Egyptian Constitution of 2014 provides that granting the right to exploit natural resources has to be for a period not exceeding 30 years.

Conclusions

It is suggested that oil and/or gas concession contracts in the Egyptian legal system currently have a hybrid/mixed legal nature as they are not pure traditional administrative contracts, due to the international changes in contract law. The influence of legal and cultural globalization phenomena is clear upon reducing the power of the state and reducing the exorbitant clauses in the contract; therefore, it is suggested that the consent of the competent minister is not required before recourse to arbitration as this legislative stipulation exists in the Egyptian Arbitration Law for only pure administrative contracts.[100] If the contract is a private law contract and does not have the administrative nature, the competent minister's consent is not required.[101] It is clear that concession contracts having hybrid/mixed legal nature are a step to achieve the unification of contract law principles and to narrow the gaps between private and public contracts. Public law barriers are beginning to deteriorate.

97 The Supreme Administrative Court is at the top of the hierarchy of the Egyptian judicial system and at the top of the judicial section of the Egyptian Conseil D'État.

98 As the administrative law substantive principles 'in administrative contracts and administrative decrees' are not yet codified until present, the Egyptian Supreme Administrative Court created, through decades, the substantive principles of administrative law in the absence of written legislation in most cases. Therefore, the Egyptian Supreme Administrative Court has invented both theories in public contracts.

99 To distinguish between both theories, see: The Supreme Administrative Court, session on 27 October 2020, Case No. 58619 of Judicial Year 62.

100 Article 1 of the Egyptian Arbitration Law as amended by law No. 9 of 1997.

101 The same legislative stipulation, but with some modifications, is required before recourse to arbitration in administrative contracts, is provided in Qatar Arbitration Law 2017. Meanwhile, The Saudi Arbitration Law 2012 stipulates in Article 10/2 that any public juristic entity before recourse to arbitration has to obtain the prime minister's consent (whether the dispute is contractual or otherwise and if it is contractual whether the dispute concerns administrative contract or private law contract).

5 Digitalization as A Tool to Achieve Global Contract Law in State Contracts

Introduction

This chapter focuses upon digitalization of public contracts which is, in the legal globalization phenomenon era, playing significant role in the unification of international states' contracts principles and is a fundamental tool to achieve unified contract law principles in both public and private (commercial) contracts. The aim of digitalization, in addition to other targets, is to achieve unified substantive contract law principles, whether in public or private (commercial) contracts. The chapter answers important questions which are: How can digitalization of public contracts create unification in substantive principles in both public and private (commercial) contracts in the international sphere? How can global contract law principles be achieved through digitalization, in light of removing the barriers between private law (commercial law) principles and public law constraints? This chapter is an attempt to highlight the significance of digitalization of public contracts in the MENA countries as implementation of such digitalization is fundamental to public contracts' reform. Such implementation will achieve remarkable advantages in the procedural phase, which is consistent with the developments of the new contractual patterns that signify the new hybrid/*dual* legal nature of '*Le contrat administratif*' traditional theory. The chapter focuses particularly on globalization and its impact upon '*Le contrat administratif*' through a successful digitalization process in Egypt and the Gulf States, in particular United Arab Emirates, the Kingdom of Bahrain, and Kuwait. It provides an in-depth analysis of the current trends in the MENA countries to adopt the free-market economy disciplines and to assess the emergence of the trends of the partnerships between public and private sectors[1] along with the current theory of compatibility with the fundamental principles

1 In public-private partnership (PPP) contracts in the MENA countries see: Mohamed A.M. Ismail, *Public Private Partnership Contracts, the Middle East and North Africa* (Routledge, 2020); and in public-private partnerships in Egypt in particular see: Said Hanafi and Khaled El Dardiry, PPPs in Egypt (ICLR 27, Part 4, Informa, Oct. 2010, pp. 432–47). In PPPs in Egypt and Arab doctrine generally see: Mohamed A.M. Ismail, *Public Economic Law and the New International Administrative Contract* (Al Halabi Publishing Co., Beirut, 2010); Ragab Mahmoud, *PPP Agreements, Comparative Study to these Contracts in French Administrative Law* (Dar Al Nahda Al Arabia, 2007), and the second edition, PPPs Agreements (Dar Al Nahda Al Arabia, 2010). For PPPs in Europe see: Christopher Bovis, *Public Private Partnerships in the European Union* (Critical Studies in Public Management, Routledge, 2014).

DOI: 10.4324/9781003466352-6

of the world leading economist Adam Smith[2] and Chicago school[3] in economics. Such a partnership is a fundamental step towards the implementation of a digitalized system for public contracts in the MENA countries. It sheds light on the constitutional developments in the MENA countries and how it is now accepting new economic ideologies to enhance public utilities' performance and to modernize public services to end-users through the intention of implementing a coherent system of digitalization of public contracts. MENA countries' constitutions do not adopt static economic ideologies but they adopt dynamic ideologies which enable legislation and regulation to adapt the new developments in state contracts' theories[4] and to promote new techniques to protect public interests and preserve public funds in these new contractual patterns. The aim of the latter techniques is to achieve the best practices in delivering public services through better management of public utilities. This chapter analyzes how the digitalization of public contracts can enhance procurement legislation and regulation in the MENA region, and how it can achieve public procurement goals and principles which are fundamental tools to achieve UN SDGs[5] and to achieve unification of substantive principles of public and private contracts. Further, it ensures that public procurement legislation in the MENA region achieves international standards and principles as it is stipulated by international organs.[6] It provides a comprehensive evaluation of the policies which underpin the potential digitalization of public contracts in the MENA countries and its compatibility as a legal framework with the international standards of states' public procurements such as the OECD MAPS[7] and the World Bank Benchmarking Report of PPPs' public procurements (2017).[8] Such compatibility is a fundamental step towards unification of global contract law principles.

Digitalization of public contracts in the MENA countries represents a specialist yet significant academic interest in international academia worldwide, and an increasing practice in international business and commercial legal environments. The volume of the market, the relative frequency of public contracts' transactions between the public and private sectors, as well as new developments in the interface between public and private sectors (public-private partnerships) amplify the

2 Adam Smith, *Wealth of Nations* (Wordsworth edition, 2012).

3 For the Chicago school see: Milton Friedman, *Milton Friedman on Economics, Selected Papers* (University of Chicago Press, 2008).

4 For the same concept in new PPP techniques in Egypt and the MENA countries see: Mohamed A.M. Ismail, *Legal Globalization and PPPs in Egypt* (EPPPL, Lexxion, 1/2010, pp. 54–67).

5 For the 2030 Agenda for Sustainable Developments Goals see: https://sdgs.un.org/2030agenda, last accessed on 27 July 2023.

6 OECD, Methodology for Assessment of the National Procurement System, OECD MAPS, 2018, available at: MAPS-Methodology-for-Assessing-Procurement-Systems.pdf, last accessed on 27 July, 2023 and in PPP procurement see: Benchmarking PPP Procurement Report: Assessing Government Capability to Prepare, Procure and Manage PPPs, The World Bank Group, 2017.

7 OECD MAPS, 2018, available at: MAPS-Methodology-for-Assessing-Procurement-Systems.pdf, last accessed on 27 July 2023.

8 *Benchmarking PPP Procurement Report: Assessing Government Capability to Prepare, Procure and Manage PPPs* (The World Bank Group, 2017).

need for an advanced legal analysis which provides theoretical and conceptual frameworks based on an assessment of the relevant law and jurisprudence in the MENA countries.

The chapter's theme, which has many distinctive features, intends to explore the new potential techniques for digitalization of public contracts to achieve significant changes in the MENA countries' legal and contractual frameworks, which pave the way for the right implementation of the international standards in public procurement legal framework in the region. The chapter's theme highlights the remarkable reform which is expected to public contracts' practices in the MENA countries in light of new digitalization to these contracts. It analyzes, when relevant to the chapter's theme, the '*value for money*' concept in public contracts' various patterns in the MENA countries. It illustrates the prospects of how digital public contracts' legislation and regulation will influence academia in the MENA countries particularly of Egypt and the relevant Gulf States. It aspires in highlighting the main features of the potential reform to public contracts' legislation, regulation, and contractual patterns which reflect transparency, equality before the law, equality before public utilities, fair competition, and fighting corruption. Such reform aims at being consistent with international standards as drawn by the relevant international organs.

The chapter envisages being a unique point of reference on issues pertinent to the current global trend in how to subject technology to serve public interests and save public funds through the implementation of digitalization of public contracts, as follows:

- Artificial intelligence (AI) offers promising opportunities to enhance the problem-solving capability of courts, but it can also have a disruptive effect. This chapter examines the existing landscape of AI tools within administrative legal protection and analyzes their impact on the development of coherent private law substantive rules, in particular Civil Codes, in international state contracts.
- How far are AI techniques subjected to achieve coherent contract law principles in international states' contracts which are consistent with global contract law principles?
- Digitalization is an important tool to enhance the efficiency of states' administrative bodies, particularly in the case of decentralization. It is a fundamental tool to enable states to introduce better services to the public and to achieve rapid and efficient performance of public utilities. Digitalization and subjecting AI in public procurement are tools to achieve better performance in international states' contracts, and to achieve unified substantive principles in such contracts, as digitalization and AI are transnational technological tools which aim to achieve transnational substantive and coherent principles of global contract law.
- It is important for MENA countries to realize the significance of creating digital infrastructure in states' contracts, not only to select the best contractor through an efficient public procurement system and to maintain better performance during the performance phase, but also to create coherent substantive

rules of international states' contracts through transnational and on-line bidding. To what extent are such rules consistent with international commercial contracts in the international sphere?

Digitalization of Public Contracts in the MENA Countries, Why?

The influence of cultural and legal globalization upon '*Le contrat administratif*' is significant and it is fundamental to clarify how the MENA countries have responded to the forces of globalization. As a result of the influence of cultural and legal globalization upon MENA countries' legal systems, there were developments in '*Le contract administratif*' legal system and the digitalization of public contracts in the MENA countries became necessary to enhance public contracts' practices, in particular contracts concerning public utilities and services.

Cultural globalization is a cultural socio-economic phenomenon. The first element that was influenced by globalization was culture. Cultural interaction is the main outcome of the flow of ideas and values into developing countries. Culture represents a set of practices, values, beliefs, and customs acquired by individuals as members of a distinctive society and resulting from interaction among people.[9] The legal globalization phenomenon is part of the cultural globalization movement. Law is a social science that performs an important role as an essential mechanism fulfilling the requirements of all human societies. On one hand, law reflects and represents the mirror image of a society, determines its common interests, and reflects its cultural traditions.[10] On the other hand, globalization has had its influence on various human societies, breaching cultural barriers through the flow of commodities, capital, people, and intangibles such as culture and values from one country to another.[11]

Information technology developments during the last two decades have facilitated the globalization process and intensified cultural interaction, especially legal cultural interaction among legal institutions in the entire world. Rigid and traditional legal patterns and traditions began to accept modifications and enhancements. Some of those patterns began to deteriorate while others created a new legal system with new characteristics as a result of cooperation among legal cultures.[12] Despite globalization movements and the flow of a new legal culture to the legal systems of developing countries, as well as to their socio-economic structure and

9 Joseph E. Stiglitz, *Globalization and Its Discontents* (W.W. Norton & Company Inc., 2004). See also Stiglitz, *Making Globalization Work* (W.W. Norton & Company, 2007); Brian Snowdon, *Globalization, Development and Transition* (Edward Elgar, 2007); Mohamed S. Wahab, *Cultural Globalization and Public Policy: Exclusion of Foreign Law in the Global Village* (Oxford: Oxford University Press, 2005, Vol. 8, p. 306).

10 Stiglitz 2004, 2007; Snowdown 2007.

11 Mohamed A.M. Ismail, *Globalization and New International Public Works Agreements in Developing Countries, An Analytical Perspective* (Routledge, 2011 and 2016).

12 Mohamed A.M. Ismail, Legal Globalization and PPPs in Egypt, EPPPL, Lexxion, 1/2010, pp. 54–67).

social traditions, it is true that some areas can still preserve their national original identity. The latter concept applies to most developing countries, particularly in the areas of family law and in social traditions in Middle Eastern societies as well as in other developing countries. Religious beliefs and social customs practiced in these countries are not influenced by cultural globalization in the socio-legal domain. Regardless of minor religious and social controversy among nationals in developing countries in areas of family law, conservative legal social cultures in Middle Eastern societies impose the same traditions and customs on the domain of human family relations.[13]

On the other hand, legal matters that are considerably influenced by legal and cultural globalization, such as the administrative contract theory ('*Le contrat administratif*') maintain some of their basic features. It is true that penalties and sanctions stipulated in the administrative contract theory have not changed to date in civil law jurisdictions, even with the existence of new trends aimed at the modernization and internationalization of the traditional theory of administrative contracts.

Accordingly, in can be said that the rigid patterns of administrative contracts as well as their substance and exorbitant features have significantly changed in the last decades in the civil legal culture, especially where infrastructure agreements with foreign private entities are concerned. These new legal patterns such as the introduction of international public works agreements; Build, Operate, Transfer (BOT); Build, Own, Operate and Transfer (BOOT); and Public Private Partnership (PPP) transactions marked the start of a new era in MENA countries' legal culture – one with unique, liberal mechanisms and stipulations.

Legal cultural globalization has had its influence on legislation, litigation, and the contractual regime of the administrative contract in the MENA region. The Arbitration Act No. 27 of 1994 in Egypt[14] and the PPP legislation that is promulgated by the Egyptian Parliament by Law No. 67 of 2010 are the direct result of legal globalization. The situation in Tunisia is markedly progressing in the area of infrastructure projects through PPPs and the exploitation of natural resources such as oil and gas with cooperation from European Mediterranean countries. PPP legislation began to appear in the MENA region.

As a result of cultural and legal globalization forces in the MENA countries, digital administration has emerged as one of the targets to be adopted by the MENA countries' governments,[15] and there is a potential for digitalization of public contracts as

13 Mohamed A.M. Ismail (EPPPL, Lexxion, 1/2010, pp. 54–67).

14 It is worth noting that Arbitration Acts began to appear in MENA countries such as: Oman in 1997; Saudia Arabia in 2012; Kingdom of Bahrain in 2015; Qatar in 2017, and United Arab Emirates in 2018.

15 Digital government in Egypt available at: https://mcit.gov.eg/en/Digital_Government; in the United Arab Emirates available at: https://u.ae/en/about-the-uae/strategies-initiatives-and-awards/strategies-plans-and-visions/government-services-and-digital-transformation/uae-national-digital-government-strategy; in Saudia Arabia available at: https://dga.gov.sa/en; in Bahrain available at: https://bahrain.bh/wps/portal/en/!ut/p/z1/pVLLbsIwEPwVLjkGb2LyoLcUUSgCUUHDwxfk

a result. There is an essential need for the digitalization of public contracts in the MENA countries to enhance public contracts' practices concerning public utilities and services. The essential need for digitalization of public contracts is not only for the legal globalization requirements, which imposes a duty upon the MEMA governments to adopt the needs and techniques required for legal globalization, but also it is a fundamental tool to achieve the essence of public procurements in academia and practice. Through achieving the targets of public procurements in MENA countries' legislation and regulatory framework, public contracts can meet the contracting authorities' expectations. It is fundamental to refer to the benefits of digitalization of public contracts and how digitalization can be implemented to achieve public procurements' targets through the procedural phase and through contract performance phases. There are many goals which public procurements aims to achieve. Among those targets are transparency, publicity, fair competition, integrity, fair treatment, and non-discrimination of contractors and suppliers, and efficiency. Some of those targets may be achieved during the procedural phase and before the contract conclusion and some others may be achieved in the performance phase. It is fundamental to refer to the Key Performance Indicators (KPIs) which indicate the qualitative measurements to evaluate the contract performance during the performance phase and whether the qualitative and quantitative outputs of the project meet the expectations of the contracting authority and the nation. It is settled in the MENA countries' constitutions that the public contracting authorities are representing the nation, therefore, satisfaction of the contracting authority is relating to the nation's satisfaction as the contracting authorities are concluding public contracts on behalf of the nation.[16] Therefore, digitalization of public

---

gDFGiR2MgfL3NeJEy6uqb2vN7M7OLCJogoike8GpEUrS3NZTEs7afQg9P_Y7MU4xJP2wMag3wWtBgMaXAMC4eQJEH9Go7ocxIPIMH_xew3uvWX6vB5DEr4Pu51sDoIWf5N94ycP5I0QQKedigaYBiyHAXuQGMQvcWkgjN1sCduthGAU-DefgZSf0XJrSrNCUcbUvlTY0nzHpQE7lQkheKSlnWwcyutJUyG1lIbiwmIpFMy0LJk1lrXZasuNP836rI_d3GzJpe5DLHa9EcO5zx-NHg6ZWaHRTqO0w3gt2QKlUurBXM_yjqW1AnUdB2UsU682GJDYAJQ37Mmjy_wTsWJ6r7HzpicxwzBHRbMk009Wdtt8rY8rtiwMOHA6HKleK56w6V4UD1ygrtbW6LpGoLNI0LWJ8dDvNZa-JayQL8n03-QZ8nIee/dz/d5/L3dHQSEvUUt3SS9nQSEh/; in Kuwait available at: https://www.e.gov.kw/sites/kgoarabic/Pages/HomePage.aspx; in Oman available at: https://omanportal.gov.om/wps/portal/index/etransformationplan/!ut/p/a1/hc7JDoIwEAbgZ-HAlQ4WCXirEBeWNCYu0IsBgwVTKAGE1xeJFxOXuf2T788MYihCrEr6giddIatEPDMzz3Snm_qGgm8BdoAsHWoYOgF6mI0gHgF8GQL_-ifEJoJhDUDtbejvQwIzfFx5dmBi1zVe4McJDzEuZDq9G5MqxRZHrMmuWZM12r0Z13nX1e1CBRWGYdC4lFxk2kWWKnyq5LLtUPQuUV1GcJuLPiCK8gB5odFR/dl5/d5/L0lDU1EvUU5RSy80SlNFL2Fy/; in Qatar available at: https://portal.www.gov.qa/wps/portal/people/!ut/p/a0/04_Sj9CPykssy0xPLMnMz0vMAfGjzOLNDCyNHH0tTEKDfJwsDDy9PUxN_dyNjA0sjPSDE4v0C7IdFQGpF6Bk/, and available also at: https://hukoomi.gov.qa/en/strategy, last accessed on 27 July 2023. In Gulf Cooperation Council (GCC) Countries, see the developments for digital government in GCC six countries United Arab Emirates, Kingdom of Bahrain, Saudia Arabia, Kuwait, Oman, Qatar, available at: https://www.egic.info/digital-transformation-in-the-gcc, last accessed on 27 July 2023.

16 The Egyptian Conseil D'État, The General Assembly for Legal Opinion and Legislation, session on 18 December 2016.

contracts is a significant tool to achieve public interest and preserve public funds, and at the same time is a tool to achieve coherent global contract law principles.

Through transparency, publicity, fair competition, integrity, fair treatment, and non-discrimination of contractors and suppliers and efficiency, a fair public procurement process can be achieved which maintains a higher threshold of protection to foreign investors. Further, a fair public procurement process procures the increase of inflow of FDI to MENA countries in various economic sectors. Harmonization and integration of MENA countries' public procurement legislation with the international standards guarantee that legislative and regulatory approaches in MENA countries shall not violate the legitimate economic expectations of private foreign investors. A fair process in public contracts' conclusion and implementation is a safeguard to achieve sustainable development goals and to achieve socio-economic goals of public contracts which is directly connected to public interests and how to maximize the economic reward for public funds.

Digitalization of Public Contracts' Award Procedures to Encourage FDI in the MENA Countries

With recognition of the critical role of investment as an engine of economic growth in the global economy, investment policies should establish open, non-discriminatory, transparent, and predictable conditions for investment, and investment policies should provide legal certainty and strong protection to investors and investments, tangible and intangible. Regulation relating to investment should be developed in a transparent manner with the opportunity for all stakeholders to participate, and should be embedded in an institutional framework based on the rule of law.

Investment policies and other policies that impact on investment such as public contracts' procedural and substantive regulatory framework should be coherent at both the national and international levels and aimed at fostering investment, consistent with the objectives of sustainable development and inclusive growth.

In light of MENA governments' right to regulate investment for legitimate public policy purposes, public contracts have special significance in this context as public contracts aim at protecting public interests. Digitalization of public contracts is an important tool which shows the interplay between protecting public interests on one hand and the aim to achieve a higher threshold of protection to foreign investors in the MENA countries on the other hand. Digitalization of public contracts is one of the main tools to promote transparency, policies for investment promotion, to maximize economic benefit, be effective and efficient, aimed at attracting and retaining investment, and matched by facilitation efforts that promote transparency and are conducive for investors to establish, conduct and expand their businesses. Those targets can be achieved only through an efficient system for the digitalization of public contracts. Investment policies should promote and facilitate the observance by investors of international best practices and applicable instruments of responsible business conduct and corporate governance, particularly during the procedural phase of public contracts and its performance phase. Such observance may be achieved through a proper system for the digitalization of public contracts.

The international community should continue to cooperate and engage in dialogue with a view to maintaining an open and conducive policy environment for investment, and addressing shared investment policy challenges. Public contracts play a fundamental role in maintaining an open and conducive policy environment for investment, and digitalization of public contracts is one of the current tools to achieve a better environment for investments. Public procurement legislative and regulatory frameworks are fundamental pillars and determining factors in any legal system which can be described as incentives to attract and increase the inward of FDI on the legislative side and on the governmental policies' side.

There is a causality link between the existence of digitalization of public contracts on one hand and the increase of the inward of FDI and the improvement of the life of ordinary citizens in MENA countries on the other.

How Can Digitalization of Public Contracts Improve Socio-economic Developments in the MENA Countries?

As public procurement legislation in the MENA countries aims at implementing fundamental principles in award procedures stipulated in international practice, it is clear that public contracts' award procedures in MENA legislation aim to create a better environment, which increases the threshold of protection to foreign investors through fighting corruption, and aims consequently to increase incentives for foreign investments which raises the inward of FDI to MENA countries. Principles of achieving public interests, integrity, objectivity, equality, equal opportunity, free competition, fair competition, publicity, and transparency are pivotal mechanisms to fight corruption and they are the same principles which procure a better environment to increase the inward of FDI to MENA countries. It is true that there is an overlapping between the principles which govern award procedures in public contracts' legislation in the MENA countries and principles which attract FDI to those countries, as they are similar principles to those which are required to maintain a clean environment in various economic sectors. Principles for both targets may cooperate to encourage digitalization of public contracts, socio-economic developments, increasing productivity, and developing infrastructure, enhancing services to MENA countries' citizens.

As public contracts' award procedures aim to achieve objectivity, integrity,[17] equal opportunity, fair competition and many other principles, it aims to enhance the life of ordinary citizens in MENA countries. Public contracts' award procedures aim to provide '*value for money*' to the government and be commercially viable for the private partner. Digitalization of public contracts enables contracting authorities during the procedural phase to select the proper contractor or supplier and during the performance phase to achieve KPIs through accurate monitoring

17 For integrity as one of the fundamental principles which govern public contracts' law and practice see: Gabriella Racca and Christopher Yukins, *Integrity and Efficiency in Sustainable Public Contracts, Balancing Corruption Concerns in Public Procurement Internationally* (Bruylant, 2014).

of the implementation of public contracts in all its phases until final completion and delivery to the state. Digitalization of public contracts is an innovative step in award procedures, the procedural phase, and during contract performance, and it is considered a pivotal tool to enhance the life of MENA countries' ordinary citizens from many angles. First, awarding public contracts aims to increase the inward of FDI to MENA countries. Increasing the inward of FDI to various economic sectors in the MENA countries is a fundamental factor to decrease the unemployment rate. The increase of the unemployment rate in MENA countries is a fundamental factor behind the increase of crime and terrorism in the MENA region. Public contracts' projects create thousands of job opportunities in MENA countries in various economic sectors. Second, public contracts' projects in the MENA countries are important factors to enhance the quality of products and services in those countries. Third, public contracts in the MENA countries maintain sustainable developments in those countries, which have a direct impact on ordinary citizens' lives and standard of living; education; health, and other public utilities' services offered by the MENA states.

Digitalization of Public Contracts and the Relevant Constitutional Principles Which Govern Public Contracts' Practice in the MENA Countries

The Egyptian Constitution of 1971 and its Amendments

Historical background: The previous Egyptian Constitution of 1971 was influenced, to a great extent, by the French Constitution of the Fifth Republic of October 1958. The previous Egyptian Constitution of 1971 was influential on all MENA countries' constitutions through decades, and played a significant role to spread the core rights as stipulated in the French Constitution of 1958 to all MEMA countries' constitutions.[18] The Egyptian Constitution of 1971 came into force in September 1971 and remained until February 2011 when the Egyptian President Hosni Mubarak relinquished power. The 1971 constitution had three amendments in 1981, 2005, and 2007. In constitutional amendments in 2007, the constitution relinquished socialists' and Marxist ideologies and started a new era of economic constitutional ideology which did not adopt a specific economic ideology and left the selection of economic ideology to each parliamentary or presidential election to select the right economic pattern for each parliamentary or presidential term. This flexibility in the constitutional economic ideology was a fundamental tool behind paving the way for the private sector's participation in all economic activities. The expansion of the private sector's role in different economic activities in the Egyptian economy was the main factor for the emergence of new patterns of administrative contracts such as BOT, BOOT, and PPP contracts. Following the aftermath of 2011 in Egypt, there were many developments to the Egyptian Constitutions when

18 Mohamed A.M. Ismail, *Arab Constitutions, Facts and Prospects* (Al Halabi Publishing Co., Beirut, 2015, p. 22, in Arabic).

the Military Council in Egypt issued the Constitutional Declaration of 2011 and in the following year Egypt promulgated the 2012 Constitution. It is worth noting that the current Egyptian Constitution of 2014 adopted the same constitutional approach, which leads to a wide participation of the private sector in all economic activities. Egypt is following considerable economic reform which has achieved significant results in establishing huge infrastructure projects and other services projects that create hundreds of thousands of job opportunities and absorb unemployment problems which are the main factor behind the increase of crime rates in particular terrorists' crimes. The Egyptian government began many projects which aim at fighting poverty, providing shelter for people below the poverty line, and creating social welfare to tens of millions of ordinary citizens. As the main target of public contracts is to achieve public interests and to preserve public funds through adopting the '*value for money*' principle, it is clear that Egypt is currently achieving considerable progress in administrative contracts' law and practice and the digitalization of public contracts, in general, whether administrative or private contracts, became an essential tool to achieve public contracts' targets and the UN Sustainable Development Goals. The Egyptian government aims to create a fully automated process in public contracts as part of the digital infrastructure national project.

Gulf States' Constitutions

Through decades, Gulf States' constitutions did not adopt any Marxist economic ideology. It was clear that Gulf States' constitutions did not adopt any economic ideology. In the United Arab Emirates' Constitution in 1971 and its amendments, the Kuwait Constitution of 1962, the Qatar Constitution of 2004, Bahrain's former Constitution of 1973, and the current Constitution in force of 2002 and the Oman Constitution of 1996, the economic ideology of these constitutions enables the private sector to participate in public contracts and to enter into PPP contracts with public actors. It is worth noting that most MENA countries' governments entered into PPP contracts before promulgation of PPP legislation in Gulf States. It is clear that there is a '*décalage*' between practice and legislation as practice came before legislation.

It is true that there is a direct link between the expansion of private sector involvement in public contracts and the digitalization of such contracts. Private sector involvement enables governments to use advanced technology, which is imported to developing countries by huge multinational companies which play a remarkable role in economic developments in the MENA region through public contracts, whether through participation with public actors, or as a contractor or supplier in traditional patterns of administrative contracts. In addition, the constructive role of the private sector enables MENA countries' governments to import technology and experience and to have an opportunity to train citizens from developing countries to use advanced technology as these countries may export expertise to the surrounding developing countries in the forthcoming years. Adopting advanced technology by MENA countries' governments, through private foreign entities, is a fundamental tool to achieve digitalization of public contracts in the forthcoming years.

Digitalization of Public Contracts in Light of the MENA Countries' Constitutions

MENA countries' constitutions have adopted the core constitutional principles which represent the basic and fundamental principles of any developed constitution worldwide, such as the principle of equality before law, equal opportunity,[19] and the principle of freedom of speech.[20] It is worth noting that transparency and publicity principles are direct results of the constitutional principle of freedom of expression.[21]

In addition, there is no prohibition in the MENA countries' constitutions to adopting digitalization of public contracts, not only in a fully digitalized process during the procedural phase and the contract performance phase, but also there are no restrictions regarding using data in the digital process to the extent permitted by legislation. MENA countries' constitutions have delegated legislation to illustrate the legislative stipulations regarding using data and whether there is a prohibition against using sensitive or personal data or not, and to what extent this prohibition is applicable. In other words, as regulations in the MENA countries' legal systems cannot contain substantive stipulations to prohibit using certain kinds of data, legislation clarifies the substantive stipulations to prohibit using some personal or sensitive data, if applicable, and legislation may, in certain cases, impose penalties.[22]

Digitalization of Public Contracts and the Legislative Principles at the Procedural Phase in the MENA Countries

How Can Digitalization of Public Contracts Implement MENA Countries' Legislation Principles at the Procedural Phase?

Public procurement legislative and regulatory frameworks in the MENA countries have adopted many principles such as transparency, equality before the law, equality before public utilities,[23] fair competition, and fighting corruption. Previous public procurement legislation in Egypt such as Law No. 9 of 1983 and Law No. 89

19 The current Egyptian Constitution of 2014, Articles 9 and 53; Kingdom of Bahrain Constitution 2002, Article 18; Kuwait Constitution, Articles 7, 8, and 29; United Arab Emirates Constitution 1971, as amended, Article 25.

20 The Egyptian Constitution 2014, Article 65.

21 Egyptian Constitution of 2014, Article 65; Kingdom of Bahrain constitution, Article 23; Kuwait Constitution, Article 36; United Arab Emirates Constitution, Article 30.

22 In the MENA countries' legal systems, regulations cannot impose penalties, in particular criminal penalties which have to be imposed only by legislation.

23 The Supreme Administrative Court, The Egyptian Conseil D'État, Principles of the Supreme Administrative Court in Egypt in 25 years, Principal No. 6865, p. 2891, session 26 June 2000, Case 4388/43. In Egypt and MENA countries public procurement legal framework see: Elleil, ASA *Methods of Concluding Administrative Contracts in Theory and Practice* (Dar Al Nahda Al Arabia, 1994, in Arabic).

of 1998 and the current state contracting Law No. 182 of 2018 are adopting same principles. In Gulf States, it is worth noting that the same principles were adopted by public procurement Law No. 36 of 2002 and its executive regulations at the Kingdom of Bahrain, Law No. 49 of 2016 as amended by Law No. 74 of 2019 in Kuwait, and Law No. 6 of 2008 of the United Arab Emirates, public procurement Law No. 24 of 2015 in Qatar and the same in many MENA countries' legislation. Digitalization of public contracts is an essential tool to achieve a proper application of public procurement basic and fundamental principles in the MENA countries. A fully digitalized process in the procedural phase is a guarantee to achieve transparency, equality, and non-discrimination during the exercise of award criteria tests and the selection of a private entity as a contractor or supplier with MENA states. Equality before law and equality before public utility are maintained through a fully digitalized process at the procedural phase. Artificial intelligence (AI) is one of the tools to achieve this target as full digitalization of the procedural phase is one of the guarantees to make a proper selection of the private contracting entity with MENA governments in light of equality before the law, equality before public utilities, transparency, and non-discriminatory principles; and AI is also one of the fundamental tools to fight corruption. Minimizing the role of human intervention is an effective approach to minimize corruption and achieve integrity, as AI in the forthcoming years can create a new fully digitalized process, which maintains innovation in the award procedures during the procedural phase. One of the fundamental requirements to improve the profile of innovation in award procedures is to invent tools which can fight corruption and minimize human intervention. Full digitalization of the procedural phase is a fundamental requirement and a guarantee to implement public procurement legislation principles which are adopted by MENA countries' legislation and regulatory framework. Fair competition is a legislative principle adopted, for instance, by competition Law No. 3 of 2005 in Egypt; Law No. 31 of 2018 in the Kingdom of Bahrain; and Law No. 4 of 2012 in the United Arab Emirates. Fair competition can be achieved in the procedural phase through adopting a fully digitalized process, with the minimum intervention of humans to avoid human mistakes and any decision which may violate fair competition principles. A structural lack of competition is due to some market structures, which are not beneficial to competition, that represent structural market failure, even in the absence of companies engaging in anti-competitive practices. For example, some markets may have systemic failures due to certain structural characteristics, such as high concentration or barriers to entry, the ability to forcibly retain customers, lack of access to data, or data accumulation. Therefore, not only is digitalization of public contracts the sole approach to maintaining fair competition, but also legislative and regulatory reforms are needed in some MENA countries to reduce barriers to enter certain markets, reduce customs duty constraints and the lack of access to data, which is considered to be the fundamental factor that enables the maintenance of fair competition. Access to data also maintains a higher threshold of protection to foreign investors.

In conclusion, a selection criterion to private entity contracting with MENA governments has to be adopted in a fully digitalized process to achieve legislative principles' goals in public procurement as illustrated in legislative and regulatory frameworks. The profile of innovation in selecting contracting entities with the MENA states in the digitalization era is expected to be unique in award procedures during the procedural phase. Traditional procedures in the MENA countries depend mainly upon human intervention. In some MENA countries, i.e Dubai and Bahrain, tender documents can be submitted via electronic means, meanwhile a fully digitalized process has not yet been achieved. A fully digitalized process maintains that public procurement legislative and regulatory frameworks are consistent with international standards as adopted by international organs.

How Can MENA Governments Achieve International Standards and Sustainable Development Goals during the Procedural Phase through Implementing AI?

AI when applied to public contracts is a fundamental tool to achieve transparency, which is an important factor to avoid conflicts of interests, risks of corruption, as AI minimizes human intervention.[24] Conflicts of interests and risks of corruption are interrelated negative practices which are directly connected to lack of transparency. AI is not only a constructive tool during the procedural phase, but it is also an important mechanism during contract performance as a tool for managing the lifecycle of public contracts (automation of repetitive tasks without added value; automation of small purchases; allowing historical contract data to be fed back to facilitate negotiations; and creation of a library of contractual clauses, etc.). AI is also a predictive justice tool in contractual litigation and arbitration which enables the contracting state to defend public interests and public funds through litigation and arbitration relating to public contracts. AI, through adopting advanced databases and algorithms, enables MENA states during public contracts' disputes to be represented in cases before administrative judiciary and arbitral tribunals in a way which guarantees the best legal and economic representation of the contracting state that minimizes the possibility of losing cases, as this is the situation in international arbitration in developing countries whether international commercial arbitration or investment arbitration. In practice, as most developing countries lose many international arbitration cases relating to public contracts,[25] AI is a constructive mechanism to minimize such risks, through minimizing the risk of corruption and bureaucracy. AI maintains good representation of contracting states legally and economically before international arbitral tribunals.

Electronic archiving is a useful tool in all public contracts phases as it maintains the right selection of the private entity and monitors contract performance until the final completion of the contract. When a dispute arises, electronic archiving is one of the fundamental pillars behind organizing a coherent and productive defense on

24 In France see: Public contracts and transparency of algorithmic processing, see for example the initiative of the city of Nantes: https://data.nantesmetropole.fr/pages/algorithmes_nantes_metropole/, last accessed on 27 July 2023.

25 For more elaboration, see: Mohamed A.M. Ismail, *International Investment Arbitration, Lessons from Developments in the MENA Region* (Routledge, 2013).

behalf of the contracting state. It is worth noting that many MENA states are currently adopting electronic archiving in governments' departments as a step towards full digital administration in the forthcoming years.[26] Some MENA countries began to use electronic identification and trust services in public contracts, such as authentication systems and electronic signatures.[27] MENA governments will achieve the target of full digital administration in the near future.

How Can MENA Governments Achieve the 'Value for Money' Concept and Select the Best Economic Offer through Implementing AI?

Implementing AI can lead to achieving the '*value for money*' concept as the latter is one of the main targets of public contracts and is directly connected to the main thematic principles behind concluding public contracts, which are public interest and preserving public funds through reducing public spending. AI as a tool for choosing the most feasible offer in public procurement and to avoid corruption (through sourcing, detection of abnormally low offers, etc.). In addition, AI is a constructive tool in the fight against fraud in public contracts and the detection of anti-competitive agreements, as both represent challenges to the economic feasibility of public contracts. '*Value for money*' is not only the economically feasible and financial challenge that public contracts need to achieve, but fighting fraud and anti-competitive agreements are two challenges directly connected to the financial challenges and related to the '*value for money*' concept, as fraud and anti-competitive agreements constitute a considerable threat to the '*value for money*' and economic feasibility of public contracts. Fraud and anti-competitive practices may increase the costs of public contracts and constitute a financial burden upon governments' budgets on one hand, and increase services' costs which governments offer to ordinary citizens through PPP contracts on the other hand. Therefore, there is a negative effect to financial offers during the procedural phase, which directly violates the '*value for money*' concept, as one of the main targets of public contracts. The main target of public contracts is to protect public interests and public funds. AI is a fundamental tool which protects public interests and public funds as it offers predictability and applies fair electronic tests that enable MENA governments to select the best economic and feasible offer.

In conclusion, Egypt has currently promulgated Law No. 182 of 2018 for State Contracting, which has a new legislative policy to achieve UN SDGs, through adopting new principles in the procedural phase, and through legislative and regulatory innovation in award procedures, to select private entities entering into contracts with the state. The profile of innovation in award procedures is clear, as

26 For instance, the Egyptian Ministry of Finance; The Ministry of Commerce, Industry and Tourism at the Kingdom of Bahrain, and many ministries in the United Arab Emirates. There are no reliable sources yet to confirm this approach from the MENA governments.

27 For instance, in Egypt see: Electronic Signature Law No. 15 of 2004; Kingdom of Bahrain Electronic Transactions Law No. 55 of 2018 and United Arab Emirates Law No. 1 of 2006.

the new legislation and its executive regulations[28] are consistent with international standards adopted by international organs such as OECD and the World Bank.[29]

Harmonizing the New Patterns of '*Le contrat administratif*' in the MENA Countries and the Potential Digitalization of Public Contracts:

New patterns of administrative contracts ('*Le contrat administratif*') began to appear in the MENA countries such as BOOT/BOT contracts and PPP contractual techniques. Egypt was the first country in the MENA region to promulgate PPP Law No. 67 of 2010. Other MENA countries have promulgated PPP legislation.[30] It is a fact that there is a '*décalage*' between practice and legislation, as in MENA countries' PPP practice having appeared through concluding PPP contracts by MENA governments before they had promulgated PPP legislation.[31] This was the case, for instance, in Egypt[32] and Dubai. Despite PPP legislation not yet having been promulgated in Bahrain, there are many PPP contracts in practice concluded by the government of Bahrain in many economic sectors.[33]. Unlike traditional administrative contracts, new patterns of administrative contracts such as BOT/BOOT and PPP have new hybrid/*dual* legal nature as they do not contain, in some cases, exorbitant clauses.[34] New international public works agreements which were concluded by the governments and private foreign entities have the same hybrid/*dual* legal nature.[35] New patterns of administrative contracts in the MENA region, which reflect the modernization and liberalization of such contracts, have introduced new contractual techniques to public sector transactions. Digitalization of public contracts is a fundamental part of the potential reform of public contracts' law and practice, and is consistent with the new developments in the legal system of administrative contracts in the MENA countries as they representing civil law

28 Executive regulations issued by decree No. 692 of 2019 from the Egyptian Minister of Finance.

29 OECD MAPS, 2018 and World Bank Benchmarking Report in PPP Public Procurement, 2017.

30 See Chapter 4 of this monograph.

31 Mohamed A.M. Ismail, *Public Private Partnership Contracts: The Middle East and North Africa* (Routledge, 2020, p. 228).

32 In Egypt for, instance, New Cairo wastewater station project in 2007 (before promulgation) PPP legislation in 2010. This project was awarded pursuant to the previous Egyptian Public Procurement Law No. 89 of 1998 and its executive regulations.

33 In the Kingdom of Bahrain, for instance, some energy and infrastructure projects adopted PPP techniques, such as Liquefied Natural Gas (LNG) Project in 2016 and Social Housing Project by the Ministry of Housing. These contracts were concluded pursuant to Bahrini Public Procurement Law No. 36 of 2002 and its executive regulations.

34 Mohamed A.M. Ismail, *PPP Contracts: The Middle East and North Africa* (Routledge, 2020, p. 229); for the same author see: International Infrastructure Agreements and PPPs in Developing Countries: Substantive Principles, With Special Reference to Arab and Latin American Countries, *European Public-Private Partnership Law Review* (EPPPL), Lexxion, 3/2011, p. 154) and also for the same author: Legal Globalization and PPPs in Egypt, EPPPL, Lexxion, 1/2010, pp. 54–67).

35 Mohamed A.M. Ismail, *Globalization and New International Public Works Agreements in Developing Countries* (Routledge, 2011), and for the same author see: *Public Private Partnership Contracts: The Middle East and North Africa* (Routledge, 2020, p. 229).

legal culture. As there were constitutional challenges to the new patterns of administrative contracts, in particular before promulgating PPP legislation in Egypt,[36] the challenges of digitalization of public contracts in the MENA region are less. The prospects of best practice of public contracts after digitalization are evident as the digitalization process maintains legislative principles and sustainable development goals' principles, and promotes the consistency of public contracts' law and practice with international commercial contracts. As new patterns of administrative contracts, in most cases, contain a foreign element, protection of intellectual property rights 'i.e secrecy agreements' is maintained through the digitalization process. Protection of foreign investors. sensitive data is a part of creating a higher threshold of protection to foreign investments in Egypt and the MENA region. Such protection is an incentive to attract foreign investments to Egypt and the region, and it is a significant step towards protection of public interests and public funds. As new patterns of administrative contracts are connected with huge infrastructure projects, public utilities' projects and services, the better implementation of contractual undertakings requires that commitments of the contracting parties are sharply defined and contractual undertakings are properly implemented during performance phase. The digitalization process is a significant step to achieve this target as an important part of public contracts' law and practice reform. New patterns of administrative contracts have remarkable influence on socio-economic life and Sustainable Development Goals as they relate to infrastructure, public utilities, and services projects. The increase of the PPP project transfers modern and advanced technologies to Egypt and the MENA countries through awarding such projects in these countries. Transfer of technology is a pivotal factor to creating highly qualified expertise and trained labor in Egypt and the MENA countries as PPP projects will create more job opportunities for citizens in the respective countries. Egypt and the MENA countries will have the opportunity to export qualified expertise and trained labor, at an economically feasible cost, to the surrounding countries and to other regions of the world as a result of awarding PPP projects in Egypt and the MENA countries.[37] Awarding PPP projects would inject billions of hard currency to Egypt and the MENA countries which maintains the stability of the foreign currency exchange rate in the respective jurisdictions, because it increases the supply of hard currency to Egypt and the MENA countries' markets against demand.

In conclusion, digitalization of public contracts is a significant incentive to encourage private foreign entities to inject FDI into PPP projects and other new patterns of administrative contracts in Egypt and the MENA region, as digitalization maintains the application of international standards in public procurement and

36 It is worth noting that without constitutional amendments of 2007 to the previous Egyptian Constitution of 1971, PPP legislation of 2010 in Egypt would not have been promulgated, as these amendments relinquished Marxism ideology for the 1971 constitution.

37 Mohamed A.M. Ismail, International Infrastructure Agreements and PPPs in Developing Countries: Substantive Principles, With Special Reference to Arab and Latin American Countries, *European Public-Private Partnership Law Review* (EPPPL, Lexxion, 3/2011).

contract performance until final completion and this is exactly what the foreign investor is looking for. In addition, digitalization will protect intellectual property rights of the foreign investor in a manner consistent with international standards. Therefore, digitalization, as part of public contracts' law and practice reform, promotes a higher threshold of protection to foreign investors in Egypt and the MENA countries.

Digitalization of public contracts will create a unified set of substantive principles of states' contracts which are consistent with international commercial contracts' principles. Such unification is paving the way to achieve global contract law principles.

Covid-19 Pandemic and the Digitalization of Public Contracts in the MENA Countries

Public contracts' digitalization had many advantaged during the Covid-19 pandemic as it minimized human interaction to a great extent. The situation in Egypt and the MENA countries was different from many countries around the world. Although the Covid-19 pandemic in Egypt and MENA countries was not considered as an event of *force majeure* which renders contracts' performance impossible, it was characterized as an event of hardship ('*L'imprévision*') or unforeseen circumstances which rendered contracts' performance onerous[38] but not impossible. There is an essential need for the fully digitalized process of public contracts in all contract phases, starting from the procedural phase and continuing until final completion.

The question is: During the Covid-19 pandemic, have MENA countries' governments created digital infrastructure platforms that can implement fully digitalized public contracts' process during the procedural phase and during contract performance until final completion of the contractual obligations?

The answer is not yet. A full digitalization of public contracts is underway, and may be achieved in a very reasonable time, through implementing digital infrastructure in MENA governments, or digital administration, by establishing a coherent digital infrastructure platform, which connects all governmental departments together and enables private entities to deal with all governmental sectors through advanced digital platforms to minimize human intervention to a considerable extent.

Digitalization of Public Contracts and Data Protection in MENA Countries' Legislation, *Transparency v. Privacy*

Personal data protection is one of the challenges to digitalization of public contracts. Many MENA countries have promulgated personal data protection legislation. The

38 For more elaboration, see: Hamdy Yassin Okahsa, *Contractual Performance During Covid-19 Pandemic and its Effect Upon Contractual Obligations*, no publisher, 2020 (in Arabic).

political will behind and the mandate of the personal data protection legislation in the MENA countries was driven by the concern that individuals' personal information was being exploited in ways that undermine privacy, infringe personal rights and, by extension, negatively affect democracy.[39] It is worth noting that protection of personal data involved in documents intended to become accessible to the public through a tendering process or during public contracts' performance until final completion is a fundamental part of the digitalization process. On the other hand, public contracts contain public data and using open data by putting data on-line, which is sometimes necessary in some public contracts, as it reflects transparency and assures the public and foreign investors that public contracts' processes are following legislative stipulations and international standards that protect public interests and preserve public funds. Therefore, absence of sanctions in the event of lack of data transparency needs legislative reform in MENA countries' legislation. Such reform is significant to public contracts' digitalization process.

In public contracts' practice through Electronic Data Interchange (EDI), there are some constraints relating to, for instance, electronic purchasing platforms, e-sourcing, inter-government data transfer, exchange of data relating to sanctions imposed upon companies, and sales contract for data relating to public contracts, etc. A legislative reform is required in Egypt and the MENA region to regulate such activities relating to EDI in the public contracts domain. Digitalization of public contracts will create a better environment for legislature in Egypt and the MENA countries to promulgate such legislation.[40]

In conclusion, public contracts' digitalization needs to achieve a sensible balance between protection of personal data and personal right of privacy on one hand, and the right of the public and foreign investors to assure that public interests are maintained and international standards are adopted. Disclosure of important data to the public and foreign investors reflects transparency and introduces higher threshold of protection to foreign investors and is an incentive to attract FDI.

Conclusions

In conclusion, there are significant developments from the digitalization process which could offer a wide spectrum of flexibility for creating a common understanding of a unified set of substantive principles of international states' contracts, in the respective jurisdictions, which are consistent with international commercial contracts. Such unification is a considerable step towards achieving global contract law principles. This chapter is an attempt to provide the academic base line of the current remarkable expected changes to the pulse and dynamics of

39 For instance, Personal Data Legislation in Egypt, Law No. 151 of 2020; Personal Data Legislation in the Kingdom of Bahrain, Law No. 30 of 2018; Personal Data Legislation in the United Arab Emirates, Law No. 12 of 2016.

40 Pursuant to MENA countries' constitutions, many stipulations and prohibitions which contain sanctions cannot be organized by regulations and they have to be organized only by legislation.

the public contracts through implementing digitalization of these contracts in the MENA countries. It provides a concrete view to the integration between the current trend of digitalization of public contracts and the substantive theory of '*Le contrat administratif*' which aims to achieve public interests and to preserve public funds. It firstly provides the innovation in implementing a coherent digital system for public contracts from constitutional, legislative, and contractual perspectives in Egypt and the MENA countries and secondly it combines those academic theories of public contracts with its digitalization approach and how such an approach will affect public contracts' practice and will create a platform of reform for such contracts. The approach of this chapter illustrates the examination of public procurement in the relevant jurisdictions, which is augmented by the scrutiny of Egyptian law as a fundamentally influential factor and legal foundation to the procedural and substantive law and policy regimes of the relevant Gulf States.

The main targets of digitalization of public contracts are to achieve public interests; to preserve public funds; to minimize public spending; to achieve the '*value for money*' concept and reflect the implementation of principles of transparency, equality before law, equality before public utilities, fair competition, and fighting corruption. Creating global contract law substantive principles is one of the main targets of digitalization of public contracts. A complete reform is expected for public contracts' practice in Egypt and the MENA countries and such reform aims at being consistent with international standards as drawn by the relevant international organs. The need for competitiveness and transparency in delivering public services through digitalization for public contracts is considered as a safeguard to achieve international standards in delivering public utilities' services. There is an essential need to achieve a fully digitalized process of public contracts in all contract phases, starting from the procedural phase and continuing until final completion, and if a dispute arises out of or in connection with the contract, a digital infrastructure in public contracts is needed. Unification of global contract law principles, whether public or private (commercial) contracts, is an important factor to guarantee the legitimate expectations of the foreign investors, and to maintain predictability to the litigation or arbitration outcomes, if a dispute arises.

A full digitalization of public contracts is underway and may be achieved in a very reasonable time through implementing digital governments or digital administration by establishing a coherent digital infrastructure platform that connects all governmental departments together and enables private entities to deal with all governmental sectors through advanced digital platforms to minimize human intervention to a considerable extent.

Digitalization of public contracts and generally digitalization of the Egyptian and MENA governments is a fundamental factor behind a better implementation of a decentralization system. The interplay between digital government and the decentralization is clear as digital infrastructure enables a better decentralization system in any state, in particular federal states. Further, digitalization is an effective tool to enhance the efficiency of the public procurement system, and in addition, contract performance during the performance phase. During the procedural phase and selection of a private entity to enter into a contract with states, a digitalized process is expected to maintain transparency, equality, equality before law, non-discrimination, equality before public utilities, fair competition, and integrity and to fight corruption and prevent conflict of interests' practices. Selecting the best feasible economic offer is maintained through a digitalized process to achieve the '*value for money*' concept and protect public interests and public funds. Pursuant to Egyptian and MENA countries' constitutions,[41] public funds belong to nation's wealth and protecting such wealth is a constitutional obligation. AI is an efficient tool to offer a high threshold of protection to public contracts, not only during the procedural phase, but also during contract performance and until final completion of contractual obligations.

A fundamental question arises, how can public contract performance be assessed? How can public contract performance achieve its substantive goals? The digitalization process maintains that KPIs can be monitored during contract performance and a digital platform is required during both the procedural phase and contract performance. During the performance phase, KPIs are a fundamental tool to monitor performance of contractual obligations ('KPIs *vis-à-vis* contract performance') and to what extent public interest is achieved through such performance. In both procedural and the performance phase, digitalization of public contracts aims to enhance the socio-economic life of the ordinary citizens in Egypt and MENA countries as public contracts mainly relate to public utilities and public services projects.

Digitalization of public contracts, if adopted, can achieve more transparency and integrity during the procedural phase of public procurement, and maintain that sustainable developments goals and international standards are adopted.

Digitalization of public contracts will create a higher threshold of protection to foreign investors and increase the inflow of FDI to Egypt and MENA countries in public contracts' projects whether in infrastructure or public utilities or services projects. If a dispute arises, digital infrastructure is an effective mechanism through electronic archiving and other electronic means which are efficient tools during administrative judiciary procedures, or while representing states before international arbitral tribunals.

Public contracts' projects in the MENA region are not only administrative contracts '*Le contrat administratif*' which contain exorbitant clauses, but they also appear in new patterns of contracts which have hybrid/*dual* legal nature such as BOOT/BOT and PPP techniques. The latter contracts, in some instances, are characterized as private (commercial) contracts. These new types of contracts, and many other new types, have new liberalized and modernized approaches which fall far beyond traditional administrative contract definition. Nevertheless, new

41 It is worth noting that Arab countries' constitutions are inspired, to a great extent, by the current French Constitution, of the Fifth Republic, promulgated in October 1958. The previous Egyptian Constitution of 1971 and the following constitutions were inspired by the French Constitution of 1958 and many Arab countries in the MENA region were directly influenced by the Egyptian Constitutions since 1971.

patterns of administrative contracts are still preserving the target to achieve public interest and to protect public funds to increase resources to the public budget. Egypt and the MENA governments, exceptionally, can also enter into pure private contracts which aim at achieving public interests.

Digitalization of public contracts is an essential mechanism to achieve an ideal system for state contracting that is consistent with the economic reform process in Egypt and the MENA countries, especially in Egypt. Delay in such a process has negative impact in the respective jurisdictions' economies.

In conclusion, digitalization of public contracts will establish unique and coherent reform to public contracts' theory and practice in Egypt and the MENA region. The expected impact of such reform to socio-economic aspects and the ordinary citizens' life in the region is remarkable. Digitalization, as a fundamental pillar to reform of public contracts in Egypt and the MENA region, is expected in a reasonable time, as some governments have already started the process and a full digitalization of public contracts is underway. Digitalization, as a tool to reform, is expected to create a unified set of substantive principles, for both public law contracts and private (commercial) contracts. Such unification is paving the way towards achieving global contract law substantive principles in the region. Digitalization will remove public law barriers and will narrow the gap between public contracts and international commercial contracts' principles. Digitalization will narrow the gap between civil law legal systems and common law jurisdictions through implementing global contract law principles.

6 Codification of Administrative Law in Egypt and MENA Countries as A Tool to Achieve Global Contract Law

Introduction

To achieve unified contract law principles in international states' contracts in Egypt and the MENA countries, which are consistent with global contract law principles, written administrative contracts' law is needed. Egyptian and Arab parliaments have to promulgate written administrative legislation in general for both administrative contracts (states' contracts in general) and administrative decrees (acts and omissions by the administration). How can coherent contract law in international states' contracts be achieved through codification? How can codification of administrative contracts' law avoid inconsistent findings (contradicted judgments) by national courts and arbitral tribunals?

This chapter has innovation in its theme as codification is one of the main fundamental factors to achieve unified and coherent international states' contract law principles, in the respective jurisdictions, which are consistent with global contract law principles and standards.

The question this chapter is attempting to answer is: Does codification of administrative law reduce the barriers and constraints to achieve unification and global contract law?

This chapter addresses the potential advantages and disadvantages of codifying the grounds of a judicial review of administrative law. The four principal legal values associated with codification are described: Certainty; clarity; democratic legitimacy; and rationality.[1] Further, this chapter examines the way administrative law became codified, the obstacles which had to be overcome, the main orientations of the codes, their evolution in time; alternatively, it explains why administrative law and in particular administrative contracts are not codified.

It is important to answer the question why. In particular why is codification of administrative law needed in Egypt and MENA countries? Normally, legal literature answers the question how? not why? Therefore, why is codification of administrative law needed in the relevant jurisdictions? is a crucial question which needs an answer. The answer is relevant at both national and international levels. It is

1 In codification of administrative law generally see: Jean-Bernard Auby (ed.), *Codification of Administrative Procedures* (Bruylant, 2014), and Felix Uhlmann, *Codification of Administrative Law, A Comparative Study on the Sources of Administrative Law* (Hart Publishing, 2023).

DOI: 10.4324/9781003466352-7

important to answer the question why? first and secondly, to answer the question of how codification of administrative law can be achieved in Egypt and MENA countries. The factual, legal, and economic results of codification for Egypt and the MENA countries are portrayed.

Codification of Administrative Law, Why?

Firstly, a crucial question arises: Why is administrative law not yet codified in Egypt and the MENA countries?

The historical background of the Conseil D'État as a unique judicial organ in Egypt was clear in Egyptian legal history. The judicial supremacy of the Egyptian Conseil D'État courts, as judicial review is exercised by administrative courts, shapes administrative law principles. This judicial review has existed in Egypt since 1946, the date of the establishment of the Conseil D'État. The case law of the Egyptian Conseil D'État courts established the doctrine of administrative law, whether in administrative contracts or administrative decrees. It may be argued that codification is triggered by the separation of powers principle as a fundamental constitutional principle. Separation of powers, as a constitutional principle, exists in the Egyptian constitutions, in particular the 1923 constitution, which was valid upon the establishment of the Egyptian Conseil D'État in 1946.[2] The same Principle exists, as one of the main pillars of the political regime in Egypt, in the current Constitution of 2014.[3] Separation of powers imposes a leading role exercised by the Conseil D'État courts in Egypt as a leading judicial organ in the MENA countries in shaping the case law of administrative law, whether in administrative contracts or administrative decrees. Until the present, there is no written administrative law (code) either in Egypt or in the MENA countries, as most supreme courts in the MENA countries follow the case law principles established by the Egyptian Conseil D'État courts.

Why is Codification Essentially Needed?

In Egypt and the MENA countries, general administrative law is clearly less codified than other areas of law. However, codification has many advantages on the national and international levels. In most countries, the implementation of administrative law lies in many hands. The administration, and different courts, may develop diverse solutions to the same problem of administrative law. Codification increases predictability and legal certainty as it avoids inconsistent findings

2 Article 23 of the 1923 Constitution provided that 'The source of all powers is the nation and the use of all powers is regulated by this Constitution.' Article 124 of the 1923 Constitution provides that the judiciary is totally independent. Article 73 of the 1971 Constitution provides that the President of the Republic shall respect separation between powers. Article 5 of the 2014 Constitution, which is valid until the present, provides that the political regime of Egypt is based on, among other principles, the separation of powers.

3 Article 5 of the 2014 Constitution.

(contradictory judgments or arbitral awards) by national courts or arbitral tribunals. Once administrative law principles, whether in administrative contracts or otherwise, are codified, a judge or arbitrator has to apply the valid legislation. Such codification will avoid the violation of legitimate expectations of the disputing parties, whether domestic or foreign investors. It is clear that codification of administrative contracts' principles, once it adopts international contract law principles and standards, is an important tool to achieve global contract law. It is assumed that codification of administrative contract law has to be consistent with international commercial contracts' principles.

Codification has to relinquish the traditional ideology of administrative contracts' principles in Egypt and the MENA countries as the traditional ideology relies mainly upon the public interest concept, the administration's power, and the public utilities' legal nature, as all of these factors imposed the need for exorbitant clauses in administrative contracts. It is suggested that codification has to implement a sensible balance between protecting investors, whether domestic or foreign, through adopting international commercial contracts principles on one hand, and the protection of public interests on the other. Therefore, there is an essential need to change the traditional ideology behind administrative contracts' law and practice and to enhance the traditional administrative contracts' patterns to be consistent with international commercial contracts' law and practice. There are many examples of substantive contractual clauses which need modifications and enhancements to be consistent with international commercial contracts' principles. Liquidated damages must relinquish its punitive nature in administrative contracts in Egypt and the MENA countries and the amount of financial fine (penalty for delay) has to be consistent with the actual loss of the contacting state. Similar to commercial contracts, *Exceptio non-adimpleti contractus* has to be permitted in administrative contracts to enable the foreign or domestic entity contracting with the state to suspend performance, and to exercise pressure upon the state, if there is a severe contractual breach by the contracting state. Further, frustration of the contract theories has to be altered. The theory of unexpected circumstances (*l'imprévision*) has to adopt the legislative approach in PPPs legislation in MENA countries to be consistent with international patterns of states' contracts, which are not necessarily administrative contracts, and which are more consistent with international commercial contracts' principles. Similar to PPP transactions, compensation to maintain the financial equilibrium of the contract can be paid by the contracting state through direct negotiations with the investors, whether domestic or foreign, and not necessarily through final judgment by courts or arbitral awards, which is a long and costly process.

It is clear that one of the main areas which needs codification is administrative contracts, as the theory of traditional administrative contracts needs substantial modifications and enhancements, in particular the exorbitant clauses, penalties, as well as the scope and extent of powers granted to the contracting state through adopting the exorbitant clauses and/or administrative decrees in administrative contracts.

Why Constitutional Law? To What Degree Does the Constitution Shape Administrative Law?

Constitutional and administrative law form two angels of public law. The division between the two areas of law is quite different from country to country. We see countries that draw a strict line, often supplemented by institutional arrangements, such as special constitutional courts, in contrast to administrative courts. Egypt and many MENA countries have such a divide. Despite the fact that the boundary between administrative and constitutional law is hard to locate on many occasions, Egypt and the MENA countries have judicial organs to exercise the judicial review upon the constitutionality of legislation and regulations, which are different from judicial organs that exercise judicial review upon administrative law and the principle of legality. The latter judicial review is exercised by the Conseil D'État courts in Egypt and the ordinary courts in most MENA countries which do not have a *dual* judicial system and separate courts for administrative disputes. It is fundamental that the administrative authorities must be subject to constitutional review for all their actions. The regulatory framework of any state, which is the regulations issued by the executive power or the administrative authorities, has to be subject to judicial review upon its constitutionality by constitutional courts and upon its legality by administrative courts. In countries with written constitutions, the courts use openly formulated constitutional provisions in a 'creative' way to implement further 'unwritten constitutional guarantees' via their case law.[4] There is an overlapping between constitutional and administrative principles in many aspects which are shaped by constitutional courts and administrative courts of Egypt and MENA countries. It is suggested that the influence of the constitution, and of human rights law on general administrative law, is growing.

How Can Codification of Administrative Law Be Achieved in Egypt and MENA Countries?

There is no generally accepted definition of a code in legislative theory. For instance, in the UK, codifying 'is understood to involve bringing together statutory law on a single subject into one legal instrument without substantially changing the boundaries between statute law and case law.' Within this scope, it is possible to distinguish between codification which comes with a substantial reform of the codified area and a mere consolidation.[5] Regardless, a common feature of codification in all countries that it is an instrument of Parliament, notwithstanding that the process may be initiated, executed, and even dominated by government or some other state actor. It is a deliberate choice to create and shape administrative law. It is an 'abstract' approach to

4 Felix Uhlmann, *Codification of Administrative Law, A Comparative Study on the Sources of Administrative Law* (Hart Publishing, 2023, pp. 392 and 393).

5 Ibid., p. 387.

administrative law, an approach of rules versus an approach by cases. In civil law countries, administrative law often forms some sanctuary for a case-based approach to law.[6]

If codes are the abstract approach to administrative law, it is quite obvious that they are the product of legislature as legislative tools. Legislation is formally enacted by Parliaments. However, this does not mean that Parliament must be the initiator, drafter, or author of the legislative text. Governments, legal scholars, or private actors often play an important role in the process of legislation by Parliament. Codification means creating a rule which is legislative, but has *dual*/hybrid legal nature, as the origins of such a rule, in administrative contracts, come from other actors, mainly courts. Therefore, codification is not purely designed by the legislature as a general rule on administrative law, in particular administrative contracts. Codification is an intentional intervention of the legislature to support or change a certain practice or an older rule on administrative law. Legislative interventions may be in favor of or in contrast to what was the legal situation beforehand.[7] Legislation in Egypt and the MENA countries is normally the product of Parliaments. It has to pass through certain procedural steps which constitute the procedural criterion to promulgate legislation. In addition, legislation has to follow an objective/substantive criterion. According to the latter criterion, legislation must contain legislative rules which are abstract in nature and which have general application. All legislation promulgated by Parliaments has to be consistent with the constitution to avoid the risk of unconstitutionality which may be decided by the Egyptian and MENA countries' constitutional courts. In Egypt and the MENA countries, it is clear that not only the government has a considerable influence on legislation, but also the legal scholars and private actors. In any jurisdiction, it is important to analyze the relationship between Parliament, the government, and the courts. There is a contrast between case law which concerns a case that has a particular factual background and abstract legislative rules which have general and abstract nature.

Private law, in both common and civil law countries, is older than administrative law and it was used to find practical solutions for administrative law questions. In many countries, the administration may conclude private law contracts. State liability may be subject to private law rules, tests, and standards. The idea of *bona fide* contracting parties often binds both private individuals and state actors whether in administrative contracts or private law contracts. Hence, private law is an important source and fundamental part of administrative law, to a varying degree from country to country. It may be directly applicable as private law, and the dispute may be subject to civil or commercial courts' jurisdiction.[8]

6 Ibid.
7 Ibid., pp. 387–9.
8 Ibid., p. 396.

Factual, Legal, and Economic Results to Codification in Egypt and MENA Countries

Administrative law, and in particular administrative contracts, is a highly complex legal topic. The main element of its complexity is the legal sources. Administrative law is different from constitutional law as it is in most countries a written constitution. The same is true of private law, which has written sources in legislation. Hence, codification has considerable effects as it offers a simplification of the existing legal order of administrative law, in particular administrative contracts. Codification may enhance access for private individuals, in particular foreign investors. It may create predictability for foreign investors at the international level. Codification may even be a result of the benchmarking of international policy.

A regulatory framework plays an important role in the simplification of legislation. However, detailed regulations offer no guarantee of a better understanding of administrative law by the public. Legislation of good quality and drafting may realistically improve the situation. The codification process is at the crossroads of three powers: the legislature, the courts, and the executive power (which is the government in Egypt and the MENA countries' legal systems).[9]

On the international contract law side, codification has many advantages as it maintains predictability of legal approaches adopted by the administration. Further, it maintains that judicial approaches adopted by courts or arbitral tribunals will not violate the economic expectations of foreign investors. Such predictability is a real implementation of the legitimate expectations of the disputing parties in any dispute between states and private foreign entities. Written administrative contract law will avoid inconsistent findings by courts and arbitral tribunals and will guarantee simplification of administrative contracts' rules which can be recognized and understood by foreign investors. It is assumed that codification of administrative contracts rules, both procedural and substantive, in a coherent legislation, will adopt international contract law principles and standards, in particular international commercial contracts' principles and practices. Codification in this manner is a considerable step towards the unification of contract law principles in Egypt and the MENA countries to be consistent with international commercial contracts' principles, and to achieve global contract law principles.

Conclusions

In civil law legal systems, there is a mixture between judicial development and selective interventions by the legislature. In Egypt and most MENA countries, in addition to case law, there is legislation for public procurement dealing with the procedural phase of administrative contracts. The administrative contracts theory, and the substantive principles of administrative contracts are regulated by private law which is Egyptian and MENA countries' Civil Codes, in addition to the case

9 Ibid., pp. 397–404.

law of the Egyptian Supreme Administrative Court and MENA countries' supreme courts. Further, there are a few pieces of administrative legislation dealing with some other activities of the administration. Generally, there is no written administrative code in Egypt and the MENA countries to regulate administrative contracts, in particular the substantive principles and performance phase, or to deal with the administration's actions. There are some actions of the administration which are connected to the administrative contracts (administrative decrees connected to the administrative contract, *Actes non-detachables*), and other actions which are not connected to the administrative contracts (decrees which are not connected, *Actes détachables*). Rules of administrative law, in Egypt and the MENA countries, often include administrative actions (decrees) and administrative law contracts.

Therefore, it is suggested that:

- Codification is a fundamental tool for the enhancements and modifications of the substantive clauses of administrative contracts to be consistent with international commercial contracts' substantive principles, which constitute the law and practice of international commercial contracts worldwide. The essential need to change the traditional ideology behind administrative contracts and to enhance the traditional administrative contracts' patterns to be consistent with international commercial contracts' principles, is a necessity.
- There are many examples of substantive contractual clauses of administrative contracts which need significant change such as, liquidated damages, *Exceptio non-adimpleti contractus*, frustration of contract such as the theory of unexpected circumstances (*l'imprévision*). The latter theory has to adopt the legislative approach in PPPs' legislation in Egypt and the MENA countries to be consistent with international patterns of states' contracts, which are not necessarily administrative contracts, and which are more consistent with international commercial contracts' law and practice.
- It is true that codification of administrative contracts' law avoids inconsistent findings (contradictory judgments) by national courts and arbitral tribunals as judges and arbitrators are obliged to apply the written legislation.
- It may be argued that codification offers no solution to the practical and theoretical problems of judicial review.[10] Codification places the content of the principles of judicial review in the hands of politicians. The answer to such an argument is that codification in Egypt and the MENA countries is a necessity to avoid inconsistent findings by state courts and arbitral tribunals, which violates the legitimate expectations of foreign investors. Further, codification is a considerable step towards achieving global contract law. Codification does not trigger the separation of powers principle as there are many constitutional guarantees in the Egyptian and MENA countries to assure that the executive or parliamentary powers are not intervening in the judiciary or in the objectivity of the legislative process.

10 Jean-Bernard Auby (ed.), *Codification of Administrative Procedures* (Bruylant, 2014).

- It is suggested that codification has to implement a sensible balance between protecting investors, whether domestic or foreigners, through adopting international commercial contracts' principles on one hand, and the protection of public interests on the other.
- It is clear that codification will not lead to a 'petrification' of administrative contracts' law and practice as the leading role of the Egyptian Conseil D'État courts shall remain in force in interpreting the legislation and, creating, shaping, and adopting new theories of administrative contracts in light of an existing legislation.
- It is assumed that codification of administrative contracts principles will adopt, in most cases, the substantive principles of international commercial contracts. As such, the gap becomes narrower between administrative law substantive principles and international commercial contracts' principles, in light of the expected unification, which is the tool to achieve global contract law. Further, Unification will narrow the gap between common law jurisdictions and civil law legal systems in the field of contract law.

7 Can Private-Public Arbitration Create Global Contract Law?

An Egyptian Case Study

Introduction

Private-public arbitration plays a significant role in creating a set of unified contract law principles in international states' contracts, whether procedural or substantive. Recourse to arbitration in private-public arbitration in Egypt and some MENA countries needs authorization from the concerned minister or the cabinet.[1] In some MENA countries, the restriction applies to states' arbitration if it enters into private-public arbitration whether in contractual disputes or otherwise,[2] and in some other MENA countries, restriction applies to only administrative contracts.[3] There is a new set of procedural legislative rules which were recently created. In addition, there are also many substantive coherent rules relating to international states' contracts and international contracts in general (whether private or public contracts); those substantive rules were created by international arbitration. New contract law rules were recently created through private-public arbitration case law. It may be argued that unification has been achieved so far, through international arbitration principles. Transnational arbitration is a phenomenon which assumes, in private-public arbitration, that a host state is a party to arbitral proceedings. Arbitrators have different backgrounds, as they are from different nationalities, reflecting civil law or common law legal culture, or a non-legal background.

To what extent are such new principles reflected in international states' contracts in the MENA region? How can states' contracts co-exist with the global diversity of international commercial contracts' principles applied by international arbitrators, who have different backgrounds?

It is worth noting that the theme of this chapter deals with the situation of private-public arbitration in Egypt. It is true that the theme of this chapter is not confined to Egypt, but it covers all MENA countries' legal systems, as Egypt played a significant role over decades to transfer extensively French legal culture to all MENA countries.

The international law paradigm and private law principles have developed the party autonomy principle, which allowed parallel choice for dispute resolution

1 Egyptian and MENA countries' arbitration legislation was influenced by Article 2060 of the French Civil Code. See: Article 1 of the Egyptian Arbitration Act 27 Of 1994, Article 10/2 of the Saudi Arbitration Act 34 of 2012, and Article 2 of the Qatari Arbitration Act 2 of 2017.

2 Article 10/2 of the Saudi Arbitration Act 34 of 2012.

3 Article 1 of the Egyptian Arbitration Act 27 Of 1994 and Article 2 of Qatar Arbitration Act 2 of 2017.

DOI: 10.4324/9781003466352-8

systems between economic actors. Regulatory convergence and norm harmonization in trade instruments such as treaties and conventions have promoted the resolution of private-public disputes through arbitration as an alternative dispute resolution system to the courts. Private actors in contractual relations with sovereign states prefer arbitration to court resolution for a number of reasons which are often attributed to negative perceptions of domestic jurisdictions. Party autonomy focuses on the parties to a contract or a transactional relation and provides optionality in dispute resolution.

International law also developed the procedural autonomy principle, which allows sovereign states to select the dispute resolution system of their preference in settling disputes related to public contracts and contractual relations between private actors and the state. Procedural autonomy focuses on the state and offers discretion in organizing resolution *fora*.

Dispute resolution through arbitration for international investment and private-public partnerships or concessions for critical infrastructure are the default option. Arbitrators, or arbitral tribunals instead of domestic courts, provide dispute resolution in grievances between the state and private actors and create *res judicata* to the applicable law. Private-public arbitration reveals law making capacities in the domestic legal order and questions the legitimacy of alternative dispute resolution systems to the democratic processes.

The permissibility of private-public arbitration is conditional upon assurances that the public interest is not compromised by channeling relevant disputes away from state-centered dispute resolution systems. States develop safeguards for the protection of public interest from the application of party autonomy principle.

This chapter covers the function of private-public arbitration in Egypt and addresses the following aspects; first, it will provide a conceptual mapping of the Egyptian Legal System by revealing its sources and influences, the evolution of its constitution and the structure and organization of the judiciary and its courts in order to position the function of dispute resolution mechanisms, either state-centered or alternative mechanisms such as arbitration; secondly, it will provide a roadmap for the development of the legal framework for the recognition and acceptance of arbitration in Egypt, including private-public arbitration; thirdly, it will attempt to deconstruct the features in the concept of administrative contract, as the base of private-public disputes, which could end up in arbitration and as the safeguard basis for the permissibility of private-public arbitration; and fourthly, it will alllude to the legal and policy lacunae which emerge from a governance perspective from the function of private-public arbitration in Egypt.

The Evolution of the Egyptian Legal System

The Egyptian legal system exudes high levels of influences from both the European systems and *Sharia'a*.[4] In particular, the French legal system has considerably

4 Sofi Abou Taleb, *Sharia'a Application in Arab Countries* (Dar Al Nahda Al Arabia, Cairo, 2006, in Arabic).

inspired the evolution of Egyptian law alongside *Sharia'a* authority as main source of national legislation. The Egyptian legal order is heavily dependent upon the implementation of French established systems, especially public law systems, which were transferred domestically though the jurisdictional organization and functioning of the Egyptian Conseil D'État.[5]

This transplant has been pivotal to the functioning of the legal order in Egypt and the relevant demarcation of public law boundaries. It is also critical to the dispute resolution organization, through either state-centered or alternative mechanisms. Thus, the concept of private-public arbitration is heavily reliant on established paradigms found in European continental legal systems.

Egypt has also acted as a conveyer of its legal system to Arab countries' legal systems, predominately in the MENA region, and thus transferred extensively French legal culture to these countries which before were relying solely on *Sharia'a* law.

Absorbance of international dispute resolution paradigms which are distinct from state-centered dispute settlement and enforcement mechanisms has relied upon international treaties and conventions on arbitration. Arbitration as a concept of dispute resolution is accepted in principle in Egypt. In private disputes, arbitration is often the norm and it is widely recognized as an efficient and effective dispute resolution mechanism which is compatible with Egypt's legal order.

Arbitration can also emerge as a dispute resolution mechanism for grievances between private actors and the state. The Egyptian legal order has been inconsistent with the treatment of private-public arbitration. As the Egyptian legal system has developed a nexus to French public law, which is by default negatively disposed to private-public arbitration, the idea of settling disputes between the state and private actors away from state-centered public law *fora* was met with relative opposition. Such opposition has also been also domestically rooted to constitutional constraints which afforded exclusive jurisdiction of all dispute emanating from administrative contractual relations to public law courts, due to the public interest nature of such relations.

However, a number of influencing factors, endogenous to the evolution of the Egyptian legal system and also external and attributed to regulatory convergence pressures from international normative sources, eroded the systemic stance of distrust by Egyptian law to private-public arbitration and attempted to align

5 After the French invasion of Egypt (1798–1801) the Egyptian legal system was considerably influenced by the French legal system, through decades, in legislation, particularly when codifying the Egyptian Constitutions and the Egyptian Civil Code. In recent decades, the influence of the French Constitution of the Fifth Republic (1958) on the previous Egyptian Permanent Constitution of 1971 was clear. The previous Egyptian Constitution of 1971 played a fundamental role in this respect as it was adopting Marxist ideology upon promulgation. The current Egyptian Constitution of 2014, which is valid until the present, adopts liberal ideology with the aim of encouraging FDI in all economic sectors. Among these sectors are public contracts which deal with infrastructure, public utilities, and services projects. It is worth noting that focusing upon administrative contracts and concession contracts, as traditional concessions are one of the administrative contracts' types, is an important angle when analyzing the theme of this chapter. Private-public arbitration, in most cases, deals with international states' contracts.

the function of private-public arbitration with legal norms and economic reality. Hence, the arbitrability of private-public disputes is conditional upon a number of features which emanate from the nature of the dispute and the character of the disputants. The Egyptian legal system has been considerably influenced by legal globalization and the flow of legal culture from common law jurisdictions.[6]

The Egyptian Constitution

The influence of the French Constitution of the Fifth Republic (1958) upon the Egyptian Permanent Constitution of 1971 was clear, in particular the fundamental rights and liberties in the latter constitution.[7] The Egyptian Constitution of 1971 had four amendments between promulgation and 2007. In the aftermath of 2011 this constitution was replaced in February 2011 with the constitutional declaration of 2011 which was issued by the Military Council in Egypt. In 2012 and 2014 new constitutions have been promulgated respectively and the 2014 Constitution is still valid. Egyptian Constitutions stipulate that *Sharia'a* Law is a main source of legislation. The 2011 Constitutional Declaration, and the 2012 and 2014 Constitutions, have adopted most of the constitutional provisions relating to fundamental rights and liberties of the 1971 Constitution, and have not adopted Marxism ideology.

The Egyptian Judiciary and Court Structure

Egypt has a remarkable history concerning its judiciary and the structure of its courts. As a legal system which relied heavily on jurisdictional transplants, the judiciary and its organization diachronically tried to align *Sharia'a* principles with pressures emanating from the country's cosmopolitan interface.

This is reflected in the establishment of the Mixed Courts' ('*Tribunaux Mixtes*') system. The Mixed Courts had codes inspired by the French Civil Code and British common law but with significant influences from Islamic principles. The Mixed Courts were settling disputes between foreign nationals and between foreigners and Egyptians.[8] The Mixed Courts led to a substantial reform of Egypt's

6 M.S, Abdel-Wahab, Cultural Globalization and Public Policy: Exclusion of Foreign Law in the Global Village (*Law and Sociology* 8, 2005), and in the legal and cultural globalization phenomena see: J. Stiglitz, *Globalization and its Discontents* (W.W. Norton, 2004); *Making Globalization Work* (W.W. Norton, 2007); B. Snowdon, *Globalisation, Development and Transition* (Edward Elgar, 2007); Mohamed AM Ismail, *Globalization and New International Public Works Agreements in Developing Countries, An Analytical Perspective* (Routledge, 2011 and 2016).

7 Fathy Fekry, *Constitutional Law* (Cairo, 2009, in Arabic). For more elaboration see: Mohamed A.M. Ismail, *Arab Constitutions Facts and Prospects* (Al Halabi Publishing Co. Beirut, 2015, in Arabic).

8 The proceedings before the Mixed Courts were held in French and judges were appointed by the Khedive from leading Egyptian and foreign candidates. The completion of the Suez Canal (1869) and the development of the cotton trade had attracted many foreign interests, business entities and foreign nationals to Egypt. See Mark S.W. Hoyle, *Mixed Courts of Egypt* (Arab Islamic Law Series, Kluwer Academic Publisher Group, 1991, England and Netherlands).

chaotic 19th-century legal system, especially after the jurisdictional separation between Consular Courts, Government Courts and Religious Courts and played a significant role towards the development of Egyptian law. [9]

The Mixed Courts played a significant role towards the development of Egyptian law[10] and their functions were transferred to a new national courts system which established the organization of justice by distinguishing between ordinary courts and administrative courts.

The ordinary courts consist of First Instance Courts, a number of Courts of Appeal[11] and the Court of Cassation which is the highest judicial authority[12] over ordinary courts in Egypt. There are also minor courts whose jurisdiction is limited by geographical coverage and the nature of disputes and finally, Family Courts which are specialized judiciary in family disputes. The Code of Civil and Commercial Procedures governs the jurisdiction of ordinary civil and commercial courts in Egypt.

The administrative courts consist of lower administrative courts vested with the power to decide over administrative disputes pertaining to administrative contracts and administrative decrees issued by government officials; there is also the Appeal Administrative Courts, which has many circuits across Egyptian governorates; the Supreme Administrative Court is the highest court in the hierarchy of administrative justice in Egypt, which has a wide jurisdiction to decide on both facts and the interpretation of law.[13] Finally, the Egyptian Conseil D'État is the ultimate judicial organ which may decide on the compatibility of administrative acts with legislation as a safeguard to the principle of legality. The Egyptian Conseil D'État consists of three sections: The Judicial section, the Legal Opinion section and the Legislation section.

In its Legal Opinion section, the General Assembly for Legal Opinion and Legislation of the Egyptian Conseil D'État has jurisdiction for the settlement of disputes between public entities.[14] It can also issue legal opinions and it is regarded as one of the main sources of administrative law in Egypt and also within the MENA countries, since administrative law has not been codified in the respective MENA legal orders. Last, the Egyptian Conseil D'État participates in the legislation promulgation process and revises laws before enactment in Egypt.

Another unique organ of the Egyptian Judiciary is the Supreme Constitutional Court[15] which has jurisdiction to decide on the constitutionality of legislation and administrative regulations to ensure their compatibility with the constitution.

9 Mark S.W. Hoyle, *The Mixed Courts of Egypt* 1886–1895 (1 Arab L.Q. 562, 1985–1986).

10 The Mixed Courts attracted significant criticism from the national movement opposing this judicial system as a *dual* system capable of violating sovereignty due to the distinction between foreign and national nature of disputes before it.

11 There are eight Courts of Appeal, one in Cairo and seven more within central governorates. Courts of Appeal, which are known as Higher Courts of Appeal, have the jurisdiction to issue final judgments on appeals concerning judgments issued by the courts of first instance.

12 The Court of Cassation has jurisdiction to issue irrevocable judgments in cases challenging judgments issued by the Courts of Appeal.

13 The Conseil D'État Law No. 47 of 1972, Article No 23.

14 Article 66/d of the Egyptian Conseil D'État, Law No. 47 of 1972.

15 The 1971 constitution in Egypt stipulated the creation of a Supreme Constitutional Court, which was established in 1979 in Cairo. See Article 175 of the 1971 Constitution.

The Legal Framework Relevant to Private-Public Arbitration in Egypt

International Instruments on Arbitration in Egypt

The international instruments of arbitration in the Egypt consist of ratifications of international conventions and treaties.

The New York Convention of 1958 on the Recognition and Enforcement of Foreign Arbitral Awards was the pillar for successful enforcement of international arbitration awards worldwide. The latter convention emphasizes the judicial nature of international arbitration and it has been a part of the Egyptian legislation since 1959.

The UNCITRAL Model Law (the Model Law) which was adopted in 1985 by the United Nations Commission on International Trade Law forms the basis of the Egyptian Arbitration Act. The ratification of the Model Law endorses the concept of party autonomy in private-private or private-public arbitration and the supportive role of courts to the arbitration process.

The UNCITRAL arbitration rules (the UNCITRAL Rules) adopted by resolution of the General Assembly of the United Nations in 1976 and amended in August 2010 are the source for the Arbitration Rules of Cairo Regional Centre for International Commercial Arbitration.

The Washington Convention of 1965 on the Settlement of Investment Disputes between States and Nationals of Other States (the ICSID Convention) has been ratified by the Egyptian legal order and is utilized as the base for settling disputes arising out of investment treaties.[16] Bilateral Investment Treaties (BITs) occupy a large space in the codification of international investment arbitration rules in Egypt as it has ratified more than 115 bilateral treaties on investment which form part of the Egyptian legislation.

The Egyptian legal order regards investment arbitration as treaty-based or contractual-based arbitration and falls within the premise of private-public arbitration. The Rules of Procedure for Arbitration Proceedings (Arbitration Rules) of the International Centre for Settlement of Investment Disputes (ICSID) are used for investment arbitration disputes.

Domestic Instruments on Arbitration in Egypt

In the Egyptian legal order, arbitration initally was governed by the Code of Civil and Commercial Procedures.[17] The Previous Constitution of 1971 did not contain any express prohibition of private-public arbitration.

Article 172 of the 1971 Constitution provides for the following: 'The *Conseil D'État* shall be an independent judiciary body and shall have the competence to decide in administrative disputes, and disciplinary actions. The law shall determine its other competencies.' The amending 2012 Constitution in Article 174 and 2014 Constitution in Article 190 contain the same legal provision.

16 For a case study on the Egyptian legal system from the ICSID case law see: *Joy Mining Machinery Limited* v. *Arab Republic of Egypt*, ICSID Case No. ARB/03/IIC 147 (2004), Paras 44–47.

17 Articles 501–513 of Law No. 13 of 1968.

Article 167 of the 1971 Constitution of Egypt stipulates: 'The law shall determine judiciary authorities and their functions, organize the way of their formation, define conditions and procedures for the appointment and transfer of their members.' As a result of implementing Article 167 of the 1971 Constitution, the Conseil D'État Law 47/1972 in Article 10 provides that the Conseil D'État courts are exclusively competent to decide on the following matters:...'Disputes pertaining to concession contracts, or public works, or supply agreements, or any other administrative contract.'

This particular legal framework on the exclusive jurisdiction of the Conseil D'État may in principle be amended but only by another law, of equal degree and rank to the Conseil D'État Law 47/1972 and pursuant to procedural and substantive stipulations (criteria) for law promulgation. The 2012 Constitution in Article 174 and the 2014 Constitution in Article 190 stipulate the same requirements for any amendments to the Conseil D'État exclusive jurisdiction over administrative contracts' dispute forum.

The Egyptian Arbitration Act no. 27/1994 stipulated that 'the provisions of the present law shall apply to every arbitration between parties of the public law or private law, notwithstanding the nature of the legal relations subject of dispute in case such arbitration is taking place in Egypt or if it is an international commercial arbitration taking place abroad, where the parties thereof agree on the present law as the governing law.'[18]

That Act provides a legislative breakthrough in the sense that it was the first piece of legislation in the MENA region which was based upon the UNCITRAL Model Law.[19] Following the Egyptian legislature, a significant number of MENA

18 Article 1 of the Arbitration Act 27/1994. Egypt and many MENA countries are part of the global arbitration community, see in international arbitration generally: N. Blackaby, C. Partasides, A. Redfern, and M. Hunter, *International Arbitration* (5th edn, Oxford University Press, 2009 and 6th edn, Oxford University Press, 2014); G. Born, *International Arbitration* (Kluwer Law International, 2012); *International Arbitration Agreements* (2nd edn, Kluwer Law International, 2014); *International Arbitration and Forum Selection Agreements* (4th edn, Kluwer Law International 2013); and *International Commercial Arbitration* (2nd edn, Kluwer Law International, 2014). In French see Philippe Fouchard, Emmanuel Gaillard, Emmanuel et Berthold Goldman, *Traité de l'arbitrage commercial international* (Paris. Litec, 1999).

19 Mahmoud Samir Al Sharkawi, *International Commercial Arbitration* (Dar Al Nahda Al Arabia, 2011, in Arabic); Fathi Wali, *Arbitration Law in Theory and Practice* (Monsha'at Al Marref, Alexandria, 2007, in Arabic); Mokhtar Beriry, *International Commercial Arbitration* (Cairo, Dar Al Nahda Al Arabia, 1995, in Arabic); Nariman Abdel Kader, *Arbitration Agreement Pursuant to Arbitration Act No. 27 of 1994* (Dar Al Nahda Al Arabia, 1996, in Arabic). Following the Egyptian legislature, some Arab countries have codified new Arbitration acts adopting directly the UNCITRAL Model Law such as: Oman (1997), Jordan (2001), Saudi Arabia (2012), Bahrain (2015), Qatar (2017), and UAE (2018). Arbitration legislation was firstly promulgated in Egypt in 1994 and it was directly influenced by the UNCITRAL Model Law. Oman, Jordan, Saudi Arabia, Qatar, and UAE were directly influenced by the Egyptian methodology and drafting in Arbitration legislation. The Kingdom of Bahrain has copied the UNCITRAL Model Law as amended in 2006 to its Official Gazette in addition to nine new promulgation articles.

countries were influenced by the Egyptian Arbitration legislation and codified Arbitration acts adopting directly the UNCITRAL Model Law.[20]

Law 9/1997 provided for an amendment to the Arbitration Act 47/1994 by explicitly stipulating that 'In all events private-public arbitration is permissible in administrative contracts' disputes with the consent of the competent minister or his *pro tempore*. Delegation of power is not permissible in this regard.'[21]

The Legal Treatment of Private-Public Arbitration in Egypt

The availability of private-public arbitration in Egypt has been ambivalent and the negative disposition of the legal regime started before the promulgation of the first Arbitration Act 1994. Even after such a development, private-public arbitration received mixed responses within public law and private law judicial *fora*. It was not until 1997 that the Arbitration Act was amended by Law No. 9/1997, which has been promulgated by the Egyptian parliament and appears to have equal status and rank with the Conseil D'État Law 47/1972 on the exclusive jurisdiction of administrative contact dispute resolution to the Conseil D'État court system.

The 1971 Constitution left the determination of judicial organization and change of jurisdiction to future law enacted by Parliament on the condition of procedural and substantive compatibility with consititional laws. The stipulation of exclusive jurisdiction of administrative contractual disputes to the Egyptian Conseil D'État[22] formed the basis for the contradictory treatment of the permissibility of private-public arbitration and reflected on a narrow and restrictive judicial interpretation of laws emanating from the 1971 Egyptian Constitution, which in fact is silent on the subject.

The Supreme Administrative Court decided[23] that private-public arbitration is not permissible as it is contrary to the exclusive jurisdiction of the Conseil D'État over administrative contracts whose nature is the attainment of public interest.[24] This case alluded to the fact that contracts where public interest is their subject matter cannot be adjudicated through private-public arbitration, since that dispute

20 Arbitration legislation directly influenced by the Egyptian Arbitration Act 47/1994 and the UNCITRAL Model Law include specific acts in Oman in 1997, Jordan in 2001, Saudi Arabia in 2012, Bahrain in 2015, Qatar in 2017, and in UAE in 2018.

21 Article 1, second clause of the Arbitration Act 27/1994 as amended by Law 9/1997.

22 Article 10 of the Conseil D'État law No. 47/1972, which was promulgated directly after the 1971 Constitution, stipulates that the Conseil D'État has the jurisdiction to settle disputes arising out of administrative contracts and all other administrative disputes.

23 Case No. 5837/44, Session 20 February 1990.

24 Egyptian doctrine highlighted the difficulties surrounding private-public arbitration before the promulgation of the Arbitration Act in 1994, see: M.M. Mahmoud, Administrative Contracts and the International Arbitration Clause, *Administrative Sciences Journal* (1993) 35(1) (in Arabic) and for the same author, Arbitrability in Administrative Contracts, Kuwait Conference for International Commercial Arbitration, 1997, p. 129 (in Arabic); and see also: M.K. Mounir, Arbitration in Administrative Contracts, *Administrative Law Journal* (1991) 33(1), p. 337 (in Arabic).

settlement mechanism cannot offer sufficient constitutional safeguards for the resolution of disputes where the state is a party.

This jurisprudence ran contrary to legal opinions of the Conseil D'État where it was held that private-public arbitration is permissible for settling administrative contracts. As early as 1989,[25] the General Assembly for Legal Opinion and Legislation of the Conseil D'État declared[26] that private-public arbitration was not explicitly prohibited by either the constitution nor acts which established jurisdictional exclusivity of the Conseil D'État over administrative contracts.

Similar reasoning was deployed by the General Assembly for Legal Opinion and Legislation in its opinion in 1993, where the Conseil D'État reiterated that the lack of explicit prohibition of having recourse to private-public arbitration by any legislative authority, constitutional or otherwise, within the Egyptian legal order cannot be overridden by procedural jurisdictional laws that provide for exclusivity of the Conseil D'État over administrative contracts.[27]

Despite the promising start in clarifying the position of private-public arbitration in Egypt, the Egyptian Arbitration Act No. 27/1994 could not break away from the restrictive constitutional interpretation of the jurisdictional exclusivity of the Egyptian Conseil D'État.

After its enactment, the General Assembly for Legal Opinion and Legislation of the Conseil D'État reversed its previous trend and in its 18 December 1996 opinion declared that private-public arbitration is not permissible for settling disputes contained in administrative contracts on the grounds that administrative contracts cannot bypass government-centered resolution mechanisms such as the Conseil D'État courts due to the prohibition of re-delegation of power from government to arbitrators in order to settle disputes. In this opinion,[28] the Conseil D'État regarded the

25 The Opinion of The General Assembly for Legal Opinion and Legislation of the Conseil D'État on 17 May 1989 merely provided that the correct interpretation to Article 10 of the Egyptian Conseil D'État law is to distinguish between the jurisdiction of the ordinary courts (civil and commercial courts) on the one hand and the Conseil D'État administrative courts on the other hand.

26 The case concerned a contract concluded between a Ministry and a private construction company which provided that the parties may refer any dispute arising from the execution or interpretation of the contract to an arbitration tribunal. The case was initially referred to the Legal Opinion of the Conseil D'État which then asked the General Assembly to deal with the issue. The General Assembly opined favorably upon the permissibility of private-public arbitration by its opinion dated 17 May 1989.

27 The Opinion of the General Assembly for Legal Opinion and Legislation of the Conseil D'État on 10 March 1993. The case regarded a contract concluded between a ministry and *Al-Ahram* Centre for Organization and Microfilming affiliated with *Al-Ahram* Institution which provided that the parties may resort to arbitration in case a dispute arises during the execution of the contract. The Ministry submitted the issue to the General Assembly for its legal opinion on the permissibility of private-public arbitration in administrative contracts. The General Assembly opined favorably upon the permissibility of private-public arbitration.

28 The case concerned a public works agreement concluded between the Supreme Council for Antiquities (a public entity) and a private foreign company (a British company). The dispute between the parties concerned the complementary works of the Nubian Antiquities Museum landscape in

arbitrability of private-public disputes as delegation of power and any settlement of disputes through arbitration arising out of administrative contracts as part of such power, which in its current order the Egyptian legal system could not permit. The Conseil D'État went further in its opinion by regarding that Article 1 of the Arbitration Act of 1994 lacked sufficient clarity as it contained legislative articles which did not provide any legal certainty.[29]

Despite that opinion, in a different section of the Egyptian judiciary, the Court of Appeal in its Commercial Circuit[30] dealing with the same case, regarded that private-public arbitration is permissible as the Egyptian Arbitration Act of 1994 is clear and there is no other interpretation in light of such express legislative provision permitting private-public arbitration. That Court maintained that private-public arbitration is a consistent approach with Egypt's international commitments through the ratification of international conventions.

The Egyptian Arbitration Act No. 27/1994 was amended in 1997 by Law 9/1997 which specifically confirmed the scope of application of the Egyptian Arbitration Act No. 27/1994 to administrative contracts, subject to the requirement of ministerial consent. Law 9/1997 envisages lifting the uncertainties arising from previous interpretation of the Egyptian Constitution on the permissibility of private-public arbitration and provides clarity and legal certainty in relation to the arbitrability conditions of private-public disputes which do not run contrary to the jurisdictional exclusivity of the Egyptian Conseil D'État.

Similar treatment afforded to the permissibility of private-public arbitration subject to ministerial consent is found in many MENA countries[31] following the enactment of Law 9/1997.

The concept of ministerial consent to have recourse to arbitration sheds light on the previous environment of vagueness deriving from both the constitutional silence on the permissibility of private-public arbitration and the restrictive and

---

Aswan. The contract contained provisions for disputes' settlement through arbitration at the Cairo Regional Centre for International Commercial Arbitration (CRCICA). The General Assembly issued its opinion (18 December 1996) where it concluded the prohibition of private–public arbitration in administrative contracts on the grounds that this administrative contract dispute fell within the Conseil D'État courts' exclusive jurisdiction.

29 In this instance, the influence of the French legal system on the opinion of the Conseil D'État was evident. Article 2060 of the French Civil Code prohibits recourse to arbitration for public entities in principle. Recourse to arbitration is allowed only by explicit legislation.

30 Cairo High Court of Appeal, Commercial Circuit 63, No. 113 of the Judicial Year 64 (unpublished). The case was the same case which went before the General Assembly of the Conseil D'État but followed a parallel route before a first instance civil /commercial court and then was submitted before the Cairo Court of Appeal which decided that private-public arbitration is permissible.

31 The Saudi Arbitration Act 2012, in Article 10/2, stipulates that any public authority cannot start private-public arbitration without the Cabinet's consent unless there is legislative provision permits arbitration. This applies to private-public arbitration in administrative contracts' disputes or otherwise. The Qatar Arbitration Act 2017 stipulates in Article 2/2 that private-public arbitration in administrative contracts is only permitted by the consent of the Prime Minister or the authority delegated by him.

narrow interpretation of jurisdictional exclusivity of administrative courts over disputes arising out of public contracts.

Law 9/1997 established a parallel jurisdiction for administrative contract disputes. It allows for contractual freedom and party autonomy to select between the Conseil D'État court system as default mechanism or to opt for arbitration.

The ministerial consent is both a procedural and substantive precondition of circumventing the jurisdictional exclusivity for the dispute resolution of administrative contracts. The consent in permitting arbitration for administrative contracts is a stipulation by the Egyptian legislature aimed at protecting the public interest. The ministerial consent will balance the probability of harm to public interest by avoiding the default legal forum of Conseil D'État courts for administrative contracts. It presumes that arbitration as a dispute resolution mechanism cannot safeguard public interest, unless certain safeguards are present.

The consent could address certain features of dispute resolution systems such as procedural issues covering the appointment of the arbitral tribunal or the arbitrator, confidentiality and secrecy of the proceedings and arbitral award, transparency of the process, hearing rules and representation, the permissibility of expert witnesses, the applicable laws for the merit of the dispute, enforcement and compliance with arbitral rulings.

The Concept of the Administrative Contract under Egyptian Law: Tug-of-War between State-Centered and Alternative Dispute Resolution Systems

The administrative contract (*Le contrat administratif*) in the Egyptian legal system is a contract between a public authority with legal personality on one hand and a private person with natural or legal personality on the other.[32] Three conditions must be cumulatively met in order for a contract to be classified as an administrative contract. These conditions are the following: a) a public authority with legal personality must be party to the contract; b) the contract must concern the running and/or the management of any of the public utilities; c) the contract must contain excessive clauses or exorbitant clauses which aim to protect public interest.

Administrative contracts fall under the exclusive jurisdiction of administrative courts in their dispute settlement.[33] Administrative contracts are regarded as a type

32 Sarwat Badawi, *Administrative Law* (Dar El Nahda El Arabia, 1985, in Arabic), and for the same author see: *Administrative Contracts* (Dar El Nahda El Arabia, 1988, in Arabic). See also: Soliman El Tamawy, *General Principles of Administrative Contracts* (5th edn, 1991, in Arabic); Soad Al Sharkawi, *Administrative Contracts* (Dar El Nahda El Arabia, 1995 and 1998, in Arabic). In French see: A. de Laubadère, F. Moderne, and P. Delvolvé, *Traité des contrats administratifs* (LGDJ, 1983, Tomes I and II); L. Richer and François Lichère, *Droits des Contrats Administratifs* (LGDJ, 2016); L. Richer, *Droits des Contrats Administratifs* (LGDJ, 2008).

33 The judicial review of administrative acts is reserved by the 1971 Constitution (Article 172), the 2012 Constitution (Article 174), and the 2014 Constitution (Article 190) to the sole jurisdiction of the Egyptian Conseil D'État.

of administrative acts, which could be unilateral ones in the form of decrees or bilateral ones in the form of administrative contracts. Unilateral administrative acts (decrees) are not arbitrable in the Egyptian legal system.[34] However, if an administrative act is connected with one or more administrative contracts, the contractual effects which arise therein are arbitrable.

Egyptian PPP Law 67/ 2010 does not consider public-private partnership contractual arrangements as administrative contracts. It excludes all PPP contracts from the State Procurement Law 89/1998 and its executive regulations, the Public Utilities' Concession Law 129/1947, and the Natural Resources' Concession Law 61/1958.

Public Utilities as entities are regarded as public authorities and their contractual relations with private actors are deemed as administrative contracts. On the other hand, State-owned companies are not regarded as public authorities and therefore their contracts are not administrative contracts in pursuit of public interest.[35]

The Notion of Public Interest as a Requisite of Administrative Contracts

The public interest concept under the Egyptian legal order serves as a principle governing administrative law. Although the concept has no specific definition, it possesses a dynamic nature as it changes its remit diachronically to encompass the interests of the nation and its people as a whole which prevail over any personal or private interests. The public interest concept is the main concept which distinguishes between administrative contracts and private law contracts. The aim of the administrative contract concerns and evolves around the pursuit of public interests. The substantive nature of the administrative contract requires the inclusion of excessive clauses which aim at creating a bias in favor of the public sector.

The concept of public interest reflects on a set of values affecting the state or the nation or the whole community of people which supersede any private or individual interest. The determination of the values for public interest takes into account established principles such as natural justice, equality, objectivity, equality of opportunity, and fairness.

Public interest has many dimensions such as economic, social, and environmental. It overlaps with the concept of public in as much as they are both dynamic concepts in the Egyptian legal order. However, public policy is different from public interest since it embraces esoteric effects of the state's essence and purpose.

Profitability in a contractual arrangement serves as a guide to determining the presence of public interest. Lack of profit as a major subject matter of a contract,

34 Soliman Al Tamawy, *The General Theory of Administrative Decrees, Comparative Study* (Dar El Fikr El Araby, 2017, in Arabic); and see also: Hamdy Yassin Okasha, *The Encyclopedia of the Administrative Decrees in the Conseil D'État Jurisprudence* (2010, three volumes, in Arabic).

35 Soad Al Sharkawi, *Administrative Contracts* (Dar El Nahda Al Arabia, 1995 and 1998, in Arabic); Mohamed A.M. Ismail, *International Construction Contracts Arbitration* (El Halabi Publishing Company, 2003, p. 31, in Arabic).

absence of commercially motivated decision making, pursuit of public service as contractual delivery are legal telltales for the presence of public interest.

The notion of public interest under Egyptian law and practice resembles the unitary concept of public interest centered upon socio-economic parameters. This approach is familiar to many European public law systems where there is a normative approach in determining minimal values which must be preserved by reference to administrative law. The unitary approach of public interest determination also reveals the principle of universality in combining social and economic aspects of interests. Public interests in private-public relations cover not only *value-for-money* considerations but also governance concerns emanating from democratic principles formed by the constitution and public law of states.

The presence of excessive clauses in administrative contracts under the Egyptian legal order serves the principle of universality and purports the safeguard of socio-economic welfare attributes which encapsulate the concept of public interest. Contractual clauses similar to the excessive clauses in Egyptian administrative contracts exist in many European jurisdictions. The contracting state reserves for itself a series of conditions that are often described as General Conditions, which cannot be negotiated or diluted on their risk implications with private actors in order to preserve its legal position and safeguard public interests.

The public interest concept also emerges as a precondition in the permissibility of private-public arbitration. Law 9/1997 confirms explicitly the scope of application of the Egyptian Arbitration Act No. 27/1994 to administrative contracts, subject to the requirement of ministerial consent. Ministerial consent is an administrative act by nature and subject to the judicial review of the Conseil D'État courts.

The ministerial consent is a legislative stipulation to ensure that private-public arbitration does not compromise public interests. The minister's power to grant or withhold consent is subject to judicial review by the Conseil D'État courts to ensure that he has applied public law principles. In addition, pursuant to administrative law principles, the plaintiff has to prove that the minister is *mala fide*.[36]

The ministerial consent is required for both domestic and international private-public arbitration on the proviso that the dispute arises as a contract-based dispute. If the dispute is not a contract-based dispute, ministerial consent is not required. Treaty-based disputes fall under a bilateral investment treaty or the ICSID Convention and as such do not require prior ministerial consent.

Ministerial consent serves as a gate-keeper feature, both in procedural and substantive terms. It acts as a precondition for circumventing the jurisdictional exclusivity for the dispute resolution of administrative contracts. Consent in permitting arbitration for administrative contracts is a stipulation of entrustment of alternative dispute resolution systems by the Egyptian legislature. It also

36 The Supreme Administrative Court, Appeal 1129/37, 15 February 1994, the Technical Bureau in the year (39) and the Supreme Administrative Court, Appeal 462/36, 9 October1994, Technical Bureau in the year (40).

verifies the compatibility of alternative dispute resolution systems with state-centered resolution systems as far as protecting the public interest is concerned. Ministerial consent lifts the *ab initio* presumption that arbitration as a dispute resolution mechanism cannot safeguard the public interest, by ensuring safeguards for public interest.

Such a feature of the Egyptian legal system has systemic governance implications. Not only could the default legal forum for administrative contracts be bypassed by the assurance of public interest preservation, the consent could have far-reaching consequences in ascertaining the compatibility of significant aspects of private-public arbitration such as procedural issues covering the appointment of the arbitral tribunal or the arbitrator, confidentiality and secrecy of the proceedings and arbitral award, transparency of the process, hearing rules and representation, the permissibility of expert witnesses, the applicable laws for the merit of the dispute, and enforcement and compliance with arbitral rulings with the Egyptian constitutional and legislative order.

Private-Public Arbitration as a Risk Feature in PPPs

The PPP legal evolution in Egypt followed European Union developments which centered on the erosion of confidence in the role of the public sector as organizer and asset holder in critical infrastructure. The inability of traditional contractual methods in delivering infrastructure projects and public services deprived the public sector of genuine value-for-money outcomes, thus did not serve the public interest. The criticism has been primarily directed towards: (i) adversarial contractual relations as a result of a competitive procurement process; (ii) inappropriate risk allocation; and (iii) poor contractual performances resulting in delayed and overbudget completions.[37]

Public-private partnerships possess distinctive characteristics when compared with traditional public-private contractual formats. These characteristics reveal a different legal ethos in public sector management. The pivotal characteristic is that the private sector partner is expected to play a strategic role in financing and delivering the infrastructure project or the public service by providing its input into the various phases such as the design, implementation, construction, completion, operation, and maintenance stages of the project. As a result, the duration of the relations between public and private sectors must reflect the need for longevity, in order to allow affordability for repayment on the part of the public sector and also the ability of the private sector to recoup its investment profitably. Another characteristic that complements both the strategic role of the private sector and its long-term engagement in delivering infrastructure and public services reflects on the distribution of risks between the public and private sectors and on the expectation that the private sector will assume substantial risks. Risk assessment in PPPs is a totally different exercise than the assessment of risk in traditional public

37 C. Bovis, *The Law of EU Public Procurement* (2nd edn, Oxford University Press, 2015).

contracts.[38] Dispute resolution is a pivotal governance feature in PPPs, mainly as a result of the risk allocation exercise between the parties.[39]

A range of different risks feature in PPPs: *construction or project risk*, which is related to design problems, building cost overruns, and project delays; *financial risk*, which is related to variability in interest rates, exchange rates, and other factors affecting financing costs; *performance risk*, which is related to the availability of an asset and the continuity and quality of the relevant service provision; *demand risk*, which is related to the ongoing need for the relevant public services; and *residual value risk*, which is related to the future market price of an asset. Finally, political risks cover a general term used to describe risks arising from external or internal factors that are determined or influenced by governments. External political risks, such as currency convertibility, war, sanctions, political instability may be avoided, mitigated, hedged, or insured against and could be significantly mitigated by actions of the state within which the PPP is structured. On the other hand, internal political risks, such as taxation, terrorism, inflation, and industrial unrest are usually uninsurable and could affect the risk allocation within PPPs. Their respective mitigation would potentially reflect on the perceptions of the parties to manage such risks.

Risk transfer from the public sector to the private sector has a significant influence on whether a PPP is a more efficient and cost-effective alternative to public investment and publicly funded provision of services. The public sector and the private sector typically adopt different approaches to pricing market risk. The public sector tends to use the Social Time Preference Rate (STPR) or some other risk-free rate to discount future cash flows when appraising projects. The private sector in a PPP project will include a risk premium in the discount rate it applies to future project earnings, where under the widely used Capital Asset Pricing Model (CAPM), the expected rate of return on an asset is defined as the risk-free rate of return plus a risk premium, the latter being the product of the market risk premium and a coefficient which measures the variance between the returns on that asset and market returns.

The enactment of Egyptian PPP Law 67/2010 on PPPs takes such arrangements between the public sector and private actors away from administrative law in both substantive and procedural terms. The treatment of PPPs as commercial contracts has been met with controversy[40] as one of the main consequences is their exclu-

38 D. Moss, *When All Else Fails: Government as the Ultimate Risk Manager* (Harvard University Press, 2004).

39 Mohamed A.M. Ismail, Private-Public Arbitration in PPPs in Egypt and MENA Region, *EPPPL*, 18(4), 2023, 4, pp. 261–5.

40 Some Egyptian scholars consider PPP contracts as an administrative contract, see: Ragab Mahmoud, *Public-Private Partnership Contracts* (Dar Al Nahda Al Arabia, 2007, in Arabic) and *Partnership Contracts between Public and Private Sectors* (Dar Al Nahda Al Arabia, 2010, in Arabic). Some other authorities consider new types of state transactions such as BOT and PPP contracts as commercial contracts, see: Hani Sarie El Din, *Legal and Contractual Regime for Infrastructure Projects Financed by Private Sector* (Dar Al Nahda Al Arabia, 2001, in Arabic); and *Legal and Contractual*

sion from the jurisdiction of the Conseil D'État courts system. In addition, the PPP contracts are not subject to competitive tendering, objectivity in partner selection, and transparency requirements for their awards.

Private-public arbitration appears as a significant feature of governance in PPPs for the reason that it is part of the dispute resolution which is one of the risks of seeking allocation among the parties. Public-private partnerships denote a sophisticated contractual interface between the public and private sectors which is based on effective risk allocation.

Dispute resolution is part of risk allocation among the parties in infrastructure projects and complex PPPs and is a *sui generis risk* which could not be treated contractually and transferred by the public sector to the private sector or retained by the party to an arrangement which is suited best to bear such risks.

The establishment of Dispute Resolution Mechanisms (DRM) in PPPs, being either state-centered systems or alternative resolution systems, reflects on endemic considerations about the relevant services and deliverables under the PPP. More specifically, perceptions related to the inefficiency of state-controlled systems, corruption and lack of independence in judiciaries, and sovereign immunity against the government or the public sector partner in a PPP erode the confidence of private actors in judicial avenues and particularly court systems.

Conclusions

Transactional complexity in critical infrastructure contracts and public-private partnerships has augmented risk allocation ineffectiveness and given rise to contractual bias, favoring arbitration as the choice for dispute resolution by private actors. Regulatory pressure to install arbitration as DRM through standardization of PPP contracts has been prompted by the loss of confidence in state-controlled systems of dispute resolution, fueled by the interpretation and application of the procedural autonomy doctrine.

The Egyptian legal system permits private-public arbitration but through the ministerial consent process it controls the observance of public interest and may deny the arbitrability of the relevant dispute arising out of administrative contracts thus reclaiming state-centered jurisdiction.

The public interest concept provides for mutual exclusivity in dispute resolution through the veil of administrative contracts which are the only contractual vehicle to ensure their preservation.

The Egyptian legal system has created a variance in treating PPPs as commercial contracts and excluding them from any public interest test for having recourse

Regime for BOT No 177 (El Ahram El Eqtisadi Book, 2002, in Arabic); Mohamed A.M. Ismail, *Globalization and New International Public Works Agreements in Developing Countries, An Analytical Perspective* (Routledge 2011 and 2016), and for the same author see: International Infrastructure Agreements and PPPs in Developing Countries: Substantive Principles, with special reference to Arab and Latin American Countries, *EPPPL* (Lexxion 3/2011).

to private-public arbitration, a test which is applicable to administrative contracts. There is no *ipso facto* control trigger to prevent arbitration as a dispute resolution mechanism in PPPs' contracts.

Private-public arbitration appears as a credible alternative of dispute resolution mechanisms in PPPs and critical infrastructure projects. However, as a *sui generis risk* category in PPPs it merits a public interest test.

The Egyptian legal system draws paradigms from both private law and public law when it comes to arbitration and in particular private-public arbitration. It is suggested that the rooted public law influences in the Egyptian legal system have instilled control mechanisms for the arbitrability of disputes arising out of private-public contractual arrangements which are based on the concept of public interest for both accountability and protection purposes.

Accountability for public interest protection is ensured by the jurisdictional exclusivity of the administrative court system for disputes arising out of private-public contractual arrangements, whereas protection of public interest is safeguarded by a control system to permit private-public arbitration.

The primacy afforded to the principle of party autonomy will typically prevent public interest controls in PPP disputes even when issues of public interest may arise in private-public arbitrations for the settlement of such disputes.

Private-public arbitration plays a significant role towards the unification of contract law principles, to achieve coherent and global substantive principles of contract law. It is worth noting that:

- The permissibility of private-public arbitration as a dispute resolution system has been transmitted to the Egyptian legal order by influencing factors such as international normative convergence and regulatory standardization. The apparent agnostic constitutional stance in relation to private-public arbitration has been the source of inconsistency in the legal treatment of alternative dispute resolutions which threaten the jurisdictional exclusivity of administrative court system.
- The prohibition of private-public arbitration was justified on the nature and character of administrative contracts as the backdrop of the relevant disputes between private actors and the state. The causal link between jurisdictional exclusivity of administrative court system and administrative contracts has been the condition of public interest which is present only in administrative contracts. On the other hand, the explicit permissibility of private-public arbitration has been conditioned on ministerial consent which serves as a system for compatibility approval of private-public arbitration with public interest, with a view to settling disputes that otherwise are reserved for the exclusive jurisdiction of administrative court system.
- A *lex lacuna* emerged by the extraction of PPP contracts from administrative jurisdiction. Such treatment of PPP contracts as commercial contracts does not run contrary to international practice, since the civil justice sector could have jurisdiction in settling disputes arising therein. The principle of party autonomy also offers the optionality of recourse to private-public arbitration,

however without any control system for public interest assurance. The *lex lacuna* reveals that private-public arbitration in PPPs merits a public interest test symbolic of good governance and best practice.

- The private-public arbitration has created, through decades, a new transnational set of substantive contractual principles, as international arbitrators have different backgrounds, whether civil law or common law, or non-legal arbitrators. Global contract law exists in practice, to a great extent, and the private-public arbitration jurisprudence is a step towards the unification of substantive principles of contract law to achieve a coherent set of substantive principles of global contract law.
- The Egyptian Cassation Court ensures on many occasions the transnational character of private-public arbitration and private-private arbitration in Egypt, and in the MENA countries, in case of enforcement of a foreign arbitral award. Provisions of the New York Convention (1958) are part of the Egyptian legislation since ratification in 1959 and such provisions prevail over any other legislative provision in Egypt. This judicial approach shows the respect to the Egyptian government's international commitments and the proper enforcement of arbitral awards.[41] Such an approach by the Egyptian Cassation Court is consistent with the international trends of unification of contract law principles.
- In the Egyptian legal system, private-public arbitration has a broad meaning, as it contains all arbitrable disputes which may arise between States (public juristic persons) and private persons, whether contract-based arbitration or otherwise, and whether commercial arbitration or investment arbitration. Meanwhile, private-private arbitration is an arbitration between two private law entities.[42]
- The Egyptian Arbitration Act No. 27/1994 was the first legislation in the MENA region to appear adopting the (United Nations Commission on the International Trade Law) UNCITRAL Model Law.[43] Egypt has long been

41 The Egyptian Court of Cassation, Case No. 10350 of the Judicial Year 65, session 1 March 1999, Technical Bureau, Civil, Year 50, vol.1, p. 327; and Case No. 2660 of Judicial Year 59, session 29 March 1996, Technical Bureau, Civil, Year 47, vol.1, p. 558.

42 It is worth noting that in the Egyptian legal system private law entities include state-owned companies as any company whether the ownership is wholly or partially owned by the state or the ownership is by private sector. State-owned companies are private law persons or private juristic entities and these private juristic entities have a commercial registration number. The result is that unlike public law persons, state-owned companies, for instance, may enter into contracts through any procedures or regulation created by the company without an obligation to use state procurement law. Thus, contracts entered into by state-owned companies are not administrative contracts (see: the Supreme Administrative Court, Case No. 4576 of Judicial Year 35, Session 6 April 1996; the *Technical Bureau* of the Conseil D'État; the Supreme Administrative Court judgments, year 42, vol. 2, p. 989. If any state-owned company is a party to any arbitral dispute with a private person, it has to be defined as a private-private arbitration dispute.

43 Mahmoud Samir El Sharkawi, *International Commercial Arbitration* (Dar Al Nahdah Al Arabia, 2011, in Arabic); Fathi Wali, *Arbitration Law in Theory and Practice* (Monsha'at Al Marref, Alexandria, 2007, in Arabic); Nariman Abdel Kader, *Arbitration Agreement Pursuant to Arbitration Act No. 27 of 1994* (Dar Al Nahda Al Arabia, 1996, in Arabic). Following the Egyptian legislature, some

ratified the New York and ICSID[44] conventions. The legislative framework governing both private-public and private-private arbitration is the Egyptian Arbitration Act No. 27/1994. The whole arbitral process is subject to party autonomy by the disputing parties.

- The Egyptian Arbitration Act No. 27/1994 is a legislative breakthrough. Prior to that law, arbitration legislative rules had been governed by the Code of Civil and Commercial Law No. 13 of 1968 in Articles 501–13. The articles of the Egyptian Arbitration Act have incorporated a number of crucial and positive aspects that are considered as driving forces behind the promotion of the international character of arbitration as a transnational phenomenon that promotes the increasing trend of achieving global contract law principles. It is important to provide the following analysis to the Egyptian Arbitration Act provisions which are applicable and relevant to both types of private-public arbitration and private-private arbitration, unless otherwise stated as an exeption.

  The follwing points reflect the international character of arbitration in Egypt, and the MENA countries, as a DRM, which plays a significant role to achieve global contract law principles:

- The Egyptian Arbitration Act pointed out that resort to arbitration is a consensual, optional, and contractual matter, through an arbitration agreement (arbitration clause, or arbitration agreement) – Part II of the said Act, namely Articles 10–14. This is an adoption of the principle of party autonomy.[45]
- The Egyptian Arbitration Act requires that the arbitration agreement has to be in writing; otherwise it is null and void (article 12).
- The Egyptian Arbitration Act stipulates in Article 13 that if there is an arbitration clause/agreement, and any of the parties starts litigation procedures before the courts, the other party may allege before the court that there is an arbitration clause/agreement. In that case, the judge must dismiss the case, and the case must be heard only in arbitration. This view is valid if the defendant alleges that there is an arbitration clause/agreement before the court starts scrutinizing substantive claims of the plaintiff.
- Article 23 of the the Egyptian Arbitration Act stipulates that the arbitration clause is an agreement independent of other contractual clauses. The nullity, rescission, or termination of the contract shall not affect the arbitration clause,

---

Arab countries have codified new Arbitration acts adopting directly the UNCITRAL Model Law such as: Oman (1997), Jordan (2001), Saudi Arabia (2012), Bahrain (2015), Qatar (2017), and UAE (2018). Arbitration legislation was first promulgated in Egypt in 1994 and it was directly influenced by the UNCITRAL Model Law. Oman, Jordan, Saudi Arabia, Qatar, and UAE were directly influenced by the Egyptian methodology and drafting in Arbitration legislation. The Kingdom of Bahrain has copied the UNCITRAL Model Law as amended in 2006 to its Official Gazette in addition to nine new promulgation articles.

44 Egypt has ratified the New York Convention since 1959 and the ICSID Convention since 1972.

45 In arbitration agreement in Egypt and MENA countries see: Samia Rashed, *Arbitration in International Private Law Relations, Arbitration Agreement* (Vol. I., Dar Al Nahda Al Arabia, 1984, in Arabic).

provided that such clause is valid *per se*. This is known in Anglo-American jurisdictions as 'Severability or Separability of Contract Clauses.' The English Arbitration Act 1996 deals with same issue in Article No.7.

- The Egyptian Arbitration Act requires that the number of arbitrators has to be an odd number, in cases where there are more than one arbitrator; otherwise the arbitral tribunal composition is void (Article 15 of the said law).
- Articles 18, 19, 20, and 21 of the Egyptian Arbitration Act regulate the procedures and grounds for the arbitrator's challenge, regarding impartiality and independence.
- Articles 20 and 21 of the Egyptian Arbitration Act regulate how to terminate the arbitrator's mandate, upon the request of any party.
- Article 22 of the Egyptian Arbitration Act regulates the principle of '*compétence/compétence*' which states that the arbitral tribunal may rule on its jurisdiction. This article corresponds to Article 30 of the English Arbitration Act 1996.
- Articles 14 and 24 of the Egyptian Arbitration Act provide for the possibility of resorting to provisional or interim measures that may be required by the nature of the dispute.
- Article 36 of the Egyptian Arbitration Act allows the arbitral tribunal to seek the opinion of technical experts when necessary.
- Article 38 of the Egyptian Arbitration Act allows arbitral proceedings before the arbitration tribunal to be suspended, upon any grounds for suspension stated in the Code of Civil and Commercial Procedures, with the consequential effects prescribed in the said law.
- In Article 39/1, the Egyptian Arbitration Act provides that the arbitral tribunal applies the parties' choice to the applicable law to the merits of the dispute. If they agree to apply the law of a specific country, the substantive rules thereof shall be applicable, and not the rules of conflict of laws ('*Renvoi*' rules are excluded),[46] unless otherwise agreed by the parties. In practice, due to sovereignty constraints, it is very difficult to apply foreign law to the merits of the administrative contract's dispute in private-public arbitration, meanwhile, a foreign law may apply to the merits of the dispute in private-private arbitration if it was the parties' choice.
- Article 39/4 of the Egyptian Arbitration Act allows the arbitral tribunal, upon an explicit authorization from the parties, to settle the merits of the dispute, pursuant to the rules of justice and equity, and to act as an *Amiable Compositeur*. This is to some extent difficult in practice in particular in private-public arbitration when a public juristic entity is a party to the dispute. It is worth noting

46 The Egyptian lawmaker followed the fundamental rules in conflict of laws in English case law, in the famous case where the parties' choice of the applicable law was valid, so long as it was in *bona fide* and not against public policy. *Renvoi* was excluded: *Vita Food Products* v. *Unus Shipping (HL)*, UKPC 7, A.C. 277 (P.C.), (1939) 63 Ll L Rep 21.

that in practical reality due to soverignty constraints in administrative contracts, it very difficult for arbitrators to act as *Amiable Compositeur.*

- Article 45 of the Egyptian Arbitration Act stipulates that, unless otherwise agreed by the parties, arbitral award is required to be issued within 12 months from the commencement date of arbitral proceedings. In all cases, the arbitral tribunal may decide to extend the said period, provided that it does not exceed six additional months, unless parties decide for a longer period.
- Article 43/2 of The Egyptian Arbitration Act provides, as a general rule, that the arbitral award must be a reasoned arbitral award, unless the parties to the arbitration agree otherwise, or the law applicable to the arbitration proceedings does not require reference to the award's reasoning.
- The arbitral award, in the Egyptian Arbitration Act, is final, binding, and enforceable. Such is the point of distinction between arbitration and mediation. Unlike court judgments, arbitration awards may not be challenged in any way prescribed in the Code of Civil and Commercial Procedures.
- Article 44 of the Egyptian Arbitration Act provides for the principle of confidentiality of the arbitral award, as a general rule. Paragraph 2 of the said article states that publishing of the arbitral award or parts thereof may not be allowed except with the approval of parties to arbitration.
- The Egyptian Arbitration Act permits the challenge of the arbitral award, as an exception to the general rule stating that the arbitral awards may not be challenged. The arbitral award can only be challenged by filing a case against it, and only in the cases enumerated in Article 53, as an exhustive list and exception to the general rule.
- The Egyptian Arbitration Act does not cause the suspension of the enforcement of the arbitral award once the nullity case is filed, unless otherwise ordered by the court before which the case is filed (Article 57 of the said law).
- The Egyptian Arbitration Act states that arbitral awards issued by virtue thereof be recognizable and enforceable, subject to the provisions prescribed therein. It is important to note that Egypt has ratified the New York Convention (1958) and this convention is considerd a part of the valid legislation in Egypt since ratification in 1959.

  The provisions incorporated in the said law are consistent with arbitration legislation of most of the major countries, in both the Anglo-American jurisdictions and civil law legal systems. The Egyptian Arbitration Law contains the principles and standards that ensure the unification and harmonization of legal approaches, and the internationalization of the arbitration process in Egypt as arbitration, in most cases, is a transnational phenomenon. In most cases, there is an assumption that a foreign investor is a party to the dispute. Thus, legal approachs in arbitration legislation in any country should not violate the economic expectations of any foreign investor.
- Arbitration Acts in Oman 1997, Saudia Arabia 2012, Bahrain 2015, Qatar 2017, and UAE 2018 adopted the same above-mentioned principles. Egyptian and MENA countries' arbitration Acts are influenced by the UNCITRAL Model Law for International Arbitration.

- Finally, private-public arbitration has created, through decades, a new transnational set of coherent substantive contractual principles, as international arbitrators have different backgrounds. Global contract law is underway in practice, due to private-public arbitration, and private-private arbitration case law which is a step towards the unification of substantive principles of contract law to achieve global contract law.

8 The Role of International Organs to Create a Global Contract Law

Introduction

International organs play a fundamental role towards achieving globally unified principles of contract law. The United Nations Commission on International Trade Law (the UNCITRAL) and the International Institute for the Unification of Private Law (the UNIDROIT), are the most important international organizations who create global instruments for the unification of global contract law principles. Both organizations implement the needs of the international community for modernizing, harmonizing, and co-ordinating private law and in particular commercial law, as between states and groups of states, and formulate uniform law instruments, principles, and rules, to achieve those objectives. Such a role of international organs has to affect international states' contracts in the MENA region, despite public law constraints.

How has the role of the UNCITRAL and UNIDROIT affects the substantive principles of international states' contracts in the MENA region? How has unification of private law (commercial law principles) affects public contracts in the MENA region, in particular international states' contracts with private foreign entities?

Unification or Harmonization of Laws, How?

The terms unification and harmonization of laws are often used interchangeably. As Moreno Rodríguez stated,

> Unification implies the adoption of common legal rules by more than one state or region. By contrast, harmonization provides flexibility; it does not necessarily refer to uniform texts but rather to the alignment of legal criteria based on common foundations, model laws, or uniform principles. Both conflict of laws rules and substantive laws can be subject to unification and harmonization. An 'international treaty' or 'convention' is the instrument traditionally used by states to adopt common rules as part of unification efforts, by building upon existing solutions or creating new ones. Indeed, many successful treaty instruments have been drafted […].[1]

1 José Antonio Moreno Rodríguez, *Private (and Public) International Law in Investment Arbitration* (Hague Academy of International Law, Offprint from *The Recueil Des Cours*, Vol. 429, Brill Nijhoff,

DOI: 10.4324/9781003466352-9

International treaties may pose limitations as they are relatively inflexible and may be incapable of responding to changes in rapidly evolving commercial practices. Therefore, the concept of 'model law' began to appear. Model law is an instrument drafted by an eminent organization that subsequently recommends its adoption by states. The UNCITRAL Model Law on International Commercial Arbitration (UNCITRAL Model Law) is a clear example of model laws as an important instrument adopted by international organs. True unification is not achieved through adopting model laws since the national legislature may revise or disregard model law provisions. States adopt additional 'soft law' legal methods which may generate a type of 'statement of the law' which are called 'principles.' Soft law may include legislative guides that offer examples of draft texts in the form of rules and regulations and other types of guides and similar instruments.[2]

Two uniform law instruments are of fundamental importance to the unification of globally accepted principles of contract law. First, the UN Convention on Contracts for the International Sales of Goods (CISG),[3] and second, the UNIDROIT Principles of International Commercial Contracts (UPICC).[4] Both instruments illustrate international commercial contracts' principles as they are globally accepted by member states and the international community in general.

It is worth noting that there are many regional unification efforts. The Principles of European Contract Law (PECL) was founded by a group of academics from all member states; a group which was created by the European Parliament. The PECL were published in 1995 (Part I), 1999 (Part I and II jointly), and 2003 (Part III). The Draft Common Frame of Reference (DCFR) is another soft law instrument, which was drafted in a similar way to PECL, and which is a purely academic document. It was presented in 2008 and welcomed by the European Parliament. It is expected that the DCFR will be an optional instrument in European contract law.

In Africa, in 2002 the Organization for the Harmonization of Business Law in Africa (OHADA) Council of Ministers began drafting a uniform act on the law of contracts with the support of the UNIDROIT. Based on the UNIDROIT Principles, the first preliminary draft encompassed only substantive contract law rules. The OHADA Council of Ministers decided to relaunch the preparation of the Uniform Act on Contract Law with the Foundation for Continental Law. OHADA and the Foundation for Continental Law created a working group that submitted a

---

Leiden/Boston, 2023, pp. 316–17). For Unification generally see: Harold J. Berman, Unification of Contract Clauses in Trade Between Member-Countries of The Council for Mutual Economic Aid, *International And Comparative Law Quarterly*, Cambridge University Press, 7(4), October, 1958, pp. 659–90; Ingeborg Schwenzer, Global Unification Of Contract Law, *Uniform Law* 21(1), Oxford Academic, March 2016, pp. 60–74.

2 José Antonio Moreno Rodríguez, *Private (and Public) International Law in Investment Arbitration*, pp. 317-18.

3 https://uncitral.un.org/sites/uncitral.un.org/files/media-documents/uncitral/en/19-09951_e_ebook.pdf, last accessed on 30 December 2023.

4 www.unidroit.org/instruments/commercial-contracts/, last accessed on 30 December 2023.

preliminary draft of the Uniform Act on the Law of Obligations for the OHADA region in 2015.[5]

The private sector has also made considerable efforts in the unification of contract law principles. 'Standard form of contract' is an important tool in the international sphere. It is worth noting that the Conditions of Contract for Works of Civil Engineering (Construction Contract) which was published in 1987 (the Red Book), and Construction Contracts 2017 (reprinted with amendments in 2002) and many other standard forms of construction contracts are prepared under the auspices of the *Fédération International des Ingénieurs-Conseils* (FIDIC). Those standard forms of contracts have been subject to many updates and amendments until the present.[6] FIDIC standard forms of contracts are very well known in international practice in the international construction contracts' field.[7]

The United Nations Commission on International Trade Law, The UNCITRAL

The importance of developing and maintaining a robust cross-border legal framework for the facilitation of international trade and investment is widely acknowledged. The UNCITRAL plays a key role in developing that framework in pursuit of its mandate to further the harmonization and modernization of the law of international trade. UNCITRAL adopts legislative and non-legislative instruments in a number of key areas of commercial law.

The UNCITRAL was established by the United Nations' General Assembly Resolution in 1966.[8] In establishing the Commission, the General Assembly recognized that disparities in national laws governing international trade created obstacles to the flow of trade, and it regarded the Commission as the vehicle by which the United Nations could play a more active role in reducing or removing these obstacles.

UNCITRAL texts are developed through an international process involving a variety of participants. UNCITRAL membership is structured so as to be representative of different legal traditions and levels of economic development, and its procedures and working methods ensure that UNCITRAL texts are widely accepted as offering solutions appropriate to many countries at different stages of economic development. To implement its mandate and to facilitate the exchange of ideas and information, UNCITRAL maintains close links with international and regional

5 José Antonio Moreno Rodríguez, pp. 327–9.

6 In the same meaning see: ibid., p. 330.

7 In FIDIC forms of contracts see: N.G. Bunni, *The FIDIC Form of Contracts* (2nd edn, Blackwell Publishing, 1997); Nael Bunni, *The FIDIC Forms of Contract* (3rd edn, Oxford: Blackwell, 2005). In the harmonization of building contracts see: Christopher S. Thomas, '*Aspects of Building Contracts: A Comparative View of English and French Law in the Light of Potential Harmonization*,' PhD thesis, School of Law, Kings College, London, 1995.

8 The United Nations General Assembly Resolution 2205(XXI) of 17 December 1966, see: https://uncitral.un.org/. Last accessed on 29 December 2023.

organizations, both inter-governmental and non-governmental, that are active participants in the work program of UNCITRAL and in the field of international trade and commercial law.

UNCITRAL is formulating modern, fair, and harmonized rules on commercial transactions. These include: conventions, model laws, and rules which are acceptable worldwide; legal and legislative guides and recommendations of great practical value; updated information on case law and enactments of uniform commercial law; technical assistance in law reform projects; and regional and national seminars on uniform commercial law.

In a legally globalized world, the importance of an improved legal framework for the facilitation of international trade and investment is widely acknowledged. UNCITRAL plays an important role in developing that framework because of its mandate to prepare and promote the use and adoption of legislative and non-legislative instruments in a number of key areas. These instruments are negotiated through an international process involving a variety of participants. As a result of this process, the UNCITRAL texts are widely accepted as offering solutions appropriate to many different countries at different stages of economic development.

The United Nations' Commission on International Trade Law is the core legal body of the United Nations' system in the field of international trade law. A legal body with universal membership specializing in commercial law reform worldwide for over 50 years, UNCITRAL's business is the modernization and harmonization of rules on international business.

UNCITRAL supports the UN SDGs. In the Addis Ababa Action Agenda, states endorsed 'the efforts and initiatives of the United Nations Commission on International Trade Law, as the core legal body within the United Nations system in the field of international trade law, aimed at increasing coordination of and cooperation on legal activities of international and regional organizations active in the field of international trade law and at promoting the rule of law at the national and international levels in this field.'[9]

The Commission carries out its work at annual sessions, which are held in alternate years at United Nations Headquarters in New York and at the Vienna International Centre in Vienna. Each working group of the Commission typically holds one or two sessions a year, depending on the subject-matter to be covered; these sessions also alternate between New York and Vienna.

In addition to Member States, all States that are not members of the Commission, as well as interested international organizations, are invited to attend sessions of the Commission and of its working groups as observers. Observers are permitted to participate in discussions at sessions of the Commission and its working groups to the same extent as members.

UNCITRAL is formulating modern, fair, and harmonized rules on commercial transactions. These include conventions, model laws and rules which are acceptable worldwide, legal and legislative guides and recommendations of great

9 https://uncitral.un.org/. Last accessed on 29 December 2023.

practical value, updated information on case law and enactments of uniform commercial law, technical assistance in law reform projects, and regional and national seminars on uniform commercial law. UNCITRAL has created, through decades, international instruments in International Commercial Arbitration, International Commercial Mediation, Investor-State Dispute Settlement, Electronic Commerce, International Sales of Goods (CISG) and related transactions, Micro, Small and Medium-Sized Enterprises, Insolvency, Security Interests, On-line Dispute Resolution, International Payment, Procurement and Public Private Partnerships, and International Transport of Goods.

The General Assembly's Sixth Committee is one of the main committees of the General Assembly and considers legal matters, including the annual report of UNCITRAL.

UNCITRAL carries out its work at annual sessions held alternately in New York and Vienna. The work at these sessions typically includes:

- Finalization and adoption of draft texts referred to the Commission by the working groups.
- Consideration of progress reports of the working groups on their respective projects.
- Selection of topics for future work or further research.
- Reporting on technical cooperation and assistance activities and coordination of work with other international organizations.
- Consideration of General Assembly resolutions on the work of UNCITRAL.
- Administrative matters.

Working Groups undertake the substantive preparatory work on topics on UNCITRAL's work program. Membership of working groups currently includes all States members of UNCITRAL. A Working Group typically meets twice a year, holding a spring session in New York and a fall session in Vienna.

The International Institute for the Unification of Private Law, The UNIDROIT

The International Institute for the Unification of Private Law (UNIDROIT)[10] is an independent intergovernmental organization with its seat in Rome. The UNIDROIT aims at studying the needs and methods for modernizing, harmonizing and co-ordinating private and in particular commercial law as between states and groups of states and formulating uniform law instruments, principles, and rules to achieve those objectives. Set up in 1926 as an auxiliary organ of the League of Nations, the Institute was, following the demise of the League, re-established in 1940 on the basis of a multilateral agreement between states. The UNIDROIT has 65 member states who have acceded to the UNIDROIT Statute, and they belong

10 www.unidroit.org/, last accessed on 30 December 2023.

to five continents and represent a variety of different legal, economic, and political systems as well as various cultural backgrounds.

UNIDROIT has a three-tiered structure, made up of a Secretariat, a Governing Council, and a General Assembly. The Secretariat is the executive organ of the UNIDROIT responsible for carrying out its work program. It is headed by the Secretary General who is appointed by the Governing Council on the nomination of the President of the Institute. The Governing Council supervises all policy aspects of the means by which the Institute's statutory objectives are to be attained and in particular the way in which the Secretariat carries out the wok program drawn up by the Council. It is constituted from one *ex officio* member, the President of the Institute, and 25 elected members, mostly eminent judges, practitioners, academics, and civil servants. The Governing Council is chaired by the President of the Institute who is a member of the Council *ex officio.* The General Assembly is the ultimate decision-making organ of the UNIDROIT as it votes for the Institute's budget each year; it approves the work program every three years; and it elects the Governing Council every five years. It is constituted from one representative from each member state. The official languages of the UNIDROIT are English, French, German, Italian, and Spanish; its working languages are English and French.

The UNIDROIT has over the years prepared more than 70 studies and drafts. Many of these have resulted in international instruments, including international conventions, model laws, principle and legal and contractual guides. International conventions are adopted by diplomatic conferences convened by member states of the UNIDROIT. UNIDROIT's work has also served as the basis for a number of international instruments adopted under the auspices of other international organizations, several of which are now already in force.

The Nature of the Instruments Drawn by the UNIDROIT

UNIDROIT's basic statutory objective is to prepare modern and harmonized uniform rules of private law understood in the broad sense. However, experience has demonstrated a need for occasional incursion into public law, especially in areas where hard and fast lines of demarcation are difficult to draw or where transactional law and regulatory law are interviewed. Uniform rules prepared by the UNIDROIT are concerned with the unification of substantive law rules; they will only include uniform conflict of laws' rules incidentally. UNIDROIT independent status among intergovernmental organizations has enabled it to pursue working methods which have made it a particularly suitable forum for tackling more technical and less political issues. UNIDROIT Principles of International Commercial Contracts (UPICC) are one of the most important instruments worldwide, in the unification of contracts' law principles, in particular international commercial contracts.[11] UPICC are recognized worldwide as unification of globally accepted

11 www.unidroit.org/instruments/commercial-contracts/, last accessed on 30 December 2023.

substantive contract law principles, which is the way to achieve a global contract law, in both private and public contracts. Such unification narrows the gap between common law jurisdictions and civil law legal systems in contract law substantive principles.

There are some factors which determine eligibility of subjects for uniform law treatment. New technologies and international commercial practices call for new, harmonized, and widely accepted solutions. The eligibility of a subject for harmonization or even unification will, to a large extent, be conditional on the willingness of states to accept changes to domestic law rules in favor of new international solutions on the relevant subject. Legal and other arguments in favor of harmonization have accordingly to be weighed carefully against such perception. Similar considerations will also tend to determine the most appropriate sphere of application to be given to uniform rules, that is to say, whether they should be restricted to truly cross-border transitions or extended to cover internal situations as well. While commercial law topics tend to make up most of the international harmonization initiatives, the broad mandate given to UNIDROIT allows the organization to deal with non-commercial matters as well.

The uniform rules drawn up by UNIDROIT have, in keeping with its intergovernmental structure, generally taken the form of international conventions, designed to apply automatically in preference to a state's municipal law once all the formal requirements of that state's domestic law for their entry into force have been completed. However, alternative forms of unification have become increasingly popular in areas where a binding instrument is not felt to be essential. Such alternatives may include model laws which states may take into consideration when drafting domestic legislation or general principles which judges, arbitrators, and contracting parties they address are free to decide whether to use or not. Generally, 'hard law' solutions (i.e. conventions) are needed where the scope of the proposed rules transcends the purely contractual relationships and where third parties' or public interests are at stake as is the case in property law. The choice of topics for the UNIDROIT work program, their priority levels and working methods, as well as the overall line of activities follow the criteria and strategic objectives of the Institute.

The UNIDROIT has long cooperated with other international organizations. It maintains its close ties of cooperation with other international organizations, both intergovernmental and non-governmental, which in many cases takes the form of cooperation agreements concluded at inter-Secretarial level. The Hague Conference on Private International Law, UNIDROIT, and the UNCITRAL; the three private law formulating agencies, are quite appropriately referred to as the 'three sisters.' By reason of its expertise on the international unification of private law, UNIDROIT is moreover at times commissioned by such other organizations to prepare comparative law studies and/or draft conventions designed to serve as the basis for the preparation and/or finalization of international instruments in those organizations.

The UNIDROIT has exercised various legislative activities and produced many international instruments such as:

- Principles of International Commercial Contracts.
- Civil Procedures.
- Model Law on factoring.
- Best Practice of Effective Enforcement.
- Rail Protocol.
- Space Protocol.
- Protocol to the Cape Town Convention on Matters Specific to Agriculture, Mining, and Construction Equipment.
- Agriculture.
- Cultural property.

Further, the UNIDROIT has a new project, in cooperation with the International Chamber of Commerce (ICC), on the unification of international investment contracts, through creating an international instrument which is suitable for all countries, whether civil law or common law legal culture.

The UNIDROIT and International Investment Contracts

In the legal globalization era, investment relations have increased in the past decades. However, there are discrepancies about the interpretation of legal concepts relevant to international investment contracts and there are no international standards to guide the contractual relationships between states and private investors. There is an essential need to unify, standardize, and harmonize the substantive principles of international investment contracts, to create a global model of such contracts, and to narrow the gaps between common law legal culture and civil law legal culture.[12]

UNIDROIT's project on International Investment Contracts (IICs) aims at developing guidance to foster the modernization and standardization of IICs. The project aims to explore the interaction between the UNIDROIT principles of international commercial contracts (UPICC) and common provisions in international investment contracts, and it seeks to address a number of recent developments in the area of international investment law, such as the increasing focus on corporate social responsibility and sustainability.

The Project is jointly undertaken by the UNIDROIT and the ICC's Institute of World Business Law (ICC Institute). This partnership combines UNIDROIT's expertise in developing international law instruments in the field of private law with the ICC Institute's expertise on investment arbitration and the development of model clauses.

In 2022, the UNIDROIT Secretariat received a proposal from the ICC Institute for a joint project on investment contracts, for inclusion in UNIDROIT's 2023–2025 work program. The Proposal aimed at exploring how international investment

12 See www.unidroit.org/work-in-progress/investment-contracts-upicc/, last accessed on 30 December 2023.

contracts could be modernized, harmonized, and standardized, particularly in light of UPICC and ICC standards, with a view to address, at the contractual level, a number of developments in the area of international investment law in the last decades, such as the trend to incorporate public policy goals in investment treaties and the increasing potential relevance of international investment contracts, also given the need to specify vague treaty norms and address legal uncertainty deriving from the lack of uniformity in arbitral decisions. The UNIDROIT Governing Council at its 101st session (June 2022) agreed on the importance of this topic and noted that it fits well with UNIDROIT's work. It welcomed the partnership with the ICC Institute and recommended including a project on IICs in the 2023–2025 work program. Following the Governing Council's recommendation, the General Assembly at its 81st session (December 2022), agreed to include this project in UNIDROIT's 2023–2025 work Program with high priority. It acknowledged that the project was ambitious and would have an impact on strengthening the contractual framework for international investments. Pursuant to the mandate provided by the UNIDROIT's governing bodies, the project will explore developments in international investment law and their impact on investment contracts. Examining the role of the UPICC in the IICs is a cornerstone of this project. UPICC's interaction with common contractual terms in IICs will highlight the need for legal guidance or adjustments to fill possible gaps. Finally, the project aims at exploring:

- The content of the envisaged project.
- Investment contracts and contract law.
- Investment contracts and foreign investment law.

The project considers developments in international investment law and confirmed the need for guidance at the contractual level. Such guidance or model contract, or whatever instrument will be adopted, is needed in the international community to achieve a global contract law in investment contracts.

The Hague Conference on Private International Law, The HCCH

HCCH is an intergovernmental organization in the area of private international law, that administers several international conventions, protocols, and soft law instruments.

The Hague Conference was first convened by Tobias Asser in 1893 in The Hague. In 1911, Asser received the Nobel Prize for Peace for his work in the field of private international law, and in particular for his achievements with respect to the HCCH. After World War II, the Hague Conference was established as an international organization.

On the initiative of Tobias Asser, the First Diplomatic Session of the HCCH was convoked in 1893. Its aim was, and remains, to 'work for the progressive unification of the rules of private international law,' including by creating, and assisting in the implementation of, multilateral conventions that promote the harmonization of the rules and principles of private international law.

The First to Fourth Diplomatic Sessions of the HCCH took place in 1893, 1894, 1900, and 1904 respectively. They resulted in a number of multilateral treaties, the Hague Conventions, that unified the rules of private international law in the areas of Marriage (1902), Divorce (1902), Guardianship (1902), Civil Procedure (1905), Effects of Marriage (1905), and Deprivation of Civil Rights (1905).

After World War I, the Fifth and Sixth Diplomatic Sessions took place in 1925 and 1928 respectively. The result of those Diplomatic Sessions was the Protocol to recognize the competence of the Permanent Court of International Justice to interpret the Hague Conventions on Private International Law.

After World War II, steps were taken to establish the HCCH as an intergovernmental organization, governed by its member states and administered by a secretariat, the Permanent Bureau. The treaty establishing the HCCH, the 'Statute of the Hague Conference on Private International Law,' was adopted during the Seventh Diplomatic Session of the HCCH in 1951, and entered into force on 15 July 1955.

The acronym 'HCCH' is derived from using the respective capitals of the phrases '*Hague Conference*' and '*Conférence de La Haye.*' It represents the bilingual nature of the HCCH, which has both English and French as its working languages.

As of March 2022, the HCCH has 91 members: 90 member states and one Regional Economic Integration Organization (REIO), the European Union.

The member states contribute to the expenses of the HCCH through their assessed contributions, which are due annually. The EU also contributes on the basis of contributions that are agreed.[13]

Since 1955, the HCCH developed 38 international conventions and protocols that establish rules on jurisdiction, applicable law, the recognition and enforcement of foreign judgments, and on legal and judicial cooperation. They are open for adoption, accession or ratification by any state, including states that are not members of HCCH.

In 2015, the HCCH adopted its first soft-law instrument, the Hague Principles on the Choice of Law in International Commercial Contracts.

The HCCH's instruments cover subject matters in the area of family law and child protection, international civil procedure and legal cooperation, as well as cross-border commercial and finance law. These areas are often referred to as the 'three pillars' of the HCCH. The following HCCH conventions are the most ratified:

- The abolition of legalization (Apostille).
- Service of process.
- Taking of evidence abroad.
- International child abduction.
- Intercountry adoption.
- Maintenance obligations.

13 The *Regulations on Financial Matters and Budgetary Practices of the Hague Conference on Private International Law* provide the details in this regard.

- Choice of Court Agreements.
- Hague Child Protection Convention.
- The law applicable to trusts.

The most recently concluded Hague convention is the Hague Judgments' Convention, adopted on 2 July 2019.

Choice of Law in International Commercial Contracts

The *Principles on Choice of Law in International Commercial Contracts* (Choice of Law Principles), the first 'soft-law' instrument of the HCCH, are designed to promote party autonomy in international commercial contracts. By acknowledging that parties to a contract may be best positioned to determine which set of legal norms is most suitable for their transaction, party autonomy in the international commercial context enhances predictability and legal certainty – important conditions for effective cross-border trade and commerce. At the same time, the principles also set reasonable boundaries to party autonomy and thus may provide a refinement of the concept where it is already accepted.

It is worth noting that the *Legal Guide to Uniform Instruments in the Area of International Commercial Contracts, with a Focus on Sales* (Legal Guide), a joint publication of the Secretariats of UNCITRAL, UNIDROIT, and the HCCH, offers an overview of the principal legislative texts prepared by each organization, such as the *United Nations Convention on Contracts for the International Sale of Goods*, the *HCCH Principles on Choice of Law in International Commercial Contracts*, and the *UNIDROIT Principles on International Commercial Contracts*. It also illustrates how these texts interact to achieve the shared goals of predictability and flexibility. The Legal Guide will be a user-friendly resource for those interested in the adoption, application, and interpretation of uniform contract law.

Conclusions

International organs play a fundamental role to achieve global contract law principles, accepted in all legal cultures, whether civil law or common law. Unification of contract law principles by the UNIDROIT, through adopting the UNIDROIT Principles for International Commercial Contracts (UPICC), as a globally recognized and accepted instrument, is paving the way to achieve standardization, harmonization, modernization, and unification of international contract law principles. Such steps taken by the international organs shall:

- Reduce public law constraints to achieve global contract law principles, accepted by both leading legal cultures in the world, common law and civil law, in particular, substantive contractual clauses which are controversial in both legal cultures, and in public and private contracts, such as liquidated damages, *Exceptio non-adempleti contractus*, and other clauses.

- Narrow the gaps between common law jurisdictions and civil law legal systems, as standardization and unification of globally accepted contract law principles will remove barriers between both legal cultures. Standardization and unification of contract law principles, whether public contracts or private contracts, will achieve global principles of contract law.

The impact of global endeavors exercised by the international organizations is clear upon Egypt and MENA countries' legal systems, as the latter jurisdictions are adopting most of the international instruments adopted by such international organs. Unification of globally accepted substantive contract law principles is the way to achieve a global contract law, in both private contracts and public contracts. Therefore, global contract law is underway in the respective jurisdictions. The role of the UNCITRAL and UNIDROIT affects the substantive principles of international states' contracts in the MENA region. Unification of private law, in particular international commercial law principles, affects public contracts in Egypt and the MENA region, in particular international states' contracts with private foreign entities.

9 The Impact of Unification of International Contract Law Principles on Egypt and MENA Countries

The aim to achieve the unification of international states' contracts' principles to be consistent with international commercial contracts' principles, has significant results for the economic developments of Egypt and the MENA countries. Unification has a great impact upon increasing foreign investments in Egypt and the MENA region.

Unification of all types of contract law principles to achieve coherent contract law principles is a fundamental tool to increase the inward of FDI to Egypt and the MENA countries. One of the fundamental tools to achieve the increase of inward of FDI is to enhance investment policies in the respective jurisdictions. Investment policies should establish open, non-discriminatory, transparent, and predictable conditions for investment. Investment policies should provide legal certainty and strong protection to investors and investments, tangible and intangible, including access to effective mechanisms for the prevention and settlement of disputes, as well as to enforcement procedures. Unification is a fundamental tool to enhance investment policies.

With the objective[1] of (i) fostering an open, transparent, and conducive national policy environment for investment; (ii) promoting coherence in national and international investment policy making; and (iii) promoting inclusive economic growth and sustainable development, the Egyptian and MENA governments aim at:

- Recognizing the critical role of investment as an engine of economic growth in the national economy, investment policies establish open, non-discriminatory, transparent, and predictable conditions for investment.
- Regulation relating to investment is developed in a transparent manner with the opportunity for all stakeholders to participate, and embedded in an institutional framework based on the rule of law.
- Investment policies and other policies that impact on investment are coherent at both the national and international levels and aim at fostering investment, consistent with the objectives of the UN SDGs and inclusive growth.
- Policies for investment promotion aim to maximize economic benefit, be effective and efficient, aimed at attracting and retaining investment, and matched by

1 'G20 Trade Ministers Meeting Statement: Annex III,' 9–10 July 2016, Shanghai, available at www.wto.org/english/news_e/news16_e/dgra_09jul16_e.pdf., last accessed on 29 October 2023.

DOI: 10.4324/9781003466352-10

facilitation efforts that promote transparency and are conducive for investors to establish, conduct, and expand their businesses.

- Cooperation between the Egyptian and MENA governments and the international community (international organs) should continue to engage in dialogue with a view to maintaining an open and conducive policy environment for investment, and to address shared investment policy challenges.
- Investment policies and other policies that impact on investment should be coherent at both the national and international levels and aimed at fostering investment, consistent with the objectives of sustainable development and inclusive growth.
- Egypt and MENA governments reaffirm the right to regulate investment for legitimate public policy purposes.
- Policies for investment promotion aim to maximize economic benefit, be effective and efficient, aimed at attracting and retaining investment, and by facilitation efforts that promote transparency and are conducive for investors to establish, conduct, and expand their businesses.
- Investment policies should promote and facilitate the observance by investors of international best practices and applicable instruments of responsible business conduct and corporate governance.
- The international community should continue to cooperate and engage in dialogue with a view to maintaining an open and conducive policy environment for investment, and to address shared investment policy challenges. This can be achieved through unification of global contract law in civil law legal systems and common law jurisdictions.

Unification of international states' contracts' principles to be consistent with international commercial contracts' principles is the fundamental pillar in any legal system which can be described as incentives to attract and increase the inward of FDI. There is a direct causal link between the existence of a unified and global international contract law legal system (whether public or commercial contracts) on one hand, and the increase of the inward of FDI and the improvement of life of the ordinary citizens in relevant jurisdictions on the other. The aim to offer a higher threshold of protection, through unification to achieve global contract law principles, to a private party in particular if it is a foreign investor, is to increase the inward of FDI in the various economic sectors and to enhance the socio-economic pattern of the ordinary citizens.

The question is: How unified can global states' international contract law principles, which are consistent with international commercial contracts' principles, offer a high threshold of protection to both domestic and foreign investors, in the respective jurisdictions?

It is true that there is an overlapping between the principles which govern international states' contracts in the relevant jurisdictions and principles which attract FDI to Egypt and MENA countries as they are similar principles which are required to maintain a better environment for various economic sectors. Principles for both targets may cooperate to encourage socio-economic developments, increasing productivity, reducing unemployment rates, and developing Egyptian and MENA economies in various ways.

Unification of international states' contracts principles, to be consistent with international commercial contracts' principles, is a pivotal tool to provide a higher threshold of protection to the private party, in particular foreign investors, and to enhance the life of Egyptian ordinary citizens. In other words, achieving global contract law in Egypt and the MENA countries is a pivotal tool to enhance the life of ordinary citizens, in the respective jurisdictions, as follows:

- Such unification aims to increase the inward of FDI to Egypt. Increasing the inward of FDI to various economic sectors in Egypt and the MENA countries is a fundamental factor to fight unemployment and reduce the unemployment rate. The increase of the unemployment rate in Egypt and the MENA countries is a fundamental factor behind the increase of crime and terrorism in the Middle East region. Oil and/or gas, renewable energy, infrastructure, services, PPP, telecommunications and other types of projects create hundreds of thousands of job opportunities in Egypt and the MENA region.
- The increase of such projects in Egypt and MENA countries enhances the quality of products and services, as in most cases the private party is a huge multinational company, which has a unique profile and distinguished experience in many economic sectors in the world. The private party injects its technological input and modern techniques, to achieve the best standards for the running and management of public utilities, as these inputs and techniques have a direct positive impact on the country.
- The increase of such projects in Egypt maintains sustainable developments in the country, which have a direct impact on ordinary citizens' lives and standard of living, education, health, and other crucial services offered by Egypt and MENA governments.
- The increase of such projects transfers modern and advanced technologies to Egypt and the MENA countries, through awarding many of these projects to multinational companies.
- Transfer of technologies is a pivotal factor to create highly qualified trained expertise and labor in Egypt and the MENA countries.
- Egypt will have the opportunity to export qualified and trained labor and expertise to the surrounding MENA countries and to other regions of the world as a result of the increase of such projects in Egypt and its leading role in the MENA region to create highly qualified expertise.
- Launching many projects would inject billions in hard currencies to Egypt, which maintains the stability of the currency exchange rate of the Egyptian Pound against the US Dollar in the country as it increases the supply of hard currency in the Egyptian markets against the demand.

In fact, unification of contract law to be consistent with global contract law principles on the legislative, regulatory, and contractual frameworks is a fundamental pillar, in any legal system, which can be described as incentives to attract and increase the inward of FDI.

How Global Contract Law in Egypt and MENA Countries Is Considered a Significant Step to Achieve Legitimate Expectations of Foreign Investors

International standards deal with legitimate expectations of foreign investors in a host state. There are many tests and standards of protection which grant a higher threshold of protection to foreign investors such as the Fair and Equitable Treatment (FET) standard. The Fair and Equitable Treatment standard is the most invoked standard of protection in investment treaty arbitration. Yet, for such a commonly invoked standard, varying applications and definitions emerged. In setting the standard of protection afforded by FET, arbitral tribunals sought to establish whether an investor's legitimate expectations have been frustrated by the host state. Reasonable minds differ, and what can be seen as a reasonable and legitimate expectation from the investor, may not be deemed as such by the state. Accordingly, conceptualizing legitimate expectations is necessary to provide clarity on what would be deemed a breach of an investor's legitimate expectations by a state.

It is important to work through the relevant sources of law to find a methodological definition of the doctrine of legitimate expectations. Further, it is important to start by questioning the very essence of legitimate expectations and their relevance as part of the FET standard, finding that the application of the doctrine is haphazard. It finds that legitimate expectations are rooted neither in treaty interpretation nor customary international law. It also avers that current case law applying the doctrine of legitimate expectations is not founded on concrete legal sources, but rather, on arbitral precedent. Finally, legitimate expectations can, most suitably, be applied as a general principle of law.

The FET standard is among the most invoked standards in investment treaty arbitration. Yet, for such a commonly invoked standard, much uncertainty surrounds it and what it entails. On appearance, the FET standard seems straightforward, obliging states to act in a 'fair' and 'equitable' manner. Nevertheless, much uncertainty surrounds the concept and its contours. This led arbitral tribunals to provide their unfettered determination of the concept, which has generated controversy. Various arbitral tribunals have found that FET encompasses protections to investors' legitimate expectations. In that regard, they enforced a standard that protects investors' expectations that a host state's legislative and regulatory framework remains stable, including any representations or assurances that have been made by the host state to the investor. It should be noted that the determination of what forms a legitimate expectation differs from one tribunal to another, and the state of the law surrounding the concept has become increasingly illusive. Host states have found themselves caught between two extremes, either to exercise their legislative and regulatory authority as sovereigns (while risking frustrating investor expectations) or to cease regulatory oversight and legislative functions just to appease investors and avoid potential claims.

Tribunals have often spoken of the need to tread the line between honoring investors' legitimate expectations while also maintaining the states' right to regulate. However, this task has proven difficult since tribunals have mostly avoided understanding legitimate expectations in a principled and coherent manner. Potestà avers that 'there has been very little attempts by arbitral tribunals to provide a systematic and rigorous framework for the consideration of legitimate expectations in investment treaty arbitration.'[2] This is dangerous. A failure to conceptualize legitimate expectations renders state actions in a twilight zone, with no way of determining whether such actions frustrate an investor's legitimate expectations. The consequences of a state's inability to regulate are drastic, often restricting the democratic process, and impeding public policy considerations.

What Are Legitimate Expectations?

What is the essence of the doctrine of legitimate expectations,[3] as it currently stands? And how far can unified principles of global contract law achieve legitimate expectations of foreign investors in Egypt and the MENA countries?

If legitimate expectations are not decreed by treaties or Customary International Law (CIL), the following question arises: How have tribunals managed to develop a consistent practice where legitimate expectations are protected? The answer is arbitral precedent. There is no doubt that case law regarding FET is distorted. This is not surprising, since tribunals have failed to apply a methodological approach to the FET standard. A common trend that may be found in case law is that tribunals pay significant regard to previously held awards. This can be illustrated in the application of legitimate expectations, where one tribunal – i.e., *Tecmed* – has provided that it forms part of the FET standard, and accordingly, many other Tribunals followed suit (for example, in *CMS* v. *Argentina*,[4] *Enron* v. *Argentina*,[5] and *Occidental* v. *Ecuador*[6]). The latter's reliance on the former's decision is completely inappropriate and misplaced.

There is no doctrine of precedent in investment treaty arbitration. This position was illustrated in *SGS* v. *Philippines* where the Tribunal explained the following: '[...] there is no doctrine of precedent in international law [...] There is no hierarchy of international tribunals, and even if there were, there is no good reason for allowing the first tribunal to resolve issues for all later tribunals.'[7]

Arbitral tribunals have attempted to attribute legitimate expectations to the FET standard, pursuant to ill-fitting sources of law. Furthermore, and perhaps more dangerously, 'tribunals are contributing to the development of a body of international

2 Michele Potestà, Legitimate Expectations in Investment Treaty Law: Understanding the Roots and Limits of a Controversial Concept, *ICSID Review* 28(1) p. 88.

3 See: Christoph Schreuer, *'Fair & Equitable Treatment,'* BIICL Investment Treaty Forum, London, 9 September 2006, 1, and Rudolf Dolzer and Christoph H. Schreuer, *Principles of International Investment Law* (2nd edn, Oxford University Press, 2012).

4 *CMS Gas Transmission Co.* v. *Argentine Republic*, ICSID Case No. ARB/01/8.

5 *Enron* v. *Argentina*, ICSID Case No. ARB/01/3, Award, 22 May 200, paras 259–60.

6 *Occidental Exploration & Production Co.* v. *Republic of Ecuador*, LCIA Case UN 3467, Final Award, 1 July 2004, paras. 190 and 196.

7 *SGS Société Générale de Surveillance S.A.* v. *Republic of the Philippines*, ICSID Case ARB/02/6, Decision of the Tribunal on Objections to Jurisdiction, 28 January 2004, para. 97.

law that is inaccurate, or at least fails to reflect a common sense in the domestic legal system.'[8]

In that regard, a more constructive and authoritative manner to correctly underpin the doctrine of legitimate expectations is to turn to its roots. In other words, a solution to correctly identifying the bounds of legitimate expectations can be ascertained through principles of domestic administrative laws, which are prevalent in several legal systems.[9] This has been supported, although in a limited manner, by several tribunals. For instance, in *Toto Construzioni Generali S.p.A* v. *Lebanon*, the Tribunal held that 'The fair and equitable treatment standard of international law does not depend on the perception of the frustrated investor but should use public international law and comparative domestic public law as a benchmark.'[10]

Through an understanding of national laws and their application of the doctrine of legitimate expectations, it will be possible to enforce their commonalities through the 'general principles of law,' which is a source of international law.

The doctrine of legitimate expectations is a form of judicial review over administrative action. Judicial review over administrative action is not unlimited. On the contrary, national laws have placed several limitations on judicial review which must be honored by the courts.

Irrespective of the degree of application of the doctrine of legitimate expectations, courts tread a very fine line when it comes to their review of administrative decrees. This is because courts do not wish to impede on matters of administrative discretion. In England, Barnett argues that 'judges are very conscious of the invisible boundary line between those matters that they regard themselves as competent to adjudicate and those matters which should be left for the democratically elected government.'[11]

In English case law, in *R* v. *Lambert* (2001), Lord Woolf stated that the judiciary 'should as a matter of constitutional principle pay a degree of deference to the view of Parliament as to what is in the interest of the public generally.'[12] Furthermore, English courts have declined to 'exercise a supervisory function over issues of high policy.' This stems from the doctrine of separation of powers, which leaves matters of public policy to the executive and not the judiciary. This was illustrated in *Nottinghamshire County Council* v. *Secretary of State for the Environment* where

8 Trevor Zeyl, Charting the Wrong Course: The Doctrine of Legitimate Expectations in investment Treaty Law, *Alta L Rev*. 49 (2011), pp. 203–10.

9 Potestà, Legitimate Expectations in Investment Treaty Law: Understanding the Roots and Limits of a Controversial Concept, *ICSID Review*, 28(1), 2013, p.91.

10 *Toto Construzioni Generali S.p.A.* v. *Lebanon*, ICSID Case No. ARB/07/12, Award (7 June 2012) para. 166

11 Hilaire Barnett, *Constitutional and Administrative Law* (13th edn, Routledge (2020), p. 610). See in the separation between powers principles in English law: Mark Elliot and Thomas Robert, *Public Law* (2nd edn, Oxford University Press (2014), p. 93).

12 Ibid., p. 610.

the court confirmed that political judgment is left to the relevant Secretary of State and the House of Commons.[13]

Finally, as general point, which can also be considered to form part of the General Principles of Laws (GPL) of Civilized Nations defining legitimate expectations, tribunals applying legitimate expectations must do so in conjunction with the doctrines of non-fettering and deference. These restrictions on administrative review (i.e., the review of governmental action) should be respected by tribunals, as they form an irrevocable element of the doctrine of legitimate expectations and its scope of application.

Economic and financial expectations constitute very important element of the legitimate expectations of any foreign investor in Egypt and the MENA countries. International contracts' financial outcome will meet the expectations of the foreign investor which he has calculated through a feasibility study (technical, financial, environmental, legal, etc.) before concluding any contract in Egypt and the MENA countries. Therefore, unification of globally accepted substantive contract law principles is a fundamental pillar to achieve legitimate expectations of foreign investors in the respective jurisdictions.

Why Can Global Principles of Contract Law Achieve Legitimate Expectations of Foreign Investors in Egypt and MENA Countries?

Unified substantive principles of global contract law can achieve legitimate expectations of the foreign investors in Egypt and MENA countries, for the following reasons:

- Unified contract law principles will not violate the legal and economic expectations of the foreign investors, and therefore, are considered a tool to increase the inward of FDI.
- Foreign investors will move with their investments and technology to increase the inward of FDI and export technology to host states, because there are globally unified principles of contract law, which create higher threshold of protection to foreign investors.
- Legitimate expectations are considered as an assurance of legal certainty and fairness between the contracting parties.
- The traditional excessive and exorbitant clauses in state administrative contracts do not exist in global contract law principles. Exorbitant clauses in administrative contracts in Egypt and the MENA region violate the economic expectations of foreign investors. Further, excessive and exorbitant clauses in such contracts are considered a motive to avoid Egypt and the MENA jurisdictions, as a destination for foreign investors, as they are one of the reasons to create unpredictability in the economic equilibrium of the contract.

13 Ibid., p. 609.

- Excessive and exorbitant clauses are a factor behind exercising the excessive power of the contracting states. Such power is a reason for the rise of many disputes through international arbitration whether commercial or investment arbitration. If there is neither a Bilateral Investment Treaty (BIT) to protect the foreign investor nor an arbitration agreement, a foreign investor would not be able to have recourse to investment or commercial arbitration, but rather he would have to start litigation procedures which might last for a longer duration as litigation is the investor's last resort. Therefore, it is assumed that exorbitant clauses do not exist in global contract law principles as they do not exist in international commercial contracts' principles.
- Unified global contract law principles would guarantee a minimum degree of certainty to arbitral or judicial processes' outcomes, as agreeing on contract law principles between civil law legal systems and common law jurisdictions would result in reducing controversial issues on the contract law and would result in reaching fair arbitral and judicial approaches in arbitral awards and courts' judgments, which will not violate the legitimate expectations of the foreign investor. Agreeing upon a minimum degree of principles will result in fair outcomes by arbitral tribunals and courts; such outcomes will be consistent with the legal and judicial approaches which are acceptable by the foreign investor.
- Arbitral tribunals and courts will avoid inconsistent findings through arbitral awards and courts' judgments final approaches, as global and unified principles of contract law minimize differences between legal approaches and legal cultures, and maintain a minimum degree of consensus between legal solutions adopted by arbitral tribunals and national courts.
- Unification of globally accepted substantive contract law principles is a factor to minimize risk allocation upon the foreign investor in international contracts concluded in Egypt and the MENA region. Unified contract law principles would undermine risk factors during contract performance, especially in long-term contracts,[14] where substantive principles of contracts have to be consistent with international commercial contracts' standards. Such consistency will create certainty and predictability during contract performance, which minimizes risk, not only for the foreign investor but also for both contracting parties and for third parties, who are not party to the main contract concluded with the foreign investor, such as sub-contractors, lenders, insurance companies, etc. Unification, in this context, meets the legitimate expectations of the foreign investor as it offers a high threshold of security during the contract performance phase.
- Unification of globally accepted substantive contract law principles is an important factor to maintain financial and economic equilibrium of the contract during performance phase of the contract. In long-term agreements, it

14 Infrastructure, construction, services, telecommunications networks, energy, renewable energy projects, and other similar projects, are normally classified as long-term contracts.

is fundamental to create contractual mechanisms that maintain the financial and economic equilibrium of the contract, during performance, such as *force majeure* clauses, stabilization clauses, hardship clauses (*L'imprévision*), etc. Adopting such contractual clauses by the contracting parties minimizes risk to foreign investors in Egypt and MENA countries, creates a higher threshold of protection and security to the foreign investor, and meets financial and economic expectations of private foreign entities.[15]

- Unification of globally accepted substantive contract law principles is a tool to achieve consensus upon limitation of liability contractual clauses which are agreed in both civil law legal systems and common law jurisdictions. Such consensus provides both contracting parties with contractual approaches which have mutual agreements despite the differences in legal cultures between the contracting parties. Narrowing the gap in contractual concepts between the contracting parties maintains a high degree of certainty and avoids unpredictability during work performance, in particular in long-term agreements, and assures fair and predictable judicial and arbitral resolutions to both contracting parties.
- Unification of globally accepted substantive contract law principles narrows the gap between common law legal culture and civil law legal culture in damages, as common law legal culture doesn't enforce penalty clauses,[16] as a general rule subject to current exceptions by English case law,[17]meanwhile, civil law legal systems in Egypt and the MENA countries enforce penalty clauses in liquidated damages clauses in states' administrative contracts.[18] Unification shall create coherent set of substantive principles of contract law that is

15 In *Parkerings-Compagniet AG* v. *The Republic of Lithuania*, the Tribunal held that: 'By deciding to invest [...], the Claimant took the business risk to be faced with changes of laws possibly or even likely to be detrimental to its investment. The Claimant could (and with hindsight should) have sought to protect its legitimate expectations by introducing into the investment agreement a stabilisation clause or some other provision protecting it against unexpected and unwelcome changes.' See: *Parkerings-Compagniet AG* v. *The Republic of Lithuania*, ICSID Case ARB/05/8, Award, 11 September 2007, para. 336.

16 Ewan McKendrick, *Contract Law* (14th edn, Macmillan Law Masters, 2021, p. 428). In new approaches to common law understanding of the administrative law see generally: Paul Daly, *Understanding Administrative Law in the Common Law World* (Oxford University Press, 2021).

17 Youssef Ismail, *Enforceability of Liquidated Damages Clauses and the Extent of Judicial and Arbitral Intervention, A comparative study between the English and Egyptian jurisdictions*, Arbitration, *The International Journal of Arbitration, Mediation, and Dispute Management*, Kluwer Law International, 2023, 89(4), pp.516–35; *Dunlop Pneumatic Tyre Co. Ltd* v. *New Garage and Motor Co, Ltd* [1914–15] All ER Rep 739; *Philips Hong Kong* v. *Attorney General of Hong Kong* [1993] 61 BLR 41 in Richard Stone and James Devenney (eds), *Texts, Cases and Materials on Contract Law* (Routledge, 2014), p. 737. For the new trends in the English case law, see: *Cavendish Square Holding BV* v. *El Makdessi; ParkingEye Ltd v Beavis* [2016] 2 All ER 519, 533.

18 For liquidated damages in administrative contracts in Egypt see: 'Supreme Administrative Court, Egyptian Conseil D'État; in Mohamed A.M. Ismail, 'Globalisation and LDs on International Public Works Agreements in Egypt: An Analytical Perspective on the Penalty for Delay Clause in Infrastructure Agreements, *The International Construction Law Review*, 2009, 26(4), pp. 506–12.

consistent with legitimate expectations for investors from common law and civil law backgrounds. Arbitration awards and courts' judgments' outcomes would not violate financial and economic expectations of the foreign investor in particular when damages enforcement and calculation are in dispute.

- Culture has a sharp edge that has been mitigated by the cultural and legal globalization forces, and unification of globally accepted substantive principles of contract law are the clear sign to narrow the gap between common law jurisdictions and civil law legal systems in international contract law and practice. It is difficult in the last decades to draw a clear line distinguishing between common law and civil law legal cultures, in many legal fields, such as international contract law, and international arbitration, whether commercial or investment arbitration.[19]

Conclusions

It is clear that the FET standard, does not encompass the doctrine of legitimate expectations. Rather, the doctrine of legitimate expectations can be rightfully invoked as a GPL. In doing so, it offers investors a degree of protection, while reviewing state conduct in the manner that they prescribed in their national laws. Invoking the doctrine of legitimate expectations through the GPL ensures a sensible balance between the conflicting interests of the investor and the state. It does so in a manner that is clear and unambiguous.

It is concluded that globally unified and accepted substantive contract law principles, which are consistent with international commercial contracts' principles, are one of the main pillars and fundamental factors to achieve the legitimate expectations of foreign investors in Egypt and MENA countries.

19 Mohamed A.M. Ismail, *Globalization and New International Public Works Agreements in developing Countries, An Analytical perspective,* with a foreword by HH Humphrey Lloyd QC (Routledge, 2011–2016, pp. 1–8).

Conclusions

Unification of international contracts' law principles to be consistent with international commercial contracts' principles to achieve global contract law is underway in Egypt and the MENA region, despite public law constraints. Courts' intervention and new patterns of administrative contracts such as PPPs are playing a fundamental role to remove public law barriers. Further, digitalization of public contracts and codification of administrative contracts' principles are fundamental tools to achieve global contract law in the respective jurisdictions. International organizations such as the UNCITRAL and UNIDROIT are playing the most important role in the international sphere to achieve unification towards new global substantive principles of contract law.

The legal globalization phenomenon mitigates public law constraints in Egypt and the MENA countries. It is evident that new substantive principles of contract law have been created through case law, legislation, and new patterns of states' contracts in Egypt and the MENA region. Digitalization of public contracts is a result of the legal globalization phenomenon and the flow of culture from common law jurisdictions to civil law legal systems, as it is a fundamental factor to minimize public law exorbitant clauses in state contracts in the respective jurisdictions. Further, it is assumed that codification of substantive principles of states' contract law will be consistent with international commercial contracts' principles and practice. Pursuant to Adam Smith's views,[1] the state role is confined to its basic functions as it has relinquished its role as an employer to be the only regulator. States in Egypt and the MENA countries are minimizing their role in states' contracts to a great extent. In PPPs, and in light of Chicago school approaches in the economy,[2] states are only a legislature. This is evident from the trajectory of states' intervention, in the respective jurisdictions, to promulgate PPP legislation. In addition, states are the only regulator in PPP contracts and in most international states' contracts, as they are trying to relinquish the classical governmental role of the traditional employer.

Culture has sharp edge that have been mitigated by the cultural and legal globalization forces, and unification of globally accepted substantive principles of

1 Adam Smith, *Wealth of Nations*, Wordsworth edition, 2012.
2 *Milton Friedman on Economics: Selected Papers*, University of Chicago Press Journal, 2008.

DOI: 10.4324/9781003466352-11

contract law is the clear sign to narrow the gap between common law jurisdictions and civil law legal systems in international contract law and practice. It has been difficult, in the last decades, to draw a clear line distinguishing between common law and civil law legal cultures, in some legal fields, such as international contract law, and international arbitration, whether commercial or investment arbitration.[3]

It is appropriate to refer to the following conclusions and recommendations achieved through this study:

1 – It is suggested that the established theories in contract financial equilibrium, whether in public or private (commercial) contracts, and whether such theories are established in legislation or by the Egyptian and MENA countries' case law, are paving the way to the unification of contract law substantive principles towards achieving global contract law. Such global contract law assumes that the substantive principles of contract law, whether public or private (commercial) contracts, in Egypt and the MENA countries, are consistent with the global diversity of contract law principles and with international commercial contracts' theory and practice.

2 – Egyptian and MENA countries' civil codes are influenced by the French Civil Code, and the Egyptian Cassation Court, and Egyptian Conseil D'État jurisprudence are influenced, to a great extent, by the French jurisprudence. Such influence reflects the civilized approaches by the Egyptian and MENA legislature and the developments of case law in Egypt and the MENA countries, as MENA countries' supreme courts are inspired, to a great extent, by Egyptian case law. MENA countries' legislatures are inspired, to a great extent, by Egyptian legislation.

3 – It is expected that the civilized legislation and developed case law in Egypt and the MENA countries will lead to a rapid and easy integration of the contract law, in the respective jurisdictions, into the global contract law principles as a new international legal order.

4 – It is clear how unification of PPP legislation in Egypt and the MENA countries, and unification of Egyptian and MENA countries' civil codes in *'L'imprévision'* theory, established a coherent and integrated set of substantive principles of contract law in both private (commercial) contracts and public contracts.

5 – In the absence of a legislative provision, frustration of contract, whether public or private (commercial) contracts, in Egypt and the MENA countries, case law in the respective jurisdictions reflects the liberalization and modernization of contract law substantive principles, as such principles are consistent with international contract law theory and practice. The Prince Theory reflects the developed approaches of the Egyptian Conseil D'État Courts

3 Mohamed A.M. Ismail, *Globalization and New International Public Works Agreements in Developing Countries, An Analytical perspective*, with a foreword by HH Humphrey Lloyd QC (Routledge, 2011 and 2016, pp. 1–8).

which adapt the French Conseil D'État case law approaches. This is fundamental step towards the unification of contract law principles to achieve global contract law.

6 – The Principle of Termination or suspension of Performance (*Exceptio non-adimpleti contractus*), needs to be codified in the Egyptian and MENA countries' legislation. There is an essential need for a legislative reform to add an extension of time to the contract duration if the state delays a contractor's payments, and to avoid payment of liquidated damages. If legislation grants the contractor the right to suspend performance, when there is a contractual breach by the state, legislative approaches in both commercial and administrative contracts would be unified.

7 – A crucial question arises on how the perceived lack of standardization appears as a deterrent in developing public contractual interfaces in MENA region. Further, is unification of contract law principles in international states' contracts, which have to be consistent with international commercial law principles, a tool to achieve standardization of public contractual interfaces in the relevant jurisdiction? It is important to achieve unified principles in case law in Egypt and the MENA countries and to achieve unification in contract law legislation in Egypt and the MENA countries' legislation. Such unification of both legislation and case law, in Egypt and the MENA countries, is the first step to achieve unification in contract law principles, whether public contracts or commercial contracts. Global contract law can be achieved if such unification in legislation and case law is adopted in the respective jurisdictions. Standardization of public contracts can be achieved through unification of public contracts' principles to be consistent with international commercial contracts' principles as globalized principles are accepted by both developed and developing legal systems, and both common law and civil law legal systems. Standardization of contractual interfaces can be achieved, in the MENA region, by narrowing gaps between public contracts and private (commercial) contracts. Removing public law barriers is an important factor to achieve standardization of contractual interfaces in the respective jurisdictions. Digitalization of public contracts is an important tool to remove public law barriers.

8 – The Egyptian Supreme Administrative Court, Egyptian Cassation Court, and MENA countries supreme courts are usually bound by the confines of the law, and its statutory provisions. That being said, courts are bound by constitutional and legislative provisions which have a mandatory nature. Meanwhile, in some circumstances, courts may rule outside of legislative provisions when the matter relates to public policy, and there is no legislative provision to govern the case, or there are legislative provisions which do not have the mandatory nature, and this allows courts to intervene in a wider scope.

9 – Courts' intervention is usually bound by the '*pacta sunt servanda'* principle in Egypt and MENA countries. It is clear that MENA courts supersede the party autonomy principle.

10 – The coexistence between the core principles of contract law in state contracts and international commercial contracts in the MENA region, on one hand, and the huge global diversity of international contracts' principles on the other hand, is a reality.

11 – In the case of unfair contract terms, courts' intervention needs further an in-depth approach to maintain priority to the party autonomy principle. Courts' approaches have to be consistent with international commercial contracts' principles.

12 – Courts' intervention in Egypt and MENA countries, if it is consistent with the global diversity of international contracts' principles, will create a suitable environment for investments in the respective jurisdictions and raise the threshold of protection granted to foreign investors. Further, it will increase the inward of FDI to the respective jurisdictions. Consequently, it will enhance the socio-economic life of the ordinary citizens in Egypt and MENA countries.

13 – Unification of PPP procedural and substantive rules, through legislation and regulations, is a significant step towards the unification of substantive principles of states' contracts, to be consistent with international commercial contracts, and to create global contract law. Establishing global contract law theory and practice, in public and private contracts, is underway in Egypt and the MENA countries.

14 – The new PPP legislation supports the innovation in substantive rules in the PPP contracts, which represent a considerable step towards the liberalization of the administrative contract, in particular traditional concessions from the rigid excessive clauses ('*Les clauses exorbitantes*'). There is an increasing trend towards unification of contract law principles, in particular PPP contracts, not only in the event of unforeseen circumstances, but also in other substantive aspects. Liberalization and modernization of administrative contracts are a considerable step towards the unification of contract law principles.

15 – MENA states' intervention reflects the high degree of flexibility in the economic ideology and legislative policy behind promulgating economic legislation, as PPP legislation is one of the most significant steps from the economic angle, because it represents the increasing trend to MENA countries to permit private sector participation in the public utilities and infrastructure projects. The economic ideology behind promulgating such liberal economic legislation is clear in the MENA constitutions and it has been implemented in the current MENA PPP legislation. This is a unified approach by Egypt and other MENA governments.

16 – States' intervention through legislation and regulation to permit PPP techniques and to formulate new policies in public utilities, services, and infrastructure projects plays a considerable role to enhance the MENA countries' ranking in the international financial institutions' reports. MENA countries are exercising new policies to create a new environment that promotes a high threshold of protection to foreign investments, and maintains better investments' atmosphere which facilitates the increase of inflow of FDI to MENA countries.

17 – MENA states' intervention through legislation and regulation to permit the participation of the private sector in public utilities, services, and infrastructure projects, through PPP techniques, is a remarkable step towards the implementation of 2030 vision goals in Egypt and the MENA countries. Many countries in the MENA region have established legal and economic frameworks and a chronology to achieve the 2030 vision goals. The role of states' intervention in economic life has been considerably minimized. The interplay between international dynamics and the unification of PPP contracts' principles in Egypt the MENA countries is portrayed.

18 – Digitalization of public contracts could offer a wide spectrum of flexibility for creating common understanding of a unified set of substantive principles of international states' contracts, in the respective jurisdictions, which are consistent with international commercial contracts. Such unification is a considerable step towards achieving global contract law principles.

19 – The main targets of digitalization of public contracts are to achieve public interests; to preserve public funds; to minimize public spending; to achieve the '*value for money*' concept and reflect the implementation of principles of transparency, equality before law, equality before public utilities, fair competition, and fighting corruption. Creating global contract law substantive principles is one of the main targets of digitalization of public contracts. A complete reform is expected for public contracts' practice in Egypt and the MENA countries and such reform aims at being consistent with international standards as drawn up by the relevant international organs.

20 – There is an essential need to achieve a fully digitalized process of public contracts in all contract phases, starting from the procedural phase and continuing until final completion, and if a dispute arises out of or in connection with the contract, a digital infrastructure in public contracts is needed. Unification of global contract law principles, whether public or private (commercial) contracts, is an important factor to guarantee the legitimate expectations of the foreign investors, and to maintain predictability to the litigation or arbitration outcomes, if a dispute arises.

21 – A full digitalization process of public contracts is underway and may be achieved in a very reasonable time through implementing digital governments or digital administration by establishing a coherent digital infrastructure platform which connects all governmental departments together and enables private entities to deal with all governmental sectors through advanced digital platforms to minimize human intervention to considerable extent. Digitalization of public contracts and generally digitalization of the Egyptian and MENA governments is a fundamental factor behind a better implementation of decentralization system. The interplay between digital government and decentralization is clear as digital infrastructure enables better decentralization system in any state, in particular federal states. Further, digitalization is an effective tool to enhance the efficiency of a public procurement system, and in addition, contract performance during performance phase.

22 – Artificial intelligence (AI) is an efficient tool to offer a high threshold of protection to public contracts, not only during the procedural phase, but also during contract performance and until final completion of contractual obligations. AI is a real implementation of a fully automated process in concluding public contracts, whether in the procedural phase or in the performance phase. AI is a considerable step towards the unification of both procedural and substantive rules of public contracts to be consistent with international commercial contracts' principles. It is an important step to achieve global contract law.

23 – Codification of administrative contracts' law is a fundamental tool for the enhancements and modifications of the substantive clauses of administrative contracts to be consistent with international commercial contracts' substantive principles, which constitute the law and practice of international commercial contracts worldwide. The essential need to change the traditional ideology behind administrative contracts and to enhance the traditional administrative contracts' patterns to be consistent with international commercial contracts' principles is portrayed.

24 – There are many examples of substantive contractual clauses of administrative contracts which need significant change such as, liquidated damages (*Exceptio non-adimpleti contractus*), and frustration of contract such as the theory of unexpected circumstances ('*l'imprévision*'). The latter theory has to adopt the legislative approach in PPPs legislation in Egypt and the MENA countries to be consistent with international patterns of states' contracts, which are not necessarily administrative contracts, and which are more consistent with international commercial contracts' law and practice.

25 – It is suggested that states' intervention, through legislation, has to be to the minimum in codifying substantive contractual clauses; therefore, liquidated damages' legislative provision in Egyptian State Contracting Law No. 182 of 2018 has to be eliminated, and to leave the penalty of delay calculation and cap to party autonomy and the decision of the contracting parties has to be left in the contract. The Kingdom of Bahrain adopted this vision in Public Procurement Law No. 36 of 2002 which didn't stipulate liquidated damages as a legislative provision and left the contracting parties (state and private person) to provide a contractual clause, if appropriate, in the contract regulating liquidated damages. It is worth noting that each contract has different nature, dynamics, factual background, and a different economic dimension. This approach is a step towards the unification of contract law principles in the region as, in most cases, private foreign entities in the MENA countries insist on inserting international commercial contracts clauses' and practice in state contracts. This is a step to narrow the gap between public and private contracts.

26 – It is assumed that codification of administrative contracts' principles will adopt, in most cases, the substantive principles of international commercial contracts. As such, the gap becomes narrower between administrative contracts' substantive principles and international commercial contracts' principles, in light of the expected unification, which is the tool to achieve global contract law.

27 – Private-public arbitration plays a significant role towards the unification of contract law principles, to achieve coherent and global substantive principles of contract law. International arbitral tribunals, through decades, have established a coherent set of substantive principles of international contracts, whether public or private contracts. Such an approach by international arbitral tribunals narrows the gap between administrative contracts' substantive principles and international commercial contracts' principles. It is a considerable step to remove the barriers and constraints of administrative contracts' traditional theory.

28 – There are many positive points, in the Egyptian and MENA countries' arbitration laws, which reflect the international character of arbitration in Egypt, and these countries, as DRM that plays a significant role to achieve global contract law principles. These positive points are considered crucial factors to ensure the international character of arbitration in Egypt, and promote a higher threshold of protection to foreign investors. Further, these points are considerable steps towards removing the barriers and constraints of public law contracts, as they are paving the way to achieve global and unified contract law principles.

29 – Global and unified contract law principles in Egypt and the MENA countries, for both public and private contracts, are consistent with the legitimate expectations of foreign investors, and are a fundamental tool to increase the inward of FDI in the respective jurisdictions. It is an important legal mechanism to avoid inconsistent findings by national courts and international arbitral tribunals. Further, it enhances the socio-economic life style of the ordinary citizens in Egypt and the MENA countries. Global contract law principles are legal mechanisms which are fundamental for the ecosystem and social developments in the MENA region.

30 – There is a direct causal link between the existence of an advanced global contract law framework on one hand and the increase of the inward of FDI and the improvement of life of the ordinary citizens in MENA countries on the other.

31 – International organs play an important role in narrowing the gap between common law and civil law legal cultures through adopting new global contract law principles which are consistent with the dynamics and practice of international commercial contracts. Further, they are removing public law constraints, in international states' contracts, through creating international instruments which aim to unify contract law principles. UNIDROIT and the ICC Institute are playing a fundamental role, through adopting an international project, to create an instrument in international investment contracts, which is always a state contract, as there is a presumption that a host state is one party to an international investment contract. Such an instrument would create a global unification of international investment contracts' principles that is suitable in its geographical scope for all states, and capable of application for the forthcoming decades. The project aims to achieve a sensible balance between protecting the public interests of host states and providing

foreign investors a higher threshold of protection, which is an important factor to increase the inward of FDI to developing countries. It is assumed that the expected instrument in international investment contracts would minimize public law constraints through minimizing exorbitant substantive clauses, which are usually in favor of the host state, and creating a better investment environment in host states that offers higher threshold of protection to foreign investors. The new international investment contracts' instrument will reduce public law constraints in states' contracts, remove public law barriers, and narrow the gap between public contracts and private contracts, to achieve global and unified contract law principles.

Annex

UNIDROIT PRINCIPLES OF INTERNATIONAL COMMERCIAL CONTRACTS 2016[1]

PREAMBLE

(Purpose of the Principles)

These Principles set forth general rules for international commercial contracts.

They shall be applied when the parties have agreed that their contract be governed by them.[2]

They may be applied when the parties have agreed that their contract be governed by general principles of law, the *lex mercatoria* or the like.

They may be applied when the parties have not chosen any law to govern their contract.

They may be used to interpret or supplement international uniform law instruments.

They may be used to interpret or supplement domestic law.

They may serve as a model for national and international legislators.

1 Reproduced by kind permission of the International Institute for the Unification of Private Law (UNIDROIT). Readers are reminded that the complete text of the *UNIDROIT Principles of International Commercial Contracts 2016* is composed of both black-letter rules and accompanying Comments. The full text is available in book form directly from UNIDROIT and is also available on the UNIDROIT website at www.unidroit.org/instruments/commercial-contracts/unidroit-principles-2016. For select case law and bibliography relating to the Principles, see www.unilex.info.

2 Parties wishing to provide that their agreement be governed by the Principles might use one of the *Model Clauses for the use of the* UNIDROIT *Principles of International Commercial Contracts* (see www.unidroit.org/instruments/commercial-contracts/upicc-model-clauses).

CHAPTER 1 — GENERAL PROVISIONS

Article 1.1

(Freedom of contract)

The parties are free to enter into a contract and to determine its content.

Article 1.2

(No form required)

Nothing in these Principles requires a contract, statement or any other act to be made in or evidenced by a particular form. It may be proved by any means, including witnesses.

Article 1.3

(Binding character of contract)

A contract validly entered into is binding upon the parties. It can only be modified or terminated in accordance with its terms or by agreement or as otherwise provided in these Principles.

Article 1.4

(Mandatory rules)

Nothing in these Principles shall restrict the application of mandatory rules, whether of national, international or supranational origin, which are applicable in accordance with the relevant rules of private international law.

Article 1.5

(Exclusion or modification by the parties)

The parties may exclude the application of these Principles or derogate from or vary the effect of any of their provisions, except as otherwise provided in the Principles.

Article 1.6

(Interpretation and supplementation of the Principles)

(1) In the interpretation of these Principles, regard is to be had to their international character and to their purposes including the need to promote uniformity in their application.
(2) Issues within the scope of these Principles but not expressly settled by them are as far as possible to be settled in accordance with their underlying general principles.

Article 1.7

(Good faith and fair dealing)

(1) Each party must act in accordance with good faith and fair dealing in international trade.
(2) The parties may not exclude or limit this duty.

Article 1.8

(Inconsistent behaviour)

A party cannot act inconsistently with an understanding it has caused the other party to have and upon which that other party reasonably has acted in reliance to its detriment.

Article 1.9

(Usages and practices)

(1) The parties are bound by any usage to which they have agreed and by any practices which they have established between themselves.
(2) The parties are bound by a usage that is widely known to and regularly observed in international trade by parties in the particular trade concerned except where the application of such a usage would be unreasonable.

Article 1.10

(Notice)

(1) Where notice is required it may be given by any means appropriate to the circumstances.
(2) A notice is effective when it reaches the person to whom it is given.
(3) For the purpose of paragraph (2) a notice "reaches" a person when given to that person orally or delivered at that person's place of business or mailing address.
(4) For the purpose of this Article "notice" includes a declaration, demand, request or any other communication of intention.

Article 1.11

(Definitions)

In these Principles

- "court" includes an arbitral tribunal;
- where a party has more than one place of business the relevant "place of business" is that which has the closest relationship to the contract and its performance, having regard to the circumstances known to or contemplated by the parties at any time before or at the conclusion of the contract;

- "long-term contract" refers to a contract which is to be performed over a period of time and which normally involves, to a varying degree, complexity of the transaction and an ongoing relationship between the parties;
- "obligor" refers to the party who is to perform an obligation and "obligee" refers to the party who is entitled to performance of that obligation;
- "writing" means any mode of communication that preserves a record of the information contained therein and is capable of being reproduced in tangible form.

Article 1.12

(Computation of time set by parties)

(1) Official holidays or non-business days occurring during a period set by parties for an act to be performed are included in calculating the period.
(2) However, if the last day of the period is an official holiday or a non-business day at the place of business of the party to perform the act, the period is extended until the first business day which follows, unless the circumstances indicate otherwise.
(3) The relevant time zone is that of the place of business of the party setting the time, unless the circumstances indicate otherwise.

CHAPTER 2 — FORMATION AND AUTHORITY OF AGENTS

SECTION 1: FORMATION

Article 2.1.1

(Manner of formation)

A contract may be concluded either by the acceptance of an offer or by conduct of the parties that is sufficient to show agreement.

Article 2.1.2

(Definition of offer)

A proposal for concluding a contract constitutes an offer if it is sufficiently definite and indicates the intention of the offeror to be bound in case of acceptance.

Article 2.1.3

(Withdrawal of offer)

(1) An offer becomes effective when it reaches the offeree.
(2) An offer, even if it is irrevocable, may be withdrawn if the withdrawal reaches the offeree before or at the same time as the offer.

Article 2.1.4

(Revocation of offer)

(1) Until a contract is concluded an offer may be revoked if the revocation reaches the offeree before it has dispatched an acceptance.
(2) However, an offer cannot be revoked
  (a) if it indicates, whether by stating a fixed time for acceptance or otherwise, that it is irrevocable; or
  (b) if it was reasonable for the offeree to rely on the offer as being irrevocable and the offeree has acted in reliance on the offer.

Article 2.1.5

(Rejection of offer)

An offer is terminated when a rejection reaches the offeror.

Article 2.1.6

(Mode of acceptance)

(1) A statement made by or other conduct of the offeree indicating assent to an offer is an acceptance. Silence or inactivity does not in itself amount to acceptance.
(2) An acceptance of an offer becomes effective when the indication of assent reaches the offeror.
(3) However, if, by virtue of the offer or as a result of practices which the parties have established between themselves or of usage, the offeree may indicate assent by performing an act without notice to the offeror, the acceptance is effective when the act is performed.

Article 2.1.7

(Time of acceptance)

An offer must be accepted within the time the offeror has fixed or, if no time is fixed, within a reasonable time having regard to the circumstances, including the rapidity of the means of communication employed by the offeror. An oral offer must be accepted immediately unless the circumstances indicate otherwise.

Article 2.1.8

(Acceptance within a fixed period of time)

A period of acceptance fixed by the offeror begins to run from the time that the offer is dispatched. A time indicated in the offer is deemed to be the time of dispatch unless the circumstances indicate otherwise.

Article 2.1.9

(Late acceptance. Delay in transmission)

(1) A late acceptance is nevertheless effective as an acceptance if without undue delay the offeror so informs the offeree or gives notice to that effect.
(2) If a communication containing a late acceptance shows that it has been sent in such circumstances that if its transmission had been normal it would have reached the offeror in due time, the late acceptance is effective as an acceptance unless, without undue delay, the offeror informs the offeree that it considers the offer as having lapsed.

Article 2.1.10

(Withdrawal of acceptance)

An acceptance may be withdrawn if the withdrawal reaches the offeror before or at the same time as the acceptance would have become effective.

Article 2.1.11

(Modified acceptance)

(1) A reply to an offer which purports to be an acceptance but contains additions, limitations or other modifications is a rejection of the offer and constitutes a counter-offer.
(2) However, a reply to an offer which purports to be an acceptance but contains additional or different terms which do not materially alter the terms of the offer constitutes an acceptance, unless the offeror, without undue delay, objects to the discrepancy. If the offeror does not object, the terms of the contract are the terms of the offer with the modifications contained in the acceptance.

Article 2.1.12

(Writings in confirmation)

If a writing which is sent within a reasonable time after the conclusion of the contract and which purports to be a confirmation of the contract contains additional or different terms, such terms become part of the contract, unless they materially alter the contract or the recipient, without undue delay, objects to the discrepancy.

Article 2.1.13

(Conclusion of contract dependent on agreement on specific matters or in a particular form)

Where in the course of negotiations one of the parties insists that the contract is not concluded until there is agreement on specific matters or in a particular form, no contract is concluded before agreement is reached on those matters or in that form.

Article 2.1.14

(Contract with terms deliberately left open)

(1) If the parties intend to conclude a contract, the fact that they intentionally leave a term to be agreed upon in further negotiations or to be determined by one of the parties or by a third person does not prevent a contract from coming into existence.
(2) The existence of the contract is not affected by the fact that subsequently
 (a) the parties reach no agreement on the term;
 (b) the party who is to determine the term does not do so; or
 (c) the third person does not determine the term,

provided that there is an alternative means of rendering the term definite that is reasonable in the circumstances, having regard to the intention of the parties.

Article 2.1.15

(Negotiations in bad faith)

(1) A party is free to negotiate and is not liable for failure to reach an agreement.
(2) However, a party who negotiates or breaks off negotiations in bad faith is liable for the losses caused to the other party.
(3) It is bad faith, in particular, for a party to enter into or continue negotiations when intending not to reach an agreement with the other party.

Article 2.1.16

(Duty of confidentiality)

Where information is given as confidential by one party in the course of negotiations, the other party is under a duty not to disclose that information or to use it improperly for its own purposes, whether or not a contract is subsequently concluded. Where appropriate, the remedy for breach of that duty may include compensation based on the benefit received by the other party.

Article 2.1.17

(Merger clauses)

A contract in writing which contains a clause indicating that the writing completely embodies the terms on which the parties have agreed cannot be contradicted or supplemented by evidence of prior statements or agreements. However, such statements or agreements may be used to interpret the writing.

Article 2.1.18

(Modification in a particular form)

A contract in writing which contains a clause requiring any modification or termination by agreement to be in a particular form may not be otherwise modified or terminated. However, a party may be precluded by its conduct from asserting such a clause to the extent that the other party has reasonably acted in reliance on that conduct.

Article 2.1.19

(Contracting under standard terms)

(1) Where one party or both parties use standard terms in concluding a contract, the general rules on formation apply, subject to Articles 2.1.20 – 2.1.22.
(2) Standard terms are provisions which are prepared in advance for general and repeated use by one party and which are actually used without negotiation with the other party.

Article 2.1.20

(Surprising terms)

(1) No term contained in standard terms which is of such a character that the other party could not reasonably have expected it, is effective unless it has been expressly accepted by that party.
(2) In determining whether a term is of such a character regard shall be had to its content, language and presentation.

Article 2.1.21

(Conflict between standard terms and non-standard terms)

In case of conflict between a standard term and a term which is not a standard term the latter prevails.

Article 2.1.22

(Battle of forms)

Where both parties use standard terms and reach agreement except on those terms, a contract is concluded on the basis of the agreed terms and of any standard terms which are common in substance unless one party clearly indicates in advance, or later and without undue delay informs the other party, that it does not intend to be bound by such a contract.

Section 2: Authority of Agents

Article 2.2.1

(Scope of the Section)

(1) This Section governs the authority of a person ("the agent") to affect the legal relations of another person ("the principal") by or with respect to a contract with a third party, whether the agent acts in its own name or in that of the principal.
(2) It governs only the relations between the principal or the agent on the one hand, and the third party on the other.
(3) It does not govern an agent's authority conferred by law or the authority of an agent appointed by a public or judicial authority.

Article 2.2.2

(Establishment and scope of the authority of the agent)

(1) The principal's grant of authority to an agent may be express or implied.
(2) The agent has authority to perform all acts necessary in the circumstances to achieve the purposes for which the authority was granted.

Article 2.2.3

(Agency disclosed)

(1) Where an agent acts within the scope of its authority and the third party knew or ought to have known that the agent was acting as an agent, the acts of the agent shall directly affect the legal relations between the principal and the third party and no legal relation is created between the agent and the third party.
(2) However, the acts of the agent shall affect only the relations between the agent and the third party, where the agent with the consent of the principal undertakes to become the party to the contract.

Article 2.2.4

(Agency undisclosed)

(1) Where an agent acts within the scope of its authority and the third party neither knew nor ought to have known that the agent was acting as an agent, the acts of the agent shall affect only the relations between the agent and the third party.
(2) However, where such an agent, when contracting with the third party on behalf of a business, represents itself to be the owner of that business, the third party, upon discovery of the real owner of the business, may exercise also against the latter the rights it has against the agent.

Article 2.2.5

(Agent acting without or exceeding its authority)

(1) Where an agent acts without authority or exceeds its authority, its acts do not affect the legal relations between the principal and the third party.
(2) However, where the principal causes the third party reasonably to believe that the agent has authority to act on behalf of the principal and that the agent is acting within the scope of that authority, the principal may not invoke against the third party the lack of authority of the agent.

Article 2.2.6

(Liability of agent acting without or exceeding its authority)

(1) An agent that acts without authority or exceeds its authority is, failing ratification by the principal, liable for damages that will place the third party in the same position as if the agent had acted with authority and not exceeded its authority.
(2) However, the agent is not liable if the third party knew or ought to have known that the agent had no authority or was exceeding its authority.

Article 2.2.7

(Conflict of interests)

(1) If a contract concluded by an agent involves the agent in a conflict of interests with the principal of which the third party knew or ought to have known, the principal may avoid the contract. The right to avoid is subject to Articles 3.2.9 and 3.2.11 to 3.2.15.
(2) However, the principal may not avoid the contract
    (a) if the principal had consented to, or knew or ought to have known of, the agent's involvement in the conflict of interests; or
    (b) if the agent had disclosed the conflict of interests to the principal and the latter had not objected within a reasonable time.

Article 2.2.8

(Sub-agency)

An agent has implied authority to appoint a sub-agent to perform acts which it is not reasonable to expect the agent to perform itself. The rules of this Section apply to the sub-agency.

Article 2.2.9

(Ratification)

(1) An act by an agent that acts without authority or exceeds its authority may be ratified by the principal. On ratification the act produces the same effects as if it had initially been carried out with authority.
(2) The third party may by notice to the principal specify a reasonable period of time for ratification. If the principal does not ratify within that period of time, it can no longer do so.
(3) If, at the time of the agent's act, the third party neither knew nor ought to have known of the lack of authority, it may, at any time before ratification, by notice to the principal indicate its refusal to become bound by a ratification.

Article 2.2.10

(Termination of authority)

(1) Termination of authority is not effective in relation to the third party unless the third party knew or ought to have known of it.
(2) Notwithstanding the termination of its authority, an agent remains authorised to perform the acts that are necessary to prevent harm to the principal's interests.

CHAPTER 3 — VALIDITY

Section 1: General Provisions

Article 3.1.1

(Matters not covered)

This Chapter does not deal with lack of capacity.

Article 3.1.2

(Validity of mere agreement)

A contract is concluded, modified or terminated by the mere agreement of the parties, without any further requirement.

Article 3.1.3

(Initial impossibility)

(1) The mere fact that at the time of the conclusion of the contract the performance of the obligation assumed was impossible does not affect the validity of the contract.

(2) The mere fact that at the time of the conclusion of the contract a party was not entitled to dispose of the assets to which the contract relates does not affect the validity of the contract.

Article 3.1.4

(Mandatory character of the provisions)

The provisions on fraud, threat, gross disparity and illegality contained in this Chapter are mandatory.

SECTION 2: GROUNDS FOR AVOIDANCE

Article 3.2.1

(Definition of mistake)

Mistake is an erroneous assumption relating to facts or to law existing when the contract was concluded.

Article 3.2.2

(Relevant mistake)

(1) A party may only avoid the contract for mistake if, when the contract was concluded, the mistake was of such importance that a reasonable person in the same situation as the party in error would only have concluded the contract on materially different terms or would not have concluded it at all if the true state of affairs had been known, and
   (a) the other party made the same mistake, or caused the mistake, or knew or ought to have known of the mistake and it was contrary to reasonable commercial standards of fair dealing to leave the mistaken party in error; or
   (b) the other party had not at the time of avoidance reasonably acted in reliance on the contract.
(2) However, a party may not avoid the contract if
   (a) it was grossly negligent in committing the mistake; or
   (b) the mistake relates to a matter in regard to which the risk of mistake was assumed or, having regard to the circumstances, should be borne by the mistaken party.

Article 3.2.3

(Error in expression or transmission)

An error occurring in the expression or transmission of a declaration is considered to be a mistake of the person from whom the declaration emanated.

Article 3.2.4

(Remedies for non-performance)

A party is not entitled to avoid the contract on the ground of mistake if the circumstances on which that party relies afford, or could have afforded, a remedy for non-performance.

Article 3.2.5

(Fraud)

A party may avoid the contract when it has been led to conclude the contract by the other party's fraudulent representation, including language or practices, or fraudulent non-disclosure of circumstances which, according to reasonable commercial standards of fair dealing, the latter party should have disclosed.

Article 3.2.6

(Threat)

A party may avoid the contract when it has been led to conclude the contract by the other party's unjustified threat which, having regard to the circumstances, is so imminent and serious as to leave the first party no reasonable alternative. In particular, a threat is unjustified if the act or omission with which a party has been threatened is wrongful in itself, or it is wrongful to use it as a means to obtain the conclusion of the contract.

Article 3.2.7

(Gross disparity)

(1) A party may avoid the contract or an individual term of it if, at the time of the conclusion of the contract, the contract or term unjustifiably gave the other party an excessive advantage. Regard is to be had, among other factors, to
   (a) the fact that the other party has taken unfair advantage of the first party's dependence, economic distress or urgent needs, or of its improvidence, ignorance, inexperience or lack of bargaining skill, and
   (b) the nature and purpose of the contract.

(2) Upon the request of the party entitled to avoidance, a court may adapt the contract or term in order to make it accord with reasonable commercial standards of fair dealing.

(3) A court may also adapt the contract or term upon the request of the party receiving notice of avoidance, provided that that party informs the other party of its request promptly after receiving such notice and before the other party has reasonably acted in reliance on it. Article 3.2.10(2) applies accordingly.

Article 3.2.8

(Third persons)

(1) Where fraud, threat, gross disparity or a party's mistake is imputable to, or is known or ought to be known by, a third person for whose acts the other party is responsible, the contract may be avoided under the same conditions as if the behaviour or knowledge had been that of the party itself.
(2) Where fraud, threat or gross disparity is imputable to a third person for whose acts the other party is not responsible, the contract may be avoided if that party knew or ought to have known of the fraud, threat or disparity, or has not at the time of avoidance reasonably acted in reliance on the contract.

Article 3.2.9

(Confirmation)

If the party entitled to avoid the contract expressly or impliedly confirms the contract after the period of time for giving notice of avoidance has begun to run, avoidance of the contract is excluded.

Article 3.2.10

(Loss of right to avoid)

(1) If a party is entitled to avoid the contract for mistake but the other party declares itself willing to perform or performs the contract as it was understood by the party entitled to avoidance, the contract is considered to have been concluded as the latter party understood it. The other party must make such a declaration or render such performance promptly after having been informed of the manner in which the party entitled to avoidance had understood the contract and before that party has reasonably acted in reliance on a notice of avoidance.
(2) After such a declaration or performance the right to avoidance is lost and any earlier notice of avoidance is ineffective.

Article 3.2.11

(Notice of avoidance)

The right of a party to avoid the contract is exercised by notice to the other party.

Article 3.2.12

(Time limits)

(1) Notice of avoidance shall be given within a reasonable time, having regard to the circumstances, after the avoiding party knew or could not have been unaware of the relevant facts or became capable of acting freely.

(2) Where an individual term of the contract may be avoided by a party under Article 3.2.7, the period of time for giving notice of avoidance begins to run when that term is asserted by the other party.

Article 3.2.13

(Partial avoidance)

Where a ground of avoidance affects only individual terms of the contract, the effect of avoidance is limited to those terms unless, having regard to the circumstances, it is unreasonable to uphold the remaining contract.

Article 3.2.14

(Retroactive effect of avoidance)

Avoidance takes effect retroactively.

Article 3.2.15

(Restitution)

(1) On avoidance either party may claim restitution of whatever it has supplied under the contract, or the part of it avoided, provided that the party concurrently makes restitution of whatever it has received under the contract, or the part of it avoided.
(2) If restitution in kind is not possible or appropriate, an allowance has to be made in money whenever reasonable.
(3) The recipient of the performance does not have to make an allowance in money if the impossibility to make restitution in kind is attributable to the other party.
(4) Compensation may be claimed for expenses reasonably required to preserve or maintain the performance received.

Article 3.2.16

(Damages)

Irrespective of whether or not the contract has been avoided, the party who knew or ought to have known of the ground for avoidance is liable for damages so as to put the other party in the same position in which it would have been if it had not concluded the contract.

Article 3.2.17

(Unilateral declarations)

The provisions of this Chapter apply with appropriate adaptations to any communication of intention addressed by one party to the other.

Section 3: Illegality

Article 3.3.1

(Contracts infringing mandatory rules)

(1) Where a contract infringes a mandatory rule, whether of national, international or supranational origin, applicable under Article 1.4 of these Principles, the effects of that infringement upon the contract are the effects, if any, expressly prescribed by that mandatory rule.
(2) Where the mandatory rule does not expressly prescribe the effects of an infringement upon a contract, the parties have the right to exercise such remedies under the contract as in the circumstances are reasonable.
(3) In determining what is reasonable regard is to be had in particular to:
  (a) the purpose of the rule which has been infringed;
  (b) the category of persons for whose protection the rule exists;
  (c) any sanction that may be imposed under the rule infringed;
  (d) the seriousness of the infringement;
  (e) whether one or both parties knew or ought to have known of the infringement;
  (f) whether the performance of the contract necessitates the infringement; and
  (g) the parties' reasonable expectations.

Article 3.3.2

(Restitution)

(1) Where there has been performance under a contract infringing a mandatory rule under Article 3.3.1, restitution may be granted where this would be reasonable in the circumstances.
(2) In determining what is reasonable, regard is to be had, with the appropriate adaptations, to the criteria referred to in Article 3.3.1(3).
(3) If restitution is granted, the rules set out in Article 3.2.15 apply with appropriate adaptations.

CHAPTER 4 — INTERPRETATION

Article 4.1

(Intention of the parties)

(1) A contract shall be interpreted according to the common intention of the parties.
(2) If such an intention cannot be established, the contract shall be interpreted according to the meaning that reasonable persons of the same kind as the parties would give to it in the same circumstances.

Article 4.2

(Interpretation of statements and other conduct)

(1) The statements and other conduct of a party shall be interpreted according to that party's intention if the other party knew or could not have been unaware of that intention.
(2) If the preceding paragraph is not applicable, such statements and other conduct shall be interpreted according to the meaning that a reasonable person of the same kind as the other party would give to it in the same circumstances.

Article 4.3

(Relevant circumstances)

In applying Articles 4.1 and 4.2, regard shall be had to all the circumstances, including

(a) preliminary negotiations between the parties;
(b) practices which the parties have established between themselves;
(c) the conduct of the parties subsequent to the conclusion of the contract;
(d) the nature and purpose of the contract;
(e) the meaning commonly given to terms and expressions in the trade concerned;
(f) usages.

Article 4.4

(Reference to contract or statement as a whole)

Terms and expressions shall be interpreted in the light of the whole contract or statement in which they appear.

Article 4.5

(All terms to be given effect)

Contract terms shall be interpreted so as to give effect to all the terms rather than to deprive some of them of effect.

Article 4.6

(Contra proferentem rule)

If contract terms supplied by one party are unclear, an interpretation against that party is preferred.

Article 4.7

(Linguistic discrepancies)

Where a contract is drawn up in two or more language versions which are equally authoritative there is, in case of discrepancy between the versions, a preference for the interpretation according to a version in which the contract was originally drawn up.

Article 4.8

(Supplying an omitted term)

(1) Where the parties to a contract have not agreed with respect to a term which is important for a determination of their rights and duties, a term which is appropriate in the circumstances shall be supplied.
(2) In determining what is an appropriate term regard shall be had, among other factors, to
  (a) the intention of the parties;
  (b) the nature and purpose of the contract;
  (c) good faith and fair dealing;
  (d) reasonableness.

CHAPTER 5 — CONTENT AND THIRD PARTY RIGHTS

SECTION 1: CONTENT

Article 5.1.1

(Express and implied obligations)

The contractual obligations of the parties may be express or implied.

Article 5.1.2

(Implied obligations)

Implied obligations stem from

(a) the nature and purpose of the contract;
(b) practices established between the parties and usages;
(c) good faith and fair dealing;
(d) reasonableness.

Article 5.1.3

(Co-operation between the parties)

Each party shall co-operate with the other party when such co-operation may reasonably be expected for the performance of that party's obligations.

Article 5.1.4

*(Duty to achieve a specific result.
Duty of best efforts)*

(1) To the extent that an obligation of a party involves a duty to achieve a specific result, that party is bound to achieve that result.
(2) To the extent that an obligation of a party involves a duty of best efforts in the performance of an activity, that party is bound to make such efforts as would be made by a reasonable person of the same kind in the same circumstances.

Article 5.1.5

(Determination of kind of duty involved)

In determining the extent to which an obligation of a party involves a duty of best efforts in the performance of an activity or a duty to achieve a specific result, regard shall be had, among other factors, to

(a) the way in which the obligation is expressed in the contract;
(b) the contractual price and other terms of the contract;
(c) the degree of risk normally involved in achieving the expected result;
(d) the ability of the other party to influence the performance of the obligation.

Article 5.1.6

(Determination of quality of performance)

Where the quality of performance is neither fixed by, nor determinable from, the contract a party is bound to render a performance of a quality that is reasonable and not less than average in the circumstances.

Article 5.1.7

(Price determination)

(1) Where a contract does not fix or make provision for determining the price, the parties are considered, in the absence of any indication to the contrary, to have made reference to the price generally charged at the time of the conclusion of the contract for such performance in comparable circumstances in the trade concerned or, if no such price is available, to a reasonable price.
(2) Where the price is to be determined by one party and that determination is manifestly unreasonable, a reasonable price shall be substituted notwithstanding any contract term to the contrary.

(3) Where the price is to be fixed by one party or a third person, and that party or third person does not do so, the price shall be a reasonable price.
(4) Where the price is to be fixed by reference to factors which do not exist or have ceased to exist or to be accessible, the nearest equivalent factor shall be treated as a substitute.

Article 5.1.8

(Termination of a contract for an indefinite period)

A contract for an indefinite period may be terminated by either party by giving notice a reasonable time in advance. As to the effects of termination in general, and as to restitution, the provisions in Articles 7.3.5 and 7.3.7 apply.

Article 5.1.9

(Release by agreement)

(1) An obligee may release its right by agreement with the obligor.
(2) An offer to release a right gratuitously shall be deemed accepted if the obligor does not reject the offer without delay after having become aware of it.

SECTION 2: THIRD PARTY RIGHTS

Article 5.2.1

(Contracts in favour of third parties)

(1) The parties (the "promisor" and the "promisee") may confer by express or implied agreement a right on a third party (the "beneficiary").
(2) The existence and content of the beneficiary's right against the promisor are determined by the agreement of the parties and are subject to any conditions or other limitations under the agreement.

Article 5.2.2

(Third party identifiable)

The beneficiary must be identifiable with adequate certainty by the contract but need not be in existence at the time the contract is made.

Article 5.2.3

(Exclusion and limitation clauses)

The conferment of rights in the beneficiary includes the right to invoke a clause in the contract which excludes or limits the liability of the beneficiary.

Article 5.2.4

(Defences)

The promisor may assert against the beneficiary all defences which the promisor could assert against the promisee.

Article 5.2.5

(Revocation)

The parties may modify or revoke the rights conferred by the contract on the beneficiary until the beneficiary has accepted them or reasonably acted in reliance on them.

Article 5.2.6

(Renunciation)

The beneficiary may renounce a right conferred on it.

SECTION 3: CONDITIONS

Article 5.3.1

(Types of condition)

A contract or a contractual obligation may be made conditional upon the occurrence of a future uncertain event, so that the contract or the contractual obligation only takes effect if the event occurs (suspensive condition) or comes to an end if the event occurs (resolutive condition).

Article 5.3.2

(Effect of conditions)

Unless the parties otherwise agree:

(a) the relevant contract or contractual obligation takes effect upon fulfilment of a suspensive condition;
(b) the relevant contract or contractual obligation comes to an end upon fulfilment of a resolutive condition.

Article 5.3.3

(Interference with conditions)

(1) If fulfilment of a condition is prevented by a party, contrary to the duty of good faith and fair dealing or the duty of co-operation, that party may not rely on the non-fulfilment of the condition.
(2) If fulfilment of a condition is brought about by a party, contrary to the duty of good faith and fair dealing or the duty of co-operation, that party may not rely on the fulfilment of the condition.

Article 5.3.4

(Duty to preserve rights)

Pending fulfilment of a condition, a party may not, contrary to the duty to act in accordance with good faith and fair dealing, act so as to prejudice the other party's rights in case of fulfilment of the condition.

Article 5.3.5

(Restitution in case of fulfilment of a resolutive condition)

(1) On fulfilment of a resolutive condition, the rules on restitution set out in Articles 7.3.6 and 7.3.7 apply with appropriate adaptations.
(2) If the parties have agreed that the resolutive condition is to operate retroactively, the rules on restitution set out in Article 3.2.15 apply with appropriate adaptations.

CHAPTER 6 — PERFORMANCE

Section 1: Performance in General

Article 6.1.1

(Time of performance)

A party must perform its obligations:

(a) if a time is fixed by or determinable from the contract, at that time;
(b) if a period of time is fixed by or determinable from the contract, at any time within that period unless circumstances indicate that the other party is to choose a time;
(c) in any other case, within a reasonable time after the conclusion of the contract.

Article 6.1.2

(Performance at one time or in instalments)

In cases under Article 6.1.1(b) or (c), a party must perform its obligations at one time if that performance can be rendered at one time and the circumstances do not indicate otherwise.

Article 6.1.3

(Partial performance)

(1) The obligee may reject an offer to perform in part at the time performance is due, whether or not such offer is coupled with an assurance as to the balance of the performance, unless the obligee has no legitimate interest in so doing.

(2) Additional expenses caused to the obligee by partial performance are to be borne by the obligor without prejudice to any other remedy.

Article 6.1.4

(Order of performance)

(1) To the extent that the performances of the parties can be rendered simultaneously, the parties are bound to render them simultaneously unless the circumstances indicate otherwise.
(2) To the extent that the performance of only one party requires a period of time, that party is bound to render its performance first, unless the circumstances indicate otherwise.

Article 6.1.5

(Earlier performance)

(1) The obligee may reject an earlier performance unless it has no legitimate interest in so doing.
(2) Acceptance by a party of an earlier performance does not affect the time for the performance of its own obligations if that time has been fixed irrespective of the performance of the other party's obligations.
(3) Additional expenses caused to the obligee by earlier performance are to be borne by the obligor, without prejudice to any other remedy.

Article 6.1.6

(Place of performance)

(1) If the place of performance is neither fixed by, nor determinable from, the contract, a party is to perform:
    (a) a monetary obligation, at the obligee's place of business;
    (b) any other obligation, at its own place of business.
(2) A party must bear any increase in the expenses incidental to performance which is caused by a change in its place of business subsequent to the conclusion of the contract.

Article 6.1.7

(Payment by cheque or other instrument)

(1) Payment may be made in any form used in the ordinary course of business at the place for payment.
(2) However, an obligee who accepts, either by virtue of paragraph (1) or voluntarily, a cheque, any other order to pay or a promise to pay, is presumed to do so only on condition that it will be honoured.

Article 6.1.8

(Payment by funds transfer)

(1) Unless the obligee has indicated a particular account, payment may be made by a transfer to any of the financial institutions in which the obligee has made it known that it has an account.
(2) In case of payment by a transfer the obligation of the obligor is discharged when the transfer to the obligee's financial institution becomes effective.

Article 6.1.9

(Currency of payment)

(1) If a monetary obligation is expressed in a currency other than that of the place for payment, it may be paid by the obligor in the currency of the place for payment unless
  (a) that currency is not freely convertible; or
  (b) the parties have agreed that payment should be made only in the currency in which the monetary obligation is expressed.
(2) If it is impossible for the obligor to make payment in the currency in which the monetary obligation is expressed, the obligee may require payment in the currency of the place for payment, even in the case referred to in paragraph (1)(b).
(3) Payment in the currency of the place for payment is to be made according to the applicable rate of exchange prevailing there when payment is due.
(4) However, if the obligor has not paid at the time when payment is due, the obligee may require payment according to the applicable rate of exchange prevailing either when payment is due or at the time of actual payment.

Article 6.1.10

(Currency not expressed)

Where a monetary obligation is not expressed in a particular currency, payment must be made in the currency of the place where payment is to be made.

Article 6.1.11

(Costs of performance)

Each party shall bear the costs of performance of its obligations.

Article 6.1.12

(Imputation of payments)

(1) An obligor owing several monetary obligations to the same obligee may specify at the time of payment the debt to which it intends the payment to be

applied. However, the payment discharges first any expenses, then interest due and finally the principal.

(2) If the obligor makes no such specification, the obligee may, within a reasonable time after payment, declare to the obligor the obligation to which it imputes the payment, provided that the obligation is due and undisputed.

(3) In the absence of imputation under paragraphs (1) or (2), payment is imputed to that obligation which satisfies one of the following criteria in the order indicated:
   (a) an obligation which is due or which is the first to fall due;
   (b) the obligation for which the obligee has least security;
   (c) the obligation which is the most burdensome for the obligor;
   (d) the obligation which has arisen first.

If none of the preceding criteria applies, payment is imputed to all the obligations proportionally.

Article 6.1.13

(Imputation of non-monetary obligations)

Article 6.1.12 applies with appropriate adaptations to the imputation of performance of non-monetary obligations.

Article 6.1.14

(Application for public permission)

Where the law of a State requires a public permission affecting the validity of the contract or its performance and neither that law nor the circumstances indicate otherwise

(a) if only one party has its place of business in that State, that party shall take the measures necessary to obtain the permission;

(b) in any other case the party whose performance requires permission shall take the necessary measures.

Article 6.1.15

(Procedure in applying for permission)

(1) The party required to take the measures necessary to obtain the permission shall do so without undue delay and shall bear any expenses incurred.

(2) That party shall whenever appropriate give the other party notice of the grant or refusal of such permission without undue delay.

Article 6.1.16

(Permission neither granted nor refused)

(1) If, notwithstanding the fact that the party responsible has taken all measures required, permission is neither granted nor refused within an agreed period or, where no period has been agreed, within a reasonable time from the conclusion of the contract, either party is entitled to terminate the contract.
(2) Where the permission affects some terms only, paragraph (1) does not apply if, having regard to the circumstances, it is reasonable to uphold the remaining contract even if the permission is refused.

Article 6.1.17

(Permission refused)

(1) The refusal of a permission affecting the validity of the contract renders the contract void. If the refusal affects the validity of some terms only, only such terms are void if, having regard to the circumstances, it is reasonable to uphold the remaining contract.
(2) Where the refusal of a permission renders the performance of the contract impossible in whole or in part, the rules on non-performance apply.

SECTION 2: HARDSHIP

Article 6.2.1

(Contract to be observed)

Where the performance of a contract becomes more onerous for one of the parties, that party is nevertheless bound to perform its obligations subject to the following provisions on hardship.

Article 6.2.2

(Definition of hardship)

There is hardship where the occurrence of events fundamentally alters the equilibrium of the contract either because the cost of a party's performance has increased or because the value of the performance a party receives has diminished, and

(a) the events occur or become known to the disadvantaged party after the conclusion of the contract;
(b) the events could not reasonably have been taken into account by the disadvantaged party at the time of the conclusion of the contract;
(c) the events are beyond the control of the disadvantaged party; and
(d) the risk of the events was not assumed by the disadvantaged party.

Article 6.2.3

(Effects of hardship)

(1) In case of hardship the disadvantaged party is entitled to request renegotiations. The request shall be made without undue delay and shall indicate the grounds on which it is based.
(2) The request for renegotiation does not in itself entitle the disadvantaged party to withhold performance.
(3) Upon failure to reach agreement within a reasonable time either party may resort to the court.
(4) If the court finds hardship it may, if reasonable,
    (a) terminate the contract at a date and on terms to be fixed, or
    (b) adapt the contract with a view to restoring its equilibrium.

CHAPTER 7 — NON-PERFORMANCE

Section 1: Non-performance in General

Article 7.1.1

(Non-performance defined)

Non-performance is failure by a party to perform any of its obligations under the contract, including defective performance or late performance.

Article 7.1.2

(Interference by the other party)

A party may not rely on the non-performance of the other party to the extent that such non-performance was caused by the first party's act or omission or by another event for which the first party bears the risk.

Article 7.1.3

(Withholding performance)

(1) Where the parties are to perform simultaneously, either party may withhold performance until the other party tenders its performance.
(2) Where the parties are to perform consecutively, the party that is to perform later may withhold its performance until the first party has performed.

Article 7.1.4

(Cure by non-performing party)

(1) The non-performing party may, at its own expense, cure any non-performance, provided that

(a) without undue delay, it gives notice indicating the proposed manner and timing of the cure;
(b) cure is appropriate in the circumstances;
(c) the aggrieved party has no legitimate interest in refusing cure; and
(d) cure is effected promptly.

(2) The right to cure is not precluded by notice of termination.
(3) Upon effective notice of cure, rights of the aggrieved party that are inconsistent with the non-performing party's performance are suspended until the time for cure has expired.
(4) The aggrieved party may withhold performance pending cure.
(5) Notwithstanding cure, the aggrieved party retains the right to claim damages for delay as well as for any harm caused or not prevented by the cure.

Article 7.1.5

(Additional period for performance)

(1) In a case of non-performance the aggrieved party may by notice to the other party allow an additional period of time for performance.
(2) During the additional period the aggrieved party may withhold performance of its own reciprocal obligations and may claim damages but may not resort to any other remedy. If it receives notice from the other party that the latter will not perform within that period, or if upon expiry of that period due performance has not been made, the aggrieved party may resort to any of the remedies that may be available under this Chapter.
(3) Where in a case of delay in performance which is not fundamental the aggrieved party has given notice allowing an additional period of time of reasonable length, it may terminate the contract at the end of that period. If the additional period allowed is not of reasonable length it shall be extended to a reasonable length. The aggrieved party may in its notice provide that if the other party fails to perform within the period allowed by the notice the contract shall automatically terminate.
(4) Paragraph (3) does not apply where the obligation which has not been performed is only a minor part of the contractual obligation of the non-performing party.

Article 7.1.6

(Exemption clauses)

A clause which limits or excludes one party's liability for non-performance or which permits one party to render performance substantially different from what the other party reasonably expected may not be invoked if it would be grossly unfair to do so, having regard to the purpose of the contract.

Article 7.1.7

(Force majeure)

(1) Non-performance by a party is excused if that party proves that the non-performance was due to an impediment beyond its control and that it could not reasonably be expected to have taken the impediment into account at the time of the conclusion of the contract or to have avoided or overcome it or its consequences.
(2) When the impediment is only temporary, the excuse shall have effect for such period as is reasonable having regard to the effect of the impediment on the performance of the contract.
(3) The party who fails to perform must give notice to the other party of the impediment and its effect on its ability to perform. If the notice is not received by the other party within a reasonable time after the party who fails to perform knew or ought to have known of the impediment, it is liable for damages resulting from such non-receipt.
(4) Nothing in this Article prevents a party from exercising a right to terminate the contract or to withhold performance or request interest on money due.

SECTION 2: RIGHT TO PERFORMANCE

Article 7.2.1

(Performance of monetary obligation)

Where a party who is obliged to pay money does not do so, the other party may require payment.

Article 7.2.2

(Performance of non-monetary obligation)

Where a party who owes an obligation other than one to pay money does not perform, the other party may require performance, unless

(a) performance is impossible in law or in fact;
(b) performance or, where relevant, enforcement is unreasonably burdensome or expensive;
(c) the party entitled to performance may reasonably obtain performance from another source;
(d) performance is of an exclusively personal character; or
(e) the party entitled to performance does not require performance within a reasonable time after it has, or ought to have, become aware of the non-performance.

Article 7.2.3

(Repair and replacement of defective performance)

The right to performance includes in appropriate cases the right to require repair, replacement, or other cure of defective performance. The provisions of Articles 7.2.1 and 7.2.2 apply accordingly.

Article 7.2.4

(Judicial penalty)

(1) Where the court orders a party to perform, it may also direct that this party pay a penalty if it does not comply with the order.
(2) The penalty shall be paid to the aggrieved party unless mandatory provisions of the law of the forum provide otherwise. Payment of the penalty to the aggrieved party does not exclude any claim for damages.

Article 7.2.5

(Change of remedy)

(1) An aggrieved party who has required performance of a non-monetary obligation and who has not received performance within a period fixed or otherwise within a reasonable period of time may invoke any other remedy.
(2) Where the decision of a court for performance of a non-monetary obligation cannot be enforced, the aggrieved party may invoke any other remedy.

SECTION 3: TERMINATION

Article 7.3.1

(Right to terminate the contract)

(1) A party may terminate the contract where the failure of the other party to perform an obligation under the contract amounts to a fundamental non-performance.
(2) In determining whether a failure to perform an obligation amounts to a fundamental non-performance regard shall be had, in particular, to whether
    (a) the non-performance substantially deprives the aggrieved party of what it was entitled to expect under the contract unless the other party did not foresee and could not reasonably have foreseen such result;
    (b) strict compliance with the obligation which has not been performed is of essence under the contract;
    (c) the non-performance is intentional or reckless;

(d) the non-performance gives the aggrieved party reason to believe that it cannot rely on the other party's future performance;
(e) the non-performing party will suffer disproportionate loss as a result of the preparation or performance if the contract is terminated.

(3) In the case of delay the aggrieved party may also terminate the contract if the other party fails to perform before the time allowed it under Article 7.1.5 has expired.

Article 7.3.2

(Notice of termination)

(1) The right of a party to terminate the contract is exercised by notice to the other party.
(2) If performance has been offered late or otherwise does not conform to the contract the aggrieved party will lose its right to terminate the contract unless it gives notice to the other party within a reasonable time after it has or ought to have become aware of the offer or of the non-conforming performance.

Article 7.3.3

(Anticipatory non-performance)

Where prior to the date for performance by one of the parties it is clear that there will be a fundamental non-performance by that party, the other party may terminate the contract.

Article 7.3.4

(Adequate assurance of due performance)

A party who reasonably believes that there will be a fundamental non-performance by the other party may demand adequate assurance of due performance and may meanwhile withhold its own performance. Where this assurance is not provided within a reasonable time the party demanding it may terminate the contract.

Article 7.3.5

(Effects of termination in general)

(1) Termination of the contract releases both parties from their obligation to effect and to receive future performance.
(2) Termination does not preclude a claim for damages for non-performance.

(3) Termination does not affect any provision in the contract for the settlement of disputes or any other term of the contract which is to operate even after termination.

Article 7.3.6

(Restitution with respect to contracts to be performed at one time)

(1) On termination of a contract to be performed at one time either party may claim restitution of whatever it has supplied under the contract, provided that such party concurrently makes restitution of whatever it has received under the contract.
(2) If restitution in kind is not possible or appropriate, an allowance has to be made in money whenever reasonable.
(3) The recipient of the performance does not have to make an allowance in money if the impossibility to make restitution in kind is attributable to the other party.
(4) Compensation may be claimed for expenses reasonably required to preserve or maintain the performance received.

Article 7.3.7

(Restitution with respect to long-term contracts)

(1) On termination of a long-term contract restitution can only be claimed for the period after termination has taken effect, provided the contract is divisible.
(2) As far as restitution has to be made, the provisions of Article 7.3.6 apply.

SECTION 4: DAMAGES

Article 7.4.1

(Right to damages)

Any non-performance gives the aggrieved party a right to damages either exclusively or in conjunction with any other remedies except where the non-performance is excused under these Principles.

Article 7.4.2

(Full compensation)

(1) The aggrieved party is entitled to full compensation for harm sustained as a result of the non-performance. Such harm includes both any loss which it suffered and any gain of which it was deprived, taking into account any gain to the aggrieved party resulting from its avoidance of cost or harm.
(2) Such harm may be non-pecuniary and includes, for instance, physical suffering or emotional distress.

Article 7.4.3

(Certainty of harm)

(1) Compensation is due only for harm, including future harm, that is established with a reasonable degree of certainty.
(2) Compensation may be due for the loss of a chance in proportion to the probability of its occurrence.
(3) Where the amount of damages cannot be established with a sufficient degree of certainty, the assessment is at the discretion of the court.

Article 7.4.4

(Foreseeability of harm)

The non-performing party is liable only for harm which it foresaw or could reasonably have foreseen at the time of the conclusion of the contract as being likely to result from its non-performance.

Article 7.4.5

(Proof of harm in case of replacement transaction)

Where the aggrieved party has terminated the contract and has made a replacement transaction within a reasonable time and in a reasonable manner it may recover the difference between the contract price and the price of the replacement transaction as well as damages for any further harm.

Article 7.4.6

(Proof of harm by current price)

(1) Where the aggrieved party has terminated the contract and has not made a replacement transaction but there is a current price for the performance contracted for, it may recover the difference between the contract price and the price current at the time the contract is terminated as well as damages for any further harm.
(2) Current price is the price generally charged for goods delivered or services rendered in comparable circumstances at the place where the contract should have been performed or, if there is no current price at that place, the current price at such other place that appears reasonable to take as a reference.

Article 7.4.7

(Harm due in part to aggrieved party)

Where the harm is due in part to an act or omission of the aggrieved party or to another event for which that party bears the risk, the amount of damages shall be reduced to the extent that these factors have contributed to the harm, having regard to the conduct of each of the parties.

Article 7.4.8

(Mitigation of harm)

(1) The non-performing party is not liable for harm suffered by the aggrieved party to the extent that the harm could have been reduced by the latter party's taking reasonable steps.
(2) The aggrieved party is entitled to recover any expenses reasonably incurred in attempting to reduce the harm.

Article 7.4.9

(Interest for failure to pay money)

(1) If a party does not pay a sum of money when it falls due the aggrieved party is entitled to interest upon that sum from the time when payment is due to the time of payment whether or not the non-payment is excused.
(2) The rate of interest shall be the average bank short-term lending rate to prime borrowers prevailing for the currency of payment at the place for payment, or where no such rate exists at that place, then the same rate in the State of the currency of payment. In the absence of such a rate at either place the rate of interest shall be the appropriate rate fixed by the law of the State of the currency of payment.
(3) The aggrieved party is entitled to additional damages if the non-payment caused it a greater harm.

Article 7.4.10

(Interest on damages)

Unless otherwise agreed, interest on damages for non-performance of non-monetary obligations accrues as from the time of non-performance.

Article 7.4.11

(Manner of monetary redress)

(1) Damages are to be paid in a lump sum. However, they may be payable in instalments where the nature of the harm makes this appropriate.
(2) Damages to be paid in instalments may be indexed.

Article 7.4.12

(Currency in which to assess damages)

Damages are to be assessed either in the currency in which the monetary obligation was expressed or in the currency in which the harm was suffered, whichever is more appropriate.

Article 7.4.13

(Agreed payment for non-performance)

(1) Where the contract provides that a party who does not perform is to pay a specified sum to the aggrieved party for such non-performance, the aggrieved party is entitled to that sum irrespective of its actual harm.
(2) However, notwithstanding any agreement to the contrary the specified sum may be reduced to a reasonable amount where it is grossly excessive in relation to the harm resulting from the non-performance and to the other circumstances.

CHAPTER 8 — SET-OFF

Article 8.1

(Conditions of set-off)

(1) Where two parties owe each other money or other performances of the same kind, either of them ("the first party") may set off its obligation against that of its obligee ("the other party") if at the time of set-off,
  (a) the first party is entitled to perform its obligation;
  (b) the other party's obligation is ascertained as to its existence and amount and performance is due.
(2) If the obligations of both parties arise from the same contract, the first party may also set off its obligation against an obligation of the other party which is not ascertained as to its existence or to its amount.

Article 8.2

(Foreign currency set-off)

Where the obligations are to pay money in different currencies, the right of set-off may be exercised, provided that both currencies are freely convertible and the parties have not agreed that the first party shall pay only in a specified currency.

Article 8.3

(Set-off by notice)

The right of set-off is exercised by notice to the other party.

Article 8.4

(Content of notice)

(1) The notice must specify the obligations to which it relates.
(2) If the notice does not specify the obligation against which set-off is exercised, the other party may, within a reasonable time, declare to the first party the obligation to which set-off relates. If no such declaration is made, the set-off will relate to all the obligations proportionally.

Article 8.5

(Effect of set-off)

(1) Set-off discharges the obligations.
(2) If obligations differ in amount, set-off discharges the obligations up to the amount of the lesser obligation.
(3) Set-off takes effect as from the time of notice.

CHAPTER 9 — ASSIGNMENT OF RIGHTS, TRANSFER OF OBLIGATIONS, ASSIGNMENT OF CONTRACTS

SECTION 1: ASSIGNMENT OF RIGHTS

Article 9.1.1

(Definitions)

"Assignment of a right" means the transfer by agreement from one person (the "assignor") to another person (the "assignee"), including transfer by way of security, of the assignor's right to payment of a monetary sum or other performance from a third person ("the obligor").

Article 9.1.2

(Exclusions)

This Section does not apply to transfers made under the special rules governing the transfers:

(a) of instruments such as negotiable instruments, documents of title or financial instruments, or
(b) of rights in the course of transferring a business.

Article 9.1.3

(Assignability of non-monetary rights)

A right to non-monetary performance may be assigned only if the assignment does not render the obligation significantly more burdensome.

Article 9.1.4

(Partial assignment)

(1) A right to the payment of a monetary sum may be assigned partially.
(2) A right to other performance may be assigned partially only if it is divisible, and the assignment does not render the obligation significantly more burdensome.

Article 9.1.5

(Future rights)

A future right is deemed to be transferred at the time of the agreement, provided the right, when it comes into existence, can be identified as the right to which the assignment relates.

Article 9.1.6

(Rights assigned without individual specification)

A number of rights may be assigned without individual specification, provided such rights can be identified as rights to which the assignment relates at the time of the assignment or when they come into existence.

Article 9.1.7

(Agreement between assignor and assignee sufficient)

(1) A right is assigned by mere agreement between the assignor and the assignee, without notice to the obligor.
(2) The consent of the obligor is not required unless the obligation in the circumstances is of an essentially personal character.

Article 9.1.8

(Obligor's additional costs)

The obligor has a right to be compensated by the assignor or the assignee for any additional costs caused by the assignment.

Article 9.1.9

(Non-assignment clauses)

(1) The assignment of a right to the payment of a monetary sum is effective notwithstanding an agreement between the assignor and the obligor limiting or prohibiting such an assignment. However, the assignor may be liable to the obligor for breach of contract.
(2) The assignment of a right to other performance is ineffective if it is contrary to an agreement between the assignor and the obligor limiting or prohibiting the assignment. Nevertheless, the assignment is effective if the assignee, at the time of the assignment, neither knew nor ought to have known of the agreement. The assignor may then be liable to the obligor for breach of contract.

Article 9.1.10

(Notice to the obligor)

(1) Until the obligor receives a notice of the assignment from either the assignor or the assignee, it is discharged by paying the assignor.
(2) After the obligor receives such a notice, it is discharged only by paying the assignee.

Article 9.1.11

(Successive assignments)

If the same right has been assigned by the same assignor to two or more successive assignees, the obligor is discharged by paying according to the order in which the notices were received.

Article 9.1.12

(Adequate proof of assignment)

(1) If notice of the assignment is given by the assignee, the obligor may request the assignee to provide within a reasonable time adequate proof that the assignment has been made.
(2) Until adequate proof is provided, the obligor may withhold payment.
(3) Unless adequate proof is provided, notice is not effective.
(4) Adequate proof includes, but is not limited to, any writing emanating from the assignor and indicating that the assignment has taken place.

Article 9.1.13

(Defences and rights of set-off)

(1) The obligor may assert against the assignee all defences that the obligor could assert against the assignor.
(2) The obligor may exercise against the assignee any right of set-off available to the obligor against the assignor up to the time notice of assignment was received.

Article 9.1.14

(Rights related to the right assigned)

The assignment of a right transfers to the assignee:

(a) all the assignor's rights to payment or other performance under the contract in respect of the right assigned, and
(b) all rights securing performance of the right assigned.

Article 9.1.15

(Undertakings of the assignor)

The assignor undertakes towards the assignee, except as otherwise disclosed to the assignee, that:

(a) the assigned right exists at the time of the assignment, unless the right is a future right;
(b) the assignor is entitled to assign the right;
(c) the right has not been previously assigned to another assignee, and it is free from any right or claim from a third party;
(d) the obligor does not have any defences;
(e) neither the obligor nor the assignor has given notice of set-off concerning the assigned right and will not give any such notice;
(f) the assignor will reimburse the assignee for any payment received from the obligor before notice of the assignment was given.

Section 2: Transfer of Obligations

Article 9.2.1

(Modes of transfer)

An obligation to pay money or render other performance may be transferred from one person (the "original obligor") to another person (the "new obligor") either

(a) by an agreement between the original obligor and the new obligor subject to Article 9.2.3, or
(b) by an agreement between the obligee and the new obligor, by which the new obligor assumes the obligation.

Article 9.2.2

(Exclusion)

This Section does not apply to transfers of obligations made under the special rules governing transfers of obligations in the course of transferring a business.

Article 9.2.3

(Requirement of obligee's consent to transfer)

The transfer of an obligation by an agreement between the original obligor and the new obligor requires the consent of the obligee.

Article 9.2.4

(Advance consent of obligee)

(1) The obligee may give its consent in advance.
(2) If the obligee has given its consent in advance, the transfer of the obligation becomes effective when a notice of the transfer is given to the obligee or when the obligee acknowledges it.

Article 9.2.5

(Discharge of original obligor)

(1) The obligee may discharge the original obligor.
(2) The obligee may also retain the original obligor as an obligor in case the new obligor does not perform properly.
(3) Otherwise the original obligor and the new obligor are jointly and severally liable.

Article 9.2.6

(Third party performance)

(1) Without the obligee's consent, the obligor may contract with another person that this person will perform the obligation in place of the obligor, unless the obligation in the circumstances has an essentially personal character.
(2) The obligee retains its claim against the obligor.

Article 9.2.7

(Defences and rights of set-off)

(1) The new obligor may assert against the obligee all defences which the original obligor could assert against the obligee.
(2) The new obligor may not exercise against the obligee any right of set-off available to the original obligor against the obligee.

Article 9.2.8

(Rights related to the obligation transferred)

(1) The obligee may assert against the new obligor all its rights to payment or other performance under the contract in respect of the obligation transferred.
(2) If the original obligor is discharged under Article 9.2.5(1), a security granted by any person other than the new obligor for the performance of the obligation is discharged, unless that other person agrees that it should continue to be available to the obligee.
(3) Discharge of the original obligor also extends to any security of the original obligor given to the obligee for the performance of the obligation, unless the security is over an asset which is transferred as part of a transaction between the original obligor and the new obligor.

SECTION 3: ASSIGNMENT OF CONTRACTS

Article 9.3.1

(Definitions)

"Assignment of a contract" means the transfer by agreement from one person (the "assignor") to another person (the "assignee") of the assignor's rights and obligations arising out of a contract with another person (the "other party").

Article 9.3.2

(Exclusion)

This Section does not apply to the assignment of contracts made under the special rules governing transfers of contracts in the course of transferring a business.

Article 9.3.3

(Requirement of consent of the other party)

The assignment of a contract requires the consent of the other party.

Article 9.3.4

(Advance consent of the other party)

(1) The other party may give its consent in advance.
(2) If the other party has given its consent in advance, the assignment of the contract becomes effective when a notice of the assignment is given to the other party or when the other party acknowledges it.

Article 9.3.5

(Discharge of the assignor)

(1) The other party may discharge the assignor.
(2) The other party may also retain the assignor as an obligor in case the assignee does not perform properly.
(3) Otherwise the assignor and the assignee are jointly and severally liable.

Article 9.3.6

(Defences and rights of set-off)

(1) To the extent that the assignment of a contract involves an assignment of rights, Article 9.1.13 applies accordingly.
(2) To the extent that the assignment of a contract involves a transfer of obligations, Article 9.2.7 applies accordingly.

Article 9.3.7

(Rights transferred with the contract)

(1) To the extent that the assignment of a contract involves an assignment of rights, Article 9.1.14 applies accordingly.
(2) To the extent that the assignment of a contract involves a transfer of obligations, Article 9.2.8 applies accordingly.

CHAPTER 10 — LIMITATION PERIODS

Article 10.1

(Scope of the Chapter)

(1) The exercise of rights governed by the Principles is barred by the expiration of a period of time, referred to as "limitation period", according to the rules of this Chapter.

(2) This Chapter does not govern the time within which one party is required under the Principles, as a condition for the acquisition or exercise of its right, to give notice to the other party or to perform any act other than the institution of legal proceedings.

Article 10.2

(Limitation periods)

(1) The general limitation period is three years beginning on the day after the day the obligee knows or ought to know the facts as a result of which the obligee's right can be exercised.
(2) In any event, the maximum limitation period is ten years beginning on the day after the day the right can be exercised.

Article 10.3

(Modification of limitation periods by the parties)

(1) The parties may modify the limitation periods.
(2) However they may not
 (a) shorten the general limitation period to less than one year;
 (b) shorten the maximum limitation period to less than four years;
 (c) extend the maximum limitation period to more than fifteen years.

Article 10.4

(New limitation period by acknowledgement)

(1) Where the obligor before the expiration of the general limitation period acknowledges the right of the obligee, a new general limitation period begins on the day after the day of the acknowledgement.
(2) The maximum limitation period does not begin to run again, but may be exceeded by the beginning of a new general limitation period under Article 10.2(1).

Article 10.5

(Suspension by judicial proceedings)

(1) The running of the limitation period is suspended
 (a) when the obligee performs any act, by commencing judicial proceedings or in judicial proceedings already instituted, that is recognised by the law of the court as asserting the obligee's right against the obligor;
 (b) in the case of the obligor's insolvency when the obligee has asserted its rights in the insolvency proceedings; or

(c) in the case of proceedings for dissolution of the entity which is the obligor when the obligee has asserted its rights in the dissolution proceedings.

(2) Suspension lasts until a final decision has been issued or until the proceedings have been otherwise terminated.

Article 10.6

(Suspension by arbitral proceedings)

(1) The running of the limitation period is suspended when the obligee performs any act, by commencing arbitral proceedings or in arbitral proceedings already instituted, that is recognised by the law of the arbitral tribunal as asserting the obligee's right against the obligor. In the absence of regulations for arbitral proceedings or provisions determining the exact date of the commencement of arbitral proceedings, the proceedings are deemed to commence on the date on which a request that the right in dispute should be adjudicated reaches the obligor.

(2) Suspension lasts until a binding decision has been issued or until the proceedings have been otherwise terminated.

Article 10.7

(Alternative dispute resolution)

The provisions of Articles 10.5 and 10.6 apply with appropriate modifications to other proceedings whereby the parties request a third person to assist them in their attempt to reach an amicable settlement of their dispute.

Article 10.8

(Suspension in case of force majeure, death or incapacity)

(1) Where the obligee has been prevented by an impediment that is beyond its control and that it could neither avoid nor overcome, from causing a limitation period to cease to run under the preceding Articles, the general limitation period is suspended so as not to expire before one year after the relevant impediment has ceased to exist.

(2) Where the impediment consists of the incapacity or death of the obligee or obligor, suspension ceases when a representative for the incapacitated or deceased party or its estate has been appointed or a successor has inherited the respective party's position. The additional one-year period under paragraph (1) applies accordingly.

Article 10.9

(Effects of expiration of limitation period)

(1) The expiration of the limitation period does not extinguish the right.
(2) For the expiration of the limitation period to have effect, the obligor must assert it as a defence.
(3) A right may still be relied on as a defence even though the expiration of the limitation period for that right has been asserted.

Article 10.10

(Right of set-off)

The obligee may exercise the right of set-off until the obligor has asserted the expiration of the limitation period.

Article 10.11

(Restitution)

Where there has been performance in order to discharge an obligation, there is no right of restitution merely because the limitation period has expired.

CHAPTER 11 — PLURALITY OF OBLIGORS AND OF OBLIGEES

SECTION 1: PLURALITY OF OBLIGORS

Article 11.1.1

(Definitions)

When several obligors are bound by the same obligation towards an obligee:

(a) the obligations are joint and several when each obligor is bound for the whole obligation;
(b) the obligations are separate when each obligor is bound only for its share.

Article 11.1.2

(Presumption of joint and several obligations)

When several obligors are bound by the same obligation towards an obligee, they are presumed to be jointly and severally bound, unless the circumstances indicate otherwise.

Article 11.1.3

(Obligee's rights against joint and several obligors)

When obligors are jointly and severally bound, the obligee may require performance from any one of them, until full performance has been received.

Article 11.1.4

(Availability of defences and rights of set-off)

A joint and several obligor against whom a claim is made by the obligee may assert all the defences and rights of set-off that are personal to it or that are common to all the co-obligors, but may not assert defences or rights of set-off that are personal to one or several of the other co-obligors.

Article 11.1.5

(Effect of performance or set-off)

Performance or set-off by a joint and several obligor or set-off by the obligee against one joint and several obligor discharges the other obligors in relation to the obligee to the extent of the performance or set-off.

Article 11.1.6

(Effect of release or settlement)

(1) Release of one joint and several obligor, or settlement with one joint and several obligor, discharges all the other obligors for the share of the released or settling obligor, unless the circumstances indicate otherwise.
(2) When the other obligors are discharged for the share of the released obligor, they no longer have a contributory claim against the released obligor under Article 11.1.10.

Article 11.1.7

(Effect of expiration or suspension of limitation period)

(1) Expiration of the limitation period of the obligee's rights against one joint and several obligor does not affect:
  (a) the obligations to the obligee of the other joint and several obligors; or
  (b) the rights of recourse between the joint and several obligors under Article 11.1.10.
(2) If the obligee initiates proceedings under Articles 10.5, 10.6 or 10.7 against one joint and several obligor, the running of the limitation period is also suspended against the other joint and several obligors.

Article 11.1.8

(Effect of judgment)

(1) A decision by a court as to the liability to the obligee of one joint and several obligor does not affect:
   (a) the obligations to the obligee of the other joint and several obligors; or
   (b) the rights of recourse between the joint and several obligors under Article 11.1.10.
(2) However, the other joint and several obligors may rely on such a decision, except if it was based on grounds personal to the obligor concerned. In such a case, the rights of recourse between the joint and several obligors under Article 11.1.10 are affected accordingly.

Article 11.1.9

(Apportionment among joint and several obligors)

As among themselves, joint and several obligors are bound in equal shares, unless the circumstances indicate otherwise.

Article 11.1.10

(Extent of contributory claim)

A joint and several obligor who has performed more than its share may claim the excess from any of the other obligors to the extent of each obligor's unperformed share.

Article 11.1.11

(Rights of the obligee)

(1) A joint and several obligor to whom Article 11.1.10 applies may also exercise the rights of the obligee, including all rights securing their performance, to recover the excess from all or any of the other obligors to the extent of each obligor's unperformed share.
(2) An obligee who has not received full performance retains its rights against the co-obligors to the extent of the unperformed part, with precedence over co-obligors exercising contributory claims.

Article 11.1.12

(Defences in contributory claims)

A joint and several obligor against whom a claim is made by the co-obligor who has performed the obligation:

(a) may raise any common defences and rights of set-off that were available to be asserted by the co-obligor against the obligee;
(b) may assert defences which are personal to itself;
(c) may not assert defences and rights of set-off which are personal to one or several of the other co-obligors.

Article 11.1.13

(Inability to recover)

If a joint and several obligor who has performed more than that obligor's share is unable, despite all reasonable efforts, to recover contribution from another joint and several obligor, the share of the others, including the one who has performed, is increased proportionally.

SECTION 2: PLURALITY OF OBLIGEES

Article 11.2.1

(Definitions)

When several obligees can claim performance of the same obligation from an obligor:

(a) the claims are separate when each obligee can only claim its share;
(b) the claims are joint and several when each obligee can claim the whole performance;
(c) the claims are joint when all obligees have to claim performance together.

Article 11.2.2

(Effects of joint and several claims)

Full performance of an obligation in favour of one of the joint and several obligees discharges the obligor towards the other obligees.

Article 11.2.3

(Availability of defences against joint and several obligees)

(1) The obligor may assert against any of the joint and several obligees all the defences and rights of set-off that are personal to its relationship to that obligee or that it can assert against all the co-obligees, but may not assert defences and rights of set-off that are personal to its relationship to one or several of the other co-obligees.
(2) The provisions of Articles 11.1.5, 11.1.6, 11.1.7 and 11.1.8 apply, with appropriate adaptations, to joint and several claims.

Article 11.2.4

(Allocation between joint and several obligees)

(1) As among themselves, joint and several obligees are entitled to equal shares, unless the circumstances indicate otherwise.
(2) An obligee who has received more than its share must transfer the excess to the other obligees to the extent of their respective shares.

References

Abdel Kader, Nariman 1996, *Arbitration Agreement Pursuant to Arbitration Act No. 27 of 1994*, Dar El Nahda El Arabia.

Abdelwahab, Mohamed Salah 2005, *Globalization Influence upon Various Areas of Law, Cultural Globalization and Public Policy: Exclusion of Foreign Law in the Global Village, Law and Sociology, 8*, Oxford University Press.

Abdelsalaam, Abdel Azim 1989, *The Effect of the Prince Theory on the Performance of Administrative Contracts.*

Abdelsalaam, Abdel Azim 1990, *The Unforeseen Circumstances and Physical Difficulties upon the Performance of Administrative Contracts.*

Abou Taleb, Sofi 2006, *Sharia'a Application in Arab Countries*, Dar Al Nahda Al Arabia.

Abul'enein, MM 1987, *Legislative Deviation and the Oversight on its Constitutionality*, Dar AL Nahda AL Arabia.

Aizawa, Motoko and Guven, Brooke 2019, *UNCITRAL's PPP Legislative Guide Must be Fit for Today's PPPs*, Columbia Center on Sustainable Development, Columbia University.

Al-Sanhoury, Abdel Razak 1984, *The General Theory of Obligations, Part 3: Expiry of Obligations.*

Al-Sanhoury, Abdel Razak 1989, *'Al-Waseet of the Civil Code', Part VII, Work and Employment Contracts*, Vol. 1, 2nd edn.

Al-Sanhoury, Abdel Razak 2010, *Al Wassit in Civil Law, Sources of Obligation*, First Part, Dar Al Shourouk.

Al Sharkawi, Soad 1993, *Constitution Liberalization and the Egyptian Constitution of 1971*, Dar Al Nahda Al Arabia.

Al Sharkawi, Soad 1995, *Administrative Contracts*, Dar Al Nahda Al Arabia.

Al Sharkawi, Soad 1998, *Administrative Contracts*, Dar Al Nahda Al Arabia.

AlSharkawi, Mahmoud Samir 2011, *International Commercial Arbitration*, Dar El Nahdah El Arabia.

Al Tamawy, Soliman 1991, *The General Principles of Administrative Contracts*, 5th edn, Ain Shams University Press.

Al Tamawy, Soliman 2017, *The General Theory of Administrative Decrees, Comparative Study*, Dar El Fikr El Araby.

Amin, Mohamed Said 1991, *General Principles for the Performance of Administrative Contracts*, Dar Al Thakafa Al Gameya.

Amin, Mohamed Said 1992, *A Brief Study on the Notion of Administrative Contracts and the Provisions of their Conclusion.*

Arrowsmith, Sue 2014, *The Law of Public and Utilities Procurement*, 3rd edn, Vol. 1, Sweet & Maxwell.

Atef, Al Bana 1984, *Administrative Contracts*, Dar Al Nahda Al Arabia.

Atef, Al Bana 1992a, *The Judicial Review Upon the Constitutionality of Regulations*, Dar Al Nahda Al Arabia.

Atef, Al Bana 1992b, *Al Wassit in Administrative Law*, Dar Al Nahda Al Arabia.

Auby, Jean-Bernard (ed.) 2014, *Codification of Administrative Procedures*, Bruylant.
Badawi, Sarwat 1954, *Le fait du Prince dans les contrats administratifs*, LGDJ.
Badawi, Sarwat 1985, *Administrative Law*, Dar Al Nahda Al Arabia.
Badawi, Sarwat 1991, *General Theory of Administrative Contracts*, Dar Al Nahda Al Arabia.
Badawi, Sarwat 1994, *General Theory of Administrative Contracts*, Dar Al Nahda Al Arabia.
Badawi, Sarwat 1994, *The General Theory of Administrative Law*, 5th edn, Dar Al Nahda Al Arabia.
Badawi, Sarwat 2007, *Hierarchies of Administrative Decrees and the Illegality Principle*, Dar Al Nahda Al Arabia.
Badawi, Sarwat 2010, *Administrative Law*, Dar Al Nahda Al Arabia.
Badie, Abdel, Mohamed Salah 1993, 'The Power of the Authority to Terminate Administrative Contract', PhD, Faculty of Law, Ain Shams University, Cairo.
Abdel, Baki and Abdel Fatah 1984, *The Encyclopedia of Egyptian Civil Law, Contract and Unilateral Acts Theory, a Comparative Study with Islamic Doctrine*.
Barnett, Hilaire 2020, *Constitutional and Administrative Law*, 13th edn, Routledge.
Beale, Hugh (ed.) 2008, *Chitty on Contracts*, 30th edn, Sweet and Maxwell.
Beriry, Mokhtar 1995, *International Commercial Arbitration*, Dar Al Nahda Al Arabia.
Berman, Harold J. 1958, *Unification of Contract Clauses in Trade between Member-Countries of the Council for Mutual Economic Aid*, Vol. 7, No. 4, October. International And Comparative Law Quarterly, Cambridge University Press, 659–690.
Bishry, Al and Tarek, Emad 2011, *Public Policy Concept in Theory and Practice, a Comparative Study between Legislation and Sharia'a Law Doctrine*, Shorouk International Library.
Blackaby, N, Partasides, C, Redfern, A and Hunter, M 2009, *International Arbitration*, 5th edn, Oxford University Press.
Blackaby, N, Partasides, C, Redfern, A and Hunter, M 2014, *International Arbitration*, 6th edn, Oxford University Press.
Born, G 2012, *International Arbitration*, Kluwer Law International.
Born, G 2013, *International Arbitration and Forum Selection Agreements*, 4th edn, Kluwer Law International.
Born, G 2014a, *International Arbitration Agreements*, 2nd edn, Kluwer Law International.
Born, G 2014b, *International Commercial Arbitration*, 2nd edn, Kluwer Law International.
Bovis, Christopher 2006, *EC Public Procurement: Case Law and Regulation*, Oxford University Press.
Bovis, Christopher 2010, 'Editorial', *EPPPL*, vol. 1.
Bovis, Christopher 2014, *Public Private Partnerships in the European Union, Critical Studies in Public Management*, Routledge.
Bovis, Christopher 2015, *The Law of EU Public Procurement*, 2nd edn, Oxford University Press.
Bruner, Phillipe Lane 1995, *Force Majeure under International Law and International Construction Contract Model Forms*, Vol. 12, Part 2, (April), ICLR.
Bunni, NG 1997, *The FIDIC Form of Contracts*, 2nd edn, Blackwell Publishing.
Bunni, Nael 2005, *The FIDIC Forms of Contract*, 3rd edn, Blackwell.
Ceruti, Marco 2017, 'Sustainable Development and Smart Technological Innovation within PPPs: The Strategic Use of Public Procurement', European *Procurement* & Public Private Partnership *Law* Review, vol. 12, no. 2., pp. 183–191.
Chabanol, D and Jouguelet, J-P 1994, *Marchés publics de travaux*, 2nd edn, Le Moniteur.
Chapus, R 1995a, *Droit Administratif Général*, vol. 2, 8th edn, Montchrestien.
Chapus, R 1995b, *Droit Administrative General*, 5th edn, Tome 2, Montchrestien.
Chapus, R 2001, *Droit Administrative General*, 15th edn, Tome 1, Montchrestien.
Chedrawe, Joseph 2017, 'LDs for Delay in the Middle East: Not Etched in Stone', *BCDR International Arbitration Review*, vol. 4, p. 99.
Chen, John C 1995, *Force Majeure in Construction Contracts*, Part 2, April, ICLR.

Clément J and Richer D 1993, *Les Marchés publics de travaux des collectivités Territoriales*, 2nd edn, Economica.
Creed, Adrian 2016, 'Dubai's New PPP Law', Construction *Law Journal*, vol. 32, no. 7, pp. 808–810.
Daly, Paul 2021, *Understanding Administrative Law in the Common Law World*, Oxford University Press.
De Barros, Monteira and Vidigal, Cecilia 2009, 'PPPs in Brazil', *International Construction Law Review*, vol. 26, Part 2, pp. 180–187.
De Cayper, Jean-Quentin 1993, *Le fait du prince libere t'il une enterprise public, revue de droit des affaires internationals, No. 8*, LGDJ.
De Cazalet, Bruno 2017, 'The Expected Benefit of CIS PPP Model Law', International Business Law Journal, vol. 2, pp. 97–114.
De Laubadère, A de, Venezia, J-C and Gaudemet, Y 1995, *Traité de droit administratif*, Tome 2, 10th edn, L.G.D.J.
De Laubadere, Andre, Moderne, Franck and Delvolve, Pierre 1983–1984, *Traite des contrats administratifs*, 2 Tomes. 2th edn, L.G.D.J.
De Richoufftz, Philippe 2015, 'The Moroccan PPP Contract', *International Business Law Journal*, 5, p. 390.
Delvolvé, J 1993, 'Multipartisme: The *Dutco* decision of the French Cour de Cassation', *International Arbitration*, vol. 9, no. 2, 197.
Delvolvé, P and Vedel ,1992, *Droit Administratif*, PUF.
Dicy, Morris and Collins 2022, *The Conflict of Laws*, Sweet and Maxwell.
Dolzer, R and Schreuer, C 2008, *Principles of International Investment Law*, Oxford University Press.
Dolzer, R and Schreuer, C 2012, *Principles of International Investment Law*, 2nd edn, Oxford University Press.
Dufau, J 1998, *Le droit des travaux publics*, Tome 1, Editions du Moniteur.
Eggleston, B 1997, *Liquidated Damages and Extensions of Time in Construction Contracts*, 2nd edn, Blackwell Science.
Egyptian Conseil D'État 1996, *Legal Principles of Administrative Contracts by the Egyptian State Council in 40 Years: Collection of Supreme Administrative Court Judgments and Legal Opinions from the General Assembly for Legal Opinion (Fatwa) and Legislation*, Egyptian Conseil D'Etat.
Egyptian Ministry of Finance 2009, *Update on the National Program for Public Private Partnership*, PPP Central Unit.
Elgamal, HA 1979, 'Legal System for the Sanctions in Public Construction Contracts', PhD thesis, Ain Shams University.
Elhaddad, H 1996, *Contracts Concluded between States and Private Foreign Persons* 1st edn, Dar El Nahda Al Arabia.
Elleil, ASA 1994, *Methods of Concluding Administrative Contracts in Theory and Practice*, Dar Al Nahda Al Arabia.
European Union Concession Directive 2014, Official Journal of the European Union, 28 March 2014, 94/1-64.
Fekry, F 2009, *Constitutional Law*, Dar Al Nahda Al Arabia.
Fouad Riad, F 1999, *Conflict of Laws, Conflict of Forum and the Effects of Foreign Judgments*, Dar Al Nahda Al Arabia.
Fouchard, Philippe, Gaillard, Emmanuel and Goldman, Berthold1999, *Traite de l'arbitrage commercial international*, Litec.
Friedman, Milton 2008, *Milton Friedman on Economics: Selected Papers*, University of Chicago Press Journal.
Ga'far, Anas 1985, *A Guide to Public Law. Principles and Sources of Administrative Law*, Dar Al Nahda Al Arabia.

Ga'far, Anas 1995, *The Theory of Unforeseen Physical Difficulties in Civil Works Contracting, a Study of the Key Economic and Legal Aspects*, Shalakany Law Firm Publications.

Ga'far, Anas and Ga'far, Ashraf Anas 2021, *Administrative Contracts*, Dar Al Nahda Al Arabia

Hamilton, Geoffrey 2009, 'FDI – The Global Crisis and Sustainable Recovery, Working Paper for Public Private Partnerships, and FDI as a Means of Securing a Sustainable Recovery', paper submitted to the Fourth Columbia International Investment Conference, Vale Columbia Centre, Columbia Law School, Columbia University, 5–6 November.

Hanafi, Said and El Dardiry, Khaled 2010, PPPs in Egypt, vol. 27, Part 4, October, ICLR.

Hartlev, K and Liljenbol, MW 2013, 'Changes to Existing Contracts under the EU Public Procurement Rules and the Drafting of Review Clauses to Avoid the Need for a New Tender', *Public Procurement Law Review*, vol. 22, pp. 51–73.

Helmy, O 1993, *Criterion for Distinguishing Administrative Contracts*, Dar Al Nahda Al Arabia.

Hiller, Alexander 2022, *Arbitrating Government Contracts in Egypt, Observations on DIPCO v. Damietta Port Authority, Association Suisse de l'arbitrage (ASA) Bulletin*, March, Kluwer.

Hoyle, Mark SW 1985–1986, 'The Mixed Courts of Egypt 1886–1895', *Arab Law Quarterly*, 1, 562.

Hoyle, Mark SW 1991, *Mixed Courts of Egypt*, Arab Islamic Law Series, Kluwer Academic Publisher Group.

Huntington, Samuel 1996, *The Clash of Civilization and the Remaking of World Order*, Free Press.

Ismail, MAM 1996, 'Appointing the Arbitral Tribunal in Multi-Party Arbitration', paper presented to the Conference on Arbitration in FIDIC Agreements held by CRCICA in May, at Nile Hilton Hotel.

Ismail, MAM 2003, *International Construction Contracts Arbitration*, Al Halabi.

Ismail, MAM 2009, 'Globalization and Liquidated Damages in the International Public Works Agreements, An Analytical Perspective for the Penalty of Delay Clause in Infrastructure Agreements', *International Construction Law Review*, vol. 26, Part 4, pp. 506–518.

Ismail, MAM 2010, 'Globalization and Contract Price in the Egyptian State Procurement Law',*International Construction Law Review*, vol. 27, Part 1, pp. 92–103.

Ismail, MAM 2010, *Globalization and Contractual Regime in International Public Works Agreements in Egypt*, ICLR, vol. 27, Part 3, pp. 363–374.

Ismail, MAM 2010, 'Legal Globalization and PPPs in Egypt: An Analytical and Comparative Perspective on the Current Legislative and Judicial Modifications to and Enhancements of the Administrative Contractual Regime on PPP Transactions', *The European Public Private Partnership Law Review*, vol. 1, pp. 54–67.

Ismail, MAM 2010, *Public Economic Law and the New International Administrative Contract*, El Halabi Publishing.

Ismail, MAM 2011, 'International Infrastructure Agreements and PPPs in Developing Countries: Substantive Principles, with Special Reference to Arab and Latin American Countries', *European Public-Private Partnership Law Review (EPPPL)*, vol. 3, pp. 147–159.

Ismail, MAM 2011, *Globalization and New International Public Works Agreements in Developing Countries: An Analytical Perspective*, Routledge.

Ismail, MAM 2016, *Globalization and New International Public Works Agreements in Developing Countries, an Analytical Perspective*, Routledge.

Ismail, MAM 2013, *International Investment Arbitration, Lessons from Developments in the MENA Region*, Routledge.

Ismail, MAM 2015, *Arab Constitutions Facts and Prospects*, Al Halabi Publishing.

Ismail, MAM 2019, *Innovation in Public Procurements in the Egyptian PPP Legislation* (With reference to PPP Legislation in Dubai and Kuwait), Public contracting and Innovation, Lessons across borders, Gabriella M. Racca, Christopher R. Yukins, Bruylant, p.567.

Ismail, MAM 2020, *Public Private Partnership Contracts: The Middle East and North Africa*, Routledge.

Ismail, MAM 2023, 'Private-Public Arbitration in PPPs in Egypt and MENA Region', *European Procurement & Public Private Partnership Law Review*, vol. 18, no. 4, pp.261–65.

Ismail, Youssef 2023, 'Enforceability of Liquidated Damages Clauses and the Extent of Judicial and Arbitral Intervention, A comparative study between the English and Egyptian jurisdictions', *Arbitration: The International Journal of Arbitration, Mediation and Dispute Management*, vol. 89, no. 4, Kluwer Law International, pp.516-35.

Jones, Douglas 1995, *Force Majeure in Australian Construction Law*, ICLR. Part 2 (April).

Kuwaiti Authority for Partnership Projects 2018, PPP Guidebook.

Lagarde, Paul and Battifol, Henri 1981, *Droit International Privé*, LGDJ.

Lalive, JF 1983, Contrats entre État ou éntreprises étatiques et personnes privées, *vol. II*, Académie de droit international.

Laubadère A de, Venezia J-C and Gaudemet Y 1995, *Traité de droit administratif*, Tome 2, 10th edn, L.G.D.J.

Leboulanger, P 1985, *Les contrats entre états et entreprises étrangères*, Economica.

Mahmoud, MM, 1993, 'Administrative Contracts and International Arbitration Clause', *Administrative Sciences Journal*, vol. 35, p. 220.

Mahmoud, MM 1997, 'Arbitrability in Administrative Contracts', Kuwait Conference for International Commercial Arbitration.

Mahmoud, Ragab 2007, *Public-Private Partnership Contracts*, Dar Al Nahda Al Arabia.

Mahmoud, Ragab 2010, *Partnership Contracts between Public and Private Sectors*, Dar Al Nahda Al Arabia.

Mark, Elliot and Robert, Thomas 2014, *Public Law*, 2nd edn, Oxford University Press.

McKendrick, Ewan 1995, *Force Majeure and Frustration of Contract*, 2nd edn, Informa, Routledge.

McKendrick, Ewan 2015, *Contract Law*, 11th edn, Palgrave Law Master.

McKendrick, Ewan 2021, *Contract Law*, 14th edn, Macmillan Law Masters.

Monteira de Barros, Cecilia Vidigal 2009, 'PPPs in Brazil', *Informa; International Construction Law Review*, vol. 26, Part 2, 180–181.

Moss, D 2004, *When All Else Fails: Government as the Ultimate Risk Manager*, Harvard University Press.

Mounir MK 1991, 'Arbitration in Administrative Contracts', *Administrative Law Journal*, vol. 33, no. 1, pp. 329–335.

Nassar, Gaber Gad 2005, *Administrative Contracts*, Dar Al Nahda Al Arabia.

OECD, *Recommendation of the Council on Public Procurement*, Directorate for Public Governance and Territorial Development.

OECD 2016, *Methodology for Assessment Procurement Systems*.

OECD 2018, *Methodology for Assessment Procurement Systems*.

OECD 2014, *Public-Private Partnerships in the Middle East and North Africa, Private Sector Development Handbook*, A Handbook for Policy Makers, OECD Publications.

Okahsa, Hamdy Yassin 2020, *Contractual Performance during Covid-19 Pandemic and its Effect Upon Contractual Obligations*.

Okasha, Hamdy Yassin 2010, *The Encyclopedia of the Administrative Decrees in the Conseil d'Etat Jurisprudence*, 3 vols.

Okasha, Hamdy Yassin 2016, '*The Encyclopedia of Practical Problems in Administrative Contracts Disputes*', 4th book.

Philippe, De Richoufftz 2015, 'The Moroccan PPP Contract', International *Business* Law Journal, vol. 5, pp. 389–398.
Potestà, Michele 2013, 'Legitimate Expectations in Investment Treaty Law: Understanding the Roots and Limits of a Controversial Concept', *ICSID Review*, vol. 28, no. 1, p. 88.
Poulsen, ST 2012, 'The Possibilities of Amending a Public Contract without a New Competitive Tendering Procedure under EU Law', *The Public Procurement Law Review*, vol. 21, pp. 167–187.
RACCA, GM and Yukins, Christopher 2014, *Integrity and Efficiency in Sustainable Public Contracts, Balancing Corruption Concerns in Public Procurement Internationally*, Bruylant.
Racca, GM, Perin, RC and Albano, GL 2011, 'Competition in the Execution Phase of Public Procurement', *Public Contract Law Journal*, vol. 41, no. 1, pp. 89–108.
Rashed, Samia 1984, *Arbitration in International Private Law Relations, Arbitration Agreement*, vol. I., Dar Al Nahda Al Arabia.
Raslaan, Anwar 1994, *Administrative Law*, Dar Al Nahda Al Arabia.
Raslan, Anwar 1980, 'The Theory of Unforeseen Physical Difficulties', *Journal of Law and Economy*, vol. 3 and 4, pp. 840–851.
Redfern, A, Hunter, M, with Blackaby, N and Partasides, C 2009, *Redfern and Hunter on International Arbitration*, 5th edn, Oxford University Press.
Redfern, A, Hunter, M, with Blackaby, N and Partasides, C 2014, *Redfern and Hunter on International Arbitration*, 6th edn, Oxford University Press.
Riad, F and Rashed, S 1988, *A Concise Guide to the Conflict of Laws and International Judicial Jurisdiction*, Dar Al Nahda Al Arabia.
Richer, L 1991, *Les Contrats Administratifs*, Dalloz.
Richer, L 1995, *Droit Des Contrats Administratifs*, LGDJ.
Richer, L 2008, *Droit Des Contrats Administratifs*, LGDJ.
Richer, L and Lichère, François 2019, *Droits des Contrats Administratifs*, 11th edn, LGDJ.
Richer, L and Lichère, François 2016, *Droits des Contrats Administratifs*, 10th edn, LGDJ.
Rivero, J and Waline, J 1994, *Droit Administratif*, 15th edn, Dalloz.
Rodríguez, José Antonio Morerno 2023, *Private (And Public) International Law in Investment Arbitration, Hague Academy of International Law, Offprint From The Recueil Des Cours*, vol. 429, Brill Nijhoff.
Sachs, Jeffrey 2008, *Common Wealth Economics for a Crowded Planet*, Penguin Books.
Sachs, Jeffrey D 2005, *The End of Poverty*, Penguin Books.
Said Amin, Mohamed 1991, *General Principles for the Performance of Administrative Contracts*.
Said, Aly 2006, *Principle of Not Executing Contract*.
Sarie El Din, Hani 1996, *Consortia Agreements in the International Construction Industry*, Kluwer Law International.
Sarie El Din, Hani 2002, *Legal and Contractual Regime for BOOT*, El Ahram El Eqtisadi Book, No. 177.
Sarie El Dine, Hani 2001, *Legal and Contractual Regim for Infrastructure Projects Financed by Private Sector*, Dar El Nahda El Arabia.
Schreuer, Christoph 2006, *Fair & Equitable Treatment*, BIICL Investment Treaty Forum, 9 September, 1.
Schwenzer, Ingeborg 2016, 'Global Unification of Contract Law', *Uniform Law Review*, vol. 21, no. 1, pp. 60–74.
Seppala, CR 1993, 'French Supreme Court Nullifies ICC Practice for Appointment of Arbitrators in Multi-Party Arbitration Cases', *International Construction Law Review*, Vol. 10, part 2, pp. 222–227.
Smith, Adam 2012, *Wealth of Nations*, Wordsworth Edition.
Smith, Katie 2019, 'A Risk Worth Taking? Practical Application of the Law on Contract Modifications in the Context of PPP Accommodation Projects', *Public Procurement Law Review*, 1, pp. 16–25.

Snowdon, B 2007, *Globalisation, Development and Transition*, Edward Elgar.
Southard, Katharine 2010, 'U.S. Electric Utilities: The First Public-Private Partnerships?' *Public Contract Law Journal*, Winter, 395.
Stanley, Jeremiah 1995, 'Insurability of Force Majeure Events in Construction Contracts', *International Construction Law Review*, Vol. 12, Part 2, (April).
Stiglitz, JE 2004, *Globalization and its Discontents*, W. W. Norton & Company.
Stiglitz, JE 2007, *Making Globalization Work*, W. W. Norton & Company.
Stone, Richard and Devenney, James (eds) 2014, *Texts, Cases and Materials on Contract Law*, Routledge.
Thomas, Christopher S 1995, 'Aspects of Building Contracts: A Comparative View of English and French Law in the Light of Potential Harmonization', PhD thesis, School of Law, Kings College, London.
Treitel, GH 1994, *Frustration and Force Majeure*, Sweet and Maxwell.
Treitel, GH 2004, *Frustration and Force Majeure*, 2nd edn, Sweet and Maxwell.
Tyler, SM 1994, 'No (Easy) Way Out: "Liquidating" Stipulated Damages for Contractor Delay in Public Construction Contracts', *Duke Law Journal*, vol. 44, p. 357.
Uhlmann, Felix 2023, *Codification of Administrative Law, a Comparative Study on the Sources of Administrative Law*, Hart Publishing.
UNCITRAL 2000, *Guide Privately Financed Infrastructure Projects.*
UNCITRAL 2020, *Legislative Guide on Public-Private Partnership.*
UNCITRAL 2020, *Model Legislative Provisions on Public-Private partnerships.*
UNCTAD 2023, *The World Investment Report.*
UNECE Guidebook on Promoting Good Governance in Public Private Partnership 2008.
United Nations Economic Commission for Europe 2008, *Guidebook on Promoting Good Governance in Public-Private Partnership.*
United Nations Sustainable Development Agenda, Department of Economic and Social Affairs, Sustainable Development.
Vedel, G 1956, 'Remarques sur la Notion de Clause Exorbitante', *L'évolution du droit public: Études en l'honneur d'Achille Mestre*, pp. 527–561, Sirey.
Vedel, G and Delvolvé, P 1992, *Droit Administratif*, 12th edn, Presses Universitaires de France.
Wali, Fathi 2007, *Arbitration Law in Theory and Practice*, Monsha'at Al Marref.
Wiwatpattarakul, Pronchai n.d. 'A Critical Examination of the Concept of Force Majeure at Thai Law and Its Impact in the Context of Construction Contracts', *International Conference on Learning Representations*, vol. 1.
World Bank 2017, 'Benchmarking PPP Procurement: Benchmarking Public-Private Partnerships Procurement: Assessing Government Capability to Prepare, Procure and Manage PPPs'.
World Bank Group 2018, *Procuring Infrastructure PPPs.*
Yehia, Abdel Wadood 1989, *Brief in the General Theory of Obligations, Sources of Obligations,* Part 1, Dar Al Nahda Al Arabia.
Yehia, Abdel Wadood 1987, *Obligation stipulations at Egyptian Civil Law*, Dar Al Nahda Al Arabia.
Zeyl, Trevor 2011, 'Charting the Wrong Course: The Doctrine of Legitimate Expectations in Investment Treaty Law', *Alberta Law Review*, vol. 49, pp. 203–210.

Index

For Product Safety Concerns and Information please contact our EU representative GPSR@taylorandfrancis.com Taylor & Francis Verlag GmbH, Kaufingerstraße 24, 80331 München, Germany